The Globalization of Industry and Innovation in Eastern Europe

The Globalization of Industry and Innovation in Eastern Europe

From Post-socialist Restructuring to International Competitiveness

Edited by

Christian von Hirschhausen and Jürgen Bitzer

DIW German Institute for Economic Research, Berlin, Germany

Edward Elgar
Cheltenham, UK • Northampton, MA, USA

Published by
Edward Elgar Publishing Limited
Glensanda House
Montpellier Parade
Cheltenham
Glos GL50 1UA
UK

Edward Elgar Publishing, Inc.
136 West Street
Suite 202
Northampton
Massachusetts 01060
USA

A catalogue record for this book
is available from the British Library

Library of Congress Cataloguing in Publication Data

The globalization of industry and innovation in Eastern Europe : from post-socialist restructuring to international competitiveness / edited by Christian von Hirschhausen and Jürgen Bitzer
    Includes bibliographical references and index.
    1. Industrial policy—Europe, Eastern. 2. Structural adjustment (Economic policy)—Europe, Eastern. 3. Europe, Eastern—Economic policy—1989-
I. Hirschhausen, Christian von, 1964– II. Bitzer, Jürgen, 1970–

    HD3616.E823 G58 2000
    338.947—dc21

                                                    99–053987

ISBN 1 84064 284 X

Printed and bound in Great Britain by Bookcraft (Bath) Ltd.

Contents

Tables   vii
Figures   ix
Contributors   xi

1. Introduction: Which Industrial and Innovation Policies are
    Appropriate for Post-socialist Eastern Europe?
    Christian von Hirschhausen and Jürgen Bitzer   1

PART I: CONCEPTUAL FRAMEWORK

2. An Evolutionary View of Post-socialist Restructuring: From Science
    and Technology Systems to Innovation Systems
    Jürgen Bitzer   13
3. Enterprise Reform and Competition Analysis in the Post-socialist
    Context: Analytical Framework and Stylized Facts
    Christian von Hirschhausen   37

PART II: EMPIRICAL ANALYSIS AND CASE STUDIES

4. The Reemergence of the Automotive Industry in Eastern Europe
    Xavier Richet and Frédéric Bourassa   59
5. Local, Regional and Global Production Networks: Reintegration of
    the Hungarian Automotive Industry
    Attila Havas   95
6. Eastern European Shipbuilding's Cruise Towards World Markets
    Christian von Hirschhausen and Jürgen Bitzer   129
7. Food Processing in Western and Eastern Europe: From
    Supply-driven Towards Demand-driven Progress
    Nick von Tunzelmann and Frédérique Charpiot-Michaud   161
8. Restructuring of the Telecommunications Sector in the West and
    the East and the Role of Science and Technology
    Jürgen Müller   185

9.   Software: New Industries and New Enterprises in Eastern Europe
     Jürgen Bitzer   227
10. The Eastern European Computer Industry: National Champions
     with a Screwdriver
     Jürgen Bitzer   257
11. Restructuring the Computer and Software Industries in Poland
     Stanislaw Kubielas   283

PART III: SUMMARY AND OUTLOOK

12. Main Findings and Perspectives for Innovation Policies in Eastern
     Europe and the West
     Christian von Hirschhausen   315

     Subject Index   337

Tables

2.1   Gross domestic expenditure on R&D as a percentage of GDP, 1991–1995   29

2.2   Sources of R&D expenditures, 1995   30

3.1   Macro-indicators for Eastern European countries, 1990–1999   52

4.1   Global car sales by region   84

4.2   Car producers by regions and strategic alliances worldwide   85

4.3   Market segments in the West European countries   86

4.4   R&D scoreboard in the world automotive industry, 1994–1996   87

4.5   Motives for investing in the Eastern European automotive industry   89

4.6   Ranking of automotive firms in Central Europe's top 100 enterprises   90

4.7   Global car production by region   91

4.8   Car production by model in the Czech Republic   92

4.9   Domestic car sales in the Czech Republic   93

4.10 Production by manufacturers in Russia   94

5.1   Major data of Magyar Suzuki, 1992–1998   100

5.2   Major data of Opel Hungary, 1992–1998   102

5.3   Performance of Audi Hungaria Motor Kft (AHM)   103

5.4   Manufacture of electrical automotive components   106

5.5   Manufacture of parts and components for motor vehicles   107

5.6   Ownership changes in the manufacture of electrical automotive components   108

5.7   Ownership changes in the manufacture of parts and components for motor vehicles   109

5.8   Outlook for Hungarian suppliers   119

5.9   Financial support for target-oriented national projects: automotive suppliers, 1994–1997   122

6.1   World ship production by region, 1990–1997   133

6.2   World shipbuilding new orders and order book by country, 1992–1997   134

6.3   Productivity estimates for shipyards   140

6.4   East European shipbuilding production, 1988–1997   141

6.5   Selected partnerships between OECD and Eastern European shipyards   144

6.6 Capitalization of the socialist Mathias Thesen Werft VEB to the
MTW Schiffswerft GmbH – a case of creating 'new' capacities 147
7.1 Percentage contribution of food, drink and tobacco to total value
added in manufacturing, 1980, 1994 and 1995 163
7.2 Comparative production structures in the 'Triad', 1988–1989 164
7.3 Percentage share of foreign investments in agriculture and food in
Hungary and Poland 176
7.4 FDI in the Czech Republic, Hungary and Poland, 1990–1996 177
8.1 Annual telecommunication revenues: selected country markets 195
8.2 Telecommunication indicators: selected country markets, 1994 197
8.3 Cost to achieve 35 percent CEE teledensity, 1991–2000 203
9.1 The software market of the EU, 1994–1998 236
9.2 Value of software markets of several Eastern European countries 240
9.3 Relation between expenditures for computers and software, 1996 241
9.4 Relation between standard and custom software in different
countries, 1996 241
9.5 Number and characteristics of Fortech experts 248
9.6 Fortech's most important cooperation partners 249
9.7 Largest firms in the software market by sales 251
10.1 The computer market in the EU, 1994–1999 260
10.2 Growth rates of different computer market segments in the EU 261
10.3 Situation on the Eastern European computer markets, 1996 267
10.4 Computer base in Eastern European countries 268
10.5 Growth rates of the Czech PC market segment in terms of value 272
10.6 Turnover of AutoCont plc, 1991–1997 272
10.7 PCs produced by AutoCont plc, 1991–1997 273
11.1 Computer equipment manufacturing – industry data, 1991–1995 291
11.2 Revenues of 200 largest IT firms by type of activity, 1994–1996 293
11.3 Main computer equipment manufacturers, 1995–1996 294
11.4 Personal computers sold in 1000 units, 1994–1996 295
11.5 Software services – industry data, 1991–1995 297
11.6 Main software producers, 1995–1996 299
11.7 Main integrators, 1995–1996 301
12.1 Survey of main results and application to sector studies 331

Figures

2.1	Stylized socialist innovation process in one sector	16
2.2	Changed tasks in the innovation process	25
3.1	Industrial production in selected Central and Eastern European countries, 1989–1997	49
6.1	Segments of the shipbuilding market	131
6.2	Regional shares of shipbuilding market segments	135
6.3	Division of the order stock of Poland, Russia and Ukraine, March 1997	142
6.4	International production and sales network of the Szczecin shipyard, 1998	151
6.5	Post-soviet shipbuilding cluster in the Leningrad oblast (Russia), 1998	156
8.1	Hierarchical value-added chain of telecommunication markets	188
8.2	GDP v. penetration in telecommunications	194
8.3	Total telecommunications investment in Russia, 1991–1995	207
9.1	Segments of the computer software market	232

Contributors

Jürgen Bitzer, Senior Researcher at DIW (German Institute for Economic Research) in Berlin, Germany; specialization in industrial economics (information technology).

Frédéric Bourassa, Research Associate at ROSES (Center for Research in Post-socialist Economic Systems, University Paris I), France; specialization in industrial economics, extensive case study work on the Eastern European automobile industry.

Frédérique Charpiot-Michaud, Lecturer in Business Administration at the University of Paris I (Sorbonne) and Research Associate at ROSES (Center for Research in Post-socialist Economic Systems, University Paris I); specialization in international trade and trade relations of Eastern European countries.

Attila Havas, Research Fellow at IKU Innovation Research Center Budapest University of Economics, and Program Director, Hungarian Technology Foresight Program at OMFB, the National Committee for Technological Development; specialization in industrial economics (automobile industry) and international investment.

Christian von Hirschhausen, Senior Researcher at DIW (German Institute for Economic Research) in Berlin and lecturer, Berlin University of Technology, Germany; specialization in industrial economics and transformation in Eastern Europe.

Stanislaw Kubielas, Professor of International Economics at Warsaw University, Poland; specialization in innovations and technology transfer.

Jürgen Müller, Professor of Economics at the Berlin School of Economics (FHW), Germany; specialization in telecommunication and regulatory economics.

Xavier Richet, Professor of Economics at the University of Paris I (Sorbonne) and Marne-la-Vallée, France; former director of ROSES (Center for Research in Post-socialist Economic Systems); specialization in industrial economics, economic systems and transformation in Eastern Europe.

Nick von Tunzelmann, Senior Researcher at the Science Policy Research Unit (SPRU), University of Sussex; specialization in the economics of technology and growth, advisor to various governmental organizations in Great Britain and the EU Commission.

1 Introduction: Which Industrial and Innovation Policies are Appropriate for Post-socialist Eastern Europe?

Christian von Hirschhausen and Jürgen Bitzer

1. THE LEGACY OF SOCIALIST INDUSTRY AND SCIENCE AND TECHNOLOGY 'POTENTIAL' IN EASTERN EUROPE

Innovation is a serious issue, and so are the innovation policies that are generally considered to enhance the innovative potential and competitiveness of enterprises or even of entire national economies. The belief in the necessity of national innovation policies and the establishment of science and technology (S&T) systems is widespread, and the literature on this subject fills entire libraries. However, in no context have these systems been considered to be so important as in the reforming economies of Eastern Europe, in their attempt to consolidate the transformation from socialism to capitalist market economies, and from the Council of Mutual Economic Assistance (CMEA) to European Union (EU) and world markets. Following the collapse of socialism and the subsequent implosion of productive capacities, many hopes for a successful transformation process were pinned on the presumption of an abundance of immaterial assets in the Eastern European countries, such as solid S&T systems, a highly qualified labor force, sound technical education, and therefore a breadth of innovative skills. An early consensus emerged around the idea that macroeconomic stabilization was necessary but insufficient to ensure the success of transformation, and that renewed economic growth dependent on the 'systemic acceptance of capabilities, including, crucially, the ability to assimilate new technology, to integrate into global production and marketing systems' (Dyker and Perrin 1997, p. 3). Hence, in the early post-socialist

1

years, say between 1990 and 1993, the *existing* technological potential was often considered to be the basis for industrial recovery and development in Eastern Europe. Subsequently, governments throughout the region came under pressure to conceive specific industrial and S&T policies in order to make use of this 'potential'. Western governments and international organizations, too, developed assistance programs for the survival and maintenance of innovation capacities in Eastern Europe.

What if the idea of a strong S&T basis inherited from socialism was only a myth? What if, as Pavitt (1997) suggested, the inherited socialist competencies had been made obsolete by the systemic change? And finally, what if the necessary process of restructuring Eastern European industries upside down owed its (partial) success to *international* networking? At the end of the century and not even ten years after the crumbling of socialism in Eastern Europe, it indeed seems normal to buy a world-class, Hungarian-made car in France, to sell Western radar technology to a shipyard in Poland which is emerging as a world market leader, or to use MS-Windows 97 software in Russian on a Russian-made personal computer (PC) in the formerly closed town of Novossibirsk. In other words, the globalization of industry and innovation seems to be under way in Eastern Europe despite the difficult initial situation. Innovation systems are restructuring all over Eastern Europe, differing in speed only (Hutschenreiter et al. 1999). The advanced reforming countries in the region have been showing sustained growth since the mid-1990s, for example, Poland, Hungary, Slovenia and Estonia, even though the former S&T structures have been torn apart. With the approaching integration of many Eastern European countries into the EU and their growing interdependence in the world economy, the issue of *national industrial and innovation policies* is an open one. Should new approaches to innovation and industrial restructuring be formulated, should existing models from the EU or elsewhere be applied, or should these policies be discontinued altogether?

This book looks at a decade of industrial and enterprise restructuring in Eastern Europe to identify the underlying reasons for change, in particular the role of national innovation policies. Based upon a conceptual framework of post-socialist industrial reform and a sample of empirical case studies, it analyzes to what extent Eastern European industries have already gone through their transformation processes, and how they are integrating themselves into global production, innovation and sales networks. Our hypothesis is that post-socialist innovation systems emerged from below rather than from top-down approaches through a process of *commercialization* (or monetization) at all levels: former research and development (R&D) institutes, academies of sciences, former socialist combines, and so on. This process was largely driven by the integration of enterprises into *existing* or *emerging* global production and sales networks or their development, leaving little space for domestic, sectorally-oriented policies. Under these conditions, it may be that *demand-oriented* innovation policies are more likely to enhance growth than a supply-oriented approach seeking to maintain obsolete capacities.

2. AN APPROACH CENTERED AROUND POST-SOCIALIST ENTERPRISE AND INDUSTRIAL RESTRUCTURING

There are two broad approaches to analyzing the role of innovation policies for industrial restructuring. The first, more traditional one is input oriented and *top down*: it measures the share of innovation expenses by public and private institutions, relates them to other macroeconomic or sectoral data (such as gross domestic product (GDP) growth, turnover of industry and business expenses), compares the results between countries, industries and regions, and then tries to identify significant relations and draw policy conclusions. Simply speaking, this approach leads to results of the type 'country X needs to expand its expenses for innovation', 'industry Y spends too much on innovation, as compared to its industry', or 'company Z has higher innovation expenses than the industry average'. The top-down approach dominated research on Eastern Europe, both in the socialist period and during the early years of post-socialism. It was commonplace for Eastern European industries and innovation researchers to contend that their respective governments' expenses for innovation lagged behind the international level. It took a lot of number-crunching and political courage to contend that Eastern European R&D expenditures were in fact *not* as low as generally assumed when compared to other countries of similar income, and that even the contrary might be the case (Auriol and Radosevic 1996; see also the survey in Chapter 2).

The second approach, *bottom up*, considers innovation to be an interactive process among technology, production and markets. This output-oriented approach puts the *industrial enterprise* (or firm) at the center of analysis, because it is at the enterprise level that the effects of innovation are best measured, for example, by increasing competitiveness. Although not easily quantifiable, the bottom-up approach is superior to the top-down approach when concrete, applicable policy conclusions are sought. Indeed, the quantitative top-down approach ignores by its very nature the specifics of the analyzed object in question, be it the industry, the country, or as in the case of Eastern Europe, the systemic change of an entire subcontinent.

Consequently, the approach adopted in this book is to analyze industrial restructuring and innovation at the *micro-level*, that is, to consider *enterprise reform* as the key to structural and technical change. This also reflects the hitherto irrefutable fact that enterprises – not countries or regions – are the pivotal element in any capitalist market economy (see Chapter 3). It is also at the enterprise level where the following three specifics that underlie and shape industrial restructuring in Eastern Europe can be detected and dealt with in policy conclusions:

- the *post-socialist* nature of transformation in Eastern Europe. The use of macro-data indeed obscures the fact that the reform process in Eastern Europe was not just another gradual structural adjustment, as had been asserted by dozens in the last two decades, mainly in Latin America. By contrast, the end of 40 years of socialism in Eastern Europe or even 70 years in the Soviet Union has opened up a period of *radical* systemic change at all economic levels, and in all enterprises, sectors, regions and nations. This radical change is linked to the replacement of socialist, non-monetary transactions by money-oriented transactions in a capitalist market environment. In a period as unstable as post-socialism, where not a single economic relation can be taken as stable, it is more important to identify the ideal types of restructuring than to interpret aggregate data of doubtful origin. Whereas the effects of systemic change on enterprise restructuring have been shown before (Bomsel 1995; Hirschhausen 1996), this book extends the post-socialist perspective to *innovation* issues;
- *industry-specific* patterns of restructuring and innovation. These are generally ignored by traditional indicator or institutional analyses, but play a crucial role when trying to separate the S&T-related factors from other determinants of restructuring. Industry-specific factors may be linked to technology (for example, resource based, engineering based, science based), capital intensity, R&D intensity, the depth of network relations upstream and downstream, and others. Without an in-depth understanding of the functioning of an industry and the patterns of competition, the identification of the specific role of innovation therein is difficult;
- last but not least, the *globalization* of industry and innovation already taking place in the rest of the industrialized world. Indeed, the restructuring of Eastern Europe is occurring in a time of increasingly complex patterns of competition and cooperation, leading to a shift in traditional modes of innovation. National innovation systems, on the front lines of economic policy and research for two decades, are increasingly being challenged from two sides: from above, that is, through the internationalization of innovation and production networks (McKelvey

1991), and from below, that is, through the regionalization of networks relying on socio-economic proximity as the driving source of competitiveness (Porter 1998). In this context, the 'Wild East' (Eastern Europe), where anything was possible during the first post-socialist years, may even be considered as a pilot case of globalization, possibly prescribing patterns that other countries may follow. Is not the fact that Eastern Europe is about to develop the most competitive car factories and shipyards in the world a sign of this development?

The main thesis and the methodology advanced in this book are themselves innovative, and thus they are controversial. To some, the globalization thesis may appear exaggerated, in particular to those who consider that old technology and bankrupt state firms still dominate Eastern Europe. Martin (1998) sees Eastern Europe in a process of internationalization into the world economy, but considers that the process of globalization, 'based on the logic of innovation ... is likely to remain partial and selective' (pp. 23–4). While acknowledging the existence of more traditional perspectives on the changes going on in Eastern Europe, we contend that the real-world approach adopted in this book tends to show the opposite. As enterprise strategies are always ahead of both politicians and researchers, it is at the enterprise and industry levels where new developments can be first identified. Precisely this perspective may lead us to a different set of conclusions, that is, that the transformation and integration of Eastern Europe into international networks is more advanced than is generally acknowledged.

3. STRUCTURE OF THE BOOK

The chapters of this book share among them a conviction that the changing nature of industry and innovation in Eastern Europe should be studied through the lens of enterprise and sectoral reform strategies in these countries, and by relating these reforms to developments elsewhere in the world. The comparative perspective was chosen deliberately in order to avoid a limitation of the analysis to a description of changes at a national level only, because as Eastern Europe and the Commonwealth of Independent States (CIS) become integrated into the world economies, so do the enterprises and national S&T institutions. The book is divided into three parts: the conceptual framework, the empirical sector analysis and case studies, and the policy conclusions.

3.1 Part I: Conceptual Framework

Part I provides a conceptual framework for analyzing the reform process in Eastern European industry and innovation systems, and reports the main developments of the last decade. Chapter 2 surveys the restructuring of innovation networks in Eastern Europe in the transformation from socialism to capitalist market economies. Whereas under socialism, science and technology and innovation were seen as having an inherent value, in capitalist economies their task is to improve – directly or indirectly – the competitiveness of enterprises. Applying a neo-Schumpeterian, evolutionary approach, it is shown that the socialist technological paths and trajectories have come to an abrupt end with the end of socialism. Following a brief description of different innovation policies in Eastern Europe, the chapter develops the concept of a 'demand-derived' innovation policy, the objective of which is the most efficient use of scarce public resources.

Chapter 3 provides a framework for analyzing enterprise restructuring in Central and Eastern Europe, and reports stylized facts on over ten years of industry reform. Its essence is to join the industrial economics analysis of competition between enterprises to the specifically post-socialist patterns of transforming socialist industrial combines into profit-oriented enterprises. As of 1999, the restructuring of most Central and Eastern European enterprises can be considered finished and leading to their integration into international networks. Most countries have recovered from the collapse of socialist production, and industrial output is showing growth. Chapters 2 and 3 also formulate hypotheses for the subsequent, empirical industry studies.

3.2 Part II: Empirical Analysis and Case Studies

Part II consists of empirical studies of industry and enterprise restructuring in Eastern Europe, including concrete case studies on the transformation of the most important enterprises. The chapters also pick up some of the conceptual issues developed in Part I. The choice of sectors was made according to a technological classification, considering that industrial sectors can be differentiated according to their technology patterns. It is assumed that particular technology patterns imply different underlying modes of innovation. The three ideal types thereof are resource-based, engineering-based and R&D-based sectors. The following sectors correspond to this broad range and are of particular interest in the context of Eastern Europe: car industry and shipbuilding (engineering based); food processing (resource based); telecommunications, software, and computers (science based). For each sector, restructuring and innovation policies are analyzed through the lens of an international competition analysis, with a particular view to the emergence of new network structures and the role of domestic and foreign technology. The empirical chapters are similar in structure, allowing cross-sectoral comparison.

Chapter 4 analyzes the restructuring of the car industry, often considered as the 'mother of all industries' due to its complex innovation and production networks and also its macroeconomic importance (employment, turnover, exports). Totally underdeveloped in the socialist period, car parts and the entire process of car assembly have flourished in the advanced reforming countries of Eastern Europe, based upon linkages to global networks through foreign direct investment, strategic alliances, mergers and sales cooperation. Thus, Eastern European car producers are providing an increasing challenge to their Western European, North American and Japanese competitors. A particularly striking case is the emergence of a car industry in Hungary (Chapter 5): the country that did not even have a car industry in the socialist period is about to become one of the most competitive car assembling countries worldwide. Traditionally considered a much 'heavier' industry, the restructuring of shipbuilding in Eastern Europe depended, in fact, on the successful integration into high-tech, information-dominated, logistically-intensive international networks (Chapter 6). Whereas two Polish shipyards are also becoming international market leaders, the industry has collapsed in Russia and Ukraine, where conversion from naval to merchant shipbuilding has failed thus far. Overcapacity all over Eastern Europe is becoming a threat to the international shipbuilding industry, which is itself suffering from a permanent restructuring crisis. The emergence of food processing in Eastern Europe (Chapter 7) is also observed with suspicion all over the world, particularly in the EU, where there are highly subsidized surpluses. However, lacking their own production and innovation networks and suffering from inefficient upstream agricultural structures, most Eastern European countries are adapting only slowly to international standards, where non-material factors (such as brand names and marketing) are at least as important as production itself.

The second section of Part II is dedicated to so-called 'future technologies', for which all countries, be they Eastern or Western, see a strategic role on the path towards a service-based economy. Chapter 8 covers telecommunication, considered a potentially booming market in Eastern Europe as it already is in the rest of the world. By deciding to adopt international standards for both telecommunication services and equipment, all Eastern European countries forced their enterprises into a radical restructuring process and increasing competition with foreign companies. Here, policy issues are technology transfer, standardization, gradual or immediate trade liberalization, and the sequencing of deregulation. Chapter 9 tests whether the Eastern European hopes in the development of a competitive software industry were justified. Indeed, Eastern European software engineers, forced to be particularly ingenious and resourceful in order to survive socialist working conditions, liked to think of themselves as a 'second India'. Reality is more complex. Chapter 10 analyzes Eastern European human and technical potential in computer technology and assembly. PC production, upon which Eastern European enterprises have concentrated, is a low-tech activity in which labor costs, logistics and market access dominate, providing favorable starting conditions for Eastern European assemblers. Whereas the integration into international supplier networks was easy in the PC segment, catching-up in higher segments (mainframes, supercomputers) may be hampered by proprietary technology. Chapter 11 provides evidence on the restructuring of the software and hardware industries in Poland, Central Europe's most populated country.

3.3 Part III: Summary and Outlook

Part III provides a summary of the main results of the book, and an outlook on the restructuring and international integration of Eastern European industry (Chapter 12). Lessons are drawn from ten years of industrial and innovation policies, and the Eastern European experience is compared with other regions of the world. The extent to which the results of the sector studies can be generalized is examined. In conclusion, the argument is presented that the restructuring of Eastern European industry also opens up new perspectives for innovation policies in the Western world, where decreasing state budgets and the globalization of R&D and production networks are challenging the rationale of domestic innovation policies.

4. ACKNOWLEDGMENTS

Thanks go primarily to the contributors to this volume, all specialists in their fields with a breadth of academic and professional background, representing both Eastern and Western Europe. We thank our discussion partners – enterprises, politicians and economists – throughout Eastern Europe, without whom the real-world perspective that we have attempted would not have been possible. The book results from a three-year research project on 'Restructuring of Science and Technology Systems in Eastern Europe', financed in part by the European Commission, DG XII within the 4th Framework's TSER-program ('Targeted Socio-economic Research'). Slavo

Radosevic (SPRU, now School of Slavonic and Eastern European Studies at the University of London) acted as the project's main intellectual and managerial driving force, David Dyker (SPRU) provided senior guidance and expertise: the book has benefitted significantly from both. Three referees have provided useful criticism. Further thanks go to Wolfgang Härle and Deborah Bowen for research assistance, preparation of the manuscript and artistic inspiration and layout, Grit Hannemann and Michael Jahn for proofreading, Dymphna Evans, Christine Boniface and colleagues at Edward Elgar for assistance and patience during the publishing process, and last but not least to Iris Semmann and Giesela Tietke for organization and secretarial support.

REFERENCES

Auriol, Laudeline and Slavo Radosevic (1996), 'R&D and Innovation Activities in Central and Eastern European Countries: Analysis Based on S&T Indicators', OECD Conference on the Implementation of Methodologies for R&D/S&T Statistics in Central and Eastern European Countries, Room Document (13), Paris, Budapest.

Bomsel, Olivier (1995), 'Enjeux industriels du post-socialisme', *Revue d'Economie Industrielle* (72).

Dyker, David and Jacques Perrin (1997), 'Technology Policy and Industrial Objectives in the Context of Economic Transition', in David Dyker (ed.), *The Technology of Transition*, Budapest: Central European University Press, pp. 3–19.

Hirschhausen, Christian von (1996), 'Lessons from Five Years of Industrial Reform in Post-socialist Central and Eastern Europe', *DIW Quarterly Journal of Economic Research*, **65** (1), pp. 45–56.

Hutschenreiter, Gernot, Mark Knell and Slavo Radosevic (1999), *Restructuring Innovation Systems in Eastern Europe*, Cheltenham, UK and Northampton, MA, USA: Edward Elgar.

Martin, Roderick (1998), 'Central and Eastern Europe and the International Economy: The Limits to Globalization', *Europe–Asia Studies*, **50** (1), pp. 7–26.

McKelvey, Maureen (1991), 'How do National Systems of Innovation Differ?', in Geoffrey M. Hodgson and Ernesto Screpanti (eds), *Rethinking Economics – Markets, Technology and Economic Evolution*, Aldershot, UK and Brookfield, USA: Edward Elgar.

Pavitt, Keith (1997), 'Transforming Centrally-planned Systems of Science and Technology: The Problem of Obsolete Competencies', in David Dyker (ed.), *The Technology of Transition*, Budapest: Central European University Press, pp. 43–60.

Porter, Michael (1998), 'Clusters and the New Economics of Competition', *Harvard Business Review*, **76** (6), November–December, pp. 77–90.

Part I

Conceptual Framework

2 An Evolutionary View of Post-socialist Restructuring: From Science and Technology Systems to Innovation Systems

Jürgen Bitzer

1. INTRODUCTION

Innovation systems are seen by many as a basis for innovation, technological development and competitiveness. The move towards a knowledge-based economy is seen as a strategy not only for industrialized Western countries during times of increasing international competition, but also for the post-socialist countries in their catching-up process. But whereas the starting points for Western market economies were well developed, with established and financed innovation systems, each of the post-socialist countries started with a fragmented and devalued *science and technology system (S&TS)*. The main question examined in this chapter is whether or not the socialist S&TS had an influence on the restructuring process of enterprises and sectors. Our hypothesis is that the socialist knowledge base and the socialist technological trajectories did not significantly influence the development of post-socialist enterprises and sectors. With the end of socialism, the technological paradigms changed abruptly; the new technological trajectories are determined by global market leaders. Thus we believe that the emerging innovation and production structures are less the product of existing fragments of the former socialist S&TS than of the absence of a functioning and competitive innovation system. We argue that domestic S&TSs have been replaced by emerging international innovation and supplier networks through which post-socialist enterprises gain access to the required knowledge.

Therefore the analysis focusses on existing demand for S&T and the sources of innovation through which this demand is satisfied.

The chapter is structured in the following way: the second section analyzes the differences between socialist S&TSs and capitalist innovation systems. The section starts with a discussion of the concept of science and technology systems with regard to the differences between socialist and capitalist economies. Following this, the different objectives and steering mechanisms of the two systems are analyzed. An analysis of various innovation policy approaches is carried out at the end of the second section. Section 3 describes the changes occurring during the transformation from the socialist S&TS to post-socialist innovation systems. This section focusses on the collapse of the socialist S&TS and the devaluation of the existing knowledge base. The analysis of the structural changes occurring in the post-socialist period explains why the socialist technological trajectory has been replaced by new technological paradigms. The section concludes with a discussion of various policy implications resulting from the post-socialist situation in Eastern Europe. Section 4 sums up the results of the chapter.

2. PRINCIPLES OF S&T CREATION IN SOCIALISM AND CAPITALISM

2.1 Science and Technology Systems: A Socialist Concept

Parallel to the theoretical developments, efforts were made as early as the 1950s and 1960s to create a statistical base for empirical research on technical change, to be used in socialist and capitalist countries alike. Following the recognition that innovation depended not just on R&D but also on a broad range of other activities such as education, training, production engineering and design quality control, UNESCO based their data-collecting and standardization work on the concept of 'science and technology'. Following the definition of UNESCO, scientific and technological activities (STA) are 'systematic activities which are closely concerned with the generation, advancement, dissemination and application of science and technical knowledge in all fields of science and technology. These include activities such as R&D, scientific and technical education and training (STET) and the scientific and technological services (STS)'.[1] Logically all institutions which are closely concerned with the S&T activities mentioned above belong to the science and technology system. This includes institutions

---

[1] UNESCO (1978).

such as enterprises that generate S&T but also institutions such as schools that disseminate it. Thus it is an approach that does not seem to be linked to a concrete economic problem.

Although the concept of S&T makes the complexity of the generation of knowledge and the range of the participating institutions clear, it is of very limited use for economic analysis and the derivation of policy recommendations. This is the result mainly of the 'neutral' definition, which considers S&T as a value in itself, independent of the surrounding economic system. This 'neutral' definition, where the *aims* of the S&T activities as well as the driving forces behind them remain unclear, makes the analysis and evaluation of S&T activities impossible. The author is aware that the definition is the result of negotiations between capitalist and socialist countries about the standardization and building-up of a statistical data base which should enable a comparison between them.[2] This explains why the two topics, aim and driving force, which comprise the difference between S&T generation and diffusion under socialism and capitalism, are absent. Neglecting these differences and treating S&T under socialism and capitalism as equal ignores the fact that the generation and diffusion of S&T in the two systems depends on completely different mechanisms. Under socialism, S&T was seen as a value in itself (Andreff 1998, p. 354, footnote 4) and the generation and diffusion was organized and steered by the state. In contrast, the ultimate objective of S&T in capitalist market economies is to enhance the competitiveness of enterprises, which are constrained by market mechanisms. To make the differences clear, we distinguish in the following between socialist S&TSs and capitalist innovation systems. The next two sections outline the differences between socialist S&TSs and capitalist innovation systems, which are important for the further analysis of the changes during the post-socialist period.

2.2 A Stylized Picture of the Socialist Science and Technology System

Under socialism, decisions concerning production and distribution of goods were made by the state/party, without any reference to monetary criteria.[3] The

---

[2]   See Freeman (1969), UNESCO (1970a and 1970b) for some insights into the origin process of the concept.

[3]   The following description of the socialist S&TS is a schematic one, which focuses on some underlying important mechanisms, more or less valid for all socialist countries. Particularities of different socialist countries are not considered because they do not contribute fundamentally new arguments to the following discussion. The description furthermore does not claim to cover all existing influences on the development and functioning of the socialist S&TS, but only the most important ones, which are at the center of the following analysis of socialist S&TS and capitalist innovation systems.

structures that evolved were therefore the result of political decisions and not of competition. Location, size and objectives of S&TS institutions were therefore more a question of *political influence* than of skills and capabilities. The division of tasks among national structures was politically determined, as was the division of tasks among the socialist East European countries. Policy, at least, was the dominant steering mechanism for the development of the socialist S&TS.

The upstream socialist S&TS was based on three pillars: the universities and institutions of higher education; the academies of sciences; and the branch research institutes and design bureaux (Freeman 1995b, p. 12). The main task of the universities and the institutions of higher education was education; only a small amount of research was carried out. The full breadth of research was carried out in the academies of sciences. The concrete development of new products and technologies was the task of the branch research institutes and bureaux of design. This included the development of products and technologies for the state, prototypes, pilot systems and experimental models (see Figure 2.1).[4]

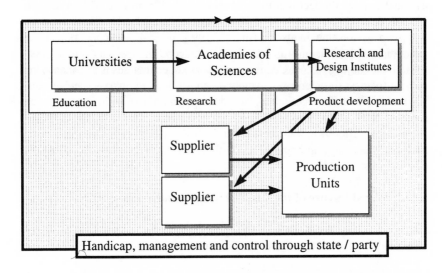

Figure 2.1 Stylized socialist innovation process in one sector

Inside the S&TS, steep hierarchies existed which were controlled by the ministries at the top. S&T institutions had no autonomy and accordingly, the

---

[4]   See Meske (1998) for a detailed description of the socialist S&TS and the division of tasks within it.

freedom of research was severely limited. The focus of the S&TS was mainly on science, and less on product and experimental development. Product refinement and testing activities in particular were inadequate (Pavitt 1997). Therefore the absorption capacities remained small. This was one reason why – despite relatively large investments in the S&TS – the pace of technological advances remained slower than in capitalist countries. Steep hierarchies hampered interactions and spillover effects between the S&T institutions (Paasi 1999, pp. 218–20).

In contrast to Western practice, product and technology development were carried out mainly in external institutions, such as the branch research institutes. The research capacities inside the *production units* were small because their task was seen to be purely in production (Radosevic 1996; Pavitt 1997; Paasi 1999). Therefore the links between the R&D institutions and the production level remained weak (Freeman 1995b, p. 12). Monetary constraints on research activities did not exist: for example, institutes were never closed for failing to achieve planned targets.

The isolation of the socialist countries through the COCOM (Coordinating Committee for Multinational Export Controls) restriction led to a two-track innovation strategy. First, an 'independent-problem-solution strategy' was carried out which tried to develop required products and technology without input from Western countries. This often led to the 'reinvention of the wheel' and to a waste of resources. Second, pure imitation was carried out to satisfy missing input from Western countries. This combination of 'independent-problem-solution-strategy' and pure imitation led increasingly to a technological backlog in most parts of the S&TS. Another reason for this technological backlog was the dominance of military research.[5] Immense resources were invested in military research, but the research results of the military–industrial complex were secret and therefore spillover effects to the civil part of the S&TS were prevented.[6] In Western countries, it may be assumed that the civil sector benefits much more from the results of military research. The allocation of immense research resources including both financial means and research personnel, as well as the interruption in diffusion of the research results prevented the socialist countries from keeping pace with the Western countries.

---

[5] Hanson and Pavitt (1987) estimate that 50–65 percent of all expenditures for R&D were used for military R&D.

[6] Even if some spillover effects exist through the production of civilian goods within the military complex, by far the overwhelming part of military research results generate no spillover effects.

2.3 Innovation Systems and Policies under Capitalism

2.3.1 Capitalist constraints as a steering mechanism of innovation generation in market economies

In contrast to the socialist S&TS, the driving force in market economies is capital constraints at the enterprise level. Thus, the situation is the complete opposite: developments in S&T are not decided by the state but determined mainly by market forces. This is reflected in the empirical fact that the majority of S&T is generated and spread by 'profit-seeking' enterprises. According to Dosi,

> in the most general terms, private profit-seeking agents will plausibly allocate resources to the exploration and development of new products and new techniques of production if they know, or believe in, the existence of some sort of yet unexploited scientific and technical opportunities; if they expect that there will be a market for their new products and processes; and, finally, if they expect some economic benefit, net of the incurred costs, deriving from the innovations. [7]

This corresponds to the empirical fact that currently the major part of R&D activities are financed and executed by the private business sector.

The search process for innovation mentioned above is based on what Dosi called 'technological paradigms', which define 'contextually the *needs* that are meant to be fulfilled, the *scientific principles* utilized for the task, the *material technology* to be used'.[8] In these paradigms, the future orientation of the innovator is reflected in the definition of the 'needs' (nothing other than the area in which the innovation should be placed). The second component that determines the technological paradigm is the innovator's 'knowledge base', which represents the combination of *information sources, knowledge* and *capabilities* on which the enterprise normally bases its search for innovation (Nelson and Winter 1982). The knowledge base is built up through accumulation, which depends heavily on the recent 'technological history' of the enterprise and determines its development along a 'technological path'. This path dependency limits the number of feasible technological opportunities because only opportunities which are suitable to the existing knowledge base can be used. Thus the technological paradigm simultaneously determines a technological trajectory for the enterprise. The result of this, as explained by Nelson and Winter (1982) and Dosi (1982 and 1988), is that the innovator's demand for (but also supply of) S&T depends heavily on its path-dependent knowledge base.

---

[7] Dosi (1988, p. 1120).
[8] Dosi (1988, p. 1127, emphasis added).

Because capitalist enterprises generate the overwhelming majority of knowledge in capitalist economies, demand and supply as well as the generation and diffusion of S&T is strongly influenced by market forces. In contrast to socialism, markets with demand and supply sides for S&T exist. Both influence each other and form sectoral, national and international innovation systems in an evolutionary process.

Demand is determined by enterprises which require S&T input. The form and size of the demand are dependent on the enterprise's technological paradigms. The required S&T can be acquired through different sources, for example, *internal capacities*, *informal sources*, *services* or *products* offered on the market. Whereas the acquisition of basic research is carried out mainly through informal sources such as publications, personal contacts and trade fairs, the demand for applied R&D can usually be satisfied only by internal capacities or on the market. In the latter case, the buyer can choose not only the source, but also the form in which he or she wants to acquire this knowledge, because it is often offered in several forms (for example, as a license or embedded in a product). The decision as to the form and degree of knowledge acquisition is again influenced by the enterprise's technological paradigm and knowledge base, as the capabilities of the demanding enterprise limit the range of acquisition opportunities significantly. Without the required capabilities, the acquisition through *embedded technologies* is often the only option. If the capabilities are not the limiting decision factor, other aspects such as cost, strategic orientation, existing production and innovation structures influence the decision process. The enterprise will create a portfolio of S&T sources according to its own specific characteristics, reflecting its particular situation. Thus an observed demand structure offers insight into the technological paradigm and trajectory of the demander.

On the supply side, it must be stated that those demanding S&T are also the main suppliers thereof. Enterprises, for example, demand S&T as an input but also offer S&T through their output. This holds true even for consumer goods, where products often stimulate innovation by competitors. Thus, all those institutions which carry out research and/or development and provide their research results as inputs are suppliers of S&T. In this case, it does not matter in which form or for which demand the results are provided. The forms in which S&T is offered on the market are manifold: services, licenses, products (embedded S&T), human capital, cooperation and publications.[9] The institutions which create the majority of S&T in any given capitalist country are universities, R&D departments of enterprises, and research institutes (public and private). The type of *knowledge provision* strongly

9   See OECD (1992, p. 37), Freeman (1995a, p.470) for different forms of knowledge acquisition.

influences the 'accessibility' and 'orientation' of S&T; therefore two different kinds of provision must be distinguished: publicly financed and privately financed knowledge. The two main differences between the two forms of financing for S&T activities are the orientation of the research – whether basic research or applied, and the difference in provision – whether as a public or a private good. According to the OECD *Frascati Manual*, basic research is 'experimental or theoretical work undertaken primarily to acquire new knowledge of the underlying foundation of phenomena and observable facts, without any particular application or use in view'.[10] Public financing of R&D permits research without an orientation towards commercial exploitation. Therefore, without further development, most of the results cannot be immediately applied for commercial uses. This usually leads to a non-existence of pecuniary demand, even if the knowledge generated is an important – even decisive – informal input for enterprises in their innovation search. Therefore basic research is carried out mainly by public institutions, and the results are *provided at no cost* as a 'public good', even though these original results do not have the characteristics of a public good as they are excludable. The state renounces its right of exclusive use, and even compels the institution to publish its results to promote quick diffusion of the newly generated knowledge. However, the research results become a public good only after publication. In contrast, profit-seeking producers of S&T carry out applied research and experimental development with a practical orientation.[11] The aim of this knowledge generation is to obtain a competitive advantage over their competitors. Therefore the enterprises use their opportunities to exclude competitors from the use of the research carried out. Enterprises represent the pecuniary supply of S&T. Because they – for the most part – want to sell their innovations in one form or another, they offer their knowledge to their customers 'ready for use' (for example, as a license or embedded in a product). Thus the supply side consists of a pecuniary and a non-pecuniary component, both of which depend mainly on the form of provision. Whereas the non-pecuniary component is influenced mainly by the state as provider, the pecuniary and major component is dominated by profit-seeking enterprises.

Corresponding to the significant but not exclusive importance of innovations for the competition of enterprises, policy-makers have discovered the innovation systems as a field of investigation. The following section compares two different approaches to carrying out an innovation policy.

---

[10] OECD (1993, p. 29).
[11] See definitions of applied research and experimental development in the OECD *Frascati Manual* (1993, p. 29).

2.3.2 Approaches to innovation policies: supply oriented vs. demand derived

Just as enterprises' R&D activities have the objective of obtaining competitive advantages, so also should the aim of innovation policies be to improve the competitiveness of enterprises. Owing to limited state budgets, the costs and benefits of possible measures have to be weighed and ranked according to priority, which in turn has to be derived from principles. S&T activities are not tasks in their own right, and if the state intervenes – in particular if the state invests money – there should ideally be a benefit for society. In market economies, these benefits are equated with the competitiveness of enterprises and with economic growth. Therefore successful commercial exploitation of the knowledge generated is a crucial secondary condition for any innovation policy. The *improvement of innovation activities* and *successful commercial exploitation* are therefore the underlying principles of innovation policies.

These principles are important guidelines for the implementation of innovation policies, but are less helpful for the concrete development of policy measures. Hence a starting point has to be chosen for further developments. Two different ways to tackle this problem can be identified: a *supply-oriented* and a *demand-derived* approach. In contrast to neo-classical and Keynesian theory, the terms 'demand' and 'supply' do not indicate the side at which the policy measures should be positioned, but the indicator which should be analyzed to derive the policy implications. Supply-oriented or supply-derived S&T policy implies that policy measures are derived from an analysis of the S&T supply. In contrast, demand-oriented or demand-derived S&T policy examines the demand side, in order to identify bottlenecks and to derive innovation policy measures.

With the supply-oriented policy approach, the government identifies so-called 'future technologies' and 'future branches' from which the state may expect above-average benefits if national enterprises are able to take over technological leadership.[12] Accordingly, an innovation policy is designed to extend the supply of S&T knowledge into these areas. Usually, this means that financial support for R&D in this area is provided and the innovation system is adapted. The main objective of this approach is to achieve a technological lead over competitors by adapting the innovation system at a very early stage of technological development. Furthermore, positive external effects are expected.

---

[12] One instrument to identify such future technologies and branches is 'technological foresight'. See Martin and Johnston (1998), for exercises in technological foresight in Britain, Australia and New Zealand.

However, this approach brings with it considerable risks. First, the question arises whether the state is able to carry out the necessary technological development control. This question can be asked at both stages, during the identification phase and the phase of implementation of the required measures. With such activities, the state has a considerable influence on the technological paradigms, as well as the technological trajectories of enterprises, sectors and possibly the entire economy.

Second, the state is dependent on the estimates of the participating agents in the innovation process, which creates a *moral hazard problem*: the state is not able to evaluate the suggestions for policy measures. Third, the state risks supporting 'wrong' technologies that in the end might have little or no potential for commercial exploitation.[13] Fourth, with regard to Eastern Europe and developing countries, the approach can be applied only by countries that have the required prevailing conditions for economic and technological development. From the outset, the supply-oriented approach is applicable only to countries that have a suitable infrastructure. Last, the supply-derived policy approach requires immense financial means due to the normal uncertainty of R&D. Therefore supply-oriented policies are applied in Western Europe particularly.

The demand-derived policy approach is oriented towards the existing demand at the enterprise level. The underlying idea is to remove the existing bottlenecks in the innovation system that result from a restriction of existing demand by supply. A crucial condition for the intervention of the state is that the enterprises are themselves unable to remove such bottlenecks efficiently. This is less exciting – and less prestigious – than taking over the 'technological steering-wheel' of an economy. However, it leaves the responsibility for the orientation of S&T to the relevant institutions, which also bear the consequences of their decisions. As mentioned, the demand for S&T is influenced by a broad range of factors that depend on the characteristics of the individual enterprise and sector. Therefore, a prerequisite for the demand-derived approach is a detailed analysis of the demand for S&T, which enables the identification of bottlenecks that reduce the competitiveness of domestic enterprises. An advantage of this approach is that *systematic* problems of different sectors are addressed by policy. This means that bottlenecks which concern all enterprises in the sector are removed. Instead of the single project support of the supply-oriented approach where the assumed spillover effects are uncertain, the demand-oriented approach guarantees that all enterprises in the sector benefit from the

---

[13]   In Germany, there have been several examples in recent years of unsuccessful future technology promotion, for example, in nuclear technology (fast breeder in Kalkar) and magnet hover technology (Transrapid).

policy measures. Furthermore, particularities of the different sectors are taken into account explicitly by the formulation of policy measures. Problems of the supply-oriented approach, such as moral hazard dilemmas, competence problems and the wrong orientation of the innovation systems are avoided by the demand-derived approach. The latter approach does, however, require a detailed analysis of the demand for S&T, implying the need for an advance preparation phase.

3. CHANGES IN EASTERN EUROPE: FROM SOCIALIST S&T SYSTEMS TOWARDS MARKET-ORIENTED INNOVATION SYSTEMS

3.1 Basic Conditions for Restructuring in Eastern Europe

With the collapse of socialism, the socialist production networks and the established links between production and the socialist S&TS collapsed as well. As a result, a fragmented S&TS without any connection to the economy remained. With the 'monetization' of the economy and the creation of capitalist market economies, the S&TSs were also monetized. Secure government funding was replaced by monetary constraints. Today, governments are no longer willing or able to finance S&TSs that have no function in the production process. Thus Eastern Europe faces the question of how to create new capitalist innovation systems, which help to improve the competitiveness of domestic enterprises, under predominantly post-socialist conditions.

Western models cannot be applied under these post-socialist circumstances because the required financial and institutional conditions do not exist. Therefore new models must be developed which take into account existing restrictions and conditions.

The post-socialist conditions in which the S&T policy has to be carried out are characterized by *limited financial means* and *high opportunity costs*. The policy-makers have to decide whether they should invest their limited funds in the creation of a new innovation system (and, if so, more precisely in which particular activities) or in the improvement of infrastructure, the creation of institutions, and so on. Expenditures, therefore, must be carefully justified. Policy-makers have to ensure that they do not hamper the necessary, continuing process of adaptation to the changed requirements of competitiveness in a post-socialist economy. Therefore the structural changes that have already occurred must be taken into account: they make it clear that the restructuring of socialist S&TSs into capitalist innovation systems in Eastern Europe is more than a question of money.

3.2 Structural Changes in the Socialist S&TS

3.2.1 Partial devaluation of human capital

Because of the former large investments in the creation of human capital, education in the Eastern European countries is of a high level. Particularly in the natural sciences, experts consider Eastern European researchers to be among the best in the world. Nevertheless, with the opening of the Eastern European markets to Western products and technologies and their quick diffusion, the great majority of Eastern European human capital was strongly devalued during transformation. This devaluation occurred particularly in the fields of *applied research* and *production* because of the far-reaching nature of the changes which took place in these fields. Examples of such changes are the introduction of new machines, new forms of organization, new forms of logistics, new input factors requiring a different use, and so on. A partial devaluation of human capital also occurred in the field of basic research because Eastern European researchers had to adapt their work procedures to international standards (for example, attention to copyright, fulfillment of standards in the case of participation in international research projects and programs). A particularly critical problem is the devaluation of human capital in the case of teaching staff, because obsolete knowledge is still being taught.

3.2.2 Changes in the division of tasks in the innovation process: from state to enterprises

Apart from this devaluation of human capital, the division of tasks in the innovation process has also changed dramatically. This led to the loss of functions in different institutions of the former S&TS. Under socialism, the state/party took over all functions, as organizer of the innovation process. The orientation of research, the application of knowledge to the development of new products and the production thereof were organized by the state/party. The distribution of products was guaranteed: competition and financial restrictions did not exist. With the introduction of capitalism as an economic principle, the application of new knowledge to new products shifted from the state to the private sector, or more precisely, to the emerging capitalist enterprises. A core task of *enterprises* in capitalist economies is seen in the use of new knowledge in the field of applied research for product development and production. This also includes commercial exploitation of products in a competitive environment and under financial restrictions.

These changes mean, as well, that the newly emerging enterprises chose their sources of innovation themselves. Often, the domestic institutes were not able to supply the required input. Therefore the enterprises chose foreign sources of innovation and the obsolete domestic sources were no longer used. Figure 2.2 shows the stylized changes.

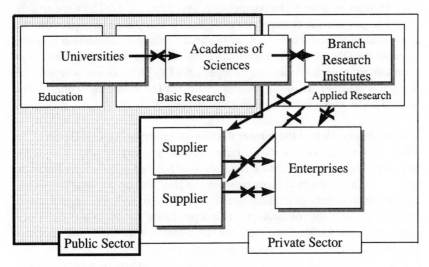

Figure 2.2 Changed tasks in the innovation process

The commercial exploitation of products in a competitive environment and under financial restrictions plays a particularly important role in the successful use of technological potential. The technological capabilities are often not the factor limiting the competitiveness of Eastern European enterprises. Competitiveness depends heavily on additional factors such as the existing market structures, the competition axes used, existing market barriers or network effects. Competitive disadvantages of Eastern European enterprises can often be found in these 'new' areas of business. Examples are a lack of quality, bad or non-existent marketing activities, low reliability, a lack of customer orientation and a lack of financing opportunities.

3.2.3 Researcher and innovation systems in international competition

With the opening of the East European markets, these countries' enterprises and national innovation institutions have entered into international competition; in the former case, this is carried out directly and in the latter case, indirectly on the product markets. Enterprises and customers are now free to decide which of the internationally available products they want to buy. The availability, high quality and high technological level of Western products led to their quick diffusion onto East European markets, but with the purchase of Western products, the services of Western innovation systems were bought as well. Through the creation of international supplier networks, East European enterprises gained access to the modern technology which they urgently need in order to be competitive. The domestic S&TSs were largely unable to provide the required technologies or knowledge as inputs for the newly emerging production. In many research fields, this comparison between Eastern S&TSs and Western innovation systems destroyed the high expectations in parts of the East European S&TS. Thus only in a handful of fields do institutions of East European S&TS have the comparative advantages to attract direct foreign investments.[14]

3.2.4 Disintegration of the former division of labor in Eastern Europe
With the collapse of socialism, both national production and innovation structures and the established CMEA production and innovation structures collapsed. The division of labor between the East European countries, which was the result mainly of political decisions and not of competition, collapsed completely with the restoration of independence of the East European countries. This further increased the problems for restructuring national S&TSs. Structures which were designed to serve the innovation and production system of the entire Eastern bloc now had to be adapted to the new domestic enterprise requirements. As a result, the size of the S&TS in most countries has been reduced significantly. Furthermore, required parts of the S&TS, which in the socialist period were located in other socialist countries, have to be recreated from scratch because they are no longer accessible.

The Baltic countries of Lithuania, Latvia and Estonia can be seen as an extreme example of this problem. As a former part of the Soviet Union, R&D for electrical engineering for civil as well as military use was a significant activity in these three countries. The capacities created were designed according to the needs of the entire Soviet S&TS, which served a population of 271 million. In comparison to the number of inhabitants of Lithuania (3.8 million), Latvia (2.6 million) and Estonia (1.6 million), the existing capacities were much too large. A further result of this division of labor was that the production of goods developed in the Baltic was usually carried out in other locations. To illustrate this, one need only refer to the production of computers, which was carried out mainly in Belarus, while the R&D took place in the Baltic countries. The former demand for the Baltic S&T services

---

[14] See Dyker (1996) for successful examples in information technology.

from within the Soviet S&TS collapsed overnight after the restoration of independence. The missing production units, now located in foreign countries, no longer demand Baltic S&T services. As a result of these developments, the size of the S&TS had to be reduced dramatically (Bitzer and Hirschhausen 1998b, pp. 510–15).

3.3 The Abrupt End of the 'Socialist Technological Trajectory' and the Emergence of New Technological Paradigms

The description above has shown that with the end of socialism, the economic and technological conditions changed abruptly. In particular, the shift in supply and demand for S&T altered the technological paradigms significantly. Coming back to Dosi, the 'needs', 'scientific principles' and the 'material technology used' have changed. Increasing international competition forced the emerging enterprises to use state-of-the-art technologies which were not available in Eastern Europe. The socialist technological paradigms were neither *competitive* nor *compatible* with the newly available technologies and therefore, their application was impractical. Empirical studies show that the overwhelming majority of East European enterprises – and often entire sectors – were not competitive and are to this day heavily dependent on Western technology transfers (Bitzer and Hirschhausen 1998a and the following chapters). The socialist knowledge base usually did not offer starting points for a promising process of catching up to global state-of-the-art technology. Therefore, the new enterprises – but also restructured production units – are using completely new technological paradigms that often have no connection to the former technological trajectories of their sector (for example, computer assembling, see Chapter 10). A particular characteristic of this change in technological paradigms is the extensive use of embedded technologies as sources of innovation, which appear in the form of imported intermediary products. For example, all components for PC assembly, with the exception of unsophisticated computer housing, are imported from the West. In the shipbuilding industry, customers demand the installation of Western state-of-the-art components, for example, radar systems, engines, control information technology and so on.

From an aggregate perspective, one could state that the 'socialist technological trajectory' ended with the collapse of socialism. The new technological paradigms have almost nothing in common with those used under socialism.

Because of the huge technological gap between Eastern European and current state-of-the-art technology, the technological paradigms and corresponding technological trajectories in Eastern Europe are widely determined by Western technological leaders.[15]

3.4 Some Empirical Facts on Restructuring of East European Innovation Systems

3.4.1 The limitations of S&T indicator analysis in Eastern Europe

S&T indicator analyses are often used to assess the situation and developments of the emerging innovation systems in Eastern Europe. But while the expressiveness of S&T indicators is already heavily debated in Western countries, S&T indicator analysis in Eastern Europe contains additional problems which call any S&T indicator in these countries into question. There are three main reasons for this. The first and most trivial, yet least respected reason is that socialist countries had other indicators which are incompatible with those of a capitalist market economy. Thus, the structural break that occurred with the collapse of socialism and the introduction of capitalism cannot be reconciled *ex post*. An S&T indicator analysis covering both the socialist and the post-socialist period is therefore questionable (Radosevic and Auriol 1998).[16]

A second problem of S&T indicator analysis in Eastern Europe is its fragile statistical base. This data is characterized by incomplete series, frequent changes of methodology, and unreliable data collection (Radosevic 1996). Whereas a comparison of East European countries in socialist times is possible, this is not the case for the post-socialist period (see notes to Table 2.1). At the beginning of the post-socialist period, each country began using a different delimitation for its S&T statistics; furthermore, the availability of data differed widely between individual countries. Today only some countries have introduced the OECD procedure for collecting S&T data, but this did not guarantee the quality and completeness of the data either.

The third problem of S&T indicator analysis in Eastern Europe is a methodical one, caused by the radical structural changes described in Section 3.2. These immense and manifold changes are reflected only partly by the S&T indicators. In Western countries, S&T indicators may be interpreted by

---

[15] See Dosi (1988, p. 1159) for a discussion of the underlying asymmetries which led to this domination.

[16] For example, the notion of GDP as an indicator for (capitalist) value added did not exist. Thus, in socialist countries, the ratio R&D/GDP did not exist. This ratio has been reapplied *ex post* by S&T statisticians ignorant of socialist reality in an attempt to fill their standardized S&T tables. This, however, is a falsification of history; the use of the R&D/GDP indicator is only possible where GDP really exists: that is, in the post-socialist period (for example, in Poland from 1990 onwards, the Czech and Slovak Republics from 1991 onwards, and the CIS countries and the Baltics from 1992 onwards, Hirschhausen 1996).

examining the gradually occurring structural changes in national innovation systems and economic structures. In contrast, in Eastern Europe it is exactly these structural changes which are the driving force of current developments. They tell the real story: to arrive at an accurate picture of the situation in the East European S&TS, it is crucial to take them into account when interpreting the figures. An interpretation of existing S&T data is difficult and should therefore not be overvalued in political and scientific discussion.

3.4.2 A careful interpretation of S&T indicators in Eastern Europe

Because of the problems of S&T indicators in Eastern Europe, an interpretation down to decimal points is out of the question. Instead, this section undertakes to interpret the observed tendencies. All countries had in common a decrease in expenditures on R&D (see Table 2.1). But in contrast to other authors, we do not agree that this decrease erodes the scientific capabilities of these countries. On the contrary, we believe that the underlying structural changes which partly caused these developments are a necessary 'purification' of the East European innovation systems. These developments are the result of the above-mentioned adaptation of the S&TS to national requirements, an increase in productivity (Kontorovich 1994; Paasi 1999), a change in the economic structure, as well as the shift of large parts of R&D to the private sector, all of which cannot automatically be viewed as negative.

Table 2.1 Gross domestic expenditure on R&D as a percentage of GDP, 1991–1995*

	1991	1992	1993	1994	1995
Czech Republic [1]	2.12	1.83	1.35	1.25	1.15
Hungary[2]	1.08	1.07	0.99	0.89	0.75
Poland[3]	1.05	0.83	0.83	0.84	0.74
Slovak Republic[4]	2.57	2.03	1.66	1.12	1.04
Russian Federation	**	0.78	0.81	0.82	0.73

Notes:
*   Defense R&D not included.
** Figure is unsuitable for S&T indicator analysis because transformation started in Russia in 1992.
[1]   Total expenditure of the R&D base, depreciation costs included.
[2]   Until 1993, including purchase of licenses, know-how and so on; break in series in 1991 due to changing methodology for calculating GDP.
[3]   Until 1993: capital expenditure in enterprises and the higher education sector not included, depreciation costs included.
[4]   Until 1993, total expenditure of the R&D base; depreciation costs included.

Sources: OECD (1996), Radosevic (1998).

The observed decrease is the result mainly of two opposite effects. On the one hand, there is a necessary reduction in publicly financed R&D, which is still at a high level (see Table 2.2) and is the result of a shift of tasks in the innovation process. On the other hand, there is a takeover of these tasks by the private sector. The international availability of products often makes independent domestic development unfeasible, in particular for enterprises that are not on the cutting edge of technology. Microprocessors are a case in point. Furthermore, the overwhelming majority of East European businesses are small and medium-sized enterprises (SMEs), which are usually only active on their domestic markets and, like SMEs in Western countries, carry out only a small part of R&D by themselves.

Table 2.2 Sources of R&D expenditures, 1995 (in percent)

	Czech Republic	Hungary	Poland	Spain	Nether- lands	Belgium
Business	63.11	39.65	31.47	44.53	46.02	64.15
Government	33.26	54.86	66.48	47.99	42.29	28.27
Private non-profit	0.29	0.48	0.36	0.79	2.38	0.63
Funds from abroad	3.34	5.01	1.69	6.69	9.31	6.94
Total	100	100	100	100	100	100*
GERD**/GDP	1.04	0.73	0.75	0.84	2.08	1.59

Notes: * Rounded to 100.
              ** Gross expenditures for research and development.

Sources: OECD (1997 and 1998); and author's calculations.

In conclusion, we believe that the reduction of expenditures on R&D is less dramatic than often perceived. It is, rather, a move towards the development of 'normal' conditions of R&D, reflecting the size of the countries and the domestic enterprises as well as the existing economic structures, which are for the first time the result of competition. The demand often made for higher expenditures on R&D must be carefully justified and cannot be based on comparisons with the expenditures of Western countries.

3.5 Elements of a Demand-oriented S&T Policy

The preceding explanations have shown the difficulties of an S&T policy in Eastern European countries. Such a policy must be targetted at the needs of newly established enterprise networks. The possible policy options are subject to severe restrictions: scarce financial resources and high opportunity costs. Scarce financial resources mean in particular that Western models, which are generally based on a supply-oriented strategy and require considerable financial expenditures, cannot be applied in Eastern Europe. The high opportunity costs which can appear in the form of investment in infrastructure or health care, prevent available funds from being invested in projects where returns are extremely uncertain and lie in the distant future.

Which strategy should a post-socialist S&T policy follow in order to construct a new innovation system and smooth out the possible short-term bottlenecks limiting the competitiveness of domestic firms? We propose several *demand-derived* policy measures, based on our conviction that monetary demand should be the dominant criteria for S&T policy decisions. The reason for this drastic proposal is that the socialist S&TSs were the product of political decisions and not of competition. Thus an economic or skill/capability-based legitimization for the different institutions cannot be demonstrated. Eastern European governments must decide whether the innovation system represents a bottleneck for the Eastern European enterprises. As described in the preceding section, often it is not the technical capacities but competitive drawbacks such as marketing that contribute to bottlenecks: thus, the existing potential is often constrained by the sales or market side. Market barriers, market conditions, but also the inability to meet the requirements of both customers and competitors can lead to the shutting down of companies and even of entire industries. Often, these conditions cannot be influenced by policies. Where technological capabilities are not the limiting factor, constructing corresponding parts of an innovation system would not have the desired effect. It has been argued frequently that demand-oriented S&T policies will lead to a loss of technological 'potential' – human capital – which might perhaps be needed in the future. But this scientific 'potential' of the Eastern European countries must be analyzed precisely in the new environment of global competitiveness to see if it is still valid.

Furthermore, the competitive institutions that are eligible for public financing must be 'filtered out'. This applies in particular to research institutions that conduct applied research, such as the academies of science and branch research institutes, which are classified as part of the corporate sector. By analyzing the new production network, one can identify innovation sources, connections to the science and innovation system and potential demand. As far as institutions are concerned, one can see whether or not the research institutions are successful in finding demand for their output. If the reorientation of the institutions is unsuitable, they should be put up for management buy-out or be closed. Holding on to obsolete institutions under the existing budget restrictions results in a lack of funds for new and innovative institutions. A demand-oriented policy approach would identify competitive advantages in particular areas of research and consequently enable targetted support. Furthermore, it is assumed that companies are in a better position than the state to assess the existing scientific potential. This policy approach additionally opens up opportunities for enlisting firms to finance parts of the innovation system from which they profit.

4. CONCLUSIONS

Reviewing the emergence and development of the socialist S&TS, it quickly becomes clear that these systems were mainly the product of political decisions – made in the absence of competition – which do not take into consideration either existing skills and capabilities or economic constraints. Whereas under socialism, S&T was seen as having a value in itself, in capitalist economies it has to perform a particular task: it must improve the competitiveness of enterprises. Therefore the systemic changes in the S&TS during transformation affected its objectives and driving forces. The collapse of socialism implied a radical change in the S&TSs of all Eastern European countries. The function and tasks of the existing institutions of the S&TS changed fundamentally. Tasks in the innovation process – which in former times were planned, steered and carried out by state/party – now had to be taken over by the private sector. Private enterprises, the new 'organizers' of innovation generation and diffusion, were now free to choose their sources of innovation. The emerging competition forced the enterprises to create innovation and supplier networks with those sources which were most effective for their business. This brought the domestic S&TS into competition with Western innovation systems. The lack of competitiveness and compatibility in the socialist technological knowledge base and paradigms quickly became obvious and led to an abrupt end of the socialist technological trajectory. New and internationally-oriented technological paradigms emerged; these remain strongly based on foreign technology transfers, mainly in the form of embedded technology. Current East European technological trajectories are therefore fixed by the leaders in Western technology. The new technological knowledge base and paradigms brought a further strong devaluation of human capital. Despite these manifold structural changes, the scope for policy measures is narrow. They must be oriented towards the conditions prevailing in Eastern Europe instead of emulating Western models, which under these conditions are doomed to failure. Instead of simply copying Western-style supply-side S&T policies, we recommend the application of a demand-derived S&T policy, which will reveal comparative advantages and help to improve the competitiveness of domestic enterprises. Furthermore, this policy approach would help to 'filter out' competitive institutions that are eligible for public financing.

REFERENCES

Andreff, Wladimir (1998), 'S&T and the Future of Economies in Transition: An Economic Perspective', in Werner Meske et al. (eds), *Transforming Science and Technology Systems – the Endless Transition?*, Nato Science Series 4: Science and Technology Policy (23), Amsterdam: IOS Press, pp. 346–60.

Bitzer, Jürgen and Christian von Hirschhausen (eds) (1998a), *Final Report – Work Package C, Industrial Restructuring, Part C.0 Conceptual Framework, Industry Studies*, TSER Project: Restructuring and Re-integration of Science and Technology Systems in Economies in Transition, Berlin: DIW.

Bitzer, Jürgen and Christian von Hirschhausen (1998b), *Industrial Restructuring and Economic Recovery in the Baltic Countries – Lithuania, Latvia, Estonia; Infrastructure Policies for Sustained Growth in the Baltic Countries*, Berlin: DIW.

Dosi, Giovanni (1982), 'Technological Paradigms and Technological Trajectories: A Suggested Interpretation of the Determinants of Technical Change', *Research Policy*, **11** (3), pp. 147–62.

Dosi, Giovanni (1988), 'Sources, Procedures, and Microeconomic Effects of Innovation', *Journal of Economic Literature*, **16** (5), pp. 1120–71.

Dyker, David (1996), 'The Computer and Software Industries in the East European Economics – A Bridgehead to the Global Economy?', STEEP Discussion Paper, (27), Sussex.

Freeman, Christopher (1969), 'The Measurement of Scientific and Technological Activities', UNESCO Statistical Reports and Studies, Paris.

Freeman, Christopher (1995a), 'The Economics of Technical Change', *Cambridge Journal of Economics*, **18** (5), pp. 463–514.

Freeman, Christopher (1995b), 'The "National System of Innovation" in Historical Perspective', *Cambridge Journal of Economics*, **19** (1), pp. 5–24.

Hanson, P. and K. Pavitt (1987), *The Comparative Economics of Research, Development and Innovation in East and West: A Survey*, Chur: Harwood Academic Publishers.

Hirschhausen, Christian von (1996), *Du combinat socialist à l'entreprise capitaliste*, Paris: l'Harmattan.

Kontorovich, Vladimir (1994), 'The Future of Soviet Science', *Research Policy*, **23** (2), pp. 113–21.

Martin, Ben R. and Ron Johnston (1998), 'Technology Foresight for Wiring Up the National Innovation System: Experiences in Britain, Australia, and New Zealand', SPRU Electronic Working Papers Series (14), Brighton.

Meske, Werner (1998), 'Towards New S&T Networks: The Transformation of Actors and Activities', in Werner Meske et al. (eds), *Transforming Science and Technology Systems – the Endless Transition?*, Nato Science Series 4: Science and Technology Policy (23), Amsterdam: IOS Press, pp. 3–26.

Nelson, Richard R. and Sidney G. Winter (1982), *An Evolutionary Theory of Economic Change*, Cambridge, MA: Harvard University Press.

Organization for Economic Cooperation and Development (OECD) (1992), *OECD Proposed Guidelines for Collecting and Interpreting Technological Innovation Data – Oslo Manual*, Paris: OECD.

Organization for Economic Cooperation and Development (OECD) (1993), *The Measurement of Scientific and Technological Activities, Proposed Standard Practice for Surveys of Research and Experimental Development, Frascati Manual*, Paris: OECD.

Organization for Economic Cooperation and Development (OECD) (1996), 'Science and Technology Statistics in the Partners in Transition Countries and the Russian Federation', *OECD Working Papers*, **4** (19) Paris: OECD.

Organization for Economic Cooperation and Development (OECD) (1997), *Basic Science and Technology Statistics*, Paris: OECD.

Organization for Economic Cooperation and Development (OECD) (1998), *Statistics Directorate, National Accounts, Main Aggregates 1960–1996*, Volume I, Paris: OECD.

Paasi, Marianne (1999), 'Efficiency of Innovation Systems in the Transition Countries', *Economic Systems*, **22** (3), pp. 217–34.

Pavitt, Keith L.R. (1997), 'Transforming Centrally Planned Systems of Science and Technology: The Problem of Obsolete Competencies', in David A. Dyker (ed.), *The Technology of Transition: Science and Technology Policies for Transition Countries*, Budapest: Central European University Press, pp. 43–60.

Radosevic, Slavo (1996), *Divergence or Convergence in Research and Development and Innovation Between 'East' and 'West'?*, Sussex: Science and Policy Research Unit (SPRU).

Radosevic, Slavo (1998), 'S&T, Growth and Restructuring of Central and Eastern European Countries, Report Based on S&T Indicators, Work

Package B', TSER Project: Restructuring and Re-integration of Science & Technology Systems in Economies in Transition, Sussex: Science and Policy Research Unit (SPRU).

Radosevic, Slavo and Laudeline Auriol (1998), 'Measuring S&T Activities in the Post-socialist Countries of CEE: Conceptual and Methodological Issues in Linking Past with Present', *Scientometrics*, **42** (3), pp. 273–97.

United Nations Educational, Scientific and Cultural Organization (UNESCO) (1970a), 'Manual for Surveying National Scientific and Technological Potential', *Science Policy Studies and Documents*, (15), Paris: UNESCO.

United Nations Educational, Scientific and Cultural Organization (UNESCO) (1970b), 'The Role of Science and Technology in Economic Development', *Science Policy Studies and Documents*, (18), Paris: UNESCO.

United Nations Educational, Scientific and Cultural Organization (UNESCO) (1978), 'Recommendation Concerning the Internationalization of Statistics on Science and Technology', Paris: UNESCO.

3 Enterprise Reform and Competition Analysis in the Post-socialist Context: Analytical Framework and Stylized Facts

Christian von Hirschhausen

1. INTRODUCTION

In this chapter, a conceptual framework for analyzing enterprise restructuring in Eastern Europe is developed, and stylized facts of ten years of industry reform are reported. In addition to looking at the meso-level, on which science and technology analysis and policies are taking place, it is necessary to look more closely at the *micro-level* transformations in Eastern Europe, that is, industrial and restructuring and technological modernization, as seen from an enterprise's point of view. Two different aspects have to be taken into account: the first is the international *competition* in which Eastern European enterprises are engaging now that trade restrictions have been largely abandoned; the second is the *post-socialist* nature of the process of systemic change in all Eastern European countries, from socialism to some kind of capitalist economy. We assume that the competition and the post-socialist aspects are closely related, leading to specific trajectories of restructuring. Thus, they should be analyzed in parallel. The framework thus brings together two different branches of research: one, derived from industrial economics theory, on competition and modes of growth of enterprises; the other, derived from the theory of systemic change in Eastern Europe. Our analysis is also based upon empirical evidence gathered in approximately 200 enterprise visits carried out personally in all Central and Eastern European countries (except Albania), Russia and Ukraine between 1990 and 1999.

This chapter is structured in the following way: Section 2 develops a methodology for analyzing inter-enterprise competition and enterprise strategies, called 'modes of growth'. The essence thereof is to distinguish enterprises not by their products (for example, cars, food processing) but by the axes on which they are in *competition* with other enterprises. The advantage of this dynamic approach is that it captures different enterprise strategies within one industrial sector. Section 3 puts this analysis in the specific post-socialist context; different modes of Eastern European enterprise restructuring are identified. Contrary to the initial euphoria for greenfield developments, comparative analysis suggests that it is rather the market-oriented use of existing enterprises and resources that explains the rapid recovery and growth of the successful transformation countries (for example, Poland, Hungary and Estonia). This, however, requires a period of *creative destruction* at the enterprise level. Section 4 provides a brief survey of macroeconomic and institutional reform in Eastern Europe over the last decade, these being important conditions for restructuring at the micro-level; some quantitative results of industrial restructuring are also presented. Section 5 concludes.

2. COMPETITION ANALYSIS AND MODES OF GROWTH OF ENTERPRISES[17]

2.1 The Enterprise as the Relevant Level of Sanctions in a Market Economy

The basic belief upon which this chapter is based is that the pivotal element of any economic system is the *enterprise* (or firm), operating under a capital constraint (or budget constraint) and (more or less) exposed to competition from other enterprises. In addition, the state sets the economic, political and some social rules for society. This distinction between the role of enterprises and the state may seem trivial to an economist working in a capitalist market environment. It is anything but trivial, though, when searching for emerging patterns of competition and industrial policies in post-socialist Eastern Europe, where this separation between business activity and the state did not exist until very recently. Also, as set out in the previous chapter, the traditional economists of science and technology like to think in terms of 'industries' rather than in terms of 'enterprises'.

---

[17] The theory of 'modes of growth', from which the competition analysis in this chapter is directly adapted, was developed at CERNA, the Center for Industrial Economics at the Paris School of Mines, under the guidance of Pierre-Noel Giraud (1991).

However, in any market economy – albeit emerging ones – the relevant object of competition analysis is not the industrial branch, but rather the enterprise level; it is also the main level where economic policy can be introduced. The reason for this is simple: in a market economy, the industrial branch is not a level where competition takes place, profits are made or sanctions can be applied. Instead, enterprises compete with their products on certain markets, and it is enterprises that operate under financial constraints. Branches are not directly in competition with each other; enterprises are. Branches cannot be closed down as such; enterprises can. Last but not least, branches do not create jobs; enterprises do.

We therefore propose to center the analysis of industry reform and innovation on the competition between individual enterprises. This does not mean that the individual enterprise is the *only* level where innovation takes place. Indeed, enterprises in a given sector compete with each other on certain axes, and may cooperate on other axes. The process of competition forces enterprises to choose their strategy using innovation as a strategic parameter. In order to detect those patterns of competition and cooperation, a tool is required to analyze the strategies of individual enterprises. This is done in the next section, by identifying the *axes of competition*.

2.2 Enterprises' Strategies between Upstream and Downstream Competition

The objective of any enterprise is to escape from market competition in order to exploit temporary monopolies in particular market segments (Schumpeter 1942). Indeed according to the very nature of a market economy, enterprises orient their strategies so as to be subject to the *least* market competition.[18] Reality shows that exactly the opposite of perfect competition prevails in most cases: enterprises pursue a variety of strategies in order to free themselves of competition and create temporary monopolies. Only temporary monopolies can assure increased prices paid by the clients (consumers), and therefore higher profits and rents that can eventually be used for R&D and innovation. Temporary monopolies can exist for a certain product or groups of products at certain points in time and at certain locations. Despite regulation, no monopoly is fixed or 'natural'. Other enterprises have to create new products with new functions in order to pre-empt such temporary

---

[18] This may seem a paradox, but it can be shown easily: in the state of perfect competition, *there is no competition*. When perfect competition prevails, all enterprises offer the same product on the same market, at the same price. On perfectly competitive markets, innovation, the motor of modernization and technical progress, does not take place. All enterprises are passive price takers. No enterprise has a reason to innovate or the means to do so.

monopolies. Curiously enough, then, competition can best be described as a series of *temporary monopolies*.

Enterprises have two levers to influence their competitive situation: one is *downstream*, that is, in their behavior towards the market side; the other is *upstream*, that is, in their orientation towards the supply side. In the following, the axes of competition that every enterprise can choose are presented. The competition process can then be characterized according to the dynamics of opening up and closing certain axes.

1. Axes of downstream competition: Downstream, that is, on the product side, an enterprise can try to create temporary monopolies on one or more of the following axes:

- *function*: varying the functions of a product by creating a new feature (for example, by adding a 'recycling' function to a car). The concept of 'functions' corresponds to the competition analysis put developed by Lancaster. The function of a product also comprises quality: there may be different market segments for the same product, if their quality differs significantly;
- *trademark*: developing a trademark image that provides an intrinsic value independent of the product (for example, 'Sony' as a synonym for high-tech, reliable, up-to-date consumer electronics);
- *time*: putting a product on the market before other competitors do;
- *place*: introducing a product at a location where it has not been offered before;
- *price*: selling a similar product cheaper than competitors.

The price axis is omnipresent in all competition processes. Other competition axes may be *open*, if competition is likely to take place on these axes, or they may be *closed*, if there is no clear product differentiation to be made on these axes.

2. Axes of upstream competition: Competition also takes place on the input side. Enterprises compete against one another for inputs on the market. They decide which inputs they should buy, and which ones they should develop in-house ('make-or-buy' decision). Whereas an enterprise clearly tends to be active on the downstream axes of competition, its relations on the input side depends on the prevailing market structure. If the supply side is characterized by a large number of producers and full competition, then the enterprise has a large degree of freedom, for example, to require high quality from suppliers in terms of technical parameters, delivery schedule, associated services and the like.[19] This is *not* the case where monopolistic supply dominates, which was precisely the case in the socialist system.

The following is a list of the axes of competition on the input side:

- *human resources*: enterprises compete against each other for human resources, either in the form of pre-defined knowledge (for example, software engineers), or in the form of developable skills. The movement of 'lean production' has increased the degree to which human resources are outsourced; yet outsourcing is limited by the extent to which the knowledge is easily transferable and a wide range of potential suppliers exist;
- *natural resources, raw materials*: competition for natural resources is mainly a question of access and reliability. In certain branches, such as metallurgy, access to a resource can be the only factor in competition, leading to an intrinsic price advantage. In those cases, one would expect a tendency to integrate vertically, and hence to oligopolistic market structures;
- *intermediate products*: in contrast to natural resources, intermediate goods already incorporate several steps of transformation. Hence, the competition for intermediate products is not limited to one product in the chain of production; instead, enterprises can compete against one another, each one being on a different level of intermediate products;
- *equipment, machinery*: competition on this axis exists when the production process is separated from the provision of the respective equipment. The specific competencies of an equipment provider are usually different from the users of the equipment; therefore, synergy effects are rare;
- *scientific and technical capacities*: this axis consists of codable knowledge available 'on the market' and useful for a wide range of enterprises, that is, non-specific knowledge. Enterprises may compete for scientific and technical capacities when they lack the means to develop them in-house. The competition for scientific and technical capacities is a key to understanding the relation between the S&T system and industrial restructuring;
- *financial resources*: in capitalist market economies, the ultimate input of production is financing; without it, nothing happens. Competition may take place between internal and external sources of financing. In post-socialist economies, financing is all the more important because the banking system and financial markets are underdeveloped.

---

[19] I am grateful to a referee for contributing this aspect.

2.3 'Modes of Growth' as an Investment Strategy to Establish Temporary Monopolistic Market Positions

Why have we developed a new theory on enterprise competition when existing concepts of corporate strategy abound (for example, Porter 1986, 1998)? First, the theory of modes of growth takes into account the specificity of enterprise behavior *within* an industrial branch. Indeed, traditional competition analysis assumes that all enterprises within one sector try to follow a 'best-practice' strategy; thus no distinction is necessary between the enterprise level and the sectoral level. However, empirical evidence shows that enterprises in one branch do not follow the same development path. Instead, there may be different groups of enterprises that compete on certain axes, and other enterprises that compete on other axes, all within the same industrial branch. When those enterprises competing on the same upstream and downstream competition axes are regrouped, *strategic groups* can be identified. A sector is then most appropriately defined as the sum of enterprises belonging to the same strategic group.

Second, the theory of modes of growth is *dynamic*, as it takes into account the changing behavior of enterprises over time. Each enterprise tries to establish a positive interaction between its stocks (capabilities) and the financial flows at its disposal. In a dynamic perspective, one can identify the competition strategy of any enterprise by its investment decisions: these are the central decisions for which the free financial flows of former periods are used. The 'mode of growth' of an enterprise or group of competing enterprises can then be characterized as the strategy pursued in order to establish temporary monopolistic market positions. Within an industrial branch, different modes of growth can co-exist.

3. THE SPECIFICS OF POST-SOCIALIST ENTERPRISE RESTRUCTURING

3.1 Structural Change as the Key to Economic Transformation

The ultimate objective of competition analysis is the identification of industrial and competition policies to enhance the competitiveness of enterprises in a market-oriented environment. This section adapts the above competition analysis to the specific post-socialist context prevailing in Eastern Europe. In this region, no 'best' policy to enhance recovery and growth has yet emerged. The reality of industrial restructuring in Eastern Europe has contradicted the expectation prevailing in the early post-socialist years that ownership changes and privatization would be sufficient to ensure the success of reforms at the micro-level (Sachs 1994; Fischer and Gelb 1991). Ten years after the end of socialism, the 'holy trinity' proclaimed in 1990, that is, stabilization–liberalization–privatization, has failed to produce the expected results. For example, countries with half-hearted privatization and high rates of inflation such as Poland are booming, whereas countries with early growth rates and low inflation are stagnating (Czech Republic, Romania); economic transformation has thus far failed in CIS countries (Russia, Ukraine, Belarus; see Table 3.1 below). Macroeconomic stabilization and monetary policies have proved to be necessary but not sufficient to assure successful transformation during the early period of systemic change. The so-called 'collapse' of investment turned out to be much less dramatic than it seemed in quantitative terms, as socialist investment had been highly inefficient.

Basing our argument upon an extensive series of case studies and the emerging literature on the obstacles to systemic change, we contend that the success of economic transformation depends heavily on the conditions for restructuring former socialist productive capacities at the level of *enterprises* and *industries*. In other words, given a minimum requirement of macroeconomic stability, it is bottom-up *structural change* that determines the economic recovery during the early years of transformation (Halpern and Wyplosz 1998; Bomsel 1995; Hirschhausen 1996a, b).

How can this demand for 'structural change' be translated into concrete policy analysis and advice? Havrylyshyn et al. (1999) have formulated three general conditions for enhancing productivity in a post-socialist context: (i) hard budget constraints must be enforced; (ii) resources must be reallocated from old (socialist) to new (market-oriented) activities; and (iii) existing firms and industries must be restructured from the bottom up according to the new capitalist market conditions. Borrowing from Schumpeter, this process was called *creative destruction*. Along the same line of reasoning and based upon personal enterprise visits, Bomsel (1995) and Hirschhausen (1996 a, b) have developed the concept of 'enterprization' to designate the transformation process from socialist industrial combines into capitalist, market-oriented enterprises. Whatever terminology is used, the important point is that the success of transformation depends upon changes at the micro-level. As the development of failed transformation countries shows (for example, Russia and Ukraine), short-term macrostabilization is not sustainable without significant structural reform.

3.2 Modes of Enterprization in Eastern Europe

The idea underlying the concepts of creative destruction and enterprization is simple: it is based on the empirical evidence that socialist factories cannot continue to operate within their old structure in a capitalist market economy. Socialist factories were designed to operate in the socialist, that is, non-monetary, non-market environment, in which the quantity and quality of inputs, the production technology and the nature of the outputs were not subject to capital constraints. The intrinsic linkage between the productive sphere and the social sphere was another uniquely socialist feature that does not exist in the post-socialist environment. In the latter, production is largely monetarized and social functions become the responsibility of the state. Hence, there is a radical break between the *socialist* logic of production, dominated mainly by the Communist Party, and the *post-socialist* production logic, dominated mainly by monetary constraints. Thus, there is also a drastic change of clients, product range, suppliers, organizational structure and employment, which every industrial unit had to cope with during the early years of post-socialism.

The different ways in which capitalist enterprises can be created in a post-socialist context have been laid out in detail elsewhere (Hirschhausen 1998, pp. 41–7). It is sufficient to recall here that greenfield creations – though in theory the easiest way to set up a new enterprise – have in practice turned out to be the *least* relevant method. By contrast, the transformation of existing socialist production structures is the main driver of enterprization. Three cases can be distinguished:

- *unbundling of former socialist combines* to allow the creation of new borders between enterprise structures by recombining existing assets. The policy challenge is to create efficient institutional conditions, that is, to allow a maximum of freedom for recombination, while at the same time avoiding premature devaluation of productive assets ('asset stripping');
- *creation of new inter-enterprise networks*, for example, industrial–financial groups or post-socialist holding companies, which appear when new enterprises institutionalize their upstream and/or downstream relations beyond simple market relations. Here the policy issue is to ensure that hard budget constraints can still be applied;
- *transformation of socialist administration into enterprises* is a process that concerns mainly 'strategic' branches, or those with a tendency towards natural monopolies (for example, energy, telecommunications and railways). While this process proceeded much faster in Eastern Europe than in the West, the problem of the industry–regulator relationship is the

same: the state has to ensure that state monopolies are not simply transformed into private ones, but that a maximum of unbundling is carried out and competition is introduced.

3.3 Competition Analysis in a Post-socialist Context

When applying the competition analysis to the emerging market economies in Eastern Europe, the post-socialist specifics have to be taken into account:

- *the instability of the observable modes of growth.* In the post-socialist context, enterprise strategies tend to be more volatile than in an established capitalist market economy. This is because during the process of enterprization, the institutional framework is still unstable, industry structures are not yet established, trade liberalization leads to more intensified competition, and so on. Even if an individual enterprise is successfully restructured, its environment continues to change quickly, thus limiting its 'strategic' behavior concerning networking and up- or downstream integration. Frequent changes in the institutional framework may have major impacts on the mode of growth. For example, an incoming foreign direct investor may redefine the mode of growth of the company completely; or the change of the privatization scheme may have a similarly fundamental effect. Hence a distinction between short-term and long-term developments may become necessary;
- *the application to post-socialist enterprise networks*: financial–industrial groups and post-socialist holding companies, as we defined them above, do have their own mode of growth, which is more difficult to identify than that of single enterprise. The theoretical question then becomes: what is the right level of analysis, for example, where are capital constraints finally sanctioned? In established economies, this is clearly the firm level; but it may well be that in post-socialist countries, in particular the CIS countries, the right level of investigation is the network as such;
- *the institutional void of the early post-socialist years, opening the way to new modes of growth unseen in the West*: indeed, in post-socialist industrial restructuring, everything is possible. The trajectories of post-socialist enterprises are wide open, and the institutional void favors radical solutions. Examples of unique solutions to new capital constraints abound: a military–industrial complex may turn its oven for steel preparation into a pizza delivery service, just as a producer of raw meat and sausage can turn his or her factory into a high-tech pharmaceutical production facility (real cases, observed in the Russian Federation and Ukraine);
- *the divergence of transformation patterns* complicates the analysis further.

Indeed, whereas the starting point of transformation was similar in all former socialist countries (that is, non-monetary socialist production structures) the reform processes proceeded quite differently afterwards, leading to different transformation processes. Advanced reforming countries in Central Europe may show very different patterns of restructuring from backward CIS countries where institutional change is still in its infancy, and the changes may include legal and economic aspects as well as the transformation of cultural attitudes. Because of the institutional specifics of different groups of countries in transformation, the diversity of systemic change is likely to grow rather than disappear in some kind of convergence toward an ideal type of systemic transformation. This will have consequences for the patterns of industrial and technological restructuring, which are difficult to forecast.

Thus, our working hypothesis in analyzing industrial and technological restructuring in Central and Eastern Europe – which is to be verified in the subsequent case studies – is that modes of growth will be specifically post-socialist and volatile, and only gradually stabilize once systemic transformation comes to an end. Indeed, the stabilization of the modes of growth can be considered as an indicator of the progress of the transformation process itself.

4. SURVEY: MACROECONOMIC AND INSTITUTIONAL FRAMEWORK FOR INDUSTRIAL RESTRUCTURING IN EASTERN EUROPE

4.1 Macro-developments

Although the necessity for creative destruction at the enterprise level applied to *all* Eastern European countries, its success was not independent of the macroeconomic and institutional framework within which it was taking place. As mentioned above, a certain interdependence exists between the structural reforms and macroeconomic stabilization. For this reason, a brief survey of macro-indicators and institutional developments completes this chapter. Indeed, recent econometric studies confirm what on-site case studies suggested some time ago: growth in transformation countries is determined by structural change and increased productivity at the enterprise level. Thus, Havrylyshyn et al. (1999) distinguish three groups of countries with regard to their structural transformation and growth patterns (see Table 3.1):

- *sustained growth* is achieved in countries with a high level of market-oriented reform and structural change, and a decreasing (albeit still important) role of the government. This is the case in most Central and Eastern European countries, as well as in Armenia and Georgia;
- *reversed growth*, that is, several years of growth followed by another recession, is caused by too little enterprise reform accompanied by too loose monetary and fiscal policies in the early phase of transformation (that is,: Romania and Bulgaria);
- *no growth* for eight (!) years, that is, since 1992, is the result of attempts to preserve unpreservable socialist industrial structures by means of state planning, protectionist trade policies, and the absence of structural reform at the local level (for example, Ukraine and Belarus).

The aftermath of the financial turmoil in Russia after the abrupt August 1998 devaluation has confirmed this classification and further aggravated the cleavage between growing and stagnating transformation countries. Indeed, whereas the fallout of the turmoil was disastrous for the core CIS countries, the advanced reforming countries of Central and Eastern Europe survived the financial instability almost unaffected. Thus, the estimated growth rates of GDP for 1999 and 2000 are *still* negative for Russia, whereas the Central and Eastern European (CEE) countries are expected to continue to grow steadily (EBRD 1999).

Another factor, largely underestimated ten years ago but well established today, is the role of *credible institutional change* at central and local government levels. This can be compared and quantified roughly, as is done regularly by the EBRD's reform-index which measures reforms in the enterprise and financial sectors, marketization and trade liberalization, as well as the share of the government in GDP (see Table 3.1). Although this indicator measures only the changes in the *formal* institutions and leaves *informal* institutions aside, some general conclusions can be drawn. For example, the initial conditions of transformation countries seem to matter little when compared to the change of institutional conditions of systemic change. There are also clearly geographical factors at play: institutional reforms are proceeding faster in countries bordering the EU, which are, not merely by chance, candidates for EU accession. The average of the institutional indicator for all CEE countries in 1998 is 3.1 (on a scale from 1[worst] to 4[best]), whereas the average of the five EU accession countries only was somewhat higher at 3.3. By contrast, institutional change is progressing much more slowly in the European CIS countries, and remains at a low level (average of institutional indicator in 1998: 2.1).

Finally, one may observe that the once-prominent issue of *privatization* has lost its pivotal role in the economic policies of transformation countries. Considered as the top priority of structural reforms in the early 1990s, most transformation countries have softened their initial privatization programs. None of the 'pure' forms of privatization, that is, voucher privatization (as attempted in the Czech Republic) or top-down privatization (as attempted in Estonia) have been carried through fully; and mixed forms have emerged rapidly. Nonetheless, none of the programs has achieved the expected results in terms of time frame and increased efficiency. Pure forms of ownership (private–public) have not emerged in the political process, while a variety of institutional forms of organizing production and distribution emerged in the post-socialist context. There seems to be no direct link between the share of privately owned enterprises and the speed of enterprization or the recovery of industrial production. Whereas ownership changes and privatization remain important elements of structural policy, they are second only to establishing conditions conducive to creating capitalist enterprises able to operate under a real financial constraint in a market competition environment.

4.2 Collapse and Recovery of Industrial Production

The quantitative development of industrial production in Eastern Europe can be summarized very bluntly: with the collapse of socialism and socialist networks, production collapsed in all countries, and then recovered more or less quickly, depending upon the external conditions and structural policies. The drastic reduction of industrial production in all post-socialist countries is the logical result of the shock of monetization, that is, the introduction of monetary constraints in the former socialist countries. Not one of these countries was spared a drop in production accompanied by a profound reorganization of productive activities: the cumulated drop in industrial production exceeded one-third for all Eastern European countries; for some of them, it was more than two-thirds (for example, Lithuania and Albania).

Figure 3.1 provides some quantitative evidence: it compares the drop in industrial production at the moment when monetary reforms and price liberalization were introduced. The curves are 'normalized' with regard to the year of monetization, indicated as t_0. In other words, the development of industrial production is shown for each country relative to the year in which socialism was abandoned (t_0).

Two common characteristics come out quite clearly: first, a large depression of output occurs in the year following monetization. Output reductions are only very moderate in the periods t_{-1}, t_{-2}, and so on, that is, in the final years of socialism, while the important slump occurs immediately after t_0, that is, after monetization. Second, the output curves then follow an elastic J-curve, with output picking up about three years after monetization. This can be seen in Figure 3.1: t_1, t_2 and, occasionally, t_3 continue the production decrease. Starting approximately from t_4 and t_5, production then witnesses the upward section of the J-curve, with slopes differing between countries.

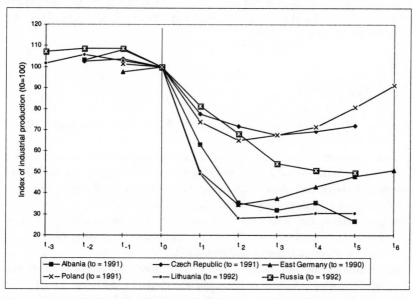

Figure 3.1   Industrial production in selected Central and Eastern European countries, 1989–1997

5. CONCLUSION

This chapter has set out a framework and some working hypotheses for the analysis of industrial and technological restructuring in Eastern Europe from a micro-level perspective. In addition to the meso-approach towards analyzing S&T policies developed in the previous chapter, we place the reforming enterprises at the center of the analysis. Based upon a model of competition, a hands-on methodology is developed and some stylized results of ten years of restructuring in Eastern Europe are presented.

The patterns of industrial restructuring have been diverse. Industrial production has recovered in most of the advanced reforming countries. But, contrary to the expectations of the early period of transformation, no 'best practice' for enterprise restructuring or industrial policy has emerged. Nor has one particular sequencing of reform steps proven to be the most efficient, optimal one (for example, unbundling–restructuring–privatization, or vice versa). Instead, almost ten years after the end of socialism, a variety of approaches to industrial and technological restructuring can be observed, and this tendency is likely to continue. By applying this framework to concrete transformation processes at the sectoral and enterprise level, the subsequent chapters of Part II will provide additional empirical evidence on post-socialist creative destruction.

BIBLIOGRAPHY

Bomsel, Olivier (1995), 'Enjeux industriels du post-socialisme', *Revue d'Economie Industrielle* (72).

Bomsel, Olivier et al. (1995), *Regional Co-operation in the European Steel Industry. Study for the EEC Commission*, Paris: CERNA Ecole des Mines.

Bomsel, Olivier and Alain Rouvez (1995), *Industrial Restructuring and Conversion*, Strategy Paper for the EU Commission, DG-I.

European Bank for Reconstruction and Development (EBRD) (various issues), *Transition Report: Economic Transition in Eastern Europe and the Former Soviet Union*, London: EBRD.

Fischer, Stanley and Alan Gelb (1991), 'The Process of Socialist Economic Transformation', *Journal of Economic Perspectives*, **5** (4), pp. 91-105.

Frydman, Roman and Andrzej Rapaczynski (1994), *Privatization in Eastern Europe: Is the State Withering Away?*, Budapest: Central European University Press.

Giraud, Pierre-Noel (1991), 'Sur le concept de mode de croissance', CERNA mimeo, Paris.

Halpern, Laszlo and Charles Wyplosz (1998), *Hungary: Towards a Market Economy*, Budapest: Central European University Press.

Havrylyshyn, Bogdan, Ivailo Izvorski and Ron van Rooden (1999), 'Recovery and Sustained Growth in Transition Economies 1990–97: A Stylized Regression Analysis', in Axel Siedenberg and Lutz Hoffmann (eds), *Ukraine at the Crossroads – Economic Reform in International Perspective*, Berlin, New York: Physica, pp. 22–57.

Hirschhausen, Christian von (1996a), *Du combinat socialist à l'entreprise capitaliste*, Paris: l'Harmattan.

Hirschhausen, Christian von (1996b), 'Lessons from Five Years of Industrial Reform in Post-socialist Central and Eastern Europe', *DIW Quarterly Journal of Economic Research*, **65** (1), pp. 45–56.

Hirschhausen, Christian von (1998), 'Arguments for a Post-socialist Horizontal Industrial Policy in Eastern Europe – Experience from Five Years of Enterprise Reforms', in Horst Brezinski and Michael Fritsch (eds), *Microeconomics of Transition and Growth,* Cheltenham, UK and Northampton, MA, USA: Edward Elgar, pp. 37–55.

Pinto, Brian (1995), 'A Primer on Enterprise Adjustment and Governance in Transition Economies. What Poland has Taught Us', in Wolfgang Quaisser, Richard Woodward and Barbara Blaszczyk (eds), *Privatization in Poland and East Germany: A Comparison*, Osteuropa-Institut München Working Papers (182/183).

Porter, Michael (1986), *Competition in Global Industry*, Boston, MA: Harvard Business School Press.

Porter, Michael (1998), 'Clusters and the New Economics of Competition', *Harvard Business Review*, **76** (6), pp. 77–90.

Sachs, Jeffrey (1994), *Poland's Jump to the Market Economy*, Cambridge, MA: MIT–Press.

Schmieding, Holger (1993), 'From Plan to Market: On the Nature of the Transformation Crisis', *Weltwirtschaftliches Archiv*, **129** (2), pp. 216–53.

Schumpeter, Joseph (1942), *Capitalism, Socialism, and Democracy*, New York: Harper & Brothers.

World Bank (1996), *From Plan to Market, Annual Report 1996*, Washington, DC: World Bank.

Table 3.1 Macro-indicators for Eastern European countries, 1990–1999

	1990	1991	1992	1993	1994	1995	1996	1997	1998	1999 (p)
Bulgaria (population: 8.4 m)										
Annual real GDP growth (%)	::	-11.7	-7.3	-2.4	1.8	2.1	-10.9	-7.4	2.0	2.0
Industrial production (%)	-16.0	-27.8	-15.0	-11.8	7.8	-6.3	-8.7	-9.1	::	::
Indicator of market-oriented reform *	::	::	::	::	::	2.6	2.6	2.8	2.8	::
Czech Republic (population: 10.3 m)										
Annual real GDP growth (%)	n.d.	-11.5	-3.3	0.6	2.7	5.9	3.9	1.0	2.0	0.0
Industrial production (%)	-3.5	-22.3	-7.9	-5.3	2.1	8.7	6.9	4.6	5.0	::
Indicator of market-oriented reform *	::	::	::	::	::	3.3	3.4	3.4	3.4	::
Estonia (population: 1.5 m)										
Annual real GDP growth (%)	n.d.	n.d.	-14.2	-8.5	-1.8	4.3	4.0	9.0	6.0	5.0
Industrial production (%)	::	::	-35.6	-18.6	-3.1	4.7	3.5	13.6	::	::
Indicator of market-oriented reform *	::	::	::	::	::	2.2	3.3	3.4	3.4	::
Hungary (population: 10.2 m)										
Annual real GDP growth (%)	-3.9	-11.9	-3.1	-0.6	2.9	1.5	1.0	4.4	5.0	4.0
Industrial production (%)	-9.3	-18.4	-9.7	4.0	9.6	4.6	3.4	6.9	10.0	::
Indicator of market-oriented reform *	::	::	::	::	::	3.4	3.4	3.5	3.5	::

	1990	1991	1992	1993	1994	1995	1996	1997	1998	1999 (p)
Latvia (population: 2.5 m)										
Annual real GDP growth (%)	n.d.	n.d.	-34.9	-14.9	0.6	-0.8	2.8	5.9	5.0	3.0
Industrial production (%)	:	-0.3	-46.2	-29.8	-7.7	0.9	3.1	6.1	6	:
Indicator of market-oriented reform *	:	:	:	:	:	2.7	3.1	3.1	3.1	:
Lithuania (population: 3.7 m)										
Annual real GDP growth (%)	n.d.	n.d.	-37.7	-24.2	1.0	3.0	3.6	6.0	3.0	2.0
Industrial production (%)	-2.8	-2.8	-50.9	-42.7	2.0	5.3	5.1	0.8	:	:
Indicator of market-oriented reform *	:	:	:	:	:	2.8	2.9	3.0	3.0	:
Poland (population: 38.6 m)										
Annual real GDP growth (%)	-11.6	-7.0	2.6	3.8	5.2	7.0	6.1	6.9	5.5	4.5
Industrial production (%)	-26.1	-11.9	3.9	5.6	13.0	9.7	8.5	10.8	9.0	:
Indicator of market-oriented reform *	:	:	:	:	:	3.3	3.3	3.3	3.3	:
Romania (population: 22.6 m)										
Annual real GDP growth (%)	n.d.	-12.9	-8.7	1.5	3.9	7.1	4.1	-6.6	-6.0	-4.0
Industrial production (%)	-23.7	-22.8	-21.9	1.3	3.3	10.0	8.2	-5.9	:	:
Indicator of market-oriented reform *	:	:	:	:	:	2.4	2.6	2.8	2.6	:
Slovak Republic (population: 4.7 m)										
Annual real GDP growth (%)	n.d.	-14.6	-6.5	-3.7	4.9	6.8	6.9	6.5	4.5	3.5
Industrial production (%)	-3.6	-17.6	-14.0	-13.5	6.4	8.3	2.5	2.0	2.0	:
Indicator of market-oriented reform *	:	:	:	:	:	3.2	3.2	3.3	3.3	:

53

	1990	1991	1992	1993	1994	1995	1996	1997	1998	1999 (p)
Slovenia (population: 4.7 m)										
Annual real GDP growth (%)	n.d.	n.d.	-5.5	2.8	5.3	4.1	3.1	3.0	3.8	3.0
Industrial production (%)	-10.5	-11.6	-12.6	-2.5	6.6	2.3	1.2	2.4	::	::
Indicator of market-oriented reform *	::	::	::	::	::	3.1	3.1	3.1	3.1	::
Central and Eastern Europe (unw. Average) (population: 107.2 m)										
Annual real GDP growth (%)	-7.8	-11.6	-11.9	-4.6	2.7	4.1	2.5	2.9	3.1	2.3
Industrial production (%)	-11.9	-15.1	-21.0	-11.3	4.0	4.8	3.4	3.2	6.4	::
Indicator of market-oriented reform *	::	::	::	::	::	2.9	3.1	3.2	3.1	::
Belarus (population: 10.2 m)										
Annual real GDP growth (%)	n.d.	n.d.	-9.6	-7.6	-12.6	-10.4	2.8	10.4	5.0	0.0
Industrial production (%)	::	1.0	-5.2	-10.5	-18.9	-10.2	3.2	17.5	::	::
Indicator of market-oriented reform *	::	::	::	::	::	2.1	1.8	1.6	1.5	::
Russian Federation (population: 147.5 m)										
Annual real GDP growth (%)	n.d.	n.d.	-14.5	-8.7	-12.6	-4.0	-4.9	-0.4	-5.0	-5.0
Industrial production (%)	-0.1	-8.0	-18.8	-16.0	-21.0	-3.3	-5.0	-1.9	::	::
Indicator of market-oriented reform *	::	::	::	::	::	2.6	2.9	2.9	2.5	::
Ukraine (population: 50.1 m)										
Annual real GDP growth (%)	n.d.	n.d.	-13.7	-14.2	-23.0	-11.8	-10.0	-3.2	-1.5	-2.0
Industrial production (%)	-0.1	-4.8	-6.4	-8.0	-27.3	-12.0	-5.1	-1.9	0.0	::
Indicator of market-oriented reform *	::	::	::	::	::	2.2	2.4	2.4	2.4	::

	1990	1991	1992	1993	1994	1995	1996	1997	1998	1999 (p)
European CIS (unw. average) (population: 207.8 m)										
Annual real GDP growth (%)	n.d.	n.d.	-12.6	-10.2	-16.1	-8.7	-4.0	2.3	-0.5	-2.3
Industrial production (%)	-0.1	-3.9	-10.1	-11.5	-22.4	-8.5	-2.3	4.6	0.0	..
Indicator of market-oriented reform *	..	..	..	..	..	2.3	2.4	2.3	2.1	..
Total Eastern Europe/CIS (unw. average) (population: 315.0 m)										
Annual real GDP growth (%)	n.d.	n.d.	-12.2	-7.4	-6.7	-2.3	-0.8	2.6	1.3	0.0
Industrial production (%)	-6.0	-9.5	-15.6	-11.4	-9.2	-1.8	0.5	3.9	3.2	..
Indicator of market-oriented reform *	..	..	..	..	..	2.6	2.7	2.7	2.6	..

Notes:
* Source: EBRD, values can vary between 1 (no reform) and 4 (market reforms accomplished).
..: not available.
n.d.: not defined.
(p): projections.

Sources: National statistics, EBRD, BMWi Dokumentation No. 420, *DIW Economic Bulletin*, March 1999.

Part II

Empirical Analysis and Case Studies

4 The Reemergence of the Automotive Industry in Eastern Europe

Xavier Richet and Frédéric Bourassa

1. INTRODUCTION

In this chapter we study how the car industry in some Eastern European transforming economies is currently undergoing restructuring. The car industry is a sector worthy of consideration, as it was previously underdeveloped in terms of quantity, standards, and technology, in comparison to capitalist Western competitors. The opening up of these economies, their integration into regional markets (primarily within the European Union) and strategies by a few of the major world car producers will, together, allow room for the future growth of this industry in Central and Eastern European Economies (CEEEs). At this point in time, the main producers have already invested in almost all these countries, some local enterprises have been integrated into larger international groups, and others are establishing industrial cooperation and strategic alliances with larger Western automobile manufacturers.

The car industry is a complex sector, being termed the 'industry of industries' by Drucker (1946) since it includes almost the entire range of possible industrial and service activities found in a developed economy: steel, electronics, finance, insurance. The nature of this industry, notably in its asset specificity and reliance on networking on the one hand and the state of development attained under the former socialist system on the other, give rise to questions which we intend to answer in this chapter. Other works (Meyer 1998; Brezinski and Flüchter 1998; Buck et al. 1996; Ruigrok and van Tulder 1999) explain how joint ventures within foreign automotive firms have been successful in establishing the performance standards of all such enterprises, which they explain by strategic investments. Few works focus on the *innovation* process and its profound influence on restructuring, or on what the role of science and technology (S&T) could potentially be. In short, these are the points we will address in the present chapter.

Our main working hypothesis is that the restructuring and catching up of enterprises in the CEEEs is accelerated more by their integration into international networks than by independent strategies. For instance, the Polish and Hungarian car industries, not to mention that of the Czech Republic, are more advanced in terms of restructuring than the Russian or the Ukrainian industries. This chapter is therefore divided into four sections. The first reviews the pattern of competition in developed market economies, while the second emphasizes the restructuring of the car industry in the CEEEs. Section 3 concentrates on two case studies: the Czech Republic and Russia. The final section draws conclusions on the most salient points drawn from this research and discusses some policy-oriented proposals.

2. ANALYSIS OF THE WESTERN AUTOMOTIVE INDUSTRY – PATTERNS OF COMPETITION AND INNOVATION

In order to analyze the Eastern European automotive industry, a preliminary understanding of the Western automotive industry is required. We also include Japan and South Korea in the Western automotive industry. This section discusses the development of the Western car industry, in addition to analyzing how the structure of the industry worldwide is developed. We shall stress outsourcing and networking in this sector and analyze the links between Western industry and science and technology systems (S&TSs).

2.1 Development of the Western Automotive Industry

Historically, car production in developed market economies has experienced three phases (Graves 1994). The first phase, namely the 'Fordist system' emphasized standard products and the development of mass production systems increasing efficiency by rationalizing production and controlling costs, while exploiting large capacities and high inventories along the production line. The second phase, which emerged during the 1950s, developed among European car manufacturers who concentrated more on product competition by engineering new motor vehicle concepts, innovative motoring, better transmission systems, brakes and so on. The number of car manufacturers and segmented markets facilitated these innovations, via a growing base of know-how and skill.

The third phase of innovation originated in Japan under the name of 'lean production'. It consisted of a combination of organizational innovations, the use of a very skilled workforce and the effort made by firms and governmental institutions to catch up with and appropriate foreign technologies, most notably through 'reverse engineering', a term coined by Freeman (1987). Lean production means avoiding the rigidity of the mass production system by establishing an alternative, less hierarchical system, and relying on the competence of different layers of workers within the factory. The skilled workforce facilitated the improvement of timing and quality control and promoted the overlapping of the various assembly line functions, traits which are contrary to the 'Taylorist model'. The combination of competence and organizational changes led to a reduction in inventory and in the time spent manufacturing motor vehicles; it also promoted continuous feedback at different levels and among the different functions performed inside the firm (R&D, production, marketing). As car manufacturers depended on suppliers for parts, the lean system developed upstream, forcing suppliers to integrate the new organizational constraint. This concept allowed incremental innovations to take place and facilitated *kaizen*, or continuous improvement, not only in Japan but also in the development of new plants abroad.

The automotive industry has developed among the Triad countries and generated a flow of cross-investments among member countries. It was one of the first industries to delocalize its activities and become truly 'global'. The principal manufacturers have set up international strategies, and are present where there is a high expectation of market growth, following the stagnant demand on the mature market of the Triad. Table 4.1 (see tables at the end of the chapter) shows that the sales in the European Union and the North American Free Trade Agreement (NAFTA) are predicted to be stable or decreasing for several years to come. Nevertheless, the main functions of the firm, namely finance, R&D and strategy, generally remain at the headquarters in the home country.

This expansion and the need to create economies of scale has resulted in the formation of an oligopolistic market with very few manufacturers per country of origin; in fact the number varies from one to five (see Table 4.2).[20] This trend will continue according to the Economist Intelligence Unit Car Forecast (1997), the utilization rate of capacities existing worldwide being approximately 75 percent,[21] with profitability in decline and the return on

---

[20] Even in the presence of very high asset specificity, high technological and finance barriers to new entrants in the last thirty years have been able to take significant market shares, first by developing a national industry (Japan, South Korea) and then by internationalizing their companies in the other regions of the Triad (North America, Western Europe).

[21] The picture is worse in some places than in others, Germany produces six million vehicles less than it would be possible (33 percent under capacity), Japan, 4 million (50 percent

investment of the big three (General Motors, Ford and Chrysler, now Daimler-Chrysler) estimated at around 5 percent. Profits have been declining regularly during the last decade. Table 4.3 shows the segmentation of Western European markets, and the relative importance of each segment. For this market-driven industry, competition through the increase of capacities must follow three major downstream competition axes.

Price is the principal axis on which the competition within the lowest segment of the range is apparent. In order to cut the costs of production, different strategies are implemented, such as delocalization in regions where production costs are lower. Additional strategies include creating economies of scale by producing increased volumes; and also the platform strategy, aimed at maximizing the use of the same bases for different models (body, engine, transmission).

Model policy is another strategy which is important in the two medium segments, tending to reduce the life cycle of each model and to add more distinct models in the manufacturer's range, resulting in heightened product differentiation. The number of non-classic segments is growing with the multi-purpose vehicles (MPVs), roadsters and off-road vehicles. This necessitates the development of the platform strategy and the merger of generalist and specialist car manufacturers. [22]

Having one model in the high segment is a wise strategy because this segment is the most profitable (Roos 1990). This implies that R&D is undertaken in order to incorporate high-tech devices in such models.

Innovation is a key upstream competition axis, aimed at reducing costs in production and design. This is true for all models. In order to remain competitive, Western car manufacturers have to exploit the available and breakthrough technologies to ultimately achieve efficiency and environmental normalization and to fulfill safety regulations. Manufacturers that have technology which satisfies new regulations have a competitive advantage[23] (OECD 1996).

Industry will have to adjust by pursuing globalization, thereby allowing the rationalization of production at different stages and producing cars for the word market. Projects of 'Global Cars' by Ford (Mondeo) and by Fiat (Paleo)

[22] under capacity) and North America 3.9 million (21 percent under capacity).
Examples of this trend are to be found in mergers of: BMW and Rover; Mercedes-Benz and Chrysler; VW with Rolls Royce and Bentley; Ford with Jaguar and Volvo; GM and Saab.
[23] The technology – safety or environmental technology, for example – usually belongs to one owner and is certified by international regulations. The first mover enjoys technological leadership. The production has to be carried out under license and the competition occurs in producing the technology for a lower price (Chanaron 1997). Innovation in this type of market-driven industry has to be in line with customers' expectations and process production.

illustrate this trend. Upstream, rationalization should reduce the number of suppliers from the thousands to a few hundred. The concentration of suppliers could lead in a few years to the generation of a first-tier supply industry with only a few actors, each of whom would have around 20 specialties (XERFI 1997).

2.2 Outsourcing and Stabilizing these Relations through Networking

Networking in automotive production has undergone a great deal of development since the last decade. Automotive production networks are characterized by their pyramidal shape. At the top of this pyramid, the manufacturer subcontracts to system suppliers (first-tier) who then subcontract to second- and third-tier suppliers. The tasks of those second- and third-tier suppliers are increasingly less complicated and their profit margins smaller, yet their delivery deadlines are tight and their quality levels are extremely high. This gives the suppliers the same opportunity to concentrate on their core business and to undertake the same type of economies of scale. With the externalization of the production of non-core parts, the externalization of some R&D tasks will also be given to suppliers.

According to Ruigrok and van Tulder's (1995) network typology, this type of network is an 'informal control hierarchy network'. In this network the core assembler (the car manufacturer) is positioned as a monopsonist, forcing all suppliers to face one powerful customer. In reality, suppliers – although developing close ties with the core firm – have other core firms as customers, too. Because the core assembler can impose tight quality requirements and very frequent deliveries, it puts suppliers in a more dependent situation. The price agreed upon may also decline over time, yet suppliers will nonetheless have to invest in R&D for new products projected by the core assembler.

2.3 Connection with the S&T System

The innovation process is primarily a process of communication and cooperation to seek technical solutions at the lowest cost to solve problems which arise in the enterprise (Moore 1997). In the car industry, this is particularly true, since innovation does not depend upon research in one specific subject (for example, biology relative to biotechnology) but it depends upon a multiplicity of small scientific discoveries and on their industrial applications. Globalization principles encourage enterprises with integrated international production networks to be flexible and find solutions from their comparative advantages, thereby producing world-class products.

- *In-house R&D*: Sources of innovation in this industry are based primarily on in-house research. Yet the resulting innovations depend to a large extent upon other industries' developments. Furthermore, almost all existing technologies are used in the design of cars (Banville and Chanaron 1991). Because the market increasingly demands quality, safety and comfort, as well as a choice of options and complex equipment in new models, costs of R&D have become proportionately more important. Table 4.4 shows that automotive firms are among the world's largest R&D investors.

- *Cooperative R&D*: There is a strong tendency for manufacturers to reduce their R&D costs. This is done by externalizing a part of R&D activities to suppliers and by cooperating with other enterprises on common research projects. This explains the growth of R&D expenses in the suppliers' budgets. The R&D organization and its links with production are soundly established. The current trend is to link the design of new models with their manufacturing concept. Naturally, the first-tier suppliers are expected to cooperate in this process, as they are specialists in their own core business. Suppliers obtain a larger value-added portion of the production in which they specialize, rendering innovation an increasingly cooperative process between different actors in a common R&D specialization.

- *Public policies*: Automotive firms are, in most cases, private stock companies, and R&D expenses are seen as a strategic investment. By and large, the results at the plant level are incremental innovations. Yet public policies are subject to extremely tight monitoring measures by competition authorities worldwide. Since the automotive industry occupies such an important place in a country's economy (accounting for more than 13 percent of the industrial production) regional authorities finance technology breakthrough projects that can assist companies in coping with upstream competition in the field of R&D.[24] It can be observed, however, that throughout the history of all Western car manufacturers, the home state has played a fundamental role in development, particularly by means of army and defense contracts.[25]

---

[24] For example, the pre-competitive technology programs BRITE/EURAM III, EUREKA, EUCAR, PROMETHEUS, ESPRIT and RACE projects. Companies from different countries can work together on specific projects at this stage in order to benefit from these discoveries and apply them to the development of new products or new systems. Peugeot, for example, has as a result been able to develop its car navigation system with the cooperation undertaken in the framework of the PROMETHEUS project financed by the European Union.

[25] Ruigrok and van Tulder (1995) see a parallel between the growth of multinational firms and state intervention. For almost all multinational firms – and automotive firms are no exception – defense and military funding were crucial in their development.

It is impossible to assess whether S&T policies regarding the Western car industry have been a success or a failure. First, it has been noted that governments have not involved themselves directly in this industry, its policies being oriented horizontally to encompass all industrial sectors. Additionally the automotive industry has a history of more than a hundred years, and has never faced any major crisis such those undergone by the textile and shipbuilding industries thirty years ago. Consequently, no emergency policies have had to be launched to remedy such a crisis. The industry has always adjusted to the business cycle either through price and employment policies or by means of innovation policies. National frontiers are disappearing in this industry and programs of international cooperation have been instituted to study future undertakings concerning pollution, traffic and safety.

3. RESTRUCTURING OF THE CAR INDUSTRY IN EASTERN EUROPE

The Eastern European automotive industry at the onset of transition clearly reveals the gap between market and planned economies resulting from four decades of socialism in Central and Eastern Europe and seven decades in Russia. The automotive industry in the region suffered from the ostracism of planners who considered cars – with the exception of limousines for *apparatchiks* – to be a luxury good representing what the system was opposed to: wealth, social aspiration, freedom and autonomy. The necessity of answering to the social needs of limited segments, given the increasing share of consumption in GDP, enabled development in this sector, often through imitation of Western products. As with other goods, the supply of cars was constrained by significant shortages, forcing consumers to wait in line for several years if they did not have access to privileged distribution channels.

3.1 Point of Departure: Socialist Industrial Structures and Transformation in the Early 1990s

There are three different modes of industrial development of the car industry in the CEEEs:

- *The development of a car industry based on domestic technology and know-how prior to the socialist system.* This is the case in the Czech Republic even though other countries such as Poland and Russia had an automotive industry sector prior to World War II. Skoda and Tatra, which were founded at the end of the last century, were able to develop their products under the former socialist system even though priority was given to heavy industry, truck manufacturing and the development of mass transportation systems. Domestic technology and the importation of foreign technology from the West (motoring, design) helped to maintain a certain level of quality and know-how in this field.

*   *The development of a car industry based on imported technology.* This is the case in Poland, Romania, Russia and Yugoslavia. Poland has imported technology and cooperated with Fiat in order to develop and build small cars for its own market and for CMEA markets. Romania also imported technology in the 1960s, notably from France (Renault, Citroen) in order to supply its own market, but also for the export of automobiles to CMEA and third world markets.[26] Russia was assisted by Ford to develop GAZ and by Fiat to develop AvtoVAZ.

*   *The absence of a domestic car industry.* This is the case in Hungary (which had a small automobile industry prior to WWII) and Bulgaria primarily for political reasons: the Soviet Union refused to permit Hungary to develop its own industry. The same constraints were placed on Bulgaria, even though this country was allowed to assemble cars on its territory much later. In spite of these restrictions, Hungary has developed a strong supply network within domestic and COMECON (Council for Mutual Economic Assistance) markets for cars, trucks and buses (Havas 1999). Bulgaria and Slovakia possessed no car industry of their own despite a very strong mechanical industry.

This constrained situation had an influence on the strategy of Western automotive manufacturers, particularly where cooperation links had existed previously, such as those between FSM and Fiat in Poland, Skoda and VW in Czechoslovakia, and Revoz and Renault in Slovenia. Yet the majority of investments made since the early 1990s in the CEEEs have been within the framework of an international expansion strategy, even in countries with no

---

[26] According to French engineers from Renault who have been involved in the technology transfer, domestic plants have never been able to match the initial standard which had been set up even after years of development. In Yugoslavia, the different Republics have imported licenses to assemble cars with different European car manufacturers (Fiat, Renault), specializing and developing some low models for home and foreign markets (Fiat-Zastava). After the disintegration of the former Federation, only the Slovenian automobile industry had been able to adjust to the new economic environment. The Croatian car industry is recovering but the Serbian one has suffered from embargo measures with the war in Croatia and Bosnia and the bombing of the Serbian Zastava plant. Know-how and competence in R&D accumulated by Zastava, the Serbian affiliate, are remarkable but the lack of markets and the economic crisis which has hit this country could have a devastating impact on the Yugoslavian plant in the future.

automobile assembling plant (Hungary, Slovakia).

3.2 Post-socialist Transformation, New Enterprise and Innovation Structures

The creation of new enterprises was achieved primarily with foreign capital through the establishment of joint ventures (JVs) and various strategic alliances (Radosevic 1998). National car manufacturers were sold directly by the state to foreign companies.[27] Foreign investors generally obtained a majority control of such enterprises, while the states themselves maintained a minority stake, in most instances. Table 4.5 summarizes motives for investing in Eastern Europe. While automotive manufacturers were undergoing privatization, governments typically played the role of negotiator, attempting to preserve the maximum employment level within these companies. The purpose of this was to keep production within the country and to increase the local content of added value (EBRD 1995). Foreign investors, however negotiated for fiscal advantages and market protection. Initially, certain market protection regulations were enforced to restrain the import of already assembled cars. These import restrictions (taxes on imports, quotas, regulation of the import of used cars) were efficient since they were accompanied by the construction of various automobile assembly plants in Poland, in the Czech Republic and in Hungary. Today, this same strategy is used to attract foreign investments in Russia. Automotive manufacturers in the CEEEs and CIS countries lack the know-how and technology necessary to upgrade their products or engineering. These countries may also lack the financial resources necessary for modernizing and developing new units and the organizational skill adequate for establishing new networks and an advanced organization of work based on the lean production model.

The former structure of R&D was created by research units located outside these enterprises, managed under the control of branch ministries and incapable of maintaining constant product innovation during the socialist period. These units did not have the proper links with the enterprises to facilitate the transfer of new technologies and their potential industrial applications. The newest technologies for applied industry were kept secret for strategic military use. Thus, the greatest weakness of socialist industry in this field was its incapacity to initiate and rely on an endogenous process of adjustment. This weak innovation system was consequently radically devalued. Some of these research units are currently operating as testing units and perform certain R&D tasks, although not so fundamentally as before. It

---

[27]   The VW group has bought Skoda in the Czech Republic. FSM in Poland was bought by Fiat and FSO by Daewoo. Renault is acquiring stakes in Dacia in Romania.

may be said that they are not acting upstream of the industry, and merely contribute by contracting orders from suppliers and car assemblers.

Foreign companies investing in the region are shaping a new car industry, taking into account local advantages (cost, technological resources, distances) in order to fit their own strategy, both locally and globally ('globalization' in Ruigrok and van Tulder 1995). They supply the domestic market but integrate local plants into the multinational's international strategy. All foreign capital car firms in CEEEs are ranked among the top 100 Eastern European enterprises (see Table 4.6).

As we have already acknowledged, the automotive industry requires a highly complex network organization. Consequently, when a manufacturer (a network leader) starts new operations in a foreign country, usually some of its suppliers follow. These enterprises establish alliances, joint ventures and other types of cooperative agreements. They proceed thereafter to function as 'network organizers' (Radosevic 1997), implementing and transferring most of their productive and R&D knowledge. Local sourcing helps in developing networks among domestic second- and third-tier suppliers. In order to take advantage of the lower costs on this market by locating potential suppliers, audits are undertaken by the foreign manufacturers, usually by foreign first-tier suppliers. These audits are intended to implement the normalization standards (ISO 9001, VDA 6.1, QS 9000) desired by foreign enterprises. An audit targetting specific normalization reveals precisely what is needed to restructure and produce world-class products. Thus, the enterprise will be able to set up its financial needs in order to finance its investment.[28] In the best-case scenario, they want to find suppliers who are able to develop products, and in order to help them, they could lend them the necessary tools and underwrite bank guarantees if loans are needed.

3.3 Review of S&T Policies in Eastern Europe

The Task Force for Structural Policy established in *Poland* suggests basing the R&D policies on those of the OECD countries experienced in the field. R&D units should be established within industrial holdings by transferring shares of R&D units to institutions of higher education and to industrial holdings. Other suggestions concern the creation of a Commission for special-purpose research projects, which would work with the State Committee for Scientific Research (KBN). Other financial aids (tax relief on investments, public aid to exporters, credit guarantees for SMEs) should be included

---

[28] Global suppliers such as Lucas, Valeo, Delphi, Bosch and VDO Instruments actively search for their suppliers. Through audits, they find out the needs of domestic suppliers in founding, evaluating, improving and training R&D and management capabilities.

among the horizontal aids to SMEs.

In the *Czech Republic*, no innovation policy has been implemented, under the Klaus government. Now, the Research and Development Council of the Government of the Czech Republic is working on the adoption of industrial policies that would promote innovation in SMEs. Managers of domestic and foreign enterprises in the Czech Republic are quite pessimistic about possible help that could come from the state. Since the 'Velvet Revolution', the economic environment has been very liberal and no work has been done to create an environment conducive to the development of SMEs.

In *Hungary*, the main target of government policies in the early 1990s was towards foreign direct investment (FDI) by multinational car manufacturers. It was partly due to these policies (including a corporate tax exemption for the first five years and government help in establishing infrastructures) that Opel, Suzuki, Ford and Audi appeared as investors in Hungary between 1991 and 1993. Special treatment for large FDIs was later abolished. Now the policy is toward general investment incentives regardless of foreign or domestic origin. However, a new incentive is a governmental subsidy to multinational firms establishing their R&D centers in Hungary. The principle is that 25 percent of the cost would be supported by the government. Serious negotiations are under way in this respect with Audi (Havas 1999).

So far, the car industry in Russia – like the rest of Russian industry – has made few efforts to adjust, even though cooperation agreements are being signed with Western manufacturers (for instance, Renault and GM). The main problem of this sector can be summarized in two points: first, the need to reorganize the car industry in order to upgrade the quality and introduce new brands of cars to meet a more sophisticated demand; and second, the need to recapitalize this sector, which lacks the capital to carry out its own modernization. As far as S&T is concerned, it falls under a more general analysis of the role of an industrial policy in this country (Hare and Richet 1997), which has not been a primary concern of the Russian government (or of the Ukrainian one).

In transforming economies, S&T policies could concentrate on the training of qualified technicians and engineers, as well as on the supply of technological knowledge to the suppliers – often SMEs – of car assemblers, in order to fill up the asymmetric gap affecting these small units. These companies have been below the minimal efficiency size. Thus, it is quite difficult for them to obtain access to the technologies that would allow them to increase the quality of their production and thus to compete more effectively. For the most part, they simply lack the financial resources to cope with the necessary investments. In Russia, the barter system makes things worse as companies have to enter specific networks in which goods are exchanged against goods.

Managers of global firms who were interviewed expressed the feeling that some infrastructural work on the part of governments is needed urgently, especially in the Czech Republic. First, SMEs are isolated because there are no efficient institutions to help circulate information. There are also no technical training seminars where new applied research techniques could be made known and transferred. There is no shared financing of research projects (as in Western countries) set up to benefit SMEs. Car industries, in these countries, do not have enough sales representation abroad. There is quite a difference between the S&T policies on paper and the reality of small enterprises. Only the Hungarian policy seems to have had a discernible result. Russian and Polish policies remain wishful thinking.

While the production networks are developing and new investments are flowing into the CEEEs, governments have remained less interventionist. A strict application of regulations against the import of used Western cars that do not match the minimal environmental regulations would be better. Those used vehicles are taking a market share of the most competitive car manufacturers in the CEEEs.

3.4 Perspectives for the Eastern European Automotive Industry

The output of plants in the CEEEs has witnessed constant growth after the general slowdown of 1993. With the exception for Tatra, Moskvitch and AvtoVAZ (which are all state owned), production has improved in terms of quantity and quality through the introduction of new models in the production line. Data Resources Incorporated (DRI)/PlanEcon forecasts constant growth for production in Eastern Europe; meanwhile, production in NAFTA and Western Europe is declining (see Table 4.7). Sales are also seeing a significant increase in all countries, but remain very sensitive to economic growth. Segmentation sales vary significantly from country to country. As markets open and incomes rise we should witness important changes in the segmentation that will eventually begin to converge towards Western European levels. Hungary, Poland, the Czech Republic and Slovenia have segmentation patterns not far from attaining Western European levels. In Russia, Bulgaria, Romania and Slovakia, lower segments are oversized in relation to other categories.

As far as industrial cooperation and restructuring is concerned, two sets of countries appear. The first one consists of the Central European countries, including the Czech Republic, Hungary, Poland, Slovenia and Slovakia. These countries started their reforms earlier, attracting more FDI, and are now more productive. Their market structures, too, are close to the Western pattern. They belong to the most advanced countries in transition. They are more capable of engaging partnerships with Western enterprises in order to learn by cooperating on technical and managerial know-how issues. Western production networks, through these partnerships, grant more responsibility to their suppliers for quality and eventually for R&D tasks.

The second group of countries includes Russia, the former Soviet Republics (Ukraine, Uzbekistan), Romania and Bulgaria. The main difference is that from the beginning, there was no real privatization undertaken in these countries, and thus, the macroeconomic environment is still highly unstable. This has led to an unclear ownership structure and the lack of any deep restructuring. These countries received only minimal FDI, and maintained a market structure quite different from that of Western Europe.

A potential obstacle to the future development of the automotive industry in the advanced reforming countries arises from the uncertain strategic policy of the foreign first-tier suppliers. It is difficult to know whether they could be used as a temporary sourcing base before the industry moves to countries with still-cheaper labor costs. This is especially true because of the agreement between the EU and the accession countries to lower import taxes to zero percent in 2002.[29] The rise in living standards and incomes in CEEEs could be an advantage for sales, but could also be an obstacle to investment in productive plants if higher productivity gains compensating the loss of labor cost advantages cannot be reached before the total opening of the borders.

4. CASE STUDIES: THE RESTRUCTURING OF THE AUTOMOTIVE INDUSTRIES IN THE CZECH REPUBLIC AND RUSSIA

These two case studies illustrate the difference between advanced and less advanced reforming countries, in terms of economic environment, enterprise restructuring and growth potential.

4.1 The Czech Republic: FDI and Rapid International Integration

The Czech Republic attracted a significant amount of the FDI inflows to

---

[29] The Cooperation Agreements between the EU and CEEEs set up a schedule to lower the restrictions and taxes on built-up car imports to zero percent in 2002. More and more disputes are arising between the CEEEs and the EU because of the non-respecting of import tariffs due to pressure from some foreign investors. A famous example is the import of already-built Korean cars, disassembled in Slovenia, shipped to Poland and re-exported into the EU by Daewoo. This Korean firm was thereby able to avoid Polish and European import duties.

CEEEs shortly after the Velvet Revolution, USD 6 billion from 1989 to 1996(CzechInvest 1998). The automotive industry, which has a century-long history in this country, benefitted from one-quarter of all foreign investment.

4.1.1 The privatization of Skoda: the integration in the VW international network

The restructuring of the automotive industry in the Czech Republic started with the setting up of the joint venture between VW and Skoda after the Czech government decided to disassemble the KAP motor branch in the early 1980s, resulting in individual companies: Liaz, Tatra, Avia, Karosa, Jawa and AZNP (Skoda). Skoda a.a.s. was created by the Volkswagen joint venture in 1991.[30] Volkswagen holds 70 percent of the shares and the Czech Agency for Property holds 30 percent. VW took over the car production plant and left Skoda's previous suppliers which were integrated into the AZNP, but has maintained business links with them.

The first effect of this joint venture is that VW's suppliers began to get involved in the new venture. Domestic suppliers were forced to cooperate, and often to merge with foreign suppliers who were also forced to locate in the Czech Republic near the assembly line. This was necessary in order to lower costs through economies of scale and to improve quality, as well as to reach the delivery standards required by the new owner. This presented an opportunity for these companies to upgrade efficiency and the quality of their production, and also to join the global VW sourcing network.[31] Sales and production growth is constant and is predicted to stabilize at a very high level around the year 2001 (see Tables 4.8 and 4.9).

In regard to downward competition axes, sales in the Czech Republic are concentrated in two segments. The first of these is the average-low segment, encompassing small, functional, low-priced cars; and the second is the average-high segment, with a lower price than its Western competitors in this segment. Skoda's priority for the latter market segment is to create a functional and sturdy car with the lowest price possible. With the opening of borders, almost all European car companies are selling on the Czech market. Opel, Fiat and Ford are the main competitors of Skoda/VW; they compete by buying market shares, sometimes at discounted prices.

Upwards on the competition axis, competition in the Czech Republic for human resources is developing because there is not much labor mobility and

---

[30] According to CzechInvest's *Annual Report 1998*, USD 900 million have already been invested in Skoda a.a.s.

[31] To save on logistical costs, six suppliers (including Rockwell, Gumotex, Siemens/Sommer Alibert and Johnson Controls) are now fully integrated and are producing on Skoda's site in Mlada Bolelav.

there are not enough good, young technicians. So Skoda has to pay its workers more than the average salary and has had to hire some guest workers from Poland.

The new channel of technology transfer is, in most cases, based on cooperation with foreign companies. Audits to obtain quality certification, a necessary precondition for business relations between Skoda and VW, are often the first step towards technical cooperation. Within a partnership with a foreign company, domestic suppliers can benefit from investments in machinery and know-how. With current overcapacity, only about 10 percent of companies will survive, because the component industry is becoming more and more global, and the main first-tier suppliers are growing. Skoda has founded a design center which works in cooperation with several Czech technical schools. Skoda's R&D department has a total of 1000 employees.

4.1.2 How domestic suppliers can benefit from foreign networks: the case of PAL Praha a.s.

PAL Praha a.s. was born out of the privatization of the PAL a.s. Company, which has amalgamated fifteen other suppliers. Privatization was achieved in 1995. During the transformation process, PAL Praha was integrated into the PAL a.s. Company and has started to adjust to the market economy environment. At first PAL Praha had a joint venture with VDO Instrument (VDO-Frankfurt) and produced under license. Since August 1996, the capital is 100 percent Czech and the partnership with VDO is finished.

A set of restructuring measures have been implemented. These included the adoption of the ISO 9001 management structure to restructure the production process and management; and the implementation of a rationalization program concerning employees. Only 50 percent of the total labor force remains compared to the 1989 level. The turnover is increasing annually, as are exports. The company exports 68 percent of its production to North America and Western Europe. It is expanding abroad, always with a majority of Czech capital. It is the first Czech system supplier for the VW group as a whole.[32]

With a foreign license, PAL Praha was able to upgrade its production quality, continuing to invest in product development. It has upgraded its equipment (tooling machines, computer equipment, computer-assisted design (CAD) software). Eighty employees work in the R&D center. Forty percent of these are technicians with backgrounds in higher education. The company has developed cooperative relations with technical universities such as Brno Technical University. Some professors and freelance researchers were hired

---

[32] To be able to set up business with international partners, quality certifications are needed. Now they have ISO 9001, QS 9000, Rate A-VW, and soon ISO 9000 and ISO14000.

as external consultants.

4.1.3 Potential role of S&T policy

Problems that arise from the current situation in the Czech Republic are the following:

- shortage on the labor market: there are not enough good technicians and not enough workers to meet the demands of industry,
- no efficient structure (that is, technological forum) granting enterprises the opportunity to exchange information on the development of new technologies,
- for local suppliers there are still governance problems inherited from voucher privatization, problems of overstaffing, shortages of technicians and shortages of the financial devices for investing which are necessary in order to improve quality and increase productivity.

Some domestic companies have been able to adjust. On the other hand, because of weak corporate governance or inflexible behavior, some companies have shut down or have had their production task downgraded by Skoda, passing from design and production to assembling parts. The significant gap between enterprises which had close cooperation with foreign firms and others which remain in old markets shows that an S&T policy is urgently needed if they want the spillover effect to be efficient. There is no innovation policy in the Czech Republic at present. The only link between enterprises and the S&T system is the Center of Excellence program managed by the Research and Development Council of the Government of the Czech Republic.[33]

All the other links that exist between S&TS and enterprises are based on individual initiatives. Universities seem to be the most effective research organ in applied research. The current university chart gives the opportunity for technical school departments (Prague Technical School has a Department of Automotive Industry) to develop cooperative relationships with industrial corporations and to keep the profits to reinvest in different laboratory tools.

---

[33] This agency is working on the design and establishment of an innovation policy for the Czech industry. The Center of Excellence Program concerns itself with the founding of cooperative research relationships between enterprises, universities and the Academy of Sciences. In some ways it could be useful, but it appears to remain too theoretical; and each program is not yet coordinated with the others. This program is developing its second version, which will be more directed towards the industry than the first one was.

4.2 Russia: Domestic Orientation in a Difficult Macro-environment

4.2.1 Point of departure: mass privatization scheme after the collapse of the USSR

The car industry in the USSR was a vital part of the military–industrial complex, and its huge production was a symbol of the power of communist industrial planning. Every car and truck producer was attached to a branch ministry and all had to produce the number of units planned without having to sell them. Only the quantity of output mattered. After the collapse of the USSR in 1991, the Russian car industry remained one of the industrial champions of the Russian economy although it lost its traditional CIS markets. Under the shock therapy prescriptions, the mass privatization plan was launched.

In contrast to the economic choices made by Hungarian, Czech and Polish governments, no privatization – at least in particular strategic sectors – was done with the help of foreign capital. Mass privatization led to the concentration of ownership in the hands of former managers, employee collectives and the government, until the recent round of privatization. Economic instability and an uncertain legislative environment has hampered the development of a real privatization program. Three major car firms, AvtoVAZ, Moskvitch and UAZ are still under the Russian state's or regional administrations' control and GAZ is held under employee collective control (insider control). The following common features of all manufacturers in Russia have slowed the restructuring process in this country:

- *Accumulated debts and soft monetary constraints have stimulated trade by bartering:* maintaining inertia in their economic behavior, car manufacturers still have not yet adjusted to the new environment. Management restructuring has not yet taken place in the organizational structure of these enterprises. Debts have accumulated in all companies, partially soaked up by the state many times, by bankruptcy suits rejected because of state intervention or by high inflation rates.
- *Overstaffing and the ownership of social structures:* the number of employees is still very high compared to Western standards, and in most of the car enterprises, no drop in employment has occurred since privatization took place. These enterprises have not changed their organization of work.
- *Inefficient governance and management structures:* it is hard to see a clear strategic pattern in the behavior of Russian car enterprises despite all declarations on restructuring programs by directors or government representatives. Politicians always try to protect employment and to

maintain their control. This behavior is nevertheless harmful to the stability of the management for long-term successes.

Without any successful privatization program leading to a new governance system and a clear division between ownership and control, it is difficult to see how some parts of the former industrial structure in this sector could be integrated efficiently into the new international production network.

Overall, the exports of Russian car producers have declined by 50 percent since 1995, and are forecast to decline further (Standard and Poor's DRI/PlanEcon 1998 and EIU 1998). This is due to the forced reorientation strategy of AvtoVAZ to sell on its domestic market instead of exporting, since some models do not conform to Western regulations concerning emission levels and safety. Russian domestic car manufacturers dominate the domestic car market with 88 percent of total new car production in 1997 (see Table 4.10). Parallel imports are frequent, but this gray area of the market is not taken into account in statistics. Sales in market segments in Russia are more concentrated in low and lower-medium segments, where the main competition axis is price. There is a growing demand for cars on the part of the emerging middle class, but domestic enterprises cannot fill this demand.

4.2.2 GAZ – the restructuring of production in the turmoil of a weak governance structure

GAZ (Gorky Avtomobila Zavod)[34] is the second-largest car producer in Russia and has the title to the most successful Russian car company. Although this company earned USD 111 million in profits in 1997, it remains among the 20 largest tax debtors to the Russian government and to the Nizhny Novgorov regional government. Production has been stabilized in 1996/97 at the level of 127,000 cars (see Table 4.10). The company is working at full capacity. GAZ does not export any of its models outside of CIS countries. The enterprise structure does not have a truly efficient governance system. It is a typical 'surviving network' from the old system. Buck et al. (1996) mention that GAZ management and employees have an interest in securing their jobs.[35]

---

[34] GAZ was founded in 1930 with the help of the Ford Motor Corporation. It was privatized in February 1993 through the mass privatization method. Ownership is held for the most part by a collective of employees (73.36 percent), after which come the institutional shareholders Avtobank (10.12 percent), GAZinvest (8.5 percent) and Menatep Bank (8.02 percent). This enterprise has 89,000 employees (106,000 in 1995) and produces 13 percent of total domestic car and light truck output. Twenty thousand employees worked in the social infrastructure in 1995. Thirty-three thousand employees were producing components in 1995. It owns 1,000 apartment blocks (Buck et al. 1996). The main plant is situated in the city of Nizhny Novgorod (formerly Gorky), and other plants are located in the region.

[35] This attitude is reflected in the internal rule regarding the transfer and selling of shares.

GAZ appears to be the Russian car manufacturer most sensitive to product development. The Volga model has been upgraded without losing any production volume (Standard and Poor's DRI/PlanEcon 1998). Now GAZ is in the process of replacing the Volga with a new car by the end of 1999. This project will be financed partly by the EBRD.

The main talent of GAZ thus far has been to attract financing from diverse sources without doing any restructuring.[36] Because of the power of employees in the control of the firm, it will be difficult to restructure work organization and reduce costs linked to the level of overstaffing. Despite this inefficient form of governance, the company was able to respond quickly to market demands with the production of an MPV, the Gazelle. It was also able to cooperate with foreign enterprises to some extent: GAZ builds engines under a production license from the Austrian Steyr–Daimler–Puch. The JV with Fiat could be an opportunity to gain some technical knowledge and, with the production of cars under the Fiat label, to earn more profits and free itself from barter trade.[37]

4.2.3 Prospects for setting an S&T policy

The Russian automotive enterprises belong to the 'survival network' type (Huber and Wörgötter 1998), which is involved in a process of 'rent extraction' in order to maintain their power in the enterprise and over regional politics. The concentration of car enterprises in different regions – AvtoVAZ in Togliatti, GAZ in Niznhy Novgorod and the industrial suburbs of Samara or even Moscow – and their control over the labor market extend over the rest of the economies of these regions, giving these enterprises a very important bargaining power with regional authorities. No communication structures such as associations of entrepreneurs seem to have been created, and local chambers of commerce, business presses, and enterprises remain isolated from one another and from the rest of the country's industry because of their closed regional networks.

In February 1998, the Russian government adopted an investment promotion policy for the automotive sector, trying to stimulate the demand of local component manufacturers. The Russian market remains very protective,

---

There is a limited internal possibility of transferring shares. This is not real privatization, as the possibility of transferring shares is not granted to owners (Buck et al. 1996). Outside investors owned only 26 percent of the shares.

36 The EBRD made two loans, of USD 20 million and USD 65 million, and a loan of USD 15 million is expected from the Avtobank, granted to GAZ by the Russian government for a five-year tax credit.

37 The project of a JV with Fiat: Fiat and GAZ will both hold 40 percent of the shares, and the remaining part will be held by the EBRD. GAZ will assemble 2,000 Fiat models a year from kits, and a new facility will be built in 1999. The JV wants to attract European and American component manufacturers.

with three different types of taxes which increase the selling price of imported models (customs duty: 30 percent, value added tax (VAT): 20 percent, and excise tax: 5 percent). The OECD (1994) proposal for a science, technology and innovation policy encouraging communication between research institutes and enterprises and financing the necessary coordination bodies still had no effect.

The effects of foreign investments in Russian automobile enterprises (manufacturers and suppliers) obtained through cooperation with foreign enterprises could be beneficial both downstream and upstream, for suppliers and marketing. Foreign enterprises could stimulate research because of their potential demand for links with research institutes. And last but not least, these foreign enterprises bring a much-needed capital investment.

The Russian government's political willingness and commitment is a real issue, as it has to exercise corporate governance on management, and as a state institution, it has to build up a better economic and industrial environment. Restructuring of car enterprises, undertaken rapidly to match profitability, will have negative and damaging effects on employment at the regional level. But there is no alternative way for them to face world competition. Maintaining employment seems to have been the main goal of management and local supervision. The August 1998 financial crisis in Russia will probably slow the pace of inflow of FDI into the country. Stabilization policies will be favored, and their microeconomic impact will be delayed.

5. PERSPECTIVES AND CONCLUSIONS

In this chapter, we have focussed on the transformation of the car industry in transition economies. This transformation process is taking place while the world car industry is restructuring and expanding into the global economy through direct investment, strategic alliances and mergers. FDI from Western companies plays an important role and is, in general, more efficient than national industrial policies implemented by governments lacking adequate competence in this area and financial resources (Hare and Richet 1997).

5.1 Restructuring at Two Speeds

The current situation shows a two-speed process of restructuring in the CEEEs:

- In Central Europe during privatization, enterprises were dismantled by selling the units separately to suppliers and concentrating on the core business. Car enterprises in the CEEEs are still more integrated than Western ones because they cannot yet rely on the market to supply everything.

• CIS countries, despite the growth in production, are stuck with serious, long-term problems to solve. The ownership structure of the four main Russian firms and the weak financial system cannot allow efficient corporate governance to take place. These enterprises are still highly vertically integrated and are doing business in an incomplete monetary economy. The level of employment has not changed much since privatization took place, and manufacturers still produce almost all components. Some strategic alliances with Western car manufacturers should help to restructure and develop new products.

On the one hand, every Eastern European country has lost its national champion since transition, with the major exception of Russia. Nevertheless, the example of the UK car industry shows that an automobile industry dominated by foreign owners – in this case, with 99 percent of output made by foreign companies, and with Japanese transplant companies who are able to transfer their industrial capacities – can be a growing sector given the existence of a very competitive environment.[38]

5.2 Filling the Gap: The Role of Public Policies

The S&T system in the CEEEs is, in particular respects, of a significantly different nature from the dominant models in Western market economies (Freeman 1987). Although the scientific level of education and research was high, the technological dimension of S&T policies is more disputable, as there were few – if any – incentives for firms to develop new products or innovate. This was the main failing of the socialist system, and probably, one of the main reasons explaining its collapse, because of its intrinsic inability to answer to the complexity of industrial organization.

Until now, with some variations, the auto industry in the CEEEs has been integrated into major world car manufacturing networks, either to supply the global market or to develop new market opportunities in the CEEEs. For some car manufacturers – Daewoo, for instance – this strategy is also a

---

[38] Today, the UK has surpassed Spain in car production, and is competing with Italy to be the third largest car manufacturer in Europe. British managers (in cooperation with suppliers) have been able to develop their skills in the new greenfield plants and have drawn from and applied some essential lessons from Japanese experience: developing an export-led strategy, exporting three-quarters of production, making quality consistent, improving the cost base, having the ability to transfer *kaizen* to suppliers by sending teams of quality and manufacturing experts into suppliers' plants, and developing good labor relations.

springboard to conquering other markets in the region. The first-mover strategy in countries such as Poland has attracted followers who are trying to take market shares either through direct investment, mergers or sales strategies (establishing retail networks). By concentrating on core businesses, as in the West, car manufacturers have made room for the expansion of subcontracting units; they also have set new standards for quality, for delivery, and also for efficiency: subcontractors have been obliged or are obliged to develop their businesses in order to match the minimum efficiency size to supply assembly lines.

S&T policies towards the car industry are at a cross-roads for different reasons. First, in the new political environment, there is no real thought on what an S&T policy should be, as most governments have followed more or less liberal policies, and there has been a lack of financial resources to implement such policies. Second, the former S&T system is almost worn out now.

Nevertheless, S&T policies generally take place upstream (at the level of national R&D expenses, the higher education system and, more generally, human capital policies). One evident task should be to examine and update the curriculum of technical schools supplying the qualified workforce. The real problem in this sector – as long as governments do not focus on a strategy of developing 'national champions' – is that S&T policies have to concentrate on helping small and medium-sized enterprises to get access to and appropriate the technology they need to meet the demands of car assemblers. It is in these segments of production that domestic companies should concentrate, as the main business is in the hands of foreign car manufacturers. The situation is quite different in Russia where the unbundling of big car companies is not yet on the agenda. In-house technology should still remain important even if development of some spin-offs could, in the near future, take place. The future of the car industry in the CEEEs and Russia is fundamentally linked to macro-stabilization and economic growth: more income distributed among the population will stimulate the demand for cars.

BIBLIOGRAPHY

Andreff, Wladimir (1995), *Le secteur public à l'Est. Restructuration industrielle et financière*, Paris: L' Harmattan.
Andreff, Wladimir and Xavier Richet (eds) (1999), *FDI in Transforming Economies*, Cheltenham, UK and Northampton, MA, USA: Edward Elgar (forthcoming).

Bangemann, Martin (1997) 'La Politique de l'Union dans le secteur automobile', *Revue du Marché Commun et de l'Union européenne* (409), June.

Banville, Etienne de and Jean-Jacques Chanaron (1991), *Vers un système automobile européen*, Paris: CPE-Economica.

Brezinski, Horst and Gabriele Flüchter (1998) 'The Impact of Foreign Investors on Enterprise Restructuring in the Czech Republic – Findings Based on a Case Study of Skoda-Volkswagen', *Center for East European Studies Working Paper,* Copenhagen Business School.

Buck, Trevor, Igor Filatotchev, Peter Nolan and Mike Wright (1996), *Change in Russian and Chinese Car Making Firms: A Matched Pair of Cases,* Banff: Academy of International Business Conference.

Comité des Constructeurs Français d'Automobiles (CCFA) (1996), *L'Industrie automobile en France*, Paris: CCFA.

Comité des Constructeurs Français d'Automobiles (CCFA) (1997), *Répertoire Mondial des activités de production et d'assemblage de véhicules automobiles*, Paris: CCFA.

Chanaron, Jean-Jacques (1997), 'Automobile: Une technologie immobile, une industrie attentiste?', *Les Cahiers du Management Technologique* (20), May/August, pp. 7–34.

CzechInvest (1998), *Annual Report 1998*, Prague.

Dasgupta, Partha and Paul Stoneman (eds) (1987), *Economic Policy and Technological Performance*, Cambridge: Cambridge University Press.

Dodgson, Mark and Roy Rothwell (eds) (1994), *The Handbook of Industrial Innovation*, Aldershot, UK and Brookfield, USA: Edward Elgar.

Drucker, Peter F. (1946), *The Concept of the Corporation*, New York: John Day.

Economist Intelligence Unit (EIU) (1998), *Motor Business International*, London: EIU.

Ergas, Henry (1987) 'The Importance of Technology Policy', in Dasgupta and Stoneman (eds) (1987).

Estrin, Saul, Mitko Dimitrov and Xavier Richet (1998), 'Enterprise Restructuring in Albania, Bulgaria and Romania', *Economic Analysis*, 1 (3), pp. 239–57.

Estrin, Saul and Xavier Richet (1999), 'A Comparison of Direct Foreign Investment in Bulgaria, the Czech Republic and Slovenia', in Andreff and Richet (eds) (1999).

European Bank for Reconstruction and Development (EBRD) (various issues), *Transition Report*, London: EBRD.

Financial Times (various issues), *World Automotive Manufacturing*, Quarterly Report.

82 Xavier Richet and Frédéric Bourassa

Freeman, Christopher (1987), *Technology Policy and Economic Performance. Lessons from Japan*, London: Pinter.

Golikova, Viktoriya and Agnessa Avilova (1997), 'State Support for the Development of Small Businesses in Russian Regions', *Communist Economy and Economic Transformation*, **9** (4), pp. 423–30.

Graves, Andrew (1994), 'Innovation in a Globalizing Industry: The Case of Automobiles', in Dodgson and Rothwell (eds) (1994).

Hanson, Philip and Keith Pavitt (1987), *The Comparative Economics of Research Development and Innovation in the East and in the West: A Survey*, Chur: Harwood Academic Press.

Hare, Paul and Xavier Richet (1997), *Firm Adjustment and Barriers to Restructuring*, Caduernos del Este (20).

Havas, Attila (1999), 'Restructuring of the Automotive Industry in Hungary', in Christian von Hirschhausen and Jürgen Bitzer (eds) *The Globalization of Industry and Innovation in Eastern Europe – From Post-socialist Restructuring to International Competitiveness*, Cheltenham, UK and Northampton, MA, USA: Edward Elgar.

Huber, Peter and Andreas Wörgötter (1998), 'Observation on Russian Business Networks', *Post-Soviet Affairs*, **14** (January–March), pp. 81–92.

KBN – State Committee for Scientific Research (1997), *Guidelines for Innovation Policy in Poland*, Warsaw.

Meyer, Klaus (1998), 'Multinational Enterprises and the Emergence of Markets and Networks in Transition Economics', *Center for East European Studies Working Paper*, (12), Copenhagen Business School.

Moore, John H. (1997), 'Science, Technology and Russia's Future: Two Legacies', *Communist Economy and Economic Transformation*, **9** (1), pp. 43–60.

Organization for Economic Cooperation and Development (OECD) (1994), *Science, Technology and Innovation Policies, Evaluation Report, Russian Federation*, Paris: OECD.

Organization for Economic Cooperation and Development (OECD) (1996), *La Mondialisation de l'industrie. Vue d'ensemble et rapports sectoriels*, Paris: OECD.

Poste d'expansion économique de l'Ambassade de France en Russie (1998), *Le Marché Automobile en Russie*, Moscow: PEE.

Radosevic, Slavo (1997), 'The Emerging Patterns of Recombination, Path-dependency and Change', Targeted Socioeconomic Research Workshop Paper, University of Sussex.

Radosevic, Slavo (1998), 'Growth of Enterprises through Alliances in Central Europe: The Issues in Controlling Access to Technology, Market and Finance', University of Sussex, Science Policy Research Unit, mimeo.

Richet, Xavier (1995), 'Restructuration, contrôle et comportement des firmes dans la transition vers le marché', in Andreff (1995), pp. 53–71.

Roos, Philippe (1990), *Pouvoir, Territoires et Métiers*, Thèse de doctorat, Ecole des Mines de Paris, CERNA.

Ruigrok, Winfried and Rob van Tulder (1995), *The Logic of International Restructuring*, London: Routledge.

Ruigrok, Winfried and Rob van Tulder (1999), 'The Integration of Central and Eastern Europe in Car Production Networks', Working Paper for Actes du GERPISA (25), Université d'Evry.

Sintserov, Leonid (1998), *The Post-Soviet Automotive Industry: First Signs of Revival*, Sixth International Colloquium, University of Evry, GERPISA.

Skoda automobilova a.s. (1998), *Annual Report 1998*.

Standard and Poor's and Data Resources Incorporated/McGraw-Hill (1998), *World's Car Industry Forecast Report*, London.

Standard and Poor's and Data Resources Incorporated/PlanEcon (1998), *East European Automotive Industry Forecast*, London.

Török, Adam (1998), *Les alliances stratégiques et la privatization. Tendances internationales, perspectives en Europe Centrale et Orientale*, Rapport ACE (94-0699 R).

Ward's World Automotive Report (various issues).

Whiston, Thomas G. (1992), *Managerial and Organizational Integration*, London: Springer-Verlag.

XERFI, Secteur 700 (1997), *L'Industrie Automobile. Base de Donnée*, Paris, Ministère de l'Économie.

Table 4.1 Global car sales by region (000s)

	1993	1995	1997	1999	2000	2001	2002	2003
W. Europe	11,263	12,032	13,413	13,576	13,831	14,104	14,211	14,198
E. Europe	1,769	1,597	2,427	2,872	3,171	3,386	3,610	3,873
NAFTA	9,640	9,454	9,312	9,100	8,915	8,774	8,872	8,973
Asia	6,651	7,227	7,530	7,198	7,580	7,863	8,075	8,321
Latin America	1,593	2,024	2,332	2,416	2,618	2,834	3,068	3,296
Other	2,062	2,491	2,533	2,446	2,506	2,546	2,564	2,627
Total	32,978	34,825	37,547	37,608	38,621	39,507	40,400	41,288

Source: Data Resources Incorporated, World Car Forecast Report, May 1998.

Table 4.2 Car producers by regions and strategic alliances worldwide

	Producer by region			Strategic alliance lines			
		European Union	Asia	'GM line'	'Ford line'	'Daimler-Chrysler line'	Independent European manufacturers
NAFTA							
GM Ford Chrysler		VW Fiat Renault BMW-Rover PSA Volvo Mercedes-Benz GM-Opel Ford-Europe Saab Jaguar	Honda Toyota Mitsubishi Daewoo Hyundai Kia Suzuki Mazda Nissan	GM (including Chevrolet, Oldsmobile, Buick, Pontiac); Toyota; Suzuki; Isuzu; Daewoo; Opel and Vauxhall; SAAB	Ford (including Lincoln, Mercury); Mazda; Kia; Jaguar; Volvo	Mercedes-Benz; Chrysler (including Jeep, Dodge, Plymouth, Neon and so on); Mitsubishi; Hyundai (through Mitsubishi); Volvo	Volkswagen-Audi-SEAT-Skoda and Rolls-Royce-Bentley; Fiat-Lancia-Alfa Romeo; Renault (Nissan); Peugeot-Citroen

Source: Török (1998). Modified and updated by the authors.

Table 4.3 Market segments in the West European countries (percentage of registrations of new cars by country)

Countries	LS	LMS	UMS	HS	Others
Austria	18	41	21	15	5
Belgium	23	34	24	17	2
Denmark	21	40	32	6	2
Finland	11	41	34	11	2
France	44	29	17	8	2
Germany	21	32	20	22	5
Greece	36	44	11	5	4
Ireland	33	40	34	5	1
Italy	50	27	12	10	2
Luxembourg	22	30	22	22	4
Netherlands	27	36	25	11	1
Portugal	56	31	8	4	0
Spain	37	38	19	6	0
Sweden	6	27	24	41	2
United Kingdom	28	34	23	12	4
European Union	32	32	19	14	3
Norway	12	42	33	11	2
Switzerland	20	30	22	22	7
Total: (17 countries)	32	32	19	14	4

Note: LS: lower segment; LMS: lower medium segment; UMS: upper medium segment; HS: high segment; Others include multi-purpose and off-road vehicles.

Source: CCFA (1996).

Table 4.4 R&D scoreboard in the world automotive industry, 1994–1996

	1997 R&D spending £000	change in %	Sales £bn	R&D as % of sales	Cost of fund (COF) £000	R&D as percent COF	1996 £000
Engineering, vehicles	23,303,024	4	560,135	4.2	14,456,546	161.2	22,462,018
General Motors, USA	4,983,591	–8	101,158	4.9	4,699,769	106	5,409,019
Ford Motor, USA	3,845,266	–7	93,368	4.1	1,706,576	225.3	4,145,497
Toyota Motor, Japan	2,106,995	16	57,232	3.7	546,862	385.2	1,818,292
Daimler-Benz, Germany	1,914,146	2	41,930	4.6	519,858	368.2	1,885,753
Volkswagen, Germany	1,487,240	10	38,278	3.9	1,100,220	135.2	1,352,037
Honda Motor, Japan	1,173,841	14	24,741	4.7	192,365	610.2	1,031,018
Chrysler, USA	1,033,183	6	34,634	3	1,265,954	81.6	972,408
Renault, France	913,068	–1	21,004	4.3	353,114	258.6	921,857
Fiat, Italy	751,445	5	26,626	2.8	830,818	90.4	718,101
Denso, Japan	710,153	16	7,596	9.3	73,891	961.1	611,395
Volvo, Sweden	663,261	5	14,065	4.7	379,619	174.7	633,541

	1997 R&D spending £000	change in %	Sales £bn	R&D as % of sales	Cost of fund (COF) £000	R&D as percent COF	1996 £000
Peugeot, *France*	615,548	3	17,444	3.5	322,103	191.1	597,363
TRW, *USA*	613,225	81	6,583	9.3	138,568	442.5	337,912
Caterpillar, *USA*	320,895	29	11,502	2.8	348,851	92	249,180
Eaton, *USA*	245,533	51	4,596	5.3	132,491	185.3	162,271
AlliedSignal, *USA*	212,106	1	8,795	2.4	298,408	71.1	209,675
Valeo, *France*	207,203	18	3,432	6	27,075	765.3	174,976
Yamaha Motor, *Japan*	203,233	18	3,978	5.1	76,761	264.8	172,270
MAN, *Germany*	197,735	2	7,218	2.7	120,683	163.8	193,679
LucasVarity, *UK*	159,000	49	4,681	3.4	127,000	125.2	106,800
Fuji Heavy Industries, *Jp*	158,505	47	5,717	2.8	71,311	222.3	107,929
Cummins Engine, *USA*	158,016	11	3,419	4.6	43,151	366.2	142,822
Northrop Grumman, *USA*	154,978	55	4,905	3.2	215,753	71.8	99,672
Textron, *USA*	134,922	20	6,408	2.1	541,510	24.9	112,435
Hyundai Motor, *S. Korea*	125,206	33	4,120	3	42,435	295.1	93,834
Pirelli, *Italy*	122,033	13	3,872	3.2	142,403	85.7	108,282
GKN, *UK*	93,000	–1	2,834	3.3	139,000	66.9	94,000

Source: Financial Times, June 25, 1998.

Table 4.5 Motives for investing in the Eastern European automotive industry

Domestic market access	VW in the Czech Republic with limited room left to other car manufacturers: Daewoo/Avia and Hyundai/Skoda-Plzen. Exporters (Renault, Citroen) are buying market shares. Control of a narrow market, Suzuki in Hungary, Daewoo in Romania
Regional market access	Different car manufacturers in Poland: Fiat, GM, Daewoo, VW-Skoda, from the Czech Republic to Poland, to Belarus, Russia, VW in Slovakia to assemble cars for the local and regional markets (Hungary, Austria, Ukraine), GM-Opel in Hungary (mainly Western markets), Daewoo in Romania, Poland, Ukraine, Hungary, the Czech Republic
Global market access	Audi in Hungary, VW-Skoda in the Czech Republic, Fiat in Poland, Renault in Slovenia produce, assemble and re-export
Building up a European base	Daewoo in Romania and in Poland; other Asian car manufacturers (Japan) already have an industrial base in Europe
Cost, technology and human resources	All countries, especially in the northern part (Hungary, the Czech Republic, Slovakia, Poland)

Table 4.6 Ranking of automotive firms in Central Europe's top 100 enterprises (by 1997 sales)

Rank 1997	Rank 1996	Enterprise	Country	Sales ($ m)	Growth rate %	Profit ($ m)	Staff	Private	Foreign investor
8	7	Skoda auto	Czech Republic	2,604	20	90.7	22,205	Yes	Yes
12	11	Fiat Auto Poland	Poland	1,890	7	28.5	11,953	Yes	Yes
21	53	Daewoo-FSO	Poland	1,304	100	16.5	13,893	Yes	Yes
40	n.a.	Audi Hungaria	Hungary	928	172	85.1	1,647	Yes	Yes
41	27	Revoz	Slovenia	928	–7	n.a.	2,561	Yes	Yes
54	45	Opel Hungary	Hungary	697	–2	172.6	1,647	Yes	Yes
61	55	VW-Bratislava	Slovakia	622	7	10.2	2,745	Yes	Yes
65	n.a.	VW-Poznan	Poland	564	94	15.1	1,950	Yes	Yes
91	88	Daewoo Motor Polska	Poland	411	6	16.5	6,502	Yes	Yes

Source: Business Central Europe, Annual Survey 1998/1999.

Table 4.7 Global car production by region (000s)

	1993	1994	1995	1996	1997	1998	1999	2000	2001	2002	2003
W. Europe	10,845	12,109	12,611	13,063	13,801	14,155	14,084	14,031	14,252	14,494	14,451
E. Europe	2,160	1,793	1,925	2,065	2,498	2,787	3,059	3,395	3,696	3,948	4,091
NAFTA	8,169	8,673	8,376	8,162	8,133	8,179	8,053	8,015	7,961	8,103	8,309
Asia	1,0645	10,222	10,455	11,097	11,900	11,112	11,500	11,578	11,774	11,866	12,111
Latin America	1,385	1,587	1,528	1,728	2,045	1,926	2,103	2,307	2,496	2,686	2,872
Other	482	516	540	564	558	593	616	636	660	681	684
Total	33,686	34,900	35,435	36,679	38,935	38,752	39,415	39,962	40,839	41,778	42,518

Source: Standard and Poor's Data Resources Incorporated/McGraw-Hill (1998).

Table 4.8 Car production by model in the Czech Republic (000s)

	1995	1996	1997	1998	1999	2000	2001	2008
Favorit/Forman	3,805	0	0	0	0	0	0	0
Felicia	189,333	238,958	296,715	290,000	260,000	0	0	0
Felicia B	0	0	0	0	45,000	320,000	320,000	330,000
Octavia	0	1,168	60,690	110,000	125,000	130,000	120,000	160,000
Model W8	0	0	0	0	0	10,000	60,000	60,000
Total Skoda	193,138	240,126	357,405	400,000	430,000	460,000	500,000	550,000
Change in %	26.8	24.3	48.8	11.9	7.5	7.0	8.7	10.0
Tatra	48	70	23	10	10	10	10	10
Total	193,186	240,196	357,428	400,010	430,010	460,010	500,010	550,010
Change in %	26.8	24.3	48.8	11.9	7.5	7.0	8.7	10.0

Source: Standard and Poor's Data Resources Incorporated/PlanEcon, April 1998.

Table 4.9 Domestic car sales in the Czech Republic (000s)

	1995	1996	1997	1998	1999	2000	2001	2008
Skoda	67,598	82,734	96,680	94,733	101,068	116,500	125,083	117,000
% market share	60.3	53.4	55.8	52.3	52.3	54.2	53.1	42.7
Tatra	50	69	23	10	10	10	10	10
Other	46	21	10	10	10	10	10	10
Total	67,694	82,824	96,713	94,753	101,088	116,520	125,103	117,020
Share in % New registration	29.6	28.4	31.3	37.8	41.6	46.6	49.5	42.4
(%) Change in %	15.1	22.4	16.8	−2.0	6.7	15.3	7.4	—

Source: Standard and Poor's Data Resources Incorporated/PlanEcon, April 1998.

Table 4.10 Production by manufacturers in Russia

	1996	1997	1998	1999	2000	2001	2009
AVTOGAZ	124,284	124,339	125,398	122,750	125,350	125,080	126,000
AVTOVAZ	680,965	740,497	594,444	654,580	682,045	686,545	667,000
AZLK	2,930	20,599	40,000	38,150	36,450	17,775	0
Daewoo	3,650	13,225	4,988	1,870	4,800	10,950	70,000
Fiat Group	0	0	0	950	1,950	12,000	113,000
Ford	0	0	0	0	0	2,200	42,000
GM	19	2,500	2,000	700	1,400	4,500	108,000
IZHMASH	9,149	5,522	5,292	500	1,500	2,750	0
KAMAZ/SEAZ	12,606	26,237	30,102	33,500	35,450	38,000	70,000
KIA	0	1,000	254	0	0	0	0
Renault	0	0	0	500	1,900	4,500	101,000
UAZ	33,701	51,411	31,932	25,500	23,975	22,670	30,000
VW Group	0	0	0	0	0	2,000	60,000
Total	867,304	985,330	834,410	879,000	914,820	928,970	1,387,000

Source: Standard and Poor's Data Resources Incorporated/PlanEcon, East European Automotive Industry Forecast Update, 1999.

94

5 Local, Regional and Global Production Networks: Reintegration of the Hungarian Automotive Industry

Attila Havas

1. INTRODUCTION[39]

The automotive industry can be regarded not only as 'the industry of industries' but also as a symbol – and a pioneer – of significant economic and social changes. Internationally, it has been the origin of major new trends in the organization of production, from the mass production developed by Ford in the 1910s to the lean production pioneered by Toyota in the past several decades. In Hungary, its radical reorganization in the 1940s was a clear sign of the introduction of a new socio-economic system. Currently it is a symbol of sweeping changes again: the performance of this sector can be regarded as a sort of proxy variable to gauge the transition process to a market economy. With the collapse of the Council for Mutual Economic Assistance (CMEA), the trading bloc of the former Soviet empire, in 1989, the privatization of the Polish and Romanian car manufacturers by foreign investors, and the war in the former Yugoslavia, Hungarian car parts suppliers lost many of their major auto assembly customers. However, foreign investors soon entered the domestic market and provided new sources of demand.[40] These projects have offered timely market opportunities to local suppliers, whose primary challenge is to seize the chance for restructuring and survival.

---

[39] This chapter is based on an extensive literature survey and interviews with managers. The author is indebted for the help of the latter.

[40] Suzuki and GM Opel have opened car assembly plants, and Opel has also built an engine assembly plant. Ford has invested in an electrical component factory, and Audi in an engine plant first, and then in car assembly as well.

Restructuring will require major changes in line with the new lean production paradigm, including the introduction of new products, processes, management and organizational culture and techniques, such as 'just in time' and total quality control. A critical question is whether just a few advanced suppliers will adopt such changes, forming a modern enclave within a declining industry, or whether these products, processes and management techniques may diffuse through second- and third-tier suppliers. A second question is whether Hungarian companies, having met the exacting demands of Audi, Ford, Opel Hungary and Magyar Suzuki, can become competitive in other export markets. A closely related fundamental issue is whether naturally evolving production linkages with the new foreign investors would lead to that stage where Hungarian scientists and engineers are involved in the global research and development efforts, or if concerted government action is also required.

The aim of this chapter is to shed some light on the restructuring process in the industry, focussing on the role and impacts of production networks, coordinated by major foreign firms, prospects and modes of growth and the scope for innovation policy. The Hungarian case clearly shows that components manufacturing – the network of first-, second- and third-tier suppliers – can be more important and more successful for a country with a small domestic market than car assembly. It also pinpoints the limits of sector-specific R&D policy and stresses the importance of the overall, more general innovation policy.[41]

Analyzing historical trends can help considerably in understanding current developments. Therefore, Sections 2 and 3 summarize the evolution of the automobile and auto parts industries in Hungary, and major developments in the transition period. Competition patterns and the role of production networks are then discussed in Section 4. The following section shifts the focus of analysis from the present to the future by looking at the different modes of growth and the prospects for Hungarian suppliers. The scope and potential impacts of government policies are examined in Section 6. Finally, conclusions are drawn in Section 7.

---

[41] Western European, US and Southeast Asian automotive companies – both car manufacturers and suppliers – are relocating their production activities to Central and Eastern European countries (i) to cut their costs, and (ii) to seize new market opportunities. Clearly, these strategic moves have crucial bearings on the Hungarian automotive industry. However, these cases are not analyzed here. A more detailed account thereof can be found in Havas (1997).

2. TRADITIONS OF THE HUNGARIAN CAR AND CAR PARTS INDUSTRIES

2.1 Production before 1945

Cars, first assembled from imported kits, have been produced in Hungary since 1903. The year 1905 saw the first car designed and built by a Hungarian engineer, János Csonka. Bus manufacturing started in 1909. Preparation for World War I sparked production of cars, lorries and engines. Ravages of war and the Great Depression hindered the sector in the 1920s. Recovery started in the 1930s, and Ford models were also produced under a license agreement. Motorcycle production commenced in the 1930s, too. First imported kits were assembled but local content had increased to 90 percent by 1935. World War II boosted production again, particularly for military vehicles (Berend and Ránki 1955, 1958). All the major car parts – engines, gears, chassis – were also produced in Hungary until the mid-1940s. In other words, Hungary's vehicle manufacturers were not mere assembly units for foreign companies, but accumulated skills in automotive engineering, building upon a long tradition in mechanical engineering.

Hungarian engineers were rather successful in R&D in the pioneering period of the industry. The most notable ones were János Csonka and Donát Bánki who substantially improved the internal combustion engine in many ways in the 1880s and 1890s. Their most significant – but hardly acknowledged – achievement was the invention of the carburetor in 1893. Bánki also designed a new engine that raised efficiency by 50 percent. These R&D results, however, were not commercialized in large-scale production in Hungary – not even the carburetor, which was reinvented by Maybach in Germany two years later, and became known in that version all over the world.

2.2 Heritage of the CMEA

Automotive production facilities were ruined during the war. Manufacturing of motorcycles, buses, lorries and other commercial vehicles resumed thereafter.[42] Car production, however, was abandoned under the new industrial policy which shaped Hungary's industrial structure to a CMEA-wide division of labor. The new policy was influenced first informally by

---

[42] Private companies – as in all other sectors, and in all other countries in the Soviet bloc – were nationalized by the late 1940s. Corollaries of nationalization and central planning – most notably lack of competition – are not sector specific, and are thoroughly analyzed in the literature, hence not discussed here.

Soviet advisors working in Hungary and then by a formal Soviet–Hungarian specialization agreement signed in 1964. The accord coordinated the two countries' industrial development projects, including automotive manufacturing, in the wider context of the CMEA. It also stipulated that Hungary would specialize in producing buses for the entire CMEA.[43] Ikarus, Hungary's bus manufacturing firm, became one of the largest in Europe, turning out some 14,000 units a year in the 1980s.[44]

Bus manufacturing provided an excellent opportunity to make use of the considerable assets and skills accumulated in auto parts manufacturing companies, despite the lack of a car manufacturing industry since the late 1940s. Hungarian suppliers also shipped car parts to other CMEA countries as of the 1960s.[45] Certain automotive components, for example, engines, axles, undercarriages and tires for commercial vehicles as well as bulbs, batteries and dashboards for cars, were also exported for hard currencies (to Western Europe, the USA and India).

As for R&D, hardly any original projects were conducted in this period, in sharp contrast to the previous one. The pace of technological improvement was set by CMEA demand. Needless to say, these requirements differed significantly compared to those of advanced countries, given the severe shortage of cars and the lack of rigorous safety and environmental regulations. The only counterbalancing factor was that CMEA car manufacturers, except Skoda, based their product development strategy on Western licenses from the 1960s onward. Hence their suppliers' products were also based on Western licenses. The most advanced product and process technologies, however, were not made available through these license agreements. In other words it was a 'safe' way to maintain or even widen the technological gap. In fact, because of the lack of incentives to innovate – no import competition; extremely long waiting periods for cars which were, in effect, 'rationed'; lack of up-to-date safety and environmental rules – CMEA car producers were happy with their technology which in the 1980s was up to

---

[43] For a detailed analysis of the impacts of the agreement and the 'Central Automotive Development Program', see Bauer et al. (1980), Bauer and Soós (1980), Soós (1980) and Tárnok and Vince (1980).

[44] Production was still at 12,350 and 11,980 units in 1988 and 1989, respectively. Collapse of the CMEA caused a dramatic drop: output fell to 7,994 in 1990, and almost every year since then has seen a further decline. Output was a mere 1,576 units in 1994 and 1,162 buses in 1998.

[45] The single most important buyer has been the (former) Soviet VAZ (Lada) factory. Other significant customers have included the Polish FSO and FSM (Polski Fiat) companies as well as Dacia in Romania. Although (the former) Yugoslavia never joined the CMEA, Hungarian parts were also shipped to its car producer, Zastava (now in Serbia) until the recent UN embargo. Given the lack of sectoral statistics, aggregate CMEA sales data are not available.

thirty years old. Hence their Hungarian suppliers had neither much of an opportunity nor the incentives to innovate.

However, those suppliers who exported their products for hard currencies had no other choice than to continuously improve their products through up-to-date Western licenses (for example, from Bosch, MAN, KNORR, ZF, Girling and Lucas) and adaptive in-house R&D projects.

3. RECENT DEVELOPMENTS

3.1 Reemerging Car Production in Hungary

3.1.1 A policy dilemma

Hungarian government officials had long intended to reestablish the car assembly industry for two basic reasons. First, the severe shortage of cars was rather annoying in the most 'liberal' and reformed planned economy – often referred to as 'goulash communism' in the Western media. This shortage resulted in an aging, obsolete generation of automobiles. Second, the government also viewed car manufacturing as a means of industrial modernization, with its exacting technical and organizational requirements. Industrialists have also backed the idea as a major step towards integration into the world economy – and as another golden opportunity to obtain immense investment funds from the government. Two consortia were set up by Hungarian companies to promote the reestablishment of the car industry in the late 1980s.

One question, however, has divided this apparently unified camp of promoters: whether to opt for large-scale manufacturing of car parts for major car producers or to assemble cars again after a rather long cessation lasting for almost 50 years.[46] It was also an open and much-debated question whether to produce cars jointly with the CMEA or in cooperation with advanced countries. While the government pondered the issue, two foreign car companies looking for favorable new locations and market opportunities 'resurrected' Hungarian car manufacturing in the early 1990s.

3.1.2 Magyar Suzuki

Magyar Suzuki, a Japanese–Hungarian joint venture located in Esztergom, some 50 km from Budapest, commenced commercial production of compact cars in October 1992. Investment had totaled USD 260 million by 1997. A further USD 146 million will be invested to produce a new small car, jointly

---

[46] These conflicting opinions are described in more detail, for example, by Somai (1993) and Varga (1990).

developed with GM, but assembled separately under Suzuki and Opel badges in Esztergom and Gliwice, Poland, respectively. Because of this project, Magyar Suzuki's output will reach 100 thousand units a year. Magyar Suzuki has increased its output, employment and productivity constantly, but made losses for four years, and its 1997 profits were still modest (Table 5.1). Yet it had become the seventh-largest exporting company in Hungary by 1997.

Table 5.1 Major data of Magyar Suzuki, 1992–1998

	1992	1993	1994	1995	1996	1997	1998
Production	992	13,021	19,412	36,453	51,777	63,630	66,351
Domestic sales (units)	929	12,659	16,065	12,178	13,594	16,039	23,788
Exports (units)	n.a.	n.a.	3,309	23,873	38,183	47,700	42,001
Sales (m Ft)	1,907	9,338	15,468	36,831	56,777	77,035	n.a.
Domestic sales (m Ft)	1,903	9,272	13,098	13,333	15,652	19,117	n.a.
Exports (m Ft)	4	66	2,370	23,498	41,125	57,918	n.a.
Profits before taxation (m Ft)	–	–6,840	–2,046	–351	887	1,651	n.a.
Employment (average)	279	487	652	1,032	1,417	1,547	1,508
Productivity (cars/employees)	n.a.	26.7	29.8	35.3	36.5	41.1	44.0

Note: n.a. = not applicable, not available.

Source: Magyar Suzuki and press reports.

From the point of view of the Hungarian suppliers (and would-be suppliers) there are two critical issues: production runs and the technical level of parts demanded by an assembler. Production data – reported in Table 5.1 – indicate that Magyar Suzuki buys parts in relatively low volumes, and hence its suppliers desperately need other business. Magyar Suzuki, however, pays special attention to the viability of its suppliers as it follows a single-sourcing strategy. Together with its Japanese suppliers, it conducts a thorough technological and financial audit, covering literally every single aspect of doing business, from purchasing inputs through production methods and machinery, to accounting, sales and management, broadly defined. Then joint efforts are made to improve the selected supplier's technical level and economic performance, when needed.

Pressing, welding, painting and assembly account for around 20–22 percent of a Suzuki Swift's value and are carried out by Magyar Suzuki itself.[47] Local content, including the above activities, was only 25 percent in

---

[47] Magyar Suzuki is also involved in producing some metal parts, and thus its share in total value added has been slightly higher, that is, 23–24 percent since 1993.

October 1992, but almost doubled (48 percent) by the end of 1993 given an extensive and rapid localization program. Since then, localization has continued at a much slower pace, reaching 53 percent by 1997.[48] Magyar Suzuki intends to keep importing high-tech, high-value-added components, such as engine transmissions and undercarriages from Japan. As these sub-systems account for around 20 percent of value added, the local content might reach 80 percent in a few years. Magyar Suzuki had 34 suppliers based in Hungary in 1995, 41 in 1996 and 45 in 1998. A further 35 suppliers shipped various parts to Magyar Suzuki in 1996 from EU countries, and three – all partly or wholly foreign owned – from Central and Eastern European countries.

Originally it seemed unlikely that Hungarian suppliers could export their products to the Japanese plants of Suzuki Motor Corp., given significant lags in productivity and substantial transportation costs, let alone the then-shrinking demand for new cars in Japan. Yet, a few years later the joint endeavor of Magyar Suzuki and its Hungarian suppliers resulted in a breakthrough: exports of rubber and plastic parts to Japan started in late 1994, while springs have been shipped since October 1995. Eight Hungarian suppliers were involved in these activities in 1995, and three others joined this 'club' in 1996.

3.1.3 Opel Hungary

Also in 1992, Opel Hungary Vehicle Manufacturing Ltd opened the other Hungarian car assembly plant and an engine factory in a customs-free zone at Szentgotthárd, close to the Austrian border. Initially GM Opel invested over DEM 400 million, and by 1997 a total of DEM 735 million. Opel Astras were produced in Hungary until December 1998. Parts purchased in Hungary initially accounted for merely 4 percent of an Astra's value, then 9.6 percent in 1995–98.

As for the engine factory, its original capacity has been doubled to 460,000 units a year (that is, around one-quarter of Opel's total European production), and cylinder heads have also been added to the product lines as a result of further investment projects completed by 1996. Actual output depends primarily on demand for Opel models in Western Europe as the vast majority of production is exported to Opel assembly plants. Because of these secure markets, Opel Hungary was already in the black in the second year of

---

[48] Parts and components produced by local suppliers include clutches, batteries, seats, seat belts, horns, windshield wipers, instrument panels, dashboards, wiring harnesses, shock absorbers, glass, paint, upholstery, rubber and plastic parts as well as small, simple pressed metal parts. In other words, these are mid-tech products at best, and thus most of them do not constitute high-value-added goods.

its operation, made the third-largest profits in Hungary in 1997, and was the fourth-largest exporter (see Table 5.2).

Table 5.2 Major data of Opel Hungary, 1992–1998

	1992	1993	1994	1995	1996	1997	1998
Car production (units)	9,401	13,344	12,282	12,488	11,255	12,700	9,700
Car exports (units)	2,736	3,220	2,254	3,956	2,480	904	1,208
Engine production (units)	20,511	75,741	160,033	266,051	310,034	368,000	417,000
Revenues (m Ft)	9,074	20,345	43,093	101,729	113,293	141,904	n.a.
Exports (m Ft)	1,691	8,402	29,151	90,178	99,761	121,832	n.a.
Employment (average)	453	482	569	701	837	1,009	1.154
Profits before taxation (m Ft)	–1,343	736	6,095	14,584	20,691	32,246	n.a.

Note: n.a. = not available.

Source: Opel Hungary and press reports.

Opel Hungary, in contrast to Magyar Suzuki, prefers to have joint ventures as its suppliers, especially between its long-established Western partners and Hungarian companies. It seeks suppliers not only for its Hungarian operations but also for other GM plants all over Europe. That means a much larger volume of several hundred thousand units a year, and thus Hungarian suppliers could rely on economies of scale. Indeed, Hungarian parts purchased for other GM plants amounted to DEM 118 million in 1994, that is, worth 7.5 times more than Hungarian parts, materials and services bought for Opel Astras assembled in Szentgotthárd. Components exports to GM factories increased substantially by 1997, reaching DEM 250 million.

The engine factory could provide good business opportunities for Hungarian suppliers, at least as far as production run is concerned, but most parts are imported, as in the case of car assembly operations. Western foundries and engineering firms, however, have set up either joint ventures or subsidiaries in Hungary given the promising market opportunities provided by the expanded Opel engine plant, and the Audi engine plant opened in late 1994.

The end of car assembly does not mean that Opel would withdraw from Hungary; on the contrary, further investment projects were launched in April 1998. Opel invested DEM 230 million to build a new gearbox factory with a capacity of 250,000 units a year. This is a new product, to be manufactured only in Hungary for a limited period. Production is planned to commence in 2001 with initially 30–35 percent local content, to be raised to 50 percent.

With this project, GM Opel's investment in Hungary would total DEM 920 million. Opel also intends to involve some local suppliers and R&D institutes in product development projects in three broad fields: engine development, modeling (for example, chassis, body) and other components.

3.1.4 Audi Hungaria Motor Kft (AHM)

A third car producer joined in 1998. Originally Audi AG invested in Hungary in a new engine manufacturing plant, its first 100-percent-owned manufacturing base outside Germany. Audi Hungaria Motor Kft (AHM), located in Gyõr, western Hungary, was opened in October 1994. It is the first engine plant in the world to manufacture five-valve, four-cylinder engines in commercial production. This new engine generation is built into Audi, Volkswagen Passat, SEAT and Skoda models. Audi invested over DEM 800 million by 1998 in several steps as output increased and further engine components were added to the product lines. Production of six- and eight-cylinder petrol engines was also relocated to Gyõr. Moreover, two new sports models, the TT Coupé and the Roadster, have been assembled at AHM since 1998 (around 14,000 units in 1998 and 40,000 units a year at full capacity). Audi Hungaria Motor assembled over 100,000 four-cylinder engines in 1995, some 200,000 units in 1996 and nearly 600,000 engines in 1997. AHM was ranked second among the top ten Hungarian exporters in 1997, and made the sixth-largest profits. It produced around 1 million engines in 1998. (See Table 5.3.)

Table 5.3 Performance of Audi Hungaria Motor Kft (AHM)

	1995	1996	1997	1998
Engines (units)	104,000	196,000	584,000	980,000
Revenues (m Ft)	27,853	54,068	188,925	410,000
Exports (m Ft)	27,853	54,025	188,735	410,000
Employment (average)	254	661	1,760	2,800
Profits before taxation (m Ft)	2,811	4,386	15,900	n.a.

Note: n.a. = not available.

Source: Audi Hungaria Motor and press reports. Data for 1998 are preliminary.

Audi AG has not committed itself to increasing the level of domestic sourcing. Local suppliers account for 5 percent of the value of engines assembled in Gyõr. All the five major components are machined in Gyõr, using imported casts. AHM managing directors intend to purchase casts and forged parts from Hungarian suppliers. So far a few local – usually at least partly foreign owned – companies have obtained orders, shipping machined parts for the engine plant and seats, aluminum and plastic parts for the car assembly plant. Casts are likely to be supplied by another German firm based in Győr (already serving an Opel engine plant operating in a nearby Austrian town).

AHM buys inputs through the Volkswagen Group purchasing department (to cut prices of raw materials and components bought in large volumes). This also means that suppliers, capable of meeting Audi requirements, could increase their chance to win further orders from other VW firms. Audi buys various products and services worth DEM 150 million a year from Hungarian companies for AHM plus various parts worth DEM 80 million for other VW subsidiaries. The latter amount is projected to increase to DEM 200 million in a couple of years.

Audi has announced the opening of a new engine development center in Győr. It seems to be an inevitable step since Győr has become the engine production base for the company. It would also be rational to perform some design and/or engineering tasks in Győr related to the two new models, as those are assembled only in Hungary.

3.2 Components Manufacturing

3.2.1 Industry definition: a methodological note

Automotive component manufacturing was not considered a separate industry in international statistics until the 1980s. In the first decades of car manufacturing, independent companies supplied parts as a side business, along with machines, instruments, and parts for other transport equipment, such as bicycles and carriages. Later, car manufacturers either acquired their suppliers or established in-house production of components. Thus information and statistics on this sector used to be subsumed under the automobile or motor vehicle industry. In the 1980s, however, automotive part production emerged as an important industry in its own right because of changes in technology, organization and trade. The role of component suppliers increased not only in production but also in design; their technical and economic performance has became a key factor in the competition among car manufacturers. Thus the sector now is a new 'entry' in statistics due to its economic significance. A simple reason is that on average between 10 and 12 thousand parts are built into a car, accounting for some 50–70 percent of the manufacturing cost of an automobile.

As a very wide range of products are used to assemble a motor vehicle – practically all industrial sectors supply the automotive industry – readily available statistics are usually too narrow in terms of coverage. In other words, quite a few automotive suppliers are classified as leather, rubber, plastics, paint, glass, cable or metal producing and processing companies, foundries, electric and electronics companies, and so on. The EU statistical classification also follows this line, that is, motor vehicle parts and accessories (NACE 34.30) excludes engine and tire manufacturers, most of the electrical and electronic components, as well as glass, plastic or certain castings and other metal parts.

The current Hungarian statistical classification system,[49] more or less in harmony with the EU methodology, identifies four automotive subsectors:

* manufacture of electric automotive components (3161);
* manufacture of motor vehicles (3410);
* manufacture of bodies for motor vehicles (3420); and
* manufacture of automotive components (3430).

3.2.2 Performance of the Hungarian automotive components suppliers

Two of these sectors are relevant for this study: manufacture of electric automotive components and manufacture of automotive components. Although these names might suggest that the two sectors cover at least the majority of the automotive suppliers, this is not the case: just as in the EU statistics on the automotive components sector, a wide range of products are excluded (for example, engines and engine components, tires, glass, plastic, castings and other metal parts as well as bulbs). For this reason, available statistics only include 150–160 firms, while experts estimate that altogether some 300–350 companies produce motor vehicle parts and components in Hungary.[50]

---

[49] It was introduced in 1992. Previously, components manufacturing, in line with the previous international methodology, was treated as part of the automotive industry. Hence no data on components manufacturing are available prior to 1992, and thus the current performance of the sector cannot be compared to the pre-1990 period. In other words, it is not possible to analyze the results of the restructuring process statistically.

[50] The primary producers are Rába (diesel engines and axles for commercial vehicles), Bakony Művek (electrical parts), MMG (instrument panels), PEMŰ, TVK, Kaloplasztik, Kunplast (all plastic parts), Perion (batteries), IMAG (seats, wiring harnesses), Videoton (printed circuits, electrical parts and wiring harnesses), Knorr-Bremse (brakes), ADA, Pre-cast and Le Belier (all foundries), GE Tungsram (lighting) and Taurus (rubber parts). Besides these long-established Hungarian companies – some of them already privatized by foreign investors as their new names suggest – well-known foreign companies have also set up their subsidiaries, for example, Akzo (paints), Ford (electrical parts), Cascade and Happich (plastic parts), Denso (fuel pumps), ITT Automotive (electrical parts and wiring harnesses), Michels Kabel (wiring harnesses), Packard Electric (electrical parts and wiring harnesses), UTA (wiring harnesses), VAW (castings) and ZF (gearboxes). The major customers are the local car assemblers, Western European car manufacturers and their first-tier suppliers, as well as North American commercial vehicle companies.

These two sectors increased their sales significantly: the 1997 output of electric automotive components was almost 20 times higher than in 1992, and the other sector – from a much higher absolute level – nearly quintupled in the period 1992–97. The export intensity of these sectors is also worth noting, particularly in the case of the electrical automotive components, where the ratio of exports to sales further increased from an already high level of 69.5 percent in 1992 to 93 percent in 1997. Thus it can be established beyond doubt that these companies face fierce competition: given the globalized nature of the automotive industry and the liberal import regime there is a strong rivalry on their domestic markets, and they also face harsh competition on their export markets, where the bulk of their output is shipped. Moreover, their financial performance has improved significantly as well, that is, they are not 'buying' export markets at the expense of their profits.[51]

Table 5.4 Manufacture of electrical automotive components (3161)

	1992	1993	1994	1995	1996	1997
Sales	2,454.2	3,013.6	7,766.2	13,010.2	89,968.5	43,544.8
of which: exports	1,705.2	2,290.1	6,610.1	11,239.9	88,034.3	40,495.8
Exports/sales (%)	69.5	76.0	85.1	86.4	97.9	93.0
Employment (heads)	1,852	2,267	2,545	3,199	4,813	6,146
Number of companies	19	23	25	25	32	34
Pre-tax profits	−175.4	64.0	671.4	1,280.3	20,122.4	6,217,8
Labor costs	624.7	703.0	1,456.0	2,203.0	12,507.6	6,941.7
Value added	–	1,118.5	2,590.2	3,684.1	35,774.1	n.a.
Sales/employee	1.3	1.3	3.1	4.1	18.7	7.1
Net profits/sales (%)	–	1.9	8.3	9.3	22.3	14.1

Note: Only double-book-keeping companies are included, and figures are in million Hungarian forint, unless otherwise indicated.

Source: Ministry of Industry and Trade and author's calculation.

Thus their significant growth in the period 1992–97 is even more impressive. Figures indicate that the underlying factor of their success is improved productivity (a nearly seven-fold increase in the case of electrical automotive equipment, and a five-fold increase in the case of automotive

---

[51] Yet, the profitability of the components sector (3430) was rather low in the entire period, that is, below 4 percent until 1996, and reaching 7.5 percent only in 1997. The other sector (3136) fares much better in this respect, too, most likely because it produces higher-value-added goods.

components), thanks to the introduction of new processes and management techniques, and to a certain extent due to the modernization of equipment, reflected in the increase of assets (see Tables 5.4 and 5.5).

Table 5.5 Manufacture of parts and components for motor vehicles (3430)

	1992	1993	1994	1995	1996	1997
Sales	26,443.9	35,495.3	44,031.9	60,117.5	75,256.7	135,010.4
of which: exports	13,950.9	17,870.1	23,016.8	36,517.1	47,446.8	95,415.4
Exports/sales (%)	52.8	50.3	52.3	60.7	63.1	70,7
Employment (heads)	17,348	17,781	16,592	15,502	15,725	18,319
Number of companies	102	112	117	124	131	144
Pre-tax profits	–17.9	708.3	989.5	2,502.2	2,612.6	10,476.4
Labor costs	6,758.8	8,462.0	10,475.6	12,197.1	15,512.8	21,935.1
Value added	–	12,876.5	15,746.6	19,322.2	23,480.0	n.a.
Sales/employee	1.5	2.0	2.7	3.9	4.8	7.4
Net profit/sales (%)	–	1.0	1.9	3.7	3.0	7.5

Note: Only double-book-keeping companies are included, and figures are in million Hungarian forint, unless otherwise indicated.

Source: Ministry of Industry and Trade and author's calculations.

3.2.3 Ownership patterns

As far as ownership is concerned, a wide variety of forms can be observed. For qualitative analytical purposes it is worth listing the actual ownership forms:

A) Dominant Foreign Ownership
    A1   Greenfield investments with 100 percent foreign ownership. For the purpose of further analysis, it is useful to identify two subsets in this group:
        A1.1 Subsidiaries of car manufacturers: AUDI Hungaria Motor Kft., Ford Hungaria, Opel Hungary
        A1.2 Subsidiaries of component manufacturers: for example, ITT Automotive Hungary, United Technologies Automotive Hungary, Denso, VAW, Michels Kabel, Keiper-Recaro.
    A2   'Brownfield' investments: former state-owned companies privatized by foreign investors, for example, Knorr-Bremse, ZF.
B) Dominant Hungarian Ownership

B1   State-owned companies.

B2   Privatized former state-owned companies: in most cases privatization has been only partial so far, usually as a combination of Employee Share Ownership Programme (ESOP) and Management Buy-Out (MBO) projects; for example, Bakony Mûvek Rt., MMG Automatika Rt., Perion Akkumulátorgyár Rt.

B3   Private companies, that is, firms established by Hungarian entrepreneurs either in the 1960s or more recently.

B4   Joint ventures with dominant Hungarian private ownership, for example, RATIPUR Car Equipment Co.

Individual companies can be classified relatively easily using these categories. As for a more rigorous quantitative analysis at a sectoral level, however, a number of methodological problems arise. First, it goes without saying that ownership changes are going on literally month by month in these sectors as well. Hence, the overall picture – that is, the ratio of different ownership forms – is constantly changing. Thus from the point of view of economic analysis, it is a 'moving target'.

Second, given the lack of readily-available statistics, it is not possible to establish the ratio of private and state ownership precisely. While seven distinct types of owners are recognized in the Hungarian statistics, namely the state, the municipalities, domestic individuals, domestic corporations, ESOP, foreigners and cooperatives, published statistics provide figures only on state-owned and foreign-owned equity. Moreover, one category of ownership – namely 'domestic corporations', that is, shareholding and limited liability companies – does not distinguish between private and state ownership.[52]

Table 5.6 Ownership changes in the manufacture of electrical automotive components (3161)

	1992	1993	1994	1995	1996	1997
Equity	2,065.8	832.6	842.7	918.4	9,624.0	2,569.6
of which: foreign ownership	121.1	166.5	276.2	505.4	9,282.7	2,200.0
state ownership	1,537.2	154.0	154.0	15.0	15.1	13.2
Share of foreign ownership (%)	5.9	20.0	32.8	55.0	96.5	85,6

Note: Only double-book-keeping companies are included, and figures are in million Hungarian forint, unless otherwise indicated.
Source: Ministry of Industry and Trade and author's calculations.

---

[52] Therefore an apparently legitimate formula, assuming that the municipality-owned assets are almost negligible, and thus the ratio of private ownership equals 100 percent minus state ownership minus 2–6 percent for municipality stakes, would lead to deceptive results.

Bearing in mind these methodological limitations, available statistics do suggest a rapidly increasing share of private (in particular foreign) ownership in both sectors (see Tables 5.6 and 5.7).

Table 5.7 Ownership changes in the manufacture of parts and components for motor vehicles (3430)

	1992	1993	1994	1995	1996	1997
Equity	19,657.8	21,831.8	22,400.9	23,598.9	27,478.5	40,173.6
of which: foreign ownership	2,517.8	3,348.1	4,029.3	6,080.8	8,669.8	22,246.8
state ownership	9,130.3	9,051.4	7,190.5	5,434.6	4,389.6	338.0
Share of foreign ownership (%)	12.8	15.3	18.0	25.8	31.6	55.4

Note: Only double-book-keeping companies are included, and figures are in million Hungarian forint, unless otherwise indicated.

Source: Ministry of Industry and Trade and author's calculations.

4. PATTERNS OF COMPETITION AND PRODUCTION NETWORKS

Although car assemblers, first- (T1), second- (T2) and third-tier (T3) suppliers are all necessary to constitute a production network and in the end all share the network's destiny, they have different responsibilities in the division of labor in a given network, and they have to face different types of risks. Therefore it is necessary to analyze them somewhat separately – while also keeping in mind the strong and close ties among them.

4.1 Evolving Strategies for Car Manufacturers to Improve Competitiveness

Car manufacturers have to face strong competition and mature markets in their traditional areas of operation. Moreover, they are not – and in the foreseeable future most likely they will not be – in a position to expect to escape from this trap by relying on any technological breakthrough. Thus they have to devise and implement other strategies:

- cutting costs in order to maintain existing markets by offering lower prices,
- introducing new features, offering new functions (for example, safety,

comfort, global positioning systems, recycling) as well as improving reliability and fuel economy,

- creating new market segments in long-established, mature, markets by introducing for example, sports models, four-wheel-drive cars, light trucks, minivans,
- finding new markets with new customers and ideally, less-intense competition,
- introducing organizational innovations to improve flexibility, and shorten lead and delivery times,[53]
- customizing mass-produced models, that is, offering the opportunity to buyers to 'design' their own cars – using, of course, a set of standardized components.[54]

In short, price is still the bottom line for competitiveness in the car industry, yet many more characteristics have become musts for car manufacturers. Two of the above strategic elements are most relevant from a Central and Eastern European point of view: cost-cutting and entering new markets.

Cost-cutting is a decisive element of basically all car manufacturers' strategies. That is why they set up their new plants in South America and Southeast Asia as well as in Central and Eastern Europe, where production costs are usually lower than in their established bases, and for the same reason they encourage their suppliers to follow them, and/or to find other ways to offer cheaper parts and components. Another way of cost-cutting is to introduce improved production equipment and vehicle components (that is, incremental technological innovations, as opposed to radical innovations) as well as more efficient production processes (organizational and managerial innovations).[55] In the lean production paradigm – as opposed to the Fordist

---

[53] Lead times – once constituting a major competitive edge for Japanese car manufacturers – have become rather short, thanks to the introduction of lean production, where T1 suppliers are involved in the design of new models, and the so-called 'rugby' approach is used – instead of the former 'relay' method – among the various departments involved in designing a new model (Graves 1991, 1994). This new phenomenon underlines the importance of organizational innovations, too.

[54] No doubt, it requires a great deal of flexibility in terms of manufacturing and logistics, and, in turn, might lead to longer delivery time and higher costs. Therefore organizational innovations, coming either from car manufacturers or T1 suppliers, are of crucial importance. Quite often, though, technological innovations are necessary preconditions for organizational innovations, for example, improved flexibility obviously requires organizational innovations, which, in turn, usually necessitate an appropriate, customized new IT tool kit and/or improved production equipment.

[55] An interesting and successful new concept of cost-cutting is the so-called 'platform strategy' whereby the basic components of 3–5 models are shared, and thus economies of scales in producing those elements and product variety – that is, apparently different models serving different markets (or segments) – can be achieved simultaneously. This concept requires the introduction of a set of interrelated technological and organizational innovations.

one – suppliers are important sources of innovations, and new products, processes and managerial techniques are spread quickly throughout the whole network (assembler, T1, T2 and T3 suppliers).

Emerging markets are also considered to be important because by definition they promise new buyers. Moreover, in the late 1980s competition among car manufacturers was practically unknown in the Central and Eastern European countries (CEECs). On the contrary, buyers had to 'compete' with one another and with distributors. Hence most cars were rather obsolete in these countries, making people even more 'hungry' for new cars. In short, it seemed to be a paradise for car manufacturers. However, this region has become fairly crowded in a very short period of time because quite a few major West European, US and Asian companies have invested in production facilities. To make it worse, optimistic sales forecasts have not materialized either, because most people cannot afford new cars, especially in the potentially largest markets, that is, in the CIS countries. The current crisis in Southeast Asia has brought car manufacturers into even more intense competition globally.

The three car manufacturers operating in Hungary apply different elements of the above strategic mix. Magyar Suzuki assembles a small car, Suzuki Swift, designed some ten years ago. In this segment, profit margins are rather low because the main competition axis is price. Suzuki also puts emphasis on fuel economy, and hence organizes special rallies where the most economical drivers are rewarded. Of course several small changes and new features have been added to Swift since its introduction – even the front has been slightly modified, that is, a 'facelift' has been applied. From time to time, small, special batches are produced to appeal to a certain customer group. A new, smaller car will be assembled in Hungary as of 2000. In that case competitiveness is also likely to be based on price and probably fuel economy.

Opel has decided to abandon car assembly in Hungary. Its new strategy is to focus on low-cost manufacturing of high-tech, high-value-added components – engine components, engines and gearboxes – as well as low-cost, high-quality R&D conducted in Hungary to help improve its overall competitiveness. In short, it is a global strategy with a carefully planned division of labor among various Opel plants across countries.

AUDI Hungaria Motor has recently started assembling two new sports models, aimed at serving a special market segment of the affluent young professionals, primarily on the Western European markets. In this segment, design – technical and aesthetic features – is the key element of competition. Yet, price should be kept as low as possible, and flexibility is even more important than in the case of 'normal' cars because of seasonal cycles in demand. Hence, compared to Germany, Hungary seems to be an ideal production base with skilled but cheap workers and fairly flexible labor regulations.

4.2 Competitive Strategies of Suppliers

T1 suppliers are increasingly similar to car assemblers in many respects, and thus they have to face a similar – competitive, global – environment. Reliable quality, continuous cost-cutting (with all its methods and prerequisites discussed above), timely delivery and the ability to innovate and manage the rest of the supply chain are all indispensable for survival. Therefore it is hardly possible to single out any competition axis. T2 and T3 suppliers, however, have fewer responsibilities; the main competition axis for them is price. Nonetheless, all of them should be able to maintain reliable quality and timely shipment of parts and introduce the technological and organizational innovations developed by assemblers or T1 suppliers.

These general observations also apply to the Hungarian case. T1 suppliers – for example, ITT, Knorr-Bremse, UTA and ZF – serve the global markets from their Hungarian production bases; only an almost negligible fraction of their output is shipped to the local car assembly plants. First their primary concern was cost-cutting in the production phase. Gradually, however, they have recognized that Hungarian engineers and researchers at various R&D units can also provide useful services for their internationalized R&D projects at a rather low cost. Therefore they have already set up their own, in-house R&D units or are planning to do so. ITT is a somewhat exceptional case. Its Hungarian R&D unit works mainly for the German subsidiary, not for the local one. The other way is to 'delegate' Hungarian engineers into the parent company's global research teams. UTA, for example, has not opened an in-house R&D unit so far; its engineers, however, are involved in a number of R&D projects run by various subsidiaries of the parent company. Sometimes they work abroad; otherwise they work from Hungary, sending and receiving data electronically.

As for the intensity of competition on the local market, it should be taken into account that some 10–12 thousand parts and components are used to build a vehicle. To put it simply, an engine manufacturer, for example, might account for a very large share of the sector's output, yet this does not mean that it would dominate a seat manufacturer, which in turn has a much smaller share of the sector's output.

As for a more qualitative overview, on the whole there is strong competition in automotive components manufacturing. Although some companies might have a relatively large domestic market share, for example, in the case of axles, batteries, bearings or lighting, they also have to face fierce competition on their export markets, and given the relatively small size of the Hungarian market as well as the importance of scale economies, they cannot avoid exporting the bulk of their output. The only exception is engine manufacturing: the combined capacity of Audi and Opel is around 1.5 million units a year, and thus it is a large enough market for their suppliers. That is why foreign foundries and machining companies are setting up their Hungarian operations (for example, ADA, Pre-cast, Le Belier, VAW and Jung). In this case there is strong competition for the 'domestic market'. The engines produced in Hungary, in turn, are shipped to the various car assembly plants of Audi, VW (including SEAT and Skoda) and GM Opel in Europe.

4.3 Production Networks: Sources of Innovation

4.3.1 Technological changes

Havas (1994) analyzed a sample of 16 Hungarian automotive suppliers from the point of view of technological changes.[56] Although only seven firms in the sample spent more than 3 percent of their sales on technology-related activities[57] in 1992 (moreover, five of them spent less than one percent), basically all of them have introduced new product and/or process technologies. Most of these *product innovations* can be regarded as new products, not only for the firms that introduced them, but for the Hungarian economy as well. Thus it really is a favorable development. Car producers or their T1 suppliers were the most frequently mentioned sources of innovations (12 cases out of 26), followed by in-house development (seven cases out of 26). Other sources have included parent companies, commissioned research, other firms (partners in innovation with no other links) and licenses. All these innovations came from the sector itself or related industries.

As for *process innovations*, however, most of them have been new only to companies introducing them. As car manufacturers require total quality management (TQM) and timely delivery, the introduction of these techniques has been the most frequent process change. Modernization of machinery has been the other dominant form of process innovations. Car producers and their

---

[56] The 16 companies in the sample were already either Magyar Suzuki or Opel Hungary suppliers in 1992 or 1993, that is, the new entrants, especially foreign-owned greenfield plants, were not covered as most of them started commercial production after 1992. In other words, Audi, Ford, ITT, UTA and other foreign investment projects, representing high-tech, high-value-added products, were not included. Thus the following summary, based on that study, provides only one part of the entire picture. Moreover, our sample was rather small, and thus one should be cautious in interpreting data obtained from it.

[57] It includes expenditures on (a) R&D and related work, (b) technical training and (c) other engineering and technical services.

T1 suppliers have again played a significant role (16 cases out of 35). A marked, and in fact a self-explanatory, difference is, though, that material and machine suppliers have also been instrumental (again, 16 cases out of 35). In other words, the diffusion of embodied technologies has contributed considerably to technological improvements. Other sources of process innovations have included in-house development, consulting services, parent companies and R&D institutes, including university departments. Similar to product changes, most process improvements also have come from the sector itself, for example, know-how to produce various parts, as well as TQM methods, or from related industries, primarily from capital goods, glass and plastic industries. Various services, however, have played a more important role than in the case of product innovations. The most important ones have been software firms and consultants specializing in quality assurance.

To conclude, *two major lessons* can be drawn. First, the Hungarian case confirms the general picture emerging from the literature, namely that car assemblers and their T1 suppliers are the most important sources of innovation for the entire production network they coordinate. Second, some buyers, or their first-tier foreign suppliers, provide licenses and know-how free of charge for T2 and T3 suppliers. The most important example is Magyar Suzuki (also offering various forms of financial assistance for tooling-up). This is the major element of an explanation to reconcile the apparent contradiction between the low level of expenditures on technology-related activities and the introduction of a relatively large number of new products and processes.[58] In other cases, however, it is a prerequisite to buy certain licenses or know-how: otherwise no business can exist.

4.3.2 Managerial innovations

As already mentioned, Hungarian automotive suppliers have to adjust to a radically altered international and domestic environment (import liberalization, loss of former markets, new players in Hungary, and so on). Thus those who want to survive have also introduced new management techniques. The most important types of these innovations are total quality management and reliable cost accounting. Foreign partners usually provide technical assistance and training courses to facilitate the introduction of these techniques.

Managerial innovations can be analyzed at a sectoral level, too, as opposed to individual company level. In lean production first-tier suppliers assume a considerable part of the responsibility for product development as well as for organizing and managing the supply chain (logistics) as they build and supply

---

[58] Another major factor is that these innovations represent low- or mid-tech technologies, rather than high-tech ones, and hence are less demanding financially.

subsystems, rather than individual components. In other words, they are responsible for second-tier – and indirectly – for third-tier suppliers' performance, too. Thus they also provide training and technical assistance to their suppliers to facilitate the introduction of appropriate quality management, cost accounting, production and delivery systems and so on. More recently, Western car manufacturers have followed this path, that is, they cut the number of their first-tier (direct) suppliers and gave them greater responsibility.

This 'tiering' hardly occurred in Hungary until the early 1990s. One should not be surprised, however, since most Hungarian companies supplied fairly simple, individual parts rather than complex subsystems to their customers. Moreover, they were not involved in product development, either, as the models produced by Audi Hungaria, Magyar Suzuki and Opel Hungary were designed prior to assembly in Hungary. One should take into account that it is a relatively new concept even for the Western European managers, who are at least accustomed to the 'normal' mechanisms and requirements of a market economy. Even so, they are far from reaching the full potential of lean production. As a recent analysis of the British automotive industry claims, British managers have a long way to go, too, on the road leading towards 'tiering':

> By collaboration, the first tier of suppliers may help to develop the value chain of a vehicle manufacturer or the progress and competitiveness of a national or regional industry. There has been little such activity so far: indeed the major UK suppliers could more accurately be called an unconnected group, rather than a first tier. (DTI and SMMT 1994, p. 11)

Their Hungarian counterparts, however, first of all had to learn even the 'simple' techniques of the market economy, not only these new principles of lean supply. And, in the meantime they have also had to struggle for survival. More recently, however, some preliminary signs of the emerging new supply system can be observed in certain cases. As subsidiaries of major Western component manufacturers are taking more Hungarian suppliers on board, a more pronounced 'tiering' can be expected, and indeed, it is already occurring in some cases. For example, Michels Kabel has chosen Videoton as its major subcontractor to produce wiring harnesses. It provides production equipment, processes and managerial techniques to Videoton, which, in turn, 'nurtures' its local suppliers in similar ways. ZF has decided to develop a supplier park around its plant in Eger, and Ford is also increasing the number of its Hungarian suppliers. In short, T1 suppliers assume responsibility in organizing the supply chain in Hungary, too, following the global patterns.

5. PROSPECTS FOR HUNGARIAN AUTOMOTIVE SUPPLIERS

5.1 Modes of Growth

Discussing the growth opportunities and various modes of growth open to the Central and Eastern European (CEE) automobile firms it is worthwhile to distinguish between different kind of countries (small vs. large; advanced vs. laggard in terms of transition; level of economic development);[59] and firms (assemblers vs. suppliers). The success of different growth strategies, in turn, depends on firms' performance *vis-à-vis* their competitors as well as the macroeconomic situation (overall demand, standard of living, taxes and other levies on cars and components, and so on) and trade policies of the respective countries. Firms operating in countries with a large domestic market – for example, Russia – can, in principle, devise strategies to serve their home markets, while firms based in small or medium-sized countries – for example, the Czech Republic, Hungary, Slovakia, Slovenia (all small) and Poland (medium sized) – must seek export opportunities should they want to grow. Globalization of the automotive industry means both opportunities and threats for these firms.

Car and commercial vehicle *assemblers* privatized by large foreign automotive companies, and thus integrated into their global technological, production and marketing networks, might expect the brightest growth opportunities, for example, VW-Skoda, Fiat Auto Poland. This is usually organic growth, that is, increased output by producing new or significantly improved vehicles. Acquisition of other – automotive or non-automotive – firms is not likely. Some commercial vehicle assemblers have been privatized by domestic investors, for example, in the Czech Republic. It remains to be seen whether these investors can succeed in bringing in capital, new technologies and markets, which are all required for organic growth. In some cases acquisitions by other, large, powerful companies have occurred, and it might be a potential way out of the problem of lack of capital. Hardly any growth – on the contrary, a contraction thereof – can be foreseen for assemblers not yet privatized.

---

[59] Different traditions in the automotive industry obviously have different impacts on growth opportunities and modes of growth, for example, the Czech car industry has been based on its own product development while the Polish, Russian, Romanian and Serbian industries have been based on licenses. Hungary represents another case by having strong traditions in commercial vehicle and automotive components manufacturing but only 'remote memories' in car assembly.

As for *suppliers*, five different modes can be identified.[60] The following taxonomy not only lists these possibilities but also discusses the relationship between a specific mode of growth and R&D.

1. *Organic or indigenous growth based on the existing product lines*, that is, increased output of the same products given extended capacity and/or improved productivity. It might only be possible in the CIS countries where basically the 'good old' cars and other vehicles are still produced and can be sold. Hardly any R&D or training and retraining – skill formation – is required. At best, some process development, training and retraining is conducted.

2. *Organic or indigenous growth based on a diversified, yet still automotive product mix*, that is, increased output thanks to further automotive products added to the existing product lines. Most suppliers, previously shipping their products to various CMEA countries, and having lost these markets by now, have to take this path, for example, producing parts for Western (including Asian) cars and/or commercial vehicles.[61] Capital and skill formation is required, yet accumulated skills and experience might provide a sound basis. New products – and then almost inevitably – new processes and management techniques should be introduced. Sources of these innovations vary widely (vehicle assemblers, T1 suppliers, other suppliers, in-house and extra-mural R&D units). The supplier in question has to be involved in the innovation process to a varying extent, depending on the source of innovation.

3. *Organic or indigenous growth based on a diversified, non-automotive product mix*, that is, increased output thanks to further non-automotive products added to the existing product lines. This option is most probable in the case of suppliers already having mixed product lines, that is, producing plastic, rubber, metal, and other parts for different industries.

---

[60] One also has to bear in mind that a wide range of distinctively different industries are to be found among automotive parts and components manufacturers, for example, chemicals (paints, plastics), rubber, glass, textiles, leather, metal, engineering, electronics, and so on. Therefore a thorough analysis should take into account technological/sectoral characteristics. Further decisive factors of growth include firm-specific factors (size, ownership, technological and managerial capabilities, and so on), role of foreign investors in the domestic automotive industry, assembler–supplier relationships and macroeconomic situation.

[61] This mode of growth clearly shows that the traditional definition of growth might not be appropriate in transition economies. For detailed, firm-level case studies it is worth considering a special definition of (or approach to) growth: given the radical restructuring in the region (collapse of the CMEA, import liberalization, privatization, and so on) sometimes survival can, and, indeed, should be regarded as growth, even in the case of contracted output compared, for example, to the mid-1980s, if the current output consists of *new products* sold to *new clients*.

Requirements are similar to the ones under point 2.

4. *Acquisition of another automotive firm*, domestic or foreign. Capital needs to be found for this action, therefore it is an existing, yet rare case. Further, production, R&D and management skills and practices need to be harmonized for success, and these are undoubtedly difficult tasks even in a stable economy, let alone in the CEECs with all the challenges of transition.

5. *Acquisition of a non-automotive firm*, domestic or foreign. This option is most probable in the case of suppliers already having mixed product lines, that is, producing plastic, rubber, metal and other parts for different industries. Requirements and challenges are similar to the ones under point 4.

5.2 Outlook for Hungarian Automotive Suppliers

Privatization of car assembly in the neighboring countries provides both challenges and opportunities for Hungarian automotive suppliers. Western European investors, on the one hand, tend to rely on their long-established suppliers. Moreover, Fiat is one of the most vertically-integrated car manufacturers. Therefore some Hungarian suppliers have lost their former businesses since Fiat took over FSM. However, even Fiat has embarked upon a new sourcing strategy: it has started divesting its in-house component manufacturing plants in Poland in order to cut costs and to focus on its core business. Thus there are new market opportunities even in this case for competitive suppliers, especially for Central European subsidiaries of well-known Western European firms, given that these suppliers can combine reputation, low production costs and favorable location.

Asian firms, on the other hand, do not have a long-established supply base in Europe. Thus they have to search for local suppliers if they want to meet the local content rule of the EU. Magyar Suzuki has rapidly increased the local content of its cars produced in Hungary, and 11 of its Hungarian suppliers have already started shipping their products to Japan.

Daewoo, investing in major car operations in joint ventures with Polish and Romanian state-owned enterprises, intends to order certain parts from Hungarian suppliers. It has also acquired a majority stake in a Hungarian automotive component manufacturer. Compared to Magyar Suzuki, Daewoo has a much more ambitious plan in terms of establishing a large production base in Central European countries, and exporting to the EU, and thus it needs even more local suppliers, and significantly larger volume of parts and components.

Table 5.8 *Outlook for Hungarian suppliers*

Ownership/ Type of plant	Technology	Size	Activities	Markets	Outlook	Impacts on Domestic R&D
Greenfield plants of car manufacturers producing components (A1.1)	*Products*: mid- or high-tech, high value added *Processes*: state-of-the-art, capital and skill intensive, but not labor intensive	1,000–2,000 employees	Specialized in automotive components	*A single customer*, but geographically spread markets (assembly plants of their parent company), 100 percent of output is exported	Rather stable markets (strong commitment from parent companies), depending on overall automotive trends and strategic moves of parent companies (e.g., sourcing, location, R&D)	Major R&D projects conducted by parent companies, minor product development projects in Hungary. Audi sets up an engine development center, an R&D unit also seems inevitable; GM Opel is to involve Hungarian R&D units in product development
Subsidiaries of component manufacturers (green- and brownfield plants: A1.2, A.2)	*Products*: typically mid-tech, some high-tech, mid- or high value added *Processes*: state-of-the-art, skill intensive, less capital and more labor intensive than for A1.1 firms	From a few hundred employees to over 1,000, further growth is rather likely in most cases	Specialized in automotive components	*A number of customers*, the vast majority of output is exported	Fairly stable business opportunities due to the long-established contacts between parent companies and customers. Smaller investment compared to A1.1 cases, hence exit might be less costly	Major R&D projects conducted by parent companies, but in-house and extra-mural R&D and engineering units have been set up, and Hungarian engineers are increasingly involved in international R&D projects, conducted in various Western European countries

Ownership/ Type of plant	Technology	Size	Activities	Markets	Outlook	Impacts on Domestic R&D
State-owned companies (B1)	*Products:* low-tech, some mid-tech, low value added. *Processes:* simple material processing, obsolete, general purpose, machinery, labor intensive	Up to 1,500–2,000 employees, shrinking can be expected	Diversified; automotive parts are of secondary importance in the case of large, multi-plant companies	*A number of customers*, usually 1–2 Western T1– or T2 suppliers as well as Magyar Suzuki. A considerable part of output is exported	Rather uncertain, their customers might find cheaper suppliers	Hardly any in-house R&D projects or demand for extra-mural ones can be expected from them
Privatized former state-owned companies (B2)	*Products:* mid- or low-tech, mid-value-added. *Processes:* similar to B1 firms, usually less obsolete	Medium or large	Medium-sized ones usually specialized in automotive components, large ones diversified, car parts often of secondary importance	Similar to B1 firms	Slightly more promising than for B1 firms. Privatization has been financed through loans, debt service might threaten their future, hardly any profits can be retained for investments	Some in-house R&D projects or demand for extra-mural ones can be expected from them

Table 5.8 analyzes the major characteristics of different types of companies in the framework of a tentative taxonomy, developed in Section 3.2.3. It also considers the most likely prospects for each group of companies.[62] Two subgroups, namely *private companies* and *joint ventures with dominant Hungarian private ownership* are not included, because firms in these subgroups differ considerably from one another, that is, their products, processes and market opportunities can vary on a very wide scale. Two distinctive features, however, can be pointed out. First, they are usually much smaller than A1–B2 companies. Second, the so-called 'aftermarket' is usually much more significant for them than for the larger ones.

6. POSSIBILITIES FOR S&T POLICY

6.1 Policy Tools in Place

The government has implemented various policy tools for joint ventures to promote foreign investments, and indirectly technological improvements. The two pioneering, large automotive investors, Magyar Suzuki and Opel Hungary have initially each been granted a Ft 250 million government subsidy for job creation, infrastructure development, technological development and retraining. Additional government policy measures also help reduce their operating costs: (a) originally a five-year tax holiday, extended for a further five years given subsequent investment projects, (b) a five-year exemption from customs duties on parts to be built into cars assembled in Hungary,[63] and (c) grants on a case-by-case basis to cover trade fairs' costs. Audi Hungaria Motor has asked for some Ft 400 million grant initially, given its larger investment project. Other forms of subsidies are also available. Magyar Suzuki, for example, has successfully applied for a favorable loan to develop and install an EDI (electronic data interchange) system connecting its assembly plant and suppliers.

OMFB, a government agency responsible for promoting technological development, operates a number of schemes to improve R&D infrastructure, financing applied to R&D and the so-called target-oriented national projects. One of the national projects is dedicated specifically to automotive suppliers. It was launched in April 1993 – in association with the Ministry of Industry

---

[62] Of course, not every single case can be captured by this taxonomy, for example, a few major state-owned companies are still in the preparation phase for privatization, and thus are to some extent still 'on the road' to becoming A2 or B2 companies. In other words, their characteristics are different from those of a 'representative' B1 firm.

[63] Further parts, that is, those above a set quota, are subjects to an 8 percent duty.

and Trade – and ended in 1997. This scheme offers grants for R&D projects (especially for product development, at most 50 percent of the total cost of the project) and favorable loans (mainly to finance investment projects required for process innovations). Applicants have to prove that an automotive firm intends to buy the parts developed with the help of this grant. Some Ft 140 million were granted for these purposes in 1994–97 (Table 5.9).

Table 5.9 Financial support for target-oriented national projects: automotive suppliers, 1994–1997 (million Ft)

1994	1995	1996	1997
53.4	16.1	33.6	36.3

Source: OMFB.

Other OMFB schemes, however, are also open for and indeed used by automotive suppliers. Some Ft 2–4 billion are spent per year in the framework of the so-called applied R&D scheme; thus it is much more significant from a financial point of view than the so-called target-oriented national projects.[64] Another scheme is aimed at promoting competitiveness of Hungarian companies in export markets through technological development.[65] A further scheme offers financial support for those Hungarian applicants who participate in the 4th Framework Program of the European Union. More than 100 projects have been subsidized by this scheme, 11 of them related to automotive and transport technologies. Finally, a new scheme was launched in early 1998 to promote the establishment of new R&D centers. Firms investing at least Ft 500 million in a new center, which employs at least 30 scientists and research engineers are eligible for a 25 percent subsidy of their costs.[66]

---

[64] There are no readily available statistics on automotive projects. As 422 applications were submitted – of which 164 have been granted – in 1997 it would be time-consuming to count all the automotive projects. Yet, the 1997 annual report of OMFB shows that this scheme also promotes automotive R&D projects, highlighting three of them as among the most significant ones.

[65] It is a major scheme as well: 65 applications were submitted, of which 47 were granted in 1997, totaling Ft 735 million. There are no readily-available data on the distribution of applications and subsidies granted by sectors. Again, the 1997 annual report of OMFB indicates that automotive suppliers use this form, too: two automotive projects are mentioned among the success stories.

[66] Three firms were granted a total of Ft 800 million in 1998, of which two are automotive companies. Knorr-Bremse currently employs 60 research engineers. It will invest Ft 1 billion to extend its current R&D facility and employ a further 30 engineers. A Ft 200 million grant from this scheme will reduce the costs of the investment. Audi Hungaria has been awarded Ft 457 million to set up a new engine development center in Hungary.

To conclude, the Hungarian government applies a set of policy tools, consisting of tax holidays, employment, infrastructure development, R&D and training grants in order to attract foreign investors. Some of these tools are geared specifically towards the automotive industry, but most of them are general ones. It should also be mentioned that these subsidies are dwarfed by the significantly larger grants available in the EU countries.[67]

Empirical and theoretical innovation studies show clearly that direct subsidies for a given project play a minor role in shaping multinational firms' R&D strategies, especially in terms of the location of their R&D centers. The most important factors are the availability of knowledge and skills – as indicators of the performance of researchers in terms of level of technological excellence and advantage over competitors to be gained, for example, in the form of shorter lead times – and ultimately the level of expected profit stemming from innovations. Therefore in order to attract major multinational firms to invest in R&D, it is more important to create favorable general conditions for R&D by maintaining an excellent education system and improving the R&D infrastructure, broadly defined, than to provide direct R&D subsidies. As the Hungarian automotive industry – and a large chunk of the economy as a whole – is controlled mainly by large foreign firms, a successful S&T policy should be devised by taking into account this basic principle. For this reason, it is worthwhile to provide a short overview of the current R&D efforts and the organizations behind them.

6.2 Research Units

Given the characteristics of the automotive industry, a number of Hungarian R&D units and university departments working on a very wide range of research issues are engaged in solving technological problems related to the sector.[68] Because of the diversity of technological issues relevant for the automotive industry, there are no readily available data on the number of projects or R&D expenditures. Comparing interviews conducted in 1992–93 and those in 1996–97 does suggest, however, that foreign investors are changing their perception of Hungarian R&D capabilities. Those who took over Hungarian companies in the early 1990s at first tended to cut back expenditures and staff of existing R&D units quite severely. More recently, however, the same foreign investors, having recognized the skills and

---

[67] Bongardt (1994) shows that around one-third of the total investment costs of the joint VW–Ford assembly plant in Portugal has been financed by various Portuguese and EU grants.

[68] The best-known – for strictly-defined automotive projects – are the Budapest Technical University, Miskolc University, Veszprém University and Győr Technical College. Yet, quite a few other units working on problems related to plastics, paints, rubber, material processing, engineering, and so on, also quite frequently provide support to the industry.

knowledge of Hungarian engineers and scientists, have been spending more on R&D in Hungary and hiring more R&D staff. ITT Automotive and Knorr-Bremse have set up joint R&D groups with the Budapest Technical University. Others, who opted for greenfield investment, are also establishing their local R&D units, closely linked to their existing global – or European-wide – research networks. Certain R&D projects conducted in Hungary are aimed at developing new products or processes for other subsidiaries of the foreign investors. Thus, in these cases, R&D is truly globalized.

7. CONCLUSIONS

Investment activities across borders have intensified significantly in recent years in attempts to cut costs via relocation of production and to move closer to the ultimate customers in emerging markets. Central Europe, the immediate neighborhood of Hungary, is also no exception: the region has again moved onto the global stage. Almost all major automotive groups, except the leading Japanese automotive firms Toyota, Nissan and Mitsubishi, have already set up operations in Central Europe. These intensified investment activities have had a crucial bearing on the Hungarian automotive industry: after a half-century cessation imposed by the CMEA-wide division of labor, car production re-emerged in Hungary in the early 1990s. Suppliers have also invested heavily in Hungary. Moreover, their motivation has not been simply to follow car assemblers to serve them from nearby plants: on the contrary, this is only a minor part of the explanation. Their principal reason for setting up subsidiaries – either green- or brownfield plants – in Hungary has been cost-cutting. Their only major local clients are the engine manufacturing plants of Audi and GM Opel, and not car assemblers: hence the vast majority of their output is exported.

These strategic moves have radically restructured the indigenous suppliers, as well. In other words, transition has been accomplished in this sector. Some suppliers have been taken over by foreign firms, others have been integrated into the global networks of major automotive groups as subcontractors. In both cases, new products, processes and management techniques have been introduced quite rapidly. Data clearly show that components manufacturing is much more important than car assembly, even from a somewhat narrow-minded macroeconomic point of view: turnover, employment and export figures are significantly larger in the former sector than in the latter. Taking a more general perspective – that of industrial development and competitiveness – suppliers, and particularly the networking activities of T1 suppliers, are still more substantial. It is mainly due to them that new technologies and organizational innovations are diffusing fast and widely in Hungary. From a policy point of view, however, it is necessary to take into account the differences between various types of suppliers. Therefore a taxonomy has been developed and applied when discussing the prospects for Hungarian companies.

Foreign investors have chosen Hungary partly because skilled labor is relatively cheap – around one-seventh of German wages. Yet, had wages alone been sufficient to improve competitiveness, Western automotive firms would have gone to Ukraine and other CIS countries where labor is even cheaper. In fact, what really matters is that Hungarian workers are highly skilled, due to a German-type vocational training system, in place for many decades. As quality, reliability and productivity are all major concerns for automotive companies, there is no need to emphasize the importance of skills and experience. In short, the real advantage is the excellence of workers coupled with low wages. Further, foreign companies find flexible employment conditions in Hungary; shift work and overtime working is a commonplace, offering investors a production regime to suit their needs. Grants and concessions offered by the government – to ease the annoying shortage of cars and facilitate industrial restructuring – has also been instrumental in attracting foreign investors.

A brief comparison of production paradigms has also shown the crucial importance of innovation, R&D and engineering skills. Given the excellence of the Hungarian higher education system, there is no shortage of engineers endowed with these skills and knowledge. Interviews suggest ever-closer relationships between automotive firms on the one hand, and university departments and other R&D units on the other. More recently, some foreign investors – for example, Audi, GM Opel, ITT, Knorr-Bremse and ZF – have also recognized the world-class knowledge of Hungarian scientists and engineers, and are setting up either in-house R&D units or joint research groups with universities. Again, besides professional excellence, there is a considerable cost advantage in this field, too. Further, R&D schemes have also been applied to foster innovation activities in the automotive industry.

A major policy lesson can be drawn by comparing general and industry-specific schemes. It is more fruitful to create an attractive, favorable environment for R&D and innovation – for example, by maintaining a sound, well-performing higher education and research system, by providing the necessary physical and institutional infrastructure, and by facilitating industrial and academic cooperation and other forms of networking – than to focus on the promotion of single projects by offering earmarked automotive R&D grants. It is also of crucial importance to coordinate investment, trade, competition, regional development, employment, education and innovation policy aims and tools.

In sum, the successful restructuring of the Hungarian automotive industry is not only due to some 'push' factors – that is, the fierce competition among automotive companies and hence the pursuit of cost-cutting via relocation of production – but also thanks to 'pull' factors, that is, the attractions of the Hungarian economic environment, broadly defined. Given the ever-changing, global nature of the automotive industry, no country can be complacent: on the contrary, continuously renewed, concerted efforts and well-devised policy measures are needed to achieve further results.

REFERENCES

Andersen Consulting (1995), *World Manufacturing Competitiveness Study*, London: Andersen Consulting.

Bauer, T. et al. (1980), 'Jármûprogram és gazdaságirányítás' (Vehicle Program and Central Economic Control), mimeo, Budapest: Institute of Economics, Hungarian Academy of Sciences.

Bauer, T. and K.A. Soós (1980), 'Kényszerpályák hálójában – Vállalatközi kapcsolatok és mûszaki fejlesztés a jármûiparban' (Forced Paths: Inter-enterprise Relationships and Technical Development in the Automotive Industry), in Tardos (ed.), pp. 149–84.

Berend, T.I. and Gy. Ránki (1955), *Magyarország gyáripara 1900–1914* (Hungary's Industry in 1910–1914), Budapest: Szikra.

Berend, T.I. and Gy. Ránki (1958), *Magyarország gyáripara a második világháború elõtt és a háború idõszakában, 1933–1944* (Hungary's Industry before and during World War II, 1933–1944), Budapest: Akadémiai Kiadó.

Bongardt, Anette (1994), 'The Auto Industry in the Setúbal Peninsula (Portugal)', mimeo, Lisboa: Centro Estudos Europeus, Universidade Católica Portuguesa.

DTI (Department of Trade and Industry) and SMMT (Society of Motor Manufacturers and Traders) (1994), *A Review of the Relationships Between Vehicle Manufacturers and Suppliers*, London: Report on the DTI/SMMT Automotive Components Initiative.

Graves, Andrew (1991), 'Globalization of the Automobile Industry: the Challenge for Europe', in C. Freeman, M. Sharp and W. Walker (eds), *Technology and the Future of Europe*, London: Pinter, pp. 261–80.

Graves, Andrew (1994), 'Innovation in a Globalizing Industry: The Case of Automobiles', in M. Dodgson and R. Rothwell (eds), *The Handbook of*

Industrial Innovation, Aldershot, UK and Brookfield, USA: Edward Elgar, pp. 213–31.

Havas, Attila (1994), *The Reemergence of Car Parts Industry in Hungary*, Report to the World Bank, Budapest: IKU.

Havas, Attila (1997), 'Foreign Direct Investment and Intra-industry Trade: The Case of Automotive Industry in Central Europe', in David A. Dyker (ed.), *The Technology of Transition*, Budapest: Central European University Press, pp. 211–40.

Jones, Daniel T. (1989), 'Corporate Strategy and Technology in the World Automobile Industry', in M. Dodgson (ed.), *Technology Strategy and the Firm: Management and public policy*, London: Longman, pp. 11-24.

Lamming, Richard (1993), *Beyond Partnership: Strategies for Innovation and Lean Supply*, New York: Prentice-Hall.

Mosoni, Judit (1994), 'Industrial Research Institutes in the Transition Period in Hungary', mimeo, Budapest: IKU.

Organization for Economic and Cooperative Development (OECD) (1992), 'The Automotive Parts Industry', in OECD, *Globalization of Industrial Activities: Four Case Studies*, Paris: OECD.

Somai, Miklós (1993), 'The Car Industry and Motorization in Hungary', Working Papers (26), Institute for World Economics, Hungarian Academy of Sciences.

Soós, Károly Attila (1980), 'Műszaki színvonal és gazdaságosság: Beruházási döntés egy központi fejlesztési program keretében' (Technical Level and Profitability: Investment Decision in the Framework of a Central Development Program), in Tardos (ed.), pp. 285–94.

Tardos, Márton (ed.) (1980), *Vállalati magatartás – vállalati környezet* (Enterprises' Behavior – Enterprises' Environment), Budapest: Közgazdasági és Jogi Könyvkiadó.

Tárnok, É. and P. Vince (1980), 'Szervezett bizonytalanság' (Organized Uncertainty), in Tardos (ed.), pp. 219–54.

Varga, György (1990), 'Mibe szállunk be? – Magyar gépkocsi-ipar' (Strategic Options for the Hungarian Automotive Industry), *Figyelő*, **34** (21).

Womack, James P., Daniel T. Jones and Daniel Roos (1991), *The Machine that Changed the World*, New York: Harper Perennial.

6 Eastern European Shipbuilding's Cruise Towards World Markets

Christian von Hirschhausen and Jürgen Bitzer[69]

1. INTRODUCTION

The world shipbuilding industry has undergone a fundamental change in recent decades: it has gone from being a 'heavy' industry to being a high-tech, information-dominated industry with over 70 percent of value added outsourced in hierarchized supplier networks. In the Western world, Asian shipyards seem to have taken the lead, with European yards keeping some market niches in the high-end segments. The arrival of Eastern European yards on international markets was anticipated with both anxiety and hope in the early 1990s: whereas some stressed the overcapacity and low labor costs as a guarantee for larger market shares of Eastern European yards, others argued that the strong military orientation and insufficient quality would prevent Eastern yards from becoming internationally competitive. This chapter analyzes the restructuring of the shipbuilding industry in Eastern Europe by relating it to developments in the industry worldwide, and discusses the scope and results of innovation policies carried out in Eastern Europe over the last ten years. Our hypothesis, derived from an industrial economic analysis of this industry, is that due both to the increasing complexity of products and production processes and to international specialization, Eastern European yards are compelled to internationalize their supply networks and develop new types of ships in order to survive on world markets.

---

[69] Thanks to David Dyker and participants of the 2nd SPRU–TSER workshop (July 1997) for comments, and diverse shipbuilding institutions in Germany and Western Europe for information and data; the usual disclaimer applies.

This chapter is structured in the following way: Section 2 provides a brief industrial economic analysis of the changing shipbuilding industry in the 'West' as observed over approximately the last 20 years. Segmentation of the market has increased, and so has regional specialization. Yet after years of 'crises' and restructuring, overcapacity still abounds worldwide and productivity gains have become crucial for yard survival. In Section 3, a survey of the Eastern European shipbuilding industry and its restructuring is provided. Starting from the breakdown of socialist shipyards, these countries have all engaged in restructuring, more or less watched over and supported by their respective governments. Today, the trough is over for the advanced shipyards in Eastern Europe, in particular those in Poland. The cooperation with Western suppliers, yards, and shipping companies is analyzed, observing that major innovation pushes come from outside the Eastern shipyards: the integration into the international innovation system seems to be more important than domestic clustering. In Section 4, an ideal type of post-socialist shipyard restructuring in East Germany is identified, and the experiences of the two major countries, *Poland* and *Russia*, are reviewed. Section 5 presents our conclusions.[70]

2. ANALYSIS OF THE INTERNATIONAL SHIPBUILDING INDUSTRY

2.1 The Shipbuilding Markets and Patterns of International Specialization

A ship is a combination of electronics, information technology and a number of different materials, constructed in a shipyard and designed to fulfill specific functions at sea. The shipbuilding sector is anything but homogeneous. Four main segments can be distinguished: the merchant, naval, inland and ship repair markets. The *merchant shipbuilding* segment, on which we concentrate in this chapter, is the largest of the four and must be subdivided into three segments, which differ with respect to their basic characteristics, such as complexity of products, production requirements, competition axes and so on (see Figure 6.1, based upon AWES 1997, pp. 27, 95).

- the first group, *low-complexity ships* (LCS) includes the most simple

---

[70] As is usual practice, we do not cover naval, military shipbuilding, for reasons of lack of information. As concerns ship repair, we consider it to be a niche activity within the sector, but which we do not cover separately.

vessels, corresponding to a compensation coefficient of between 0.25 and 1.85 (for example,: crude oil tankers, bulk carriers, combined carriers). This group accounts for 37.2 percent of world ship production in terms of compensated gross tons (CGT) in 1996;

- the second group, *medium-complexity ships* (MCS) corresponds to intermediate compensation coefficients of between 0.45 and 2.05. This includes product and chemical ships, general cargo ships, full container ships, car carriers, and liquid natural gas carriers. This group made up 48.8 percent of the world ship production in 1996;
- the third group, *high-complexity ships* (HCS) contains the remaining high-value ships, including ferries, fishing ships and passenger cruisers (14 percent in 1986).

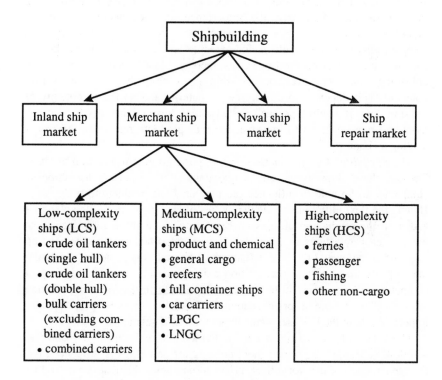

Figure 6.1 Segments of the shipbuilding market

Competition on the shipbuilding market is very strong: shipping companies can purchase their ships all over the world in a large number of fairly similar yards. Overcapacity throughout the world further intensifies this situation. The following can be identified as axes of active competition (see Borla 1995, pp. 81–94):

- price,
- quality,
- product innovation,
- delivery period,
- meeting of deadlines,

- customer service,
- flexibility,
- reputation, and
- financing services.

The foremost factor of competition in all market segments is *price*. In particular, in the segment LCS – ships which are produced in greater numbers as standardized products – the price is the most important axis of competition. With increasing complexity, the importance of price decreases and the importance of quality increases. Product innovations are a key factor in competition when they result in, for example, a reduction in the number of crew required, lower maintenance costs, increased load capacities, or reduced unloading times. However, not all ship types have the same innovation potential. This depends on the degree of maturity and on the complexity of the ship type. If a ship type has reached a high level of maturity it becomes more and more difficult to improve, for example, with respect to the ship's loading technology.[71]

The *flexibility* of shipbuilders is very important in the production of HCS. Because these ships are mostly single units, it is important for shipping companies to be able to influence the planning and production of the ship. Having the flexibility to integrate the wishes of the customer into the planning and even the production process is therefore a competitive advantage. Last but not least, questions of financing play an important role for demanding shipping companies. Offers of assistance or special conditions for financing the ship are an important competition axis. Such services can constitute a competitive disadvantage in terms of price because in the medium and long term they work like a price reduction. Financial services play a more important role in the HCS segments than in the LCS segments.

The demand for new ships has to be divided into replacement demand and additional demand. The replacement demand for new ships is influenced by: the age structure of the world fleet; prices of new ships; interest rates; product innovations; and international legislation. In particular, the age structure of the world fleet is decisive for the replacement demand. Product innovation

---

[71] In the case of container ships, the innovation potential is still high because this ship type originated only in the 1980s. On the other hand, oil tankers have existed for longer and therefore it is more difficult to make improvements.

and the international legislation (International Maritime Organization: IMO) can lead to an increase in the replacement demand. The additional demand is influenced by the development of seaborne trade; of returns on shipping activities; of transport efficiency; of transport alternatives; and by product innovations. Additional demand is required to serve the steadily growing seaborne trade. Thus the development of this demand is closely connected to the development of world trade activities and to seaborne trade as well. The additional demand is negatively influenced by the increase in transport efficiency and in alternative transport possibilities. Developments in logistic management as well as in transportation technology lead to an increase in transport efficiency, which lowers the growth rates of additional demand.[72]

The different regions of the world participated differently in this increase in production in recent years (see Tables 6.1 and 6.2). Because shipyards all over the world compete against one another, the situation on the world markets has recently changed: strong shifts between the market shares of different countries can be observed. The push of the countries of Central and Eastern Europe on the world shipbuilding markets increases this tendency.

Table 6.1 World ship production by region, 1990–1997

	1990	1991	1992	1993	1994	1995	1996	1997
AWES*	3,285	3,158	3,396	3,010	2,902	3,705	4,304	4,009
Market share in %	28.2	27.4	28.0	24.3	23.0	25.9	26.0	23.7
Japan	4,456	4,417	4,379	4,854	5,177	5,644	5,991	6,298
Market share in %	38.2	38.3	36.1	39.2	41.0	39.4	36.2	37.2
South Korea	1,564	1,729	1,995	1,835	2,104	2,887	3,549	3,983
Market share in %	13.4	15.0	16.5	14.8	16.7	20.2	21.4	23.5
Others	2,351	2,222	2,346	2,681	2,453	2,089	2,706	2,647
Market share in %	20.2	19.3	19.4	21.7	19.4	14.6	16.4	15.6
Total	11,656	11,526	12,116	12,380	12,636	14,325	16,550	16,937

Note: * From 1995 including Poland.

Source: AWES, Annual Report: various issues.

---

[72] World seaborne trade grew steadily by about 27 percent (average: 3.5 percent) from 3,977 million tons in 1990 to 5,074 million tons in 1997; in the same period, world ship production grew by about 45 percent (average: 5.5 percent). The largest single transported good is still crude oil, followed by coal, ion ore, oil products and grain.

Table 6.2 World shipbuilding new orders and order book by country,
1992–1997 (1,000 CGT)

	1993		1994		1995		1996		1997	
	(a)	*(b)*	*(a)*	*(b)*	*(a)*	*(b)*	*(a)*	*(b)*	*(a)*	*(b)*
Belgium	17	134	54	118	3	96	1	28	1	4
Denmark	390	698	382	596	109	299	269	651	257	610
Finland	515	791	277	961	178	855	384	881	133	728
France	227	569	240	678	66	513	111	448	118	370
Germany	1,029	1,600	1,034	1,591	1,714	2,290	799	1,952	924	1,724
Greece	7	44	0	104	1	13	0	1	0	0
Ireland	0	0	0	0	0	0	0	0	0	0
Italy	511	1,039	345	1,029	1,081	1,860	662	1,843	585	2,049
Netherlands	305	386	343	442	460	600	542	811	421	764
Norway	252	371	263	411	235	360	293	389	466	536
Portugal	6	46	44	76	64	112	98	156	3	60
Spain	360	476	404	668	378	735	345	668	661	1,156
Sweden	1	0	0	0	12	25	99	99	19	465
UK	66	321	39	212	107	192	86	182	122	164
W. Europe	3,686	6,475	3,425	6,886	4,408	7,950	3,689	8,109	3,710	8,630
Bulgaria	42	142	64	149	134	199	40	148	42	132
Croatia	153	511	270	466	58	430	321	505	364	720
Poland	191	1,014	678	999	1,085	1,685	491	1,455	128	969
Romania	150	861	140	944	203	972	104	761	129	726
Russia	358	779	170	887	81	770	101	550	154	446
Ukraine	291	426	397	702	191	737	90	554	21	491
E. Europe	1,185	3,733	1,719	4,147	1,752	4,793	1,147	3,973	838	3,484
Others	57	318	154	413	196	493	245	571	241	549
Europe	4,928	10,526	5,298	11,446	6,356	13,236	5,081	12,653	4,789	12,663
China	437	1,257	547	1,262	837	1,446	1,226	1,924	1,381	2,937
Japan	4,681	6,256	6,688	8,000	5,898	8,173	6,294	8,480	8,797	10,955
Korea	3,673	4,793	3,088	5,867	4,114	6,845	3,744	6,872	6,180	8,973
Subtotal Asia	8,791	12,306	10,323	15,129	10,849	16,464	11,264	17,276	16,358	22,865
Rest of world	807	1,960	1,132	2,384	2,361	1,159	1,159	2,295	1,336	2,484
Total world	14,526	24,792	16,753	28,959	19,566	30,859	17,504	32,224	22,483	38,012

Notes: (a) New orders; (b) Order-book, on December 31 of the named year.
Source: AWES, Annual Report: various issues.

The share of the AWES countries[73] dropped from 28 percent in 1990 to 23.7 percent in 1997.[74] In contrast, South Korea's market share increased from 13.4 percent in 1990 to 23.5 percent in 1997. The market leader, Japan, more or less held its market share, which is about 38 percent. The top five shipbuilding countries in the world are Japan, South Korea, Germany, China and *Poland*. Together they held a market share of 75.5 percent in terms of CGT in 1997.[75]

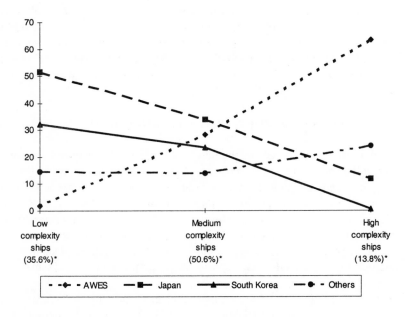

Note: *Share of market segment of total shipbuilding market.

Source: AWES (1998, p. 91).

Figure 6.2 Regional shares of shipbuilding market segments

An analysis of the market segments for different ship types shows specialization in different countries and regions of the world (see Figure 6.2). With a change in the level of complexity, the shares of labor and material

---

73 AWES countries are the European Community (EC) countries plus Norway and Poland.
74 The increase of the AWES market share in 1995 results mainly from the accession of Poland
    to the AWES organization.
75 VSM (1996, p. 34).

costs shift. The share of labor costs for LCS is higher than for HCS, where the equipment raises the share of material costs. It can be observed that most countries with low labor costs and often also low productivity are located in the market segment LCS. Countries with high labor costs try to use their productivity advantages and technological knowledge to compete with the low labor cost countries. Therefore the high labor cost countries are mostly engaged in HCS market segments. Figure 6.2 shows that Japan (51.4 percent) and South Korea (32.3 percent) dominate the market segment LCS; this market segment accounts for 35.6 percent of the produced CGT in the world (AWES 1998, p. 91). In 1997 for the first time, Japan also took a clear lead in the market segment MCS (34 percent), ahead of the AWES countries (28.4 percent). In the market segment HCS, the AWES countries are market leaders with a 63.3 percent market share and a large margin compared to the second country, Japan (12 percent).

2.2 Structure of Production Networks and State Policies

Contrary to popular belief, shipbuilding is no longer a labor-intensive, mainly blue-collar 'heavy' industry. In reality, shipbuilding has developed to become a capital-intensive, high-technology industry, with a high dependency upon upstream R&D and innovation activities. Its high-technology content, rapid pace of product and process innovation, and deep linkages upstream and downstream make it a key industry for many coastal industrialized countries. Furthermore, the increasing outsourcing level which has taken place in recent decades reduces the shipyard to a location for planning, coordinating and assembling.

A large portion of R&D is carried out externally by the suppliers. In particular, technologically complex components (for example, motors, radar systems, computers, software and so on) are developed outside the shipyard. The suppliers come from different industrial sectors, such as software, computers, machine tools, and electrical and mechanical engineering, and bring knowledge with them which is used for the specific tasks of shipbuilding. The shipyards depend upon the knowledge of their suppliers for (i) components built into the ships, but also (ii) production equipment such as robots, docks, plasma cutting machinery and cranes. The internal R&D experts carry out mainly project and ship design and construction plans as well as the development of optimal production organization. Recently, a shift in the focus of internal R&D activities has become observable in Western countries. Whereas until now the product was the main focus of internal R&D activities, today questions of organization, logistics and the optimal degree of outsourcing are at the center of R&D efforts.[76] The external R&D institutes and universities which carry out the majority of basic research as well as a significant portion of applied research are a third source of innovation in the shipbuilding industry.[77] The research fields extend from hydrodynamics to CAD design applications. These institutions and research programs are often publicly funded.[78]

Given the intensification of competition on European and international markets, different strategies of diversification and cost reduction can be observed in the shipyards. Depending upon which strategies are chosen by the respective yard, the sources and loci of innovation will vary. One tendency is *outsourcing* and the reduction of 'core activities' (the so-called 'shipbuilding only' strategy). As in automobile or machine production, Western capitalist shipbuilding has adopted the concept of 'lean production' over the last decade. Today, over 70 percent of a ship's value added may come from suppliers outside the yard; this tendency is increasing. The shipyard is reduced to purchasing and assembling (as the so-called 'system leader'). Its productivity gain no longer comes from its own R&D, but mainly from optimizing the assembly procedure through 'simultaneous engineering'. The suppliers organize themselves in hierarchical order, so that the largest suppliers themselves become 'system suppliers', including R&D and services. This also implies close information integration between shipyard and system suppliers, and between system suppliers and simple suppliers.[79] The issue of outsourcing is related to the changing paradigm in shipbuilding: away from individual production and towards automated assembly production in so-called 'compact yards'.[80] Another tendency that is gaining momentum in Europe is the concentration of shipbuilding and the increasing specialization of production in individual shipyards.[81] Yard specialization can improve productivity and yield economies of scale, both in design and assembly. Also, the takeover of shipyards may facilitate the gradual reduction of capacity, as

---

[76] VSM (1998, p. 55).

[77] See Bitzer and Hirschhausen (1997, pp. 15–17), for a detailed description of the German sectoral innovation system.

[78] For example, the EU provides a substantial amount for R&D in maritime technology, within its ECU 14 m '5th Framework Program for Research and Development' for the years 1999 to 2004; VSM (1998, p. 60).

[79] The 400 German supply enterprises, for example, employ about 70,000 people, and have a turnover of DEM 13 bn (EUR 7 bn), 60 percent of which is exported. At the same time, the German shipbuilding industry employs only 22,000 people and has a turnover of DEM 5 bn (EUR 2.8 bn).

[80] The idea is to standardize the production process as much as possible, and to establish half-automated assembly lines. The three most modern shipyards under construction in East Germany were conceived as compact yards (Warnemünde, MTW Wismar and Peene Werft Wolgast).

[81] Röller and Hirschhausen (1996, p. 19).

the closure of any one yard can be gradually prepared for within a group (it is not an 'all-or-nothing' decision, as in the case of single-yard firms).[82] Finally, the strategy of downstream integration to ensure captive markets has become increasingly popular. Capital participation in shipping companies may be a means for a shipbuilder to ensure captive markets, but also to maintain a close relationship to the client's potential demand and technology changes.[83]

In practice, one can observe very different institutional settings of production, which may also imply different links with the innovation system. We distinguish three 'ideal types' of linking the process of shipbuilding to the upstream suppliers and downstream clients:

- *the individual, non-integrated shipyard* in Europe has no stable capital or other relationships, either with suppliers or with clients. Its strategy is mainly cost reduction, production differentiation and specialization towards the high-complexity range of ships (for example, gas and chemical tankers, passenger ships). It obtains productivity gains internally through automation of production and externally by integrating its suppliers' innovations.[84] Many Western European shipyards can be characterized as individual and non-integrated.
- *the Danish maritime cluster* is an attempt to institutionalize innovation in a competition-oriented environment. The peculiarity of the cluster is that it is downstream oriented: the driving forces are the shipping companies that have accumulated the capital participation of particular shipyards. This does not impede competition between Danish and foreign yards; it does imply, though, that shippers and shipyards cooperate closely in the development of *new technologies* and *new types of ships*. If an innovative order is at stake, a shipper will place the order with 'his' shipyards. Furthermore, the Danish maritime cluster stretches to system suppliers, financial institutions, and the state. Policy instruments of 'clustering' are research programs, financed partially by the Danish Ministry of Industry, in which shippers, shipyards, suppliers and other firms participate.
- *the Japanese model of state/industry 'co-competition'* is based on an

---

[82] Examples of concentration are the Norwegian Kvaerner group until its sell-off in 1999, and that underway in Northern Germany (Thyssen Industrie, combining Blohm+Voss and the Thyssen Nordseewerke, which Preussag's Howaldtswerk Deutsche Werft AG may join).

[83] Capital ownership may be in both directions (that is, shipyards owning shipping companies, for example, the 50 percent stake that Bremer Vulkan held in the shipper Senator/DSR Reederei, or shipping companies owning shipyards (as in the Danish case, A.P. Moeller owning Odense shipyard and J. Lauritzen owning Danyard).

[84] Being a non-integrated shipyard does not imply the total absence of cooperation: the relations between almost all individual shipyards are characterized by some form of 'co-competition': while they compete for smaller, individual contracts, they cooperate in larger contracts, for which a single yard is too small.

important role of pre-competitive research (state financed, carried out in a 'National Institute for Shipbuilding') and a long-term, unwritten cooperative understanding between the state, the yards and the shipping companies. In times of crisis (for example, the 1976–79), the state watches over the restructuring of the shipbuilding industry and ensures its survival; in expansionary times, the shipyards actually compete against one another. Shipyards usually belong to a larger industrial group (*'Keiretsu'*). In 1993, eight of the world's 11 largest shipyards were Japanese.

A few examples show that development and competition in the shipbuilding industry are greatly influenced by public policies all over the world. As a result of regional differences in public subsidies, the shipbuilding industry is characterized by a high distortion of competition. The efforts in the European Union to harmonize the conditions of public support resulted in the Seventh Council Directive on Shipbuilding (90/684/EEC), which regulates public support in the EU.[85] In contrast to this, the attempt to reach harmonization within the framework of the OECD (including Japan, South Korea and the United States) failed.[86]

Information about the financial support granted to the shipbuilding industry in the *Asian* countries (Japan, South Korea, China) is handled very restrictively. In the 1980s, the shipbuilding industry placed priority on industrial policy; the investment risk was reduced by the government's guarantee of support to the branch in economic crises.[87] In South Korea, the shipbuilding industry was strongly supported by the government through the 1980s and the early 1990s. After the successful international establishment of the industry, government support was reduced and industrial priorities shifted to other branches. Governments usually also fund a national shipbuilding research institute and grant financing to special projects.

---

[85] *Operating aid* is granted as a percentage of the contract value before aid. Each year the EC determines a ceiling for public aid, which results from a comparison between the most competitive Community shipyards and their main competitors (mostly from the Far East). In recent years the ceiling was fixed at 9.9 percent. *Restructuring aid* includes investment aid, aid for closures and aid for research and development. The aim of this aid is to narrow the gap between the least and most efficient shipyards. Another aim is the reduction of overcapacity in the industry. Furthermore, the EC funds R&D programs for maritime technology.[85] In addition to this, every national government in the EC can fund further R&D projects in its own country. In 1996, Germany spent about DM 45 million on R&D projects in maritime technology (VSM 1997, p. 51).

[86] The 'OECD Agreement on Normal Competitive Conditions in the Commercial Shipbuilding and Repair Industry', which should already have been enforced at the end of 1995, had still not come into force by 1999; the United States have not ratified the agreement and therefore prevent its enforcement.

[87] Arthur D Little (1993, p. VIII).

3. RESTRUCTURING OF SHIPBUILDING IN EASTERN EUROPE

3.1 Point of Departure: The Breakdown of Socialist, Multifunctional Shipyards

Under socialism, shipbuilding was first and foremost a military, strategic activity. Civil shipbuilding was considered secondary. The structure of the shipyards and the modes of production reflected the principles of socialist production: shipyards were multifunctional units, in which the production of ships was but one objective; other functions were the provision of social services to employees (such as housing, education, culture, access to consumer goods and so on) and the maintenance of some political activity and control. With respect to ship production, a socialist shipyard was characterized by enormous production depth, that is, the in-house fabrication of ship outfits and machinery equipment including winches, steering gear, accommodation, electrical equipment, switchboards, and so on.[88]

Employment in socialist shipyards was very high, when compared on a man/CGT basis. Direct employment was three to four times higher than in capitalist, Western European shipyards in the 1980s.[89] Table 6.3 shows average estimates for labor productivity in shipbuilding in the early 1990s (Russia and Ukraine are representative of other post-socialist countries). While the difference between the good world averages and the good European averages is already striking (almost 1:2), post-socialist countries lagged far behind at about 0.05–0.075 employee per CGT.

Table 6.3 Productivity estimates for shipyards (early 1990s)

Country	Productivity (in '000 employee years/CGT)
Russia/Ukraine	50–75
Good European	22–28
Good World	11–17

Sources: AWES, VSM, OECD (1995a).

---

[88] Integration was pushed to the limits in the Krasnoje Sormovo shipyard (Nizhny Novgorod), which had its own steel production and rolling mills.

[89] In East Germany, for example, where the restructuring from socialist to capitalist shipyards took place extremely quickly, direct employment in the five largest yards was reduced from 21,000 to about 6,000, with no significant reductions in CGT output. However, given the increasing degree of outsourcing in capitalist shipyards, and the vast non-productive activities in socialist shipyards, this direct comparison has to be interpreted with care.

In contrast to the deep integration of all productive activities, the socialist shipyard had little proper design or innovation capacity. Design offices were independent units, though they usually belonged to the same ministry. The shipyards themselves were largely reduced to being assemblers. Thus, their capacity for product differentiation and innovation was limited.

With the end of socialism, the socialist industrial structures fell apart, too. Monetization and the abandonment of party-dominated, non-monetary production led to the implementation of new constraints. As with all socialist productive structures, the multifunctional shipyards also lost their *raison d'être*. Capital constraints and increasing national and international competition required a radical restructuring of the 'industrial ruins of socialism'. Indeed, it turned out that none of the socialist shipyards in Eastern Europe would be economically viable as such.

3.2 Sectoral Survey: The Situation in the Eastern European Shipbuilding Industry

The restructuring of Eastern European yards is also reflected in the macro-statistics which we summarize here for the entire region (Table 6.4). As a rule of thumb, with the end of socialism and the Cold War, the figures of Eastern European ship production *dropped* in all Eastern European countries. Several years after this breakdown, production usually rises again, and today Poland, and to some extent Romania and Croatia, are serious competitors on the world ship market; Russia and Ukraine may become competitors in the future.

Table 6.4 East European shipbuilding production, 1988–1997

Production – ships completed	1988	1989	1990	1991	1992	1993	1994	1995	1996	1997	% of world market
Bulgaria	n.a.	n.a.	n.a.	71	62	71	79	77	86	57	0.3
Poland	344	238	177	223	306	264	345	474	480	522	3.1
Romania	n.a.	n.a.	n.a.	126	147	72	22	150	149	95	0.6
USSR	56	227	482	365							
Russia					22	156	91	82	145	109	0.6
Ukraine					119	153	210	158	183	69	0.4
Yugoslavia	230	328	293	240							
Croatia					238	104	165	97	257	90	0.5
Eastern Europe	630	793	952	1,025	894	820	912	1,038	1,300	942	5.5

Sources: AWES Annual Reports 1992–1998, EEC Report of the Commission to the Council on the state of the shipbuilding industry, COM (95) 38 final, Table 5a.

In 1997, Poland, the largest ship producer of the East European countries, held a market share of 3.08 percent in terms of worldwide CGT production. It was followed by Russia, Romania, Croatia, Ukraine and Bulgaria. Together they accounted for about 5.56 percent (1996: 7.85 percent) of the CGT produced worldwide in 1997. The production of the three dominant countries, that is, Poland, Russia, and Ukraine, shows very different structures: with its rapid reorientation to Western markets, *Poland* was able to become competitive in some segments of the shipbuilding market. In 1996 it was able to attract 10 percent of worldwide orders in the container ship segment. *Russia* was able to stabilize its shipbuilding production in the period 1994–97; however, the order stock has decreased steadily since 1993. The development of *Ukrainian* shipbuilding was characterized by relatively steady production in the years 1993–96 and a drop in production in 1997; simultaneously, the attraction of new orders and the order stock have dropped substantially since 1994. Whereas the Polish shipyards are mainly active in the MCS market segment, Ukraine's shipbuilding industry is active mainly in the LCS segment. Russia's shipbuilding industry focusses mainly on LCS and MCS, where both segments have a similar importance. *None* of the Eastern European countries were able to enter the high-complexity segment significantly (see Figure 6.3).

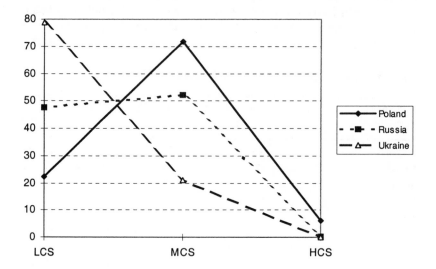

Figure 6.3   Division of the order stock of Poland, Russia and Ukraine, March 1997

3.3 A Taxonomy of East–West Cooperation in Shipbuilding

Cooperation with foreign enterprises is a major determinant of the success of enterprization. The breakdown of the CMEA and the restructuring of post-socialist yards (including China) have indeed given a major impetus to international cooperation in shipbuilding. Cooperation between 'developing' and 'developed' shipyards is increasing all over Eastern Europe. Motivation is bidirectional: developing shipyards need the technology transfer, design and access to markets that developed shipyards can offer. In the other direction, developed shipyards are looking for opportunities to outsource parts of, or even the bulk of the production process. The proximity between Eastern and Western European shipyards, the relatively high level of capabilities in Eastern European yards, and the EU–CEE wage differential suggest that East–West cooperation is bound to increase.

The term 'cooperation' designates regular business contacts that are to some extent institutionalized, either between two or more shipyards (horizontally), or between suppliers, shipyards, and customers (vertically).

Table 6.5 shows how fast East–West cooperation has developed in the 1990s: almost non-existent in socialist times, Eastern European shipyards today account for over 40 percent of all registered cooperation of OECD shipyards; when considering only the European OECD yards, this ratio is as high as 2:3. East–West cooperation can be classified according to the degree of integration between the two partners:[90]

1. *Regular supply of components* means regular or exclusive agreements with suppliers and/or shipyards in another country. In general, the 'components' should be of a certain value or technological content, such as entire hull sections, outfitting, electronics, or motors.
2. *Subcontracting* and *licensed production* become more intense once the technological level of the developing shipyards is rising. Examples are labor-intensive steel work, diesel engine production, but also shared production of entire ships.
3. *Technological cooperation and training* can be done by exchanging personnel and/or codified knowledge such as design or software blueprints. One common strategy of 'catching-up' for developing shipyards is to participate in the production of a prototype ship in a developed shipyard, and to 'copy' the design and production process with its own means thereafter. Developed yards have an interest in this 'second-

---

[90] Developed from OECD (1996).

Table 6.5 Selected partnerships between OECD and Eastern European
shipyards

	'Western shipyard' (or maritime company)	'Eastern shipyard'
1	Astilleros de Huelva (Spain)	Baltija Shipyard, Klaipeda (Lithuania)
2	Kvaerner Group (Norway)	Severnaya Shipyard (Russia)
3	Fosen Mek. Verkst. A/S (Norway)	Galatz (Romania)
4	Damen B.V., Gorinchem (Netherlands)	Sev-Mash Predpriyatiye, Severodvinsk (Russia)
5	Estaleiros Navals (Vianayard (Portugal)	Yards in Russia and Ukraine
6	HDW, Kiel (Germany)	Shipyard in Poland
7	Lloyd Werft, BHV (Germany)	Pregol-yard, Kaliningrad (Russia)
8	Mützelfeldtwerft, CUX (Germany)	Romanian shipyard
9	FATA, Torino (Italy)	Kershon Shipyard (Ukraine)
10	Mariotti (Italy)	Okean Shipyard (Ukraine)
11	Fassmer&Co, Mothen (Germany)	Yantar Shipyard, Kaliningrad (Russia)
12	Several smaller yards	Poland
13	Several smaller yards	Romania
14	British marine equipment suppliers, London	Ukraine
15	Burmeister & Wain (Denmark)	Szczecin (Poland)
16	Vulkan*, Bremen (Germany)	Severnaya, St. Petersburg (Russia)
17	Kvaerner Group (Norway)	Sever Shipyard, Archangel (Russia)
18	Kvaerner Group (Norway)	Vyborg Yard (Russia)
19	Cassens Yard (Emden, Germany)	Petrosawodsk (Rep. Karelia, Schlisselburg, Aksai)
20	ILS (Finland)	Leninskaya Kusnita Kyiv (Ukraine)
21	Daewoo (Korea)	Romanian shipyard; Mangalia (Romania)
22	Arminus Werke (Germany)	Withe Sea&Onega Shipping Co., St. Petersburg
23	Arminus, Stinnes (Germany)	North Western Shipping Co., St. Petersburg (Russia)
24	Cassens yard (Germany)	Volgo-Don Shipping Co., Rostov/Don (Russia)
25	Elbewerft Boizenburg (Germany)	Zelenodolsk, Tatarstan (Russia)
26	H. Peters, Wewelsfleth (Germany)	Slip Shipyard, Rybinks (Russia)
27	Mittelst. Serienschiffbauges (MSG)	Shipyard ventures (Russia)
28	Kvaerner Group (Norway)	Vyborg Shipyard, St. Petersburg (Russia)
29	Fram Shipping, Pepsi Co.	Saliw, Kertsch (Ukraine)
30	Odense Staalskibsvaerft (Denmark)	Loksa shipyard, Tallinn (Estonia)
31	Mc Dermott (USA)	MacAmur (Russia)

Notes: * Liquidated in 1996.
(1) Supply of components.
(2) Subcontracting/licensed production.
(3) Technological cooperation.
(4) Capital participation/joint ventures.

Type of cooperation				Remarks	
(1)	(2)	(3)	(4)		
	x			Subcontracting of outfitting works	1
x				Licensing production	2
x	x				3
x				Hull production in Sev-Mash	4
x	x			Subcontracting of hulls, licensing production	5
x	x			Supplier of components	6
x			x	Ship repair	7
x	x			Subcontracting of hulls	8
x				Fast built ferries	9
x	x			Hull-production in Okean	10
	x			Aluminum construction	11
	x				12
	x				13
	x			Technology transfer, equipment	14
		x		Joint production of 25 river vessels	15
		x	x	Small vessels	16
		x	x	Conversion to civilian production	17
		x	x		18
	x	x		Joint production of 25 river vessels	19
		x		Joint development of passenger ferries	20
		x	x	Know-how training	21
			x	'Onega Arminus Shipbuilders'	22
			x	'New Newskij Shipyard'	23
			x	'Don Cassens shipbuilders'	24
			x	Joint construction/operation	25
			x	Design by Peters, built in Rybinks	26
			x	Outsourcing	27
			x	Direct investment	28
			x	Joint development and marketization of oil tankers	29
			x	Purchased for hatch-cover production	30
			x		31

best' cooperation, as competition between them for markets and
subcontractors in developing countries is fierce.

4. *Capital participation* and *joint ventures* are the most explicit forms of
cooperation, with one partner taking direct influence on the other. Joint
ventures are by far the most developed type of cooperation, as transaction
costs are lower than for capital participation. This is particularly the case
in countries where the legal framework is unstable or non-existent.

4. CASE STUDIES: EAST GERMANY, POLAND, RUSSIA

Within Eastern Europe and the CIS, we have identified two fundamentally
different patterns of enterprization: (i) the *Polish* rapid enterprization process.
which is to some extent representative for other CEE countries, such as
Romania or Croatia; and (ii) the *Russian* slowed-down enterprization with
significant state intervention (which is also observed in Ukraine). As an
additional reference, we add the extreme case of East Germany, because its
restructuring process is already finished.

4.1 Reference Case Study: East Germany[91]

The restructuring of the East German shipbuilding industry was a radical case
of enterprization, as the socialist shipyards had become economically non-
viable the very day of monetary union with West Germany, that is, July 2,
1990. Deprived of their former clients in the Soviet Union, all seven
shipyards ran substantial losses in 1990 and 1991 (amounting to several
hundred million Deutschmarks). The only way to maintain some shipbuilding
capacity – and thus some employment in the depressed shore-region of the
Baltic Sea (Mecklenburg-Vorpommern) – was to inject massive investments
and to create, practically from scratch, new shipyards. This meant that the
Treuhandanstalt (THA), the German Ministry charged with restructuring East
German industry, had to provide massive subsidies to attract external
shipyards to take over some of the remnants of the East German yards, and to
invest in new operations.

Table 6.6 shows a typical, representative case of restructuring a post-
socialist shipyard. The Mathias Thesen Werft VEB ('factory of the people')
in East Germany, once employing 6,000 for a capacity of 135,000 socialist
CGT, was closed down. On the same site, a new shipyard was built and
opened in November 1998, financed mainly by state subsidies. It is one of the

---

[91] This section draws on case studies carried out by one of the authors, as reported in Röller
and Hirschhausen (1996, pp. 13–21).

most modern 'compact yards' in Europe, featuring an entirely new product range.[92]

Table 6.6   Capitalization of the socialist Mathias Thesen Werft VEB to the MTW Schiffswerft GmbH – a case of creating 'new' capacities

	Under socialism (1989)	After restructuring (1998)
Name	Mathias Thesen Werft VEB (factory of the people)	MTW Schiffswerft GmbH
Owner	Schiffbau-Kombinat Rostock, controlled by the Communist Party and its 'Plan'	Norwegian private industrial group AKER
Berths	2 small open building berths for ship sizes 87x25 m (5,000 t) and 206x32 m (8,000 t)	New dry dock, 340x67 m; compact yard
Product range	Fishing vessels and refrigerator ships; multi-purpose transport vessels; container ships	Very large crude carriers, specialized container vessels, passenger vessels, chemical tankers
Maximum size ships	40,000 dead weight tons	300,000 dwt
Markets, competition	Bartered with USSR; competition: none	Mainly European markets, competition with West European, and, increasingly, Polish shipyards
Employment	6,000 (including social functions)	1,200
Capacity	135,000 CGT 'socialist' capacity	ca. 100,000 CGT 'new' capacity

Source: Röller and Hirschhausen (1996, p. 32).

In the other East German shipyards, the transformation to capitalism proceeded similarly. As a result, five new shipyards were created in East Germany with a nominal capacity of 327,000 CGT, but capable of producing well beyond 400,000 CGT.[93] As all five yards were taken over by West

---

[92] The new MTW Werft GmbH employs about 1,200 people directly; another 900 permanent jobs may be created in 26 new small and medium enterprises around the site (for example, in anti-corrosion, construction, concrete, part assembly; rigging (takelage); mechanical works, craftsmen, and so on). Only the following types of activities were kept as 'core business' within MTW: shipbuilders, welders, mechanical engineering, pipe builders, electricians and equipment personnel.

[93] When accounting THA expenditures and Art. 92 state aid, total expenses amount to DM 6.3

German or Western European groups, they were all immediately integrated into existing production and sales networks. This resolved the issue of a particular S&T or innovation policy. Innovation in the capitalist yards comes from the same sources as innovation in any Western yard. In the East German case, the only 'S&T policy' was to facilitate the unbundling of the former combines and the creation of specialized SMEs.

4.2 Restructuring and Integration in International Networks in Poland

4.2.1 An industry in which the post-socialist period has ended

The starting point was difficult in 1989 when Poland was still a socialist country: the three main shipyards (Szczecin, Gdynia, Gdansk) still produced mainly for Polish and Soviet Union clients. Product specialization was low, but so, too, were the maximum sizes of the ships (30,000 dwt maximum at Szczecin, Gdynia being an exception). Exports to non-socialist countries already existed, but their absolute volume was limited (around 20 percent). The monetarization of the economy on January 1, 1990 triggered the end of socialist production and forced restructuring on all yards. Socialist networks fell apart, and within two to three years, market- and capital-oriented strategies had to be adapted by the newly emerging (state-owned) stock companies. Common elements of the process of enterprization were the following:

- *product specialization*; once generalists, the Polish yards sought to become competitive in the low-end segments, mainly container ships, general cargo vessels and tankers. Sixty percent of Polish production is in this segment, where Polish yards have obtained a world market share of 11 percent; in the segment of 900–1,750 TEU container ships, Polish yards are even said to hold 35 percent of the world market (mainly due to Szczecin and Gdynia)!;[94]
- *outsourcing* could not proceed as quickly as in the East German case, but the Polish yards started to emulate the Western strategy of concentrating on core business.[95] The unbundled enterprises became independent economic entities, though generally they remained in the sphere of a larger 'holding' company for some time;[96]

---

bn (ca. EUR 3.5 bn)! About DM 350 m private investment was attracted, and about 5,000 permanent jobs created in the shipyards.
[94] BfAI (1996).
[95] For example, Szczecin increased the external value added to 16 percent (1995) and rising, the other two increased to 10 percent, see OECD (1996, p. 5).
[96] For example, the holding company that emerged in Szczecin comprised the whole range of a 'maritime cluster', including shipbuilding, shipping, financial and insurance services and a

- *labor shedding* was not as radical as in East Germany, but remained significant nonetheless. In the 1980s, employment in shipbuilding was about 40,000; in 1996, direct employment had fallen to about 22,000 (of which: Szczecin: 6,000; Gdynia: 6,000; Gdansk: 7,000) and is estimated to be below 20,000 in 1998. To this, several thousand subcontractors have to be added;
- *computerization* and *process automation* was an integral part of the adaptation process. Computer hardware and software was purchased to enhance design and optimize production, but also for management information systems (MIS);
- the yards tried to enhance their *design* capacities through in-house development and/or by purchasing foreign equipment and knowledge. Expanding design capacities was a critical factor for product diversification;[97]
- solving the issue of *outstanding debts and credits* was the major non-technical obstacle to obtaining liquidity for new investment. While the Polish government officially claimed not to support its shipbuilding industry, it did subsidize its development – indirectly – through the generous takeover of debts (amounting to several tens of millions of dollars).[98]

As of late 1998, the Polish shipbuilding industry seems to have overcome the worst traps of post-socialist restructuring and embarked upon an ambitious catching-up process. The specific post-socialist creative destruction of all shipyards can be regarded as being at an end. Two yards, Szczecin and Gdynia, have established themselves as profitable (in 1996 and 1997) and are among the most competitive in Europe.

4.2.2 Enterprization and network integration of the Szczecin shipyard, 1990–98

The enterprization of the Szczecin shipyard is a good example of how rapid enterprization and the reorientation of production can lead to international competitiveness in post-socialist shipbuilding. In socialist times, the Szczecin

---

[97] fuel company.
A good example is the expansion of the product range observed in the Gdynia yard, which purchased Swedish design software (Kockum Steerbear program) and adapted it to the Polish environment. Together with the prevalent engineering potential, the yard was thus able to construct a larger container ship of 5,000–6,000 TEU.

[98] In September 1994 the government decided for the first time to grant guarantees for credit extended by a bank to the Gdansk shipyard. In October 1995 the government further decided to grant financial support of USD 600 million for increasing the competitiveness of their shipyards. This policy raised fears about whether the Polish government would adopt the same habits as shipbuilding nations around the world.

yard was the most backward of the three large Polish yards, and could produce only medium-sized ships. It was oriented mainly towards Eastern European clients, most of whom canceled their orders after 1990 or did not pay for finished ships. Hence, in late 1991, bankruptcy was considered to be the only solution. Only the fact that it was still state owned and the major employer in the region guaranteed its survival. The turnaround came with *specialization* on a small segment of low-value-added ships (mainly container vessels), the development of new, Western clients, and increased outsourcing and cooperation with multiple suppliers. The key operation may have been the acquisition of an extremely long series of contracts for the B-183 container vessel (1,000 TEU), for which the first order was received in 1989. Since 1991, no less than 30 (!) vessels of this type were built, enabling the shipyard to organize efficient production structures, cut new building times and reduce costs. Following this success story, Szczecin has become a major international player in container shipbuilding.[99]

As concerns the organizational structure, *outsourcing* and the development of *new supplier relations* meant that Szczecin specialized in shipbuilding and abandoned some of its former activities (for example, software production, which is now imported). Investments were made in automation, expansion of operations, and increased technical and productive capacities. The key condition for success, however, was the integration of Szczecin not only in international production networks but also *downstream*, that is, finance and sales. Figure 6.4 shows the emerging network of the Szczecin shipyard, with regard to both suppliers and clients. We estimate that most of the sources of innovation are external. Upstream, Szczecin was able to support the modernization of the motor supplier HCP and the conversion of the FAMAK machines and appliances factory (Kluczbork), a former mining supplier.[100] Downstream, Szczecin was divided among several shipping companies' networks, both domestic (PZM shipping with five orders on stock in 1997) and international.[101]

The 'shipbuilding' policy of the Polish government was largely limited to offering indirect financial support, and – as the owner of some yards – to exercising soft budget constraints. An earlier divestiture of state stock might

---

99 A revealing case study that had already forecast a positive development in the early 1990s is provided in Johnson et al. (1995).

100 Steel is purchased both in Poland (Czestowchowa) and abroad, whereas most of the navigation and radar systems are imported. In the case of capacity bottlenecks, Szczecin can also subcontract to two smaller yards with which it has cooperation agreements (Ustka and Odra). On the horizontal axis, participation in its equity (30 percent) of two large banks (Polski Bank Rozwoji and Bank Handlowy) and the purchase of an insurance company have strengthened Szczecin's financial capabilities.

101 The yard has established itself as Germany's largest single suppliers: two-thirds of the final demand is accounted for by German shipping companies.

have accelerated restructuring without worsening the social consequences (this applies particularly to the Gdansk yard). In contrast, very little is known about the government's S&T policy, if taken in a more restricted sense.[102] This may be explained by the fact that there is indeed not much room for an S&T policy targetted specifically at shipbuilding. The integration into international networks assures the necessary transfers of technology and know-how. The absorptive capacities of Polish yards are large, as the cases of Szczecin and Gdynia show. Bottlenecks in yard diversification and restructuring could be overcome by integrating suppliers' knowledge.

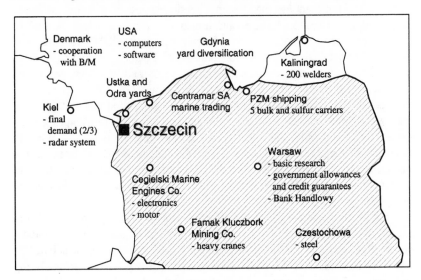

Figure 6.4   International production and sales network of the Szczecin shipyard, 1998

Conversely, shipbuilding has become an opportunity for Polish equipment suppliers: former mining equipment companies have survived by diversifying to shipbuilding. The major policy issue regarding Polish shipbuilding is not S&T, but *industrial policy*: ever since the mid-1990s, the idea of a 'Polish shipbuilding holding group' has been high on the agenda: the idea of joining together the large yards (Szczecin, Gdynia, possibly even the remainders of Gdansk) and of adding the most important suppliers. The industrial logic would be to complement Szczecin's strength in small-size, standardized ships

---

[102] In particular, no publications made any reference to the destiny of the former socialist 'institutes'.

(now up to 50,000 dwt) with Gdynia's large-size capacities (now up to 400,000 dwt). As of 1999, the future of this plan is open.

4.3 Russia: From a Post-socialist to a Post-Soviet Maritime Cluster?

4.3.1 The collapse of socialist shipbuilding leads to a state-planned S&T-policy

During the socialist period, the Soviet Union boasted the largest employment in shipbuilding worldwide (about 1 million people), producing one-third of naval ships and among the leading producers of civil ships as well. Shipbuilding for seaborne and inland transport was carried out in a total of 260 (!) yards and a large number of equipment units, R&D institutes and design institutes. Thus, with the breakdown of Soviet shipbuilding, Russia inherited a quite heterogeneous mixture of yards and auxiliary producers, without a clear pattern of specialization. Ship production fell drastically to a mere 56 ships in 1996; capacity utilization was estimated at about 40 percent; and worse, few signs of deep technological and financial restructuring were evident. Consequently, the S&T potential in shipbuilding was radically devalued. The traditional linkage between independent R&D institutes, design institutes and fully integrated shipyards was broken up. Shipyards tried to develop their own R&D capacity and diversify their product range through in-house design.

Faced with the unprecedented decline, not only of the shipyards but also of the entire maritime industry plus suppliers, the Russian government adopted a series of policy measures aimed at 'maintaining and developing the scientific–technical potential and the productive potential of the Russian shipbuilding industry'.[103] This was done through direct and indirect support to Russian enterprises, which can be considered the Russian S&T policy on the sector.[104] The angle of attack of these S&T programs is similar: by supporting one or more elements in the maritime industry (yards, suppliers, shippers) it sought to establish a competitive, vertically-integrated 'Russian' shipbuilding industry. The following concrete S&T elements were defined:

- yard restructuring and modernization: financial support to modernization and increased yard capacity to 'regain Russia's position as a leading

---

[103] Cited from the Federal Program 'Russian Yards', government decree No. 96 of 26/09/1995.

[104] The four main government programs are: (i) the 'Program on reviving the commercial fleet', adopted in 1993, was aimed at modernizing the structure of the Russian fleet, which had reached a critical state; (ii) the federal program 'Russian Yards' was developed by the State Committee of Defense in 1994/95 and adopted by the government in September 1995; (iii) the 'Federal program to develop the Russian fishery industry to the year 2000 (Ryba)'; and (iv) the 'Program for modernizing the fleet of help- and rescue ships' (about 1996).

shipbuilding nation';

- reorientation of product types, in particular development of large product and chemical tankers (thus competing with the Okean yard in Kherson, Ukraine, which specialized in these types during the Soviet period);
- support to the vertical integration of yards as a means of deep restructuring; the most prominent example is the attempt to merge the three St. Petersburg yards Baltisky, Admirality and Severnaya into one holding, sizable enough to host a new compact yard;
- strengthening the Russian network of suppliers to the shipbuilding industry. A list of 240 pieces or systems has been put together (it is unclear whether by ministerial bureaucrats or industrial lobbyists) which should be developed by *Russian* suppliers;
- particular emphasis placed on the development of new capacities in *R&D* as well as on *design for civil shipbuilding*. It is acknowledged that while the extensive socialist knowledge in military applications has been lost, new fields of R&D in civil shipbuilding are required (examples are environment, safety standards, new materials research, and so on). The same applies to design capacities as well;[105]
- furthermore, a trade policy is contained in the 'S&T package': a flat import tariff of 30 percent on ships is supposed to protect domestic producers. The 20 percent VAT plus a 'special tax' of 1.5 percent are applied to imports as well.

However, although the list of S&T policy measures is long, there are practically no tangible results to be observed as of today. Plan fulfillment ratios were deceptively low, with only small fractions of the four governmental programs carried out in reality.[106] In 1998, none of the objectives of 'Russian yards' were fulfilled, either in terms of output, yard restructuring, or competitiveness of suppliers. The 'Program on reviving the commercial fleet' did not succeed in increasing the share of Russian new orders placed domestically; instead, even the Russian Ministry of Transport placed over 50 percent of its orders with foreign yards (38 out of 73)!

Though still weak, alternative ways to gain competitiveness *do* exist even in post-Soviet Russia. Successful enterprise restructuring is systematically linked, either (i) to a Russian company becoming a supplier in an international network or importing technology from it, or (ii) to a Russian

---

[105] The program 'Russian Yards' foresees specific scientific programs for R&D Institutes (amounting to RUR 110–140 bn, approx. RUR 40–50 m Euro per year). As regards design, a reduction of design cycles and the development of 92 new shipyards is supported with RUR 15 bn (ca. EUR 5 m, unclear whether in absolute terms or yearly) for selected design institutes.

[106] Since no official data exists on this matter, only tentative conclusions can be drawn.

shipyard obtaining financing from Russian or (mainly) foreign banks.[107] Russian equipment suppliers can also rely upon *technology transfers* and networks for modernization.[108] At the yard level, modernization is achieved most efficiently through integration with foreign suppliers and/or yards. All Russian yards are trying to establish relations with Western system suppliers: the import rate of systems has increase to 70 percent.[109] The best opportunity for individual Russian suppliers is to subcontract for Western system suppliers, who in turn sell their products to Russian yards. At the level of R&D and design institutes, too, survival and restructuring can work where direct, solvent demand exists and some international cooperation is implemented.[110] The few examples of demand-dominated restructuring show that there is really no scope for a purely national S&T policy. The Russian maritime industry, despite its ongoing recession, is slowly starting to integrate into international production and technology networks (though to a much lesser degree than that in Poland). Once the financial conditions in the country stabilize, demand-oriented restructuring can also be supported by domestic actors, but for the time being Western (mainly public) financial institutions dominate.

4.3.2 Perspectives of shipbuilding in the Leningrad oblast: enterprization or vertical (re)integration?

The city of St. Petersburg and the surrounding Leningrad oblast host the largest concentration of shipbuilding and related activities worldwide. In 1997, even after five years of depression, output reduction and closures, it

---

[107] The most frequently used approach is securing *export credit guarantees* from Western European countries (for example, Baltisky savod obtained funds from Norway and Germany for Lukoil-tankers) to finance the import of technology. Collateral may be provided through ownership of the ship in production, built on existing orders of a (Western or Russian) shipping company. Thus, a direct market outlet for a ship is a condition for producing and obtaining technology.

[108] An example is the St. Petersburg-based 'Transas Marine', a former supplier of radar systems to the Soviet military. It is now providing its specific design to a UK manufacturer, who also markets the products worldwide (navigation equipment, simulators, electronic chart systems). Transas is in the process of being audited for ISO 9001 quality standards, a necessary condition to participate in international competition. Transas pieces are also used by the American company Trandes Corp., a system integrator of navigation equipment. Obliging Transas to 'buy Russian' or 'deliver Russian' in order to save Russian S&T potential would be highly counterproductive.

[109] According to estimates in (BfAI 1995): rescue equipment: 70 percent, diesel auxiliary engines: 60 percent, cranes and pumps: 50 percent, winds and rudders: 30 percent, navigation equipment: 20 percent.

[110] At shipyard level, the 'Krylov Shipbuilding Research Institute" (St. Petersburg), together with the engineering 'Shipbuilding Technical Institute' have reoriented themselves to a few concrete projects. These consist mainly in adapting foreign technology to local conditions. A major project is the design of a compact yard in the Leningrad oblast.

still comprises seven yards, 14 enterprises for equipment and mechanical engineering, the main R&D and design institutes of the country, several inland and international shipping companies, electronics firms, and so on. Direct employment in new civil building and repair alone exceeded 20,000; indirect employment is estimated at more than 100,000. Some of the yards, equipment suppliers and institutes have engaged in international cooperation and joint-ventures; yet the Leningrad shipbuilding cluster is largely internally-focussed and has still to recover from the post-socialist depression. By 1998, almost all shipyards were commercialized into stock companies, parts of which are held by private capital owners. However, capitalist constraints are not enforced by the (state) owners: none of the large yards were forced to reduce capacity, let alone to close down.[111] During the Soviet period, most of the shipyards benefitted from the services of the large institutes such as the Krylov Research Institute (maritime research, ship design) and the Shipbuilding Technical Institute (conception of shipyards). However, experience shows that these services can rapidly be replaced by imports: most of the ships exported to Western countries use Western design institutes.[112] Instead of a capitalist 'cluster' (in the positive Western sense), the Leningrad shipbuilding cluster has to be regarded as 'post-socialist', that is, yet to be restructured. Figure 6.5 shows the main elements of that cluster and the emerging links with foreign enterprises.

In principle, two different development options are imaginable: (i) *accelerated enterprization* would imply letting each shipyard find its own strategy, and increasing the capital constraint through strengthened governance structures. This strategy would oblige shipyards to engage more quickly in international competition. But it would also lead to intensified competition *within* the Russian yards. By contrast, (ii) *state-coordinated integration* would be an attempt to join local forces in order to create a truly competitive cluster. This solution implies the fusion of several shipyards into a holding company, to which some strategic suppliers would be added. A bank and shipping companies would complete the holding company.

---

[111] The announced shut-down of the Severnaya shipyard, for example, was revoked only months after its closure; Severnaya is now back in business.

[112] The most recent example is the Baltisky yard's plans for liquefied petroleum gas (LPG) tankers, for which it will use the design from the SRS Design Bureau in Oslo (Norway).

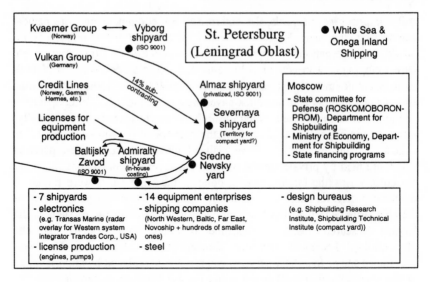

Figure 6.5   Post-Soviet shipbuilding cluster in the Leningrad oblast
(Russia), 1998

5. CONCLUSIONS

Shipbuilding is no longer a low-tech, 'heavy industry', but has developed to become a high-tech, information-dominated, logistically intensive production process. In the Western world, most of the ship is currently developed and produced outside of the shipyard. The supplier network therefore plays a crucial role in the development and the production of the ship. In this chapter, we have analyzed the restructuring of East European shipyards within the framework of international developments in this sector. With the collapse of socialism, the centralized, vertically integrated socialist mode of ship production collapsed. Not only did the Eastern European countries lose their traditional outlet, which was mainly the Soviet Union; the S&T potential of the entire production network was devalued as well. Production had to be reoriented towards international markets where Eastern European yards now compete with Western capitalist yards worldwide. Therefore the restructuring from highly integrated shipyards towards non-integrated production structures with an efficient supplier network is the basic condition for successful restructuring.

A technological gap did exist between post-socialist and capitalist yards, but it was not a hampering factor for restructuring. For all developing shipbuilding countries, the use of modern maritime technology is a precondition for competition on world markets. This technology is now freely available to all Eastern yards. Technology transfer was a necessary but not sufficient condition for the restructuring of Eastern European yards. *Innovation* in the Eastern European shipbuilding industry comes from internal (for example, design bureaus, R&D departments and so on) as well as from external (for example, suppliers, research institutes and so on) sources. Through their suppliers, Eastern European shipyards use domestic and foreign S&T systems. In particular, foreign suppliers and their S&T systems are utilized by Eastern European shipyards to access modern maritime technologies. The result is that the shipbuilding industry in Eastern Europe is no longer dependent on national S&T systems. There is little evidence of market failures which would warrant state support to national shipbuilding; nor can the lack of absorptive capacity justify direct support to local or national production networks.

The specific *institutional aspects* play a role in shipyard restructuring: the financial conditions where large sums of cash flow are needed, have made it difficult for post-socialist yards to begin production from scratch; high investment rates, weak banks and underdeveloped financial markets added to the dilemma. Privatization and strengthened corporate governance seem to have accelerated restructuring. Little effect can be expected from the continued state support to vertical integration, which is high on the policy agenda: Polish yards have integrated international supplier and downstream networks (shipping companies, finance) and are competing successfully on international markets. Neither technology nor financing seem to be limiting factors to enterprises' success any longer. By contrast, Russian and Ukrainian yards are for the time being blocked in their enterprization by the institutional framework (such as non-monetized economies, rigidities of local labor markets and unstable legal conditions), leading to high costs and low international competitiveness. Import tariffs for equipment and local-content obligations should be abandoned: they reduce the competitiveness of domestic shipyards rather than support. An acceleration of the enterprization process is needed if shipbuilding is to have a future. A diversification from low- to medium-complexity ships seems to be necessary, as the competitiveness of Eastern European yards in the low-complexity segment is at risk.

The prospects for shipbuilding in Eastern Europe and the CIS are good, though this does not apply to all shipyards equally. The example of Poland, which emerged as the fifth-largest shipbuilding country worldwide shows that the 'potential' can be put to work once the external conditions to restructuring become favorable. Last but not least, the Eastern European countries may even have a unique opportunity to set a standard for the Western shipbuilding industry: whereas shipbuilding is a heavily subsidized activity in *all* Western producing countries around the world, Eastern European countries may be able to show that shipbuilding is not *per se* an unprofitable business.

ABBREVIATIONS

AWES	Association of Western European Shipbuilders
CGT	Compensated gross tons
DWT	Dead weight tons
GT	Gross tons
HCS	High-complexity ships
LCS	Low-complexity ships
MCS	Medium-complexity ships
TEU	Tonnage equivalent unit

BIBLIOGRAPHY

Arthur D. Little (1993), 'Der Einfluß der japanischen und der südkoreanischen Schiffbaupolitik aud die internationale Wettbewerbsfähigkeit der westdeutschen Werftindustrie', Gutachten im Auftrag des Bundesministers für Wirtschaft, Berlin.

Association of Western European Shipbuilders (AWES) (various issues), Annual Reports.

Bitzer, Jürgen and Christian von Hirschhausen (1997), 'The Shipbuilding Industry in East and West: Industry Dynamics, Science and Technology Policies and Emerging Patterns of Co-operation', DIW Discussion Papers (151), Berlin.

Böhme, Hans (1997), 'Weltseeverkehr: Das Tonnagenangebot bleibt marktbestimmend', *Kieler Diskussionsbeiträge*, Institut für Weltwirtschaft Kiel (299/300) Kiel.

Borla, Andrea L. (1995), *Globale Wettbewerbsstrategien für die deutsche Schiffbauindustrie*, St. Gallen: University of St. Gallen

Bundesstelle für Außenhandelsinformationen (BfAI) (1995), *Markt in Kürze: Rußland Schiffbau*, Köln: BfAI.

Europäische Kommission (1995), 'Bericht der Kommision über den Stand der Schiffbauindustrie in der Europäischen Union', Stand 1993, in Kommision der Europäischen Union, Bericht der Kommision, KOM (95) 38, final version, Brüssel.

Europäische Kommission (1998), *Panorama of European Industry*, Luxemburg.

European Commission (1990), 'Council Directive of 21 December 1990 on Aid to Shipbuilding (90/684/EEC)', *Official Journal of the European Communities* (L380), pp. 27–32.

Hirschhausen, Christian von (1996), 'Lessons from Five Years of Industrial Reform in Post-socialist Central and Eastern Europe', *DIW Quarterly Journal of Economic Research*, **65** (1), Berlin, pp. 44–56.

Jaszowski, Wladyslaw (1994), 'Schlüsselindustrie: Entwicklungstendenzen der polnischen Schiffbauindustrie', *Schiff & Hafen*, **46** (8), pp. 19–34.

Johnson, Simon, David T. Kotchen and Gary Loveman (1995), 'How One Polish Shipyard Became a Market Competitor', *Harvard Business Review*, **6**, pp. 53–72.

Kurth, Wilhelm (1995a), 'The Shipbuilding Market in the Years Ahead', *HANSA – Schiffahrt – Schiffbau – Hafen*, **132** (7), pp. 6–8.

Kurth, Wilhelm (1995b), 'An Agreement on Shipbuilding', *OECD Observer*, (192), Paris, pp. 44–6.

Lloyd's Register of Shipping (various issues), World Fleet Statistics.

Lloyd's Register of Shipping (various issues), World Shipbuilding Statistics.

Organization for Economic Cooperation and Development (OECD) (1995a), 'The Polish Shipbuilding Industry: Present Condition and Development Perspectives', Council Working Party on Shipbuilding, unpublished papers, (C/WP6(95)4), Paris.

Organization for Economic Cooperation and Development (OECD) (1995b), 'The Romanian Shipbuilding Industry, Working Party on Shipbuilding', unpublished papers, (C/WP6(95)22), Paris.

Organization for Economic Cooperation and Development (OECD) (1995c), 'The Shipbuilding Industry in Russia and the Ukraine, Council Working Party on Shipbuilding', unpublished papers, (C/WP6(95)2), Paris.

Organization for Economic Cooperation and Development (OECD) (1996), 'Outward Co-operation of OECD Shipyards', Working Party on Shipbuilding, unpublished papers, (C/WP6(96)3), Paris.

Repetzki, B. (1996), 'Strukturwandel in Polens Schiffbau ungewiß', Nachrichten für Außenhandel, April 10, 1996.

Röller, Lars-Hendrik and Christian von Hirschhausen (1996), 'State Aid, Industrial Restructuring and Privatization in the New German Länder: Competition Policy with Case Studies of the Shipbuilding and Synthetic Fibres Industries', WZB Discussion Papers (FS IV 96-13), Berlin.

Ruwe, Hans Friedrich (1995), 'Rußland, Schiffbau', in Bundesstelle für Außenhandelsinformationen (BfAI), Markt in Kürze, Bd. 4435.

Verband für Schiffbau und Meerestechnik e.V. (VSM) (various issues), Jahresbericht.

Witte, Philipp (1995), 'Kernfähigkeit und Diversifikation: Probleme, Lösungsansätze und Handlungsempfehlungen untersucht am Beispiel der Werftindustrie', Dissertation, No. 1763, St. Gallen: University of St. Gallen.

7 Food Processing in Western and Eastern Europe: From Supply-driven Towards Demand-driven Progress

Nick von Tunzelmann and
Frédérique Charpiot-Michaud

1. INTRODUCTION

Food processing is often overlooked as a major segment of manufacturing industry in the West. It is largely ignored in accounts of industrialization for most countries, it is seen as rather traditional and backward looking, and it is rarely investigated as having possibilities for spearheading industrial change in an era of glamorous high-tech industries. On the supply side, its resources are finite and subject to diminishing returns (for example, in agriculture and so on) and its technologies are conservative. On the demand side, it tends to be written off as having restricted possibilities thanks to 'Engel's law', which proposes that the income elasticity of demand for food is low, and that consumers will shift their budgets away to spending on other goods and services as development proceeds.

Such perspectives do the industry little justice. Closer assessment of the historical experience would show that it has been central to the industrialization of a number of now advanced countries, particularly some smaller ones (for example, Switzerland and Denmark). Moreover, it would show that, despite the long history of the industry, it continues to evolve and to provide some impetus for growth. As we shall show below, it stands on the threshold of a new lease of life, in which possibilities drawn from the high-tech industries have the potential to promote a new wave of expansion in the industry. More surprisingly, perhaps, the nature of demand for its products is in the midst of dramatic change in advanced (high-income) countries, to the extent that the writing-off of its prospects may have been premature.

These issues are studied in the present chapter. Our basic finding is that branches of food processing in the CEECs are having to aim at a 'moving target': although there is some indication of a shift from a supply-driven towards a more demand-driven system in Eastern Europe, the industry in the West has at the same time shifted even further towards a demand-driven system, so the gap may even be increasing. Food processing does nevertheless offer some prospects as a route to development for many of the CEECs, but increasingly this may become contingent on resolving what we call the 'network failures', originating in socialist production and still endemic in the post-socialist system of production in the industry. The alternative is to become increasingly dependent on the West, either for imports or for production by subsidiaries of multinational companies (MNCs).

2. COMPARISONS OF THE FOOD-PROCESSING INDUSTRY, CAPITALIST AND SOCIALIST[113]

2.1 Scale and Competitiveness of the Industry

The scale of the industry even in advanced countries is a primary reason why it deserves further attention. It is in fact one of the largest of the secondary industries (that is, manufacturing) even in the advanced countries, if measured by output or employment at the SIC 2-digit level (food, drink and tobacco grouped together). Table 7.1 gives data from the World Bank on the share in value added in all manufacturing. It can be seen that in Western countries, its share ranges from about one-tenth to one-quarter of the total value added in manufacturing. There is little indication of an impact from Engel's law over the period from the beginning of the 1980s to the mid-1990s; indeed there are more cases of increase of share over this period than decrease. The shares are typically higher still in Eastern Europe and again, even allowing for miscounting of the limited 1980 figures, there is no sign of substantial decline. Furthermore, the industry is crucial for employment: in 1993, it employed over 2.3 million people in Western Europe. Governments can thus scarcely afford to overlook such a major contributor to the generation of income and employment.

---

[113] The discussion of the Western European industry in this section draws extensively on Christensen et al. (1996), especially the contributions of von Tunzelmann to that report.

Table 7.1 Percentage contribution of food, drink and tobacco to total value added in manufacturing, 1980, 1994 and 1995, Western and Eastern Europe

Country (Western Europe)	1980 %	1994 %	1995 %	Country (Eastern Europe)	1980 %	1994 %	1995 %
Austria	16	17	15	Bulgaria	–	20	19
Belgium	17	17	18	Croatia	–	24	–
Denmark	24	23	–	Hungary	11	21	21
Finland	12	13	11	Latvia	–	–	39
France	13	15	14	Macedonia	–	29	24
Greece	18	27	28	Poland	12	31	31
Ireland	28	27	25	Romania	–	22	27
Italy	9	10	10	Russia F.	–	20	17
Netherlands	23	24	24	Slovak R.	–	–	13
Norway	15	23	23	Slovenia	–	18	15
Portugal	13	–	15				
Spain	16	19	18				
Sweden	10	10	9				
Switzld	–	10	10				
UK	13	14	14				

Source: World Bank (1997 and 1998).

This need to attend to the progress of the food-processing industry is acute in Western Europe, which produces about one-third of the world total (Charpiot-Michaud 1998a, p. 5), and where the industry is one of the region's major sources of comparative advantage. Davies and Lyons (1996) assess sectoral differences in comparative advantage across the 'Triad' of Europe, North America and Japan, as set out in Table 7.2. Most of the effort in Western European innovation programs and the like has gone into the high-tech activities, yet as Table 7.2 shows, high-tech industries are, by and large, an area of comparative disadvantage for this region. It is the food industry which represents its clearest comparative advantage. The reasons for this will be considered further when we turn to the organization of the industry. It may also be noted that the industry is a comparatively profitable one for Western Europe. In 1993, when the world was beginning to recover from the depression of the early 1990s, the profit/turnover ratio of the industry was 7.7 percent, as compared with 5.3 percent in the much-favored chemical industry and 4.7 percent in automobiles. The industry, with its relatively consistent demand patterns, tends to have a stabilizing effect on the business cycle.

Table 7.2 Comparative production structures in the 'Triad', 1988–1989

Sectors in %	EU	N. America	Japan
Food, drink & tobacco	16.6	14.9	11.4
Chemicals	14.5	13.2	11.3
Engineering	21.4	22.6	32.0
Transport equipment	12.7	15.2	14.4
Minerals	3.9	2.6	3.6
Metals	12.9	11.0	11.7
Textiles & clothing	7.0	5.5	4.8
Wood, paper, printing	9.7	14.1	9.7
Rubber	1.1	1.0	1.1
Total	100*	100*	100

Note: * Rounded to 100.

Source: Davies and Lyons (1996, p. 14), based on UNCTAD data.

2.2 A 'Low-tech' Industry?

The large relative size of the industry makes its supply characteristics of serious practical concern. The disfavor with which it is met in many assessments of sectoral industrial policies for development arises in large part out of its supposedly 'low-tech' character. The OECD classifications of manufacturing sectors judge the level of sectoral technology according to two criteria: (i) their level of R&D activity, (ii) their purchases of high-tech intermediate goods. According to this schema, food processing comes out fairly and squarely in the low-tech stratum, with values of R&D intensity (that is, R&D relative to turnover) well below 1 percent (OECD 1995). However, the OECD itself has also pointed out that this may underestimate the valuable contribution the industry can make (OECD 1988).

Because of the structure of the industry and its relations with other (supplier) industries, to be discussed below, food-processing firms do not generally carry out much of their innovation 'in-house', and therefore relatively little in the form of R&D as usually measured for OECD purposes. Innovations in the industry have predominantly been process innovations, at least until recent times. These process innovations may take place in-house, that is, inside the firm, but rarely involve R&D of the conventional kind. As we shall see later, it is this area in which the CEE industry is conspicuously weak. Alternatively, the process technologies may be acquired from suppliers, in which case they ought to appear in the OECD's classification of intermediate technology purchases, but it seems likely that the OECD figures underestimate the knowledge flows represented by these supplier networks, because of reliance on (probably rather dubious) data on purchased hardware. Finally, the product innovations, which are becoming more numerous as we shall see below, involve much expenditure that is not covered by orthodox outlays on R&D. It has often been argued that the high advertising and marketing expenditures laid out by this industry ought to be regarded as tantamount to technology expenses in other industries, given the amount of product development they assist (Galizzi and Venturini 1996, p. 3). Such expenditures are very much 'in-house', and they can be regarded in part as equivalent to R&D in other sectors as being endogenously determined by corporate strategies (Davies and Lyons 1996; see the path-breaking work of Sutton 1991, 1998).

The EU's Community Innovation Survey (CIS) used questionnaires to firms to assess the number of firms that claimed to innovate. Innovations were divided between those that were new to the particular firm – which could include considerable imitation of other firms' innovations – and those that were new to the industry, more like the usual notion of innovation. According to the replies, between 31 percent (Italy) and 100 percent (Portugal) of the firms claimed to have been innovative in the former sense, that is, introducing innovations new to the firm, while between 15 percent (Italy) and 40 percent (Portugal) of firms claimed to be innovative in the second, narrower sense. Obviously there is a high degree of doubt about relying on the firms' own assessments, and the figures for Portugal are suspiciously high. Moreover, there were big differences in coverage in this first CIS survey, with that in Italy being easily the broadest – hence accounting for the apparently lower innovativeness of Italian firms.[114] When compared with other industries, which no doubt suffered from similar limitations of data quality, food processing does not emerge as conspicuously non-innovative, at least when the conspicuously high-tech sectors are excluded. In terms of outcomes, both labor productivity and turnover have been rising sharply in Western Europe, despite the low R&D (Charpiot-Michaud 1998a, p. 5).

The supposed backwardness of food processing is harder still to reconcile with its recent permeation by advanced technologies, such as biotechnology, pharmaceuticals, instrumentation, advanced materials and other high-tech

---

[114] The second CIS survey, currently in progress, has achieved much wider coverage and its forthcoming results should be much more reliable.

activities. The nature of this prospectively dramatic shift of direction will be examined below, after we have first recounted the nature of the organization of the industry, to put it in context.

2.3 Organization

The food-processing industry has been characterized as a 'supplier-dominated' industry according to the much-used taxonomy of Pavitt (1984). This has rested on two foundations. One is its dependence on machinery, supplied to it by the mechanical engineering industry, from which it was clearly separated in organizational terms. In this respect, the industry conformed to the paradigm of manufacturing technology established in the 'First Industrial Revolution', of being mechanical (machinery based) in nature. So powerful has this paradigm been, that technology and machinery are often popularly equated with each other. The machinery paradigm, though added to by other technological paradigms in the Second Industrial Revolution of the late 19th century (the chemical, the electrical, the automotive, and so on), has continued to be important and even dominant until recent times (Patel and Pavitt 1994).

In organizational respects, the key point about the machinery paradigm is that the production of machinery remained distinct from the production of the products based on that machinery, such as processed food (or textiles, or vehicles, and so on). At an early stage, the machinery production 'spun off' upstream from the production of the goods and established a separate identity. In addition, the production of machine tools, that is, tools for the production of machinery, spun off upstream from the production of the machinery itself into separate firms (Rosenberg 1963). Thus, there arose a system of technology (physical capital) flows which was hierarchical but vertically disintegrated. This was true of the Soviet system of production, but it was almost equally so in most capitalist systems, in Western Europe or North America.

This meant that the food-processing industry, along with other such supplier-dominated industries, was externally dependent for its technological advances on what was supplied to it by the machinery industry. Technological change was removed, at least in organizational terms, from the scene of its applications. This had the advantage of encouraging horizontal spillovers of technological know-how within the mechanical engineering industry, so that producers of machinery for the food-processing industry benefitted from advances in machinery destined for quite different user industries. But it had the disadvantage of breeding a rather passive attitude to technology in the food-processing industry itself, and somewhat limited the amount of vertical feedback to its machinery suppliers. In this sense, a supplier-dominated perspective was accentuated.

The other 'supplier-dominated' dimension of consequence was that which came down the food chain from agriculture, acting as the raw material inputs into the processing industries. In capitalist countries, again a vertical division usually cut across the links between growers and processors. Here the power imbalance ran strongly the other way – farmers, at least of staple crops, were typically small producers in competitive conditions, whilst processors were often large producers in oligopolistic or even monopolistic market conditions. Farmers produced commodities which would be graded for quality by independent assessments or by the purchasers themselves, whereas food-processing companies aimed to produce branded products in which the brand name was intended to act as differentiating the product in the eyes of final consumers. In cash crops, the processors, whose productive contribution might be rather minimal (for example, in bananas), could integrate backwards into their agricultural suppliers by buying up plantations and so on. Food-processing firms were often to be found among the earliest examples of divisionalized hierarchical corporations (Chandler 1990), and the prevailing trend now in Western Europe seems to be towards growing concentration of the large firms amidst a fringe of numerous small ones (Charpiot-Michaud 1998a, p. 10).

Under centrally-planned socialism, the situation was, however, normally different from this. With the collectivization of agriculture in most (though not all) socialist countries, together with 'scissors' crises in agricultural prices and similar eventualities (which were often the motivation for collectivization), agriculture ceased to be competitively organized. It is not for us to debate here the merits and demerits of agricultural collectivization, but it had substantial effects on the organization of food processing, which became largely subservient to agriculture in many of its staple branches (ibid., pp. 22–5). In other words, the imbalance of power which favored the manufacturing end in capitalist countries, instead favored the agricultural end in collectivized socialist countries.

Rather more precisely, the food-processing industry in centrally-planned economies more generally tended to split into two parts – an 'upstream' part driven in this way by its suppliers of materials, and another more 'downstream' part that related to products other than staple foodstuffs. The latter segment, applying to tobacco products and many beverages as well as to non-staple foodstuffs such as sugar, was typically organized as a state-owned monopoly or oligopoly. Here the direct or sometimes indirect influence of the centralized state protected the power of the processors, though not necessarily in the best interests of consumers.

Neither branch managed to establish itself as a nucleus for innovation in the socialist system of production. The 'upstream' branch tended to remain under the thumb of agriculture and was essentially an appendage to agricultural production. In the state-monopolized 'downstream' branch, distribution tended to take precedence over innovation. A stagnating, supply-driven industry was left to be revitalized primarily by the inflow of foreign technology following transition.

In a number of Western countries, the suppliers of either kind no longer dominate food manufacturing. Instead the balance of power has shifted well downstream to the retailers. In countries like the UK, the oligopolistic supermarket chains now effectively dominate the whole food supply chain, to the point where they have supplanted the processors in directly controlling even the growing phase in agriculture (Senker 1988; Galizzi and Venturini 1996, chs 3, 5; Dumonteil 1997; Charpiot-Michaud 1998a, pp. 12, 19). This is a reflection of the way in which the Western industry has shifted from being supplier dominated to being demand driven. To see this more broadly, we therefore turn to developments in the West before coming back to the prospects in the CEECs.

3. INNOVATION IN WESTERN COUNTRIES

We have briefly mentioned the wide range of new technologies currently being applied to food processing in the advanced Western countries – among them biotechnology and pharmaceuticals, electronics and advanced instrumentation and advanced and smart materials – in other words, all of the major new paradigms of technological advance in the West. In this section we show how this represents the confluence of science-based and process innovation on the supply side, and product innovation in all major fields on the demand side.

3.1 Scientific Advance

The food-processing industry had a long tradition in the West of solving its problems mainly by empirical means. If any science was involved, and often it was somewhat minimal, it tended to happen after rather than before the technical changes, as in pasteurization leading microbiology, or refrigeration leading cryology. From an early stage, attempts were made to increase the scientific content of food production, but mostly these earned a bad reputation. Food science (often known as 'domestic science') was seen as a 'soft' subject for women to study, in an era in which it was believed that women's brains should not be overtaxed. It shied away from developing *a priori* methods of scientific investigation in fields such as those just noted, on the grounds that this was too 'hard'. But nowadays it has come to be accepted by most that the science required is essential to developments in food technology, and that it is indeed 'hard' and exacting science that is required. Moreover, in order to be applied practically to the circumstances of the food industry, it needs to be multidisciplinary in approach, which further increases its complexity. The following illustrations give a brief outline of examples of this new food-related science.

1. *Mathematics*. Predictive modeling in areas such as microbiology and contamination has been going on for over 60 years. The poor performance of these models in practice, as shown up for instance in underestimating outbreaks of food poisoning or the consequences of Chernobyl, have led to models encompassing a much wider range of variables, requiring more advanced mathematics (for example, computational fluid dynamics) and multivariate statistics. The inherently complex nature of the food being modeled adds to the difficulty of the procedures.
2. *Computer science*. For real-time analysis, interpretation of data as used, for example, in spectroscopy requires very fast computing power, but with modern computers this is becoming feasible. Computer science in the form of linking databases remains a key problem even with networked computing systems, and software remains a critical bottleneck. The inherent 'fuzziness' of food data favors learning-oriented software systems such as in neural networks.
3. *Physics*. Basic processes in food manufacturing are heavily dependent on understanding the physics of heating and cooling. Fields such as optics and sonics are being developed in imaginative ways to deal with some of the more intractable problems of the industry. New areas such as irradiation of food to destroy bacteria have been developed, but their use remains costly and rather controversial (Galizzi and Venturini 1996, ch. 2).
4. *Chemistry*. Chemistry has traditionally been the dominant science in the food-processing industry, especially in applying wet chemistry to food analysis. The pharmaceutical industry has become a major source of safe reagents for chemical means of modifying proteins, and in general the pharmaceutical industry continues to be the first port of call for problems arising in food production.
5. *Biotechnology*. In recent years, attention has switched to biological rather than chemical means of modification. The food industry has been the main location of simple biotechnology since time immemorial (baking, brewing, and so on), but it is the potential of latest-generation biotechnologies

which has attracted most attention. The first enzyme products from genetically engineered organisms entered the market in 1989. Protein engineering, at the heart of recent developments in biotechnology, appears an especially attractive prospect, for example, in replacing purification techniques, but much remains to be discovered of the basic science itself. Biotechnology has now become the most controversial of all the sciences for consumers and for regulators of the food industry.

As we shall see, much of this science continues to be developed upstream from food manufacturing itself. But the industry needs extensive understanding of what is developing, because it faces an increasing multiplicity of techniques for helping to solve its problems. In many circumstances it is compelled to choose from among these techniques; for example, the modification of milk to produce healthier butter can now be undertaken alternatively by physical means, by chemical means, by biotechnological means, or by agricultural means (changing what is fed to the cows). These methods have to be brought together, and the user needs to be able to draw comparisons. This also highlights the urgency of the need to develop networks of communication, which ought to run horizontally as well as vertically. Past links between, say, nutritionists and toxicologists have been poor even in advanced countries.

3.2 Process Innovation

Aside from understanding the techniques, they achieve little unless they are carefully integrated into the production process. The basic processes of heating and cooling are being fundamentally transformed by these scientific and technological advances in best-practice operations. Examples of some key operations include the following.

1. *Cooking*. Here the main objectives are to shorten the process and to increase its flexibility (adaptability to different products). High-temperature short-time (HTST) processing is coupled with the development of ultra-high-temperature (UHT) processes and products, such as long-life milk. In using microwaves and similar methods in industry, great care has to be exercised to get the right balance between too short an exposure (which would fail to destroy bacteria) and too long (which would harm product quality). A major shift in methods for cereals, snacks, and so on has been from rotary ovens to extruders, which greatly increase the speed (pass-through time is typically 30 to 90 seconds) and permit continuous rather than batch processing, all in a smaller area. The

shift from single-screw to twin-screw extruders allows 'co-extrusion', permitting combinations of ingredients (for example, in convenience foods). Because the extruder can conduct a range of other processes (such as grinding, mixing, compressing, sterilizing, deodorizing, texturing, drying and cutting), the flexibility permits economies of scope as well as dynamic economies of scale. The question of such adaptability is nowadays seen as more crucial than that of time-saving.

2. *Freezing*. As with cooking, the basic objectives in improving processing are economies of time and space, reliability and flexibility. Very rapid freezing techniques (cryogenics) have been employed for certain purposes, such as 'crust freezing', but require exceptional care in monitoring the process. The main issue has been the switch from frozen to chilled products, in response to shifts in consumer demand, as these methods require continuous monitoring, right up to the point of final sale.

3. *Production integration*. Aside from the individual processes, their overall integration remains a major difficulty. With the combined ingredients behaving very differently under the various processes to which they are subjected, sophisticated methods are being developed for early extraction and later recombination into the product (for example, in brewing a common method is to process a bland 'base beer' and add bitterness, hop aroma, color and foam only at the end of the processing). The complexity of the material being processed meant that early information technology (IT)-based methods were inadequate. Although modern microprocessors and computerization have the potential capacity, the development of sensors has lagged behind. Advanced instrumentation such as both low-intensity and high-intensity ultrasonics can be borrowed from other industries, but their application to food still requires much 'art' as well as 'science'.

4. *Packaging*. Advances in packaging are as diverse as those in the core production processes. Packaging has moved from being an afterthought to being a driving force for innovation. Most technologically demanding have been the requirements for chilled foods and ready meals, which can involve the use of smart materials (for example, susceptor packaging to react to the heat treatment), and more commonly controlled or modified atmosphere packaging (combatting oxidization within the package). The packaging of liquids and semi-liquids has moved away from the tin can and the glass bottle to a range of plastic and other materials.

Process technology is in the midst of a change from being driven mostly by supply factors, such as reducing costs, to being driven more by demand factors, especially increased variety of products. This has implied a shift away from a vertically downward flow of technology from the machinery suppliers to a vertically upward flow from consumer demands. Automation is shifting from the machinery to the product itself, which involves closely coupling process innovation to product innovation. It is such process technologies and their coupling with product innovation that domestic producers in the CEECs seem to have found hardest to grasp.

3.3 Product Innovation

The new demand-led orientation of the industry has meant replacing the old conservatism about product changes, derived from stable loyalties to brand names, with new pressures for product innovation. Again, these cover the full spectrum of possibilities, as follows.

1. *New products*. This in turn covers a range of changes:

- more exotic foods, particularly in ready-made dishes;
- more prepared foods (especially the rise of ready meals, chilled foods *and* 'ambient products' such as sauces, for example, in foods for microwaving);
- more casual foods (snacks and so on);
- healthier foods (low-calorie and low-fat foods, organically produced foods).

2. *New materials (ingredients)*. These include:

- substitution of 'natural' for 'artificial' ingredients (for example, replacing 'E-number' additives, searching for 'nature-identical' flavorings);
- replacing qualities lost by removing 'bad' ingredients (for example, protein alternatives to fats, alternatives to sugar).

3. *Quality and safety*. Given the obvious safety problems raised by infected foods, the control of quality right along the food chain should be an area of key concern. Contamination scandals even in advanced countries (such as the UK beef crisis) indicate the crucial importance of quality and safety control to sustaining production and exports. Food processors are only partly responsible for the deficiencies which remain evident, but the pressure is on to improve standards considerably. Traditional methods to test safety in-house in such firms usually involve 'wet chemistry', but these suffer from being both too slow (the results are not usually available until well after the tested product has been eaten) and too unreliable (samples

from the edges of food products may not reflect their centers). Methods of advanced instrumentation have been recruited from biomedical operations, including DNA assays, but need to become more user friendly for relatively unskilled workers and also less expensive. In any case, many aspects cannot be covered even by advanced instruments and are generally assessed by panels of experts (taste and so on). Regulatory standards are rising, both through the establishment of specifically responsible organizations and through trying to implement better manufacturing practices through ISO 9000 and other standards. As elsewhere, meeting rising demands for food quality involves competence in handling multiple techniques and approaches, and being able to achieve that in real time.

3.4 Demand Factors

Virtually all of the above-mentioned changes in processes have shifted away from being mainly supply driven (faster speeds, reduced costs, and so on) to being more consumer driven. For example, in packaging, the new processes are designed to meet consumer demands for (i) ease of use (for example, ring-pull cans and tear-strip openings), (ii) new eating habits (as for the ready-made meals), (iii) food safety (for example, avoiding the 'migration' of packaging into the product), (iv) environmental friendliness (for example, avoiding non-biodegradable and wasteful packaging). In those respects, the process changes have aligned with the product innovations just noted, as responses to shifting consumer demands.

The socio-economic ('lifestyle') sources of demand change can be itemized as follows:

1. Global competition among producers for market share, which has restructured tastes towards greater international homogeneity (for example, Coca-Cola, McDonald's) as well as increased competition for national producers.
2. Rising incomes and embourgeoisement of the social structure, involving diversification as well as homogenization of tastes ('love of variety', for example, demands for ethnic dishes), plus acquisition of associated consumer goods (for example, freezers, microwave ovens);
3. Rising employment of married women in the workforce, encouraging purchase of ready-made meals, once-weekly or after-hours shopping and so on.
4. Increased pressure and stress in life, resulting in resort to 'snacking', avoidance of long food preparation and cooking and so on;

5. Changing age distribution of populations, especially 'graying' demographic profiles (increasing demands for health foods, 'functional foods' and so on).
6. Demands for healthier lifestyles, encouraging search for healthier foods (as opposed to health foods), for example, low-calorie, low-fat, low-cholesterol or low-sodium foods.
7. Environmental pressures, especially affecting packaging.

Food manufacturers are to some extent caught between the Scylla of reducing additives, for example, and the Charybdis of increased risk of food contamination by micro-organisms. They cannot, however, escape the widening impact of these shifts in demand, and the consequent need to pursue innovations oriented downstream towards consumers rather than their old upstream reliance on suppliers.

4. FOOD PROCESSING IN THE CEECS UNDER TRANSITION

We have already noted how the transition economies inherited systems from centrally-planned socialism which reflected a dualistic organizational structure, with the dominance of agricultural suppliers in many of the upstream branches of food processing on the one hand, and that of state monopolies or oligopolies in many of the downstream branches on the other. Both were inadequate for meeting these new pressures for improvement and innovation coming from the demand side. To be sure, the levels of demand in the CEECs were well below those in the advanced Western countries in per capita terms, and gave a further breathing space from their fall in the early transition period.

However the pressures of demand could not be avoided completely, even while income per capita was low. For one thing, many of the CEECs were dependent in part on exports to maintain their agro-food sectors. With the collapse of the CMEA, and particularly the USSR (where parts of the Union had acted as specialized farms, for example, Estonia in pigs and milk), they were pushed into trying to export to Western countries to preserve this source of revenue. But there they found that the quality of the foods they produced limited them to narrow ranges of the market. The quality of the processed foods was in general far too low to meet Western standards, and that of agricultural products low enough that they could find niches only at the very bottom of Western markets. In effect, to reestablish themselves in exports they needed to raise the quality of their goods. Moreover, their own domestic markets were flooded by better Western products, so they could not even rely on falling back on the home market. All of this required concerted efforts on the part of both product and process development, in accord with, if not necessarily to the same levels as the developing Western standards described above.

4.1 Problems in Transition

Food processing was one of the worst-performing industries in the CEECs in the early years of transition, because of a lack of resources and the presence of obsolete physical assets and processes (Duponcel 1998, p. 14). It had to look abroad to break out of the deadlock imposed by past weaknesses and present disintegration of demand.

In the upstream branches of the sector, the former agricultural state enterprises (now privatized) and cooperatives withdrew from their previous role as system integrators. Problems within agriculture were serious enough without taking on the added burdens of sectors such as processing, technological development and non-food operations for which they had previously been responsible. Enterprise development destroyed many of the old vertical relationships (Charpiot-Michaud 1998a, pp. 25–6).

In the downstream branches, the former state-owned enterprises (SOEs) had for the most part performed poorly, suffering from overconcentration and limited competition, paying little attention to prices and costs, having few incentives for innovation, underinvesting, being harried by administrative interference and so on. Just prior to transition, in the late 1980s, some 75 percent of Hungarian food production came from 138 large SOEs, and about 80 percent of Polish production from 196 of them (Duponcel 1998, p. 21).

4.2 Changes in Organization

Privatization and the varied forms it has taken are too large a subject for us to be able to do more than treat superficially here. The extent of success of privatization as a means of curing the economic ills remains highly controversial. The ways in which privatization has panned out in the wake of the various rounds are, however, of crucial importance to us. In some countries, it has still made only limited headway, most obviously in the CIS countries as compared with the EU 'accession countries' (Bitzer and Hirschhausen 1998; Charpiot-Michaud 1998a, pp. 33–4). From what has been said above, a key issue has been the control from upstream, downstream and outside exercised by the new forms of ownership and governance.

From the upstream side, efforts were made in many of the CEECs to reassert the role of agricultural producers and cooperatives in the privatized food manufacturers (Hungary was an important exception to this strategy). Although this appeared to be in line with stakeholder interests passing down the food supply chain, it does not seem to have been a particularly successful strategy in those countries in which it has been studied. It remains significant primarily in a few of the upstream branches of processing, such as milk, where locational issues (like transportability and perishability) plus technological issues (the levels of technological sophistication or their absence), tend to favor it. Accordingly, the pattern seemed to be shifting to a more Western one of arm's-length relationships along the food chain.

4.3 The Role of FDI

One possible reason for the low impact of agriculture on food production was that FDI did not favor joining ownership structures in which local cooperatives played a big part, for example, in countries like Estonia (Duponcel 1998; see also Table 7.3 below). Contrary to most expectations, the industry – or at least some of its branches – did, however, prove attractive to inflows of FDI, at least in certain countries, although agriculture did not. Table 7.4 shows a rather diversified impact by branch, though differing across the three countries considered.

Table 7.3 Percentage share of foreign investments in agriculture and food in Hungary and Poland

	Hungary		Poland	
Year	Agriculture	Food	Agriculture	Food
1992	7.1	19.3	n.a.	n.a.
1993	1.2	16.6	n.a.	n.a.
1994	1.2	16.0	0.3	28.7
1995	1.2	12.1	0.3	17.5

Source: Charpiot-Michaud (1998b, p. 6), based on OECD data.

The assumption that FDI would not be attracted to food was based on the belief that low processing costs would be the main inducement to such FDI, but these low costs would have to be set against low efficiency and quality. The latter indeed proved correct, but low costs turned out not to be the main inducement. The main motivation for this FDI appears quite clearly to have been to obtain market share (Duponcel 1998, p. 15; Charpiot-Michaud 1998b, p. 7) to annex firm and assured markets, often with the added barrier of import protection.[115] This explains its particular attraction to the larger or relatively wealthier Eastern countries.

FDI was usually directed at particular branches (see Table 7.4), generally avoiding the old export-oriented activities where the cost factors might have been important but market vulnerability was high and market structure indeterminate, and favoring branded products and the old state monopolies, in which control of the market was greatest (Duponcel 1998, p. 17).

Table 7.4 FDI in the Czech Republic, Hungary and Poland, 1990–1996 (in million USD)

Branch	Czech Republic	Hungary	Poland
Meat	–	–	8
Ready-made meals	4	10	28
Dairy	–	152	90
Ice cream	–	10	38
Flour, bread and pasta	–	22	75
Biscuits and cakes	35	–	30
Potato products	3	–	35
Snacks	–	20	–
Sugar	23	91	30
Confectionery	–	82	186
Vegetable oil	–	–	25
Margarine	32	–	–
Fruit and vegetables	–	230	28
Tobacco	–	32	227
Soft drinks	–	22	60
Coffee	–	8	27
Beer	14	22	6
Wines and spirits	–	102	–
Total	111	803	893
Per capita food FDI	10.65	78.04	23.12

Source: Duponcel (1998, p. 17).

---

[115] This was not the case in Estonia, where a free-trade policy was pursued, but Estonia was attractive in any case for its proximity to the Russian market.

In some cases, FDI helped launch new product areas, for example, in baby foods, mineral water and ice cream (Charpiot-Michaud 1998a, p. 31), and it is evidently still the main source of product and quality innovation of the kinds taken further in Western countries (Charpiot-Michaud 1998c, pp. 5, 8). But its contribution to improving indigenous technological standards, for instance towards product diversity, is as yet unclear.

4.4 Market Structure and Technology

The impact of FDI was not limited to the direct repercussions of more efficient foreign-based suppliers, as there were spillover effects on domestic suppliers, through heightened competition. On the other hand, to the extent that FDI grabbed market share, it could alternatively lead to increased concentration. The effects thus varied between branches of the industry and across countries. FDI in Hungary appears to have increased monopolization in branches such as sugar and vegetable oil, and decreased in others such as cigarettes, soft drinks and confectionery.

Overall, there appears to have been a significant decline in concentration since the socialist era, but some branches have shown significant reconcentration. Some of the latter, such as Czech beer-brewing, reflect strong domestic capabilities; others, such as biscuits in Hungary, the impact of foreign MNCs (Duponcel 1998). There is no convincing evidence as yet, either way, as to whether changes in concentration and competition have increased efficiency significantly.

The downstream branches of the industry have been restructured more intensively than most of the upstream branches, under the impact of FDI and so forth, as described above. There is an urgent need for increased standards of food quality and safety all along the food chain, in order to retain or increase market shares both at home and abroad. This will be exacerbated by accession of the chosen countries to the EU, which will self-evidently intensify competition. At the same time, the awarding of EU licenses may be expected to upgrade standards, and this is particularly necessary in upstream branches such as dairy and meat products. Such improvements require the attention to product and process improvement being addressed in the Western industry, as described in Section 3 above.

4.5 Network Failure

Bitzer and Hirschhausen (1998) show the complete lack of continuity between the former, top-down socialist S&T system and the new one beginning to emerge in bottom-up fashion from the evolution of enterprises ('enterprization'). In this view, the former national systems of innovation are irrelevant to the new requirements, which need to be market oriented. These authors reject the view that the former run 'deeper' than the new foreign-led networks, which are often alleged to be 'shallower', in arguing that both are rather shallow in view of the disconnectedness of the old systems. The extent of depth or shallowness is a controversial one, and the subject is still open to further investigation.[116]

The policy implication is what to rely upon for industrial development, in this instance of the food-processing industry. Bitzer and Hirschhausen argue that the view that existing stocks of human capital, in the form of large numbers of highly trained people, represent 'potential' for redevelopment is too facile. According to them, it is the realities of actual competition rather than starry-eyed views of a new 'Silicon Valley' that should weigh upon policy-makers.

Their argument is a powerful one. However it could also be said that, in our industry, the target of competition is a moving one. The Western industry, in this old 'low-tech' sector, is shifting rapidly towards high-tech methods and products, in the ways we have described. This leaves the industry in the East either retreating into the remaining 'low-tech' niches, or instead trying to imitate the up-market shift of the Western industry.

In our view, persevering with existing low standards and encountering diminishing market niches ought not to be considered as a serious option for the CEECs. We thus see little effective alternative to adapting the food manufacturing sector in the East towards higher-tech operations. Where we do agree with the Bitzer–Hirschhausen view is in seeing the existing 'potential' as inadequate in itself for achieving this.

Our detailing of Western developments showed that the areas of scientific advance include those in which the CEECs have a particularly high reputation, such as mathematics and physics. However it also includes fields such as biotechnology, in which its record is considerably poorer. Nevertheless, the growing needs of the industry for highly skilled scientists ought to be a 'potential' for future CEEC comparative advantage in at least some of these activities.

The major disadvantage of the old Eastern systems is that which results from the shift in the West to demand-driven production and innovation. This has proved difficult enough for Western countries, despite their long history of market-based competition. It is evidently more difficult still for the rarefied, top-down, military-oriented research systems in the CEECs. We agree totally with the Bitzer–Hirschhausen view that emerging S&T systems

---

[116] Slavo Radosevic and a group from SPRU, including the present author, have been awarded a UK ESRC grant to re-examine this issue.

in the East must be market driven, and our industry of choice shows this all too clearly. We therefore see a severe breakdown, even a schism, between the scientific 'potential' and the new scientific need for applications.

This schism can be described as 'network failure'. It results from the basic deficiencies of the old Soviet system for S&T, which treated technology as a question of 'information' rather than of 'knowledge', and hence adopted the principle of division of labor to locate it far away from the operation of production (von Tunzelmann 1995, ch. 9). The outpouring of modern work on innovation studies shows that technology is in practice mostly about 'knowledge', including uncodified tacit knowledge, and this needs to be accumulated in user firms adopting the technology as well as in supplier firms responsible for producing it. Bitzer and Hirschhausen (1998) point to the devaluation of the human capital 'potential' consequent on transition, and contrary to the initial expectations that this could form the foundation for new growth. The politically-imposed division of labor collapsed, including that in S&T systems (for example, in the Baltic countries, which had previously carried out much of the USSR's R&D in electrical engineering). Production and R&D now became further divorced thanks to the creation of new countries, which separated the two across new national boundaries.

The need is overwhelming to integrate production with technological development, which will mean not reverting to the old S&T systems and their vertical division of labor, but establishing a new demand-driven system similar to that described by Bitzer and Hirschhausen. The open question is whether the accumulated stock of human capital from the old system has any relevance to the new one. We, more optimistically than they, think that it might (not least because the cost of developing a new stock would be astronomical). They themselves point to some encouraging harnessing of such skills in new areas such as software (ibid. 1998, p. 37). We see the overwhelming need for a reorganization of networks in such ways as to realign existing stocks with emerging market-driven demands.

All of this may require major investments in building institutions and their interconnections. It will not come cheaply, or without serious social consequences. It is also deeply opposed by some of the architects of the new market-based economies, on the grounds that networks sound uncomfortably like the discredited cooperatives and collectives.[117] The fluid and flexible market-driven networks which are coming to dominate many areas of production in Western Europe and North America (see, for example, Best 1998) are, however, a far cry from the centrally-planned and stagnant collectives of Eastern days gone by.

---

[117] This view was frequently expressed to von Tunzelmann in interviews in Estonia in 1998.

5. CONCLUSION: CAN THE CEE INDUSTRIES BECOME DEMAND DRIVEN?

For the CEECs, the shift to being demand driven would involve a very 'big push'. A motivating force in Western countries is the growing power of consumers; voiced, however, not through the Adam Smith mechanism of the 'invisible hand' so much as the 'visible hand' of powerful retailers and others. Post-socialist countries have no past experience and little present strength to go in for organizing consumer voice. Although there is now a fierce struggle being waged for control of the food chain in countries like Hungary, the retail chains are less important in this than in Germany or the UK (Charpiot-Michaud 1998c, p. 7). Moreover, better vertical coordination of the producer networks in the West rests in part on the new technologies (such as biotechnologies) which allow greater exercise of control over production all along the chain (Galizzi and Venturini 1996, p. 7), but for countries lacking such technologies this is little encouragement. Furthermore, the attainment of reasonable standards of product acceptability for customers requires a close coupling of process with product innovation, and the transition economies have a weak record in process technologies, and even weaker in demand-driven process technologies. The CEECs require simultaneous development of both the technologies and the modes of organization, as well as of the marketing in which they are so deeply deficient.

However, we do not feel that the prospects for using food processing as a means to economic development in the CEECs are entirely dire. The most critical shortcoming is the poor quality of the product. The means adopted in Western countries to remedy such deficiencies are, however, similar to those that follow naturally from the surviving S&T systems in Eastern countries: namely technological development in laboratories and firms that are separated from the milieu of production. According to one survey, 72 percent of Western food-processing firms use external sources of innovation (Charpiot-Michaud 1998a, p. 13). In other words, like the failed Soviet system for S&T, the current Western system in this industry involves partly separating technological development from production. This is where the question of 'potential' is resurrected. Compared with possible rivals outside the advanced countries, the CEECs do possess acknowledged high-quality stocks of trained personnel, as a leading source of 'potential' comparative advantage.

The issue remains as to whether this potential can be harnessed to the needs of a modernizing industry. The deficiencies in this respect lie not just on the science side, for instance in the underdevelopment of biological and other such sciences, but also – and above all – on the network interactions between producer firms and the upstream technological institutes and contract research firms. This involves a fundamental reappraisal from seeing technology as information to seeing technology as knowledge, in which users as well as suppliers must participate. The development of markets has had its disadvantages as well as its advantages in this respect – it has promoted a flourishing of contract research institutes on the one side, which have become much more customer driven, but it has fostered arm's-length transactional relationships in place of continuing contact on the other.

Western firms depend on in-house capabilities to master the new technologies as well as external technology suppliers (Rama 1996). Domestic firms in the CEECs have undertaken some product diversification into the new fields we have detailed, but still lack the command of process control to produce adequate qualities of these products at viable prices (Charpiot-Michaud 1998c, p. 9). Also the networked links to local suppliers of technology have largely been bypassed by the reinvigoration of food processing in the CEECs emanating from FDI, but may need to be resuscitated (or in many cases activated for the first time) if branches of the industry are to achieve international and not just national success, or even not to wither in the face of foreign competition in the domestic markets.

REFERENCES

Best, M.H. (1998), 'Production Principles, Organizational Capabilities and Technology Management', in J. Michie and J. Grieve Smith (eds), *Globalization, Growth and Governance*, Oxford: Oxford University Press, pp. 13–29.

Bitzer, Jürgen and Christian von Hirschhausen (1998), 'Final Report – Work Package C, "Industrial Restructuring"', *TSER Project: Restructuring and Re-integration of Science & Technology Systems in Economies in Transition*, Berlin: DIW.

Chandler, A.D. jr (1990), *Scale and Scope: The Dynamics of Industrial Capitalism*, Cambridge, MA: Belknap Press.

Charpiot-Michaud, Frédérique (1998a), 'Restructuring the Food-processing Industry in Eastern Europe for International Competition: Final Summary Paper' (ed. by N. von Tunzelmann), Work Package C.3.1, *TSER Project: Restructuring and Re-integration of Science & Technology Systems in Economies in Transition*, Université de Paris-1: ROSES.

Charpiot-Michaud, Frédérique (1998b) 'The Food-processing Industry in Eastern Europe: a Sectoral Survey' (ed. by N von Tunzelmann), Work Package C.3.2, *TSER project: Restructuring and Re-integration of Science*

& *Technology Systems in Economies in Transition*, Université de Paris-1: ROSES.

Charpiot-Michaud, Frédérique (1998c), 'Case Study: Restructuring the Food-processing Industry (With Special Reference to S&T Policy) in Hungary' (ed. by N. von Tunzelmann), Work Package C.3.3, *TSER Project: Restructuring and Re-integration of Science & Technology Systems in Economies in Transition*, Université de Paris-1: ROSES.

Christensen, J.L., R. Rama and N. von Tunzelmann (1996), *Industry Studies of Innovation Using CIS Data: Study on Innovation in the European Food Products and Beverages Industry*, EC, Luxembourg: EIMS/SPRINT.

Davies, S. and B. Lyons (1996), *Industrial Organization in the European Union: Structure, Strategy, and the Competitive Mechanism*, Oxford: Clarendon Press.

Dumonteil, C. (1997), 'Agriculture and Environment: the Environmental Implications of the Changing Relations Between Supermarkets and Growers in the UK', DPhil thesis, SPRU, University of Sussex, UK.

Duponcel, M. (1998), 'Restructuring of Food Industries in the Five Central and Eastern European Front-runners Towards EU Membership (CEEC-5)', *Center for Economic Reform and Transformation (CERT) Discussion Paper*, (98/6), Heriot-Watt University, Edinburgh.

Galizzi, G and L. Venturini (eds) (1996), *Economics of Innovation: The Case of the Food Industry*, Heidelberg: Physica-Verlag.

Organization for Economic Cooperation and Development (OECD) (1988), *Industrial Revival through Technology*, Paris: OECD.

Organization for Economic Cooperation and Development (OECD) (1995), *Classification of High-technology Products and Industries*, Paris: OECD.

Patel, P. and K. Pavitt (1994), 'The Continuing, Widespread (and Neglected) Importance of Improvements in Mechanical Technologies', *Research Policy*, **23**, pp. 533–46.

Pavitt, Keith (1984), 'Sectoral Patterns of Technical Change: Towards a Taxonomy and a Theory', *Research Policy*, **13**, pp. 343–74.

Rama, R. (1996), 'Empirical Study on Sources of Innovation in the International Food and Beverage Industry', *Agribusiness*, **12**, pp. 123–34.

Rosenberg, N. (1963), 'Technological Change in the Machine Tool Industry, 1840–1910', *Journal of Economic History*, **23**, pp. 414–46.

Senker, J. (1988), *A Taste for Innovation: British supermarkets' influence on food manufacturers*, Bradford: Horton.

Sutton, J. (1991), *Sunk Costs and Market Structure*, Cambridge, MA: MIT Press.

Sutton, J. (1998), *Technology and Market Structure: Theory and History*, Cambridge, MA: MIT Press.

von Tunzelmann, G.N. (1995), *Technology and Industrial Progress: The Foundations of Economic Growth*, Aldershot, UK and Brookfield, USA: Edward Elgar.

World Bank (various issues), *World Development Indicators*, Washington, DC: World Bank.

8 Restructuring of the Telecommunications Sector in the West and the East and the Role of Science and Technology[118]

Jürgen Müller

1. INTRODUCTION

The telecommunications sector plays a crucial role in modern economies because it facilitates not only communication, but also trade, transactions and international specialization. Telecommunication services include not only simple voice telephony but also emerging multimedia services which allow the integration of data and image in either specialized or flexible multimedia networks and thus also cover the networks used for broadcasting (including satellite and cable TV networks) and the specialized networks for data communication.

In the *socialist* economies these telecommunication services and the underlying equipment sector were poorly developed, except for some special military applications. With the move to a decentralized, market-oriented system, the importance of telecommunications has grown. This is obvious not only because of the increased need to coordinate transactions between businesses nationally and internationally, but also to satisfy the fast-growing

[118] This chapter would not have been possible without the constant encouragement and support within the TSER team and especially its local Berlin members Jürgen Bitzer and Christian von Hirschhausen at the DIW, a place where I was myself able to conduct much of the background research for this study. Thanks are also due to the many experts in the equipment and service sector who have provided me with their own assessment of the development in the industry and have helped me to obtain access to industry data sources and commercial studies that are normally not easy to find. The final analysis is mine, however, so I remain responsible for any errors or misinterpretations of data or sector scenarios that others have shared with me.

demand of private households. At the same time the sector is undergoing fundamental changes, due to liberalization, privatization and globalization.

The aim of this chapter is to show how the restructuring process is being achieved in the service and equipment sector and what are its determinants. Among these, we focus specifically on the role the research and development institutions (science and technology systems, S&TSs) play and to what extent they are contributing to this process. The question of technology transfer both for the equipment industry and for the service sector will therefore have to be considered in greater detail, especially since the telecommunications sector has been much more advanced in Western countries, helped by rapid technical change on the one hand and market liberalization on the other. Further questions are can the restructuring process in the West serve as a model for the restructuring process of the enterprises in the post-socialist economies or will competition and industry structure evolve differently?

The convergence between telecommunications and data processing, the associated digitalization of services and the rapid globalization of the sector, first for equipment and more recently for services, has accelerated the speed of technical change in the industry. The competitive environment, in which the industry operates, and the associated legal and regulatory structure are crucial for the realization of this growing technology potential, as is the overall macroeconomic environment. However, this leads to a growing technology gap *vis-à-vis* countries that are still trying to complete this transformation process. Their difficult macroeconomic conditions increase the already large capacity gap with respect to their telecommunications infrastructure. As a consequence, financing policies and technology transfer, in addition to a liberal regulatory environment, become more crucial then S&TS policies, that is, to some extent the path of change also becomes demand driven – it is dictated by the overall investment into the telecommunications service sector and in turn by the resulting derived demand for telecommunications equipment. When considering the ongoing sectoral transformation in the post-socialist countries we therefore start with the following working hypothesis:

Limited growth and investment restricts the role of S&T policies, as the sector uses up only its current stock of network equipment.

This means that we have to look at aggregate demand for services as one of the major variables that drives technical change. The potential for change is limited if the sector is essentially stagnant and exists only from the current capital stock and technology basis. For the equipment sector, it is the derived demand that plays this role, except for equipment that is used along with services.

The form and product distribution of aggregate demand also has important implications, especially for the derived demand. This is reflected in our second working hypothesis:

Skewed demand for modern telecommunication services is oriented mostly towards imported technology from the West.

The first task therefore will be to analyze these overall market trends before being able to see how firms and scientific institutions have behaved in this changing framework and what role public policy plays.

We shall focus on Russia, the Baltics (particularly Latvia) and Hungary. These countries have all fundamentally reorganized the sector, but have adopted very different approaches. The policies pursued range from opening the market to dominant foreign investors, as in Latvia and Hungary, to a much more state-controlled approach in Russia. In addition, we also observe very different levels of aggregate demand for services in these countries, allowing us to look in greater detail at the effect the overall economic development has on progress and technology transfer in the telecommunications sector.

First we analyze the evolution and industry structure of the service and equipment sector in the West, in order to establish a reference model for sectoral transformation. Special attention is given to the major axis of competition, as well as to other determinants of sectoral change (Section 2). We then review the development of the sector during the previous socialist period (Section 3), before looking in detail at the three countries themselves (Section 4). The chapter concludes with an assessment of the lessons to be learned for the development of the sector in other post-socialist countries (Section 5).

2. THE GLOBAL TELECOMMUNICATIONS INDUSTRY AND ITS LINKS TO THE NATIONAL AND INTERNATIONAL S&TSs

2.1 The Products and their Markets in the Value-added Chain

We may divide the telecommunications sector broadly into the *equipment* sector and the *service* sector but they are all part of a larger vertical value-added chain. Figure 8.1 helps to give a perspective to the different vertical activities; it describes the increasing amount of value added at each higher level of the value-added chain in the sector, starting with components production at the bottom and ending with telecommunication and value-added services at the top. Each higher level in the vertical supply chain represents a larger amount of value added, thereby representing the figure of an inverted cone.

At the bottom of the hierarchical value-added chain we have the production of telecommunications equipment and components which are being assembled into telecommunications equipment or products. On the basis of these products, telecommunication networks can be constructed and serve as a basis for supplying telecommunication services. At the top of the hierarchy are value-added services (VAS) which use telecommunication networks as an important input for production. This vertical supply chain serves to illustrate two important points.

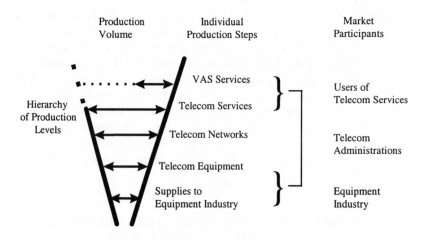

Figure 8.1 Hierarchical value-added chain of telecommunication markets

First, in order to produce telecommunication services efficiently, the different hierarchy levels of the vertical supply chain have to be integrated and interlinked effectively. For this reason some telecommunication companies were in the past almost completely vertically integrated (such as AT&T, providing both equipment and telecommunication services within one company). However, this traditional picture of the industry has changed gradually. With the emergence of many more service applications and business innovations in the different product groups, several platforms for products and different interfaces are being developed, which allow for the telecommunication services to be offered in different ways and with various product philosophies. A full vertical integration is no longer seen as a strategic advantage.

Second, as the use of information technology and telecommunications in the economy grows, the cone becomes larger, representing an increasing share of value added in the telecommunications sector in the overall economy, as it encompasses more and more activities. With the digitalization of telephone services and its convergence with the computer sector, telephony applications are increasing enormously. At the moment most of the telephone service applications are still in voice, but data, image and enhanced services, that is, those supported by 'intelligent network software' such as call forwarding, voice mail, teleconferencing, fax-store-and-forwarding and e-mail and so on are growing fast. An important role is played in this connection by new product providers which reconfigure the telecommunication products and provide them in a more user-friendly form (such as internet services, electronic commerce and so on) and help to push up the level of economic activity in the telecommunications service sector. This change is to some extent also demand driven, that is, dictated by the overall investment into the telecommunications service sector and in turn the resulting derived demand for telecommunications equipment.

This concept of the vertical supply chain, covering the products in the equipment sector and the services that they help to create, makes it easier to identify the individual markets in which the firms operate, and the links to the S&TS sector. While it is beyond the scope of this chapter to look at the determinants of the market structure in each submarket, and the detailed S&TS links that influence technical change, we shall try to identify them in the most important equipment and service markets. We start with an analysis of the major service sectors, to be followed by the equipment sectors.

2.2 Changing National and International Market Structure in the Service Sector

In the past, telephone services were organized either as national or as regional monopolies. Privately operated services were under close state regulation, but in general they were publicly owned activities, usually in the form of national PTT (Post, Telephony and Telegraph) ministries. With deregulation and liberalization of the telecommunications market this is changing rapidly.

Former state-owned companies became commercialized and privatized and entry by private companies is encouraged under the framework of a new regulatory structure. Nevertheless, the old industry form of dominant national telephone operators is still present in today's liberalizing telephony world. It looks at the moment as if most of the industry restructuring will take place through entry and different internal growth rates of the entrants compared to the incumbent, plus through alliances among existing national operators. The radical restructuring which has taken place in the USA with the help of governmental policy (divestiture of AT&T) is *less likely* to happen elsewhere in the world.

Some restructuring has nevertheless taken place through entry in the form of *mobile* service provision. In most countries mobile licenses were awarded to the traditional voice monopoly carrier (the wire line carrier) in addition to one or two other entrants. But in some countries, mobile licenses were awarded exclusively to new entrants, thereby bringing about much more rapid structural change.

The liberalization in some countries of some of their non-voice markets, mainly for non-reserved and mobile services, led to new international investment opportunities. These are increasingly taken up by all the important players in the market, but initially by those which were already private (like AT&T and British Telecom) or had already been commercialized (France Telecom, Deutsche Telekom and so on).[119] The full liberalization of these markets provides further investment opportunities. These resulted in strategic investments by some operators into foreign fixed linked markets (which were sometimes not yet liberalized) and to strategic alliances to provide more global service options.

2.3 Axis of Competition in the Service Sector

Service companies have no history of *downstream vertical* competition as usually they have had exclusive service territories. Where downstream competition has recently been allowed, namely for non-reserved services, the competition has been mainly of the quality type – usually more advanced services that were provided by new entrants from data processing rather than from the telecommunication firms.

The other area that has recently been liberalized, mobile services, also has had some quality competition. Initially the axis of competition was mainly through rebates for handsets or for large corporate customers. As the number of mobile licenses in each market increased, price competition developed

---

[119] See Elixmann (1996) for details.

more strongly. Important non-price parameters for competition are international roaming facilities, add-on services, number portability and so on.

In the past (in Europe up to the 1980s) when telephone companies encouraged national champions in the production of telecommunications equipment, there was also very little *upstream vertical* competition. Markets tended to be isolated by national procurement policies and standards. However, this is changing rapidly, as the market for telecommunications equipment too has become global. The vertical links or quasi-vertical links which existed between national network companies and national equipment manufacturers have more or less been broken, because of a significant shake-out in the equipment industry. Equipment manufacturers must now be credible suppliers to a number of customers, especially as the forces of competition are being felt by the service providers downstream. For them, access to crucial inputs like billing software or network optimization models can consequently yield an important competitive advantage. Keeping in mind the vertical value-added chain, we can see a direct link between the competition in the service market and the increased intensity of competition in the upstream equipment market.

Considering elements of *horizontal* competition, we have argued above that the service market is very much demand driven. Governmental regulation is important in allowing this demand to be matched by supply. If the regulatory environment provides for flexibility of entry for new competitors and as a consequence choice for the customer, then the greater is the ability of the customer and his or her service supplier to take advantage of the available technology and to improve it in an ongoing learning process. In a liberalized competitive network environment, the ways in which access to the network and interconnection for competing networks is regulated are therefore crucial. Access to capital and long-term finance is also a crucial parameter to help service providers meet emerging demand.

Competition in *international telephony* services, which is just beginning, had first centered on price competition, mainly to fill available network capacity and to utilize economies of density and scale. As this market matures and the international alliances are being formed, global presence and one-stop shopping also become important as elements of non-price competition. The ability to provide the latest transmission technology for corporate networks, with a focus on flexible bandwidth and higher speed of network delivery, is also seen as crucial to competition.

2.4 Axis of Competition in the Equipment Sector

Since in the past national buyers required specific *national* standards or specifications, it was difficult for foreign equipment suppliers to enter these markets, given the high adjustment cost (for the user and the producer) of moving from one type of technology or standard to another. On the other hand, some axes of horizontal competition, namely the exploitation of economies of scale and learning, allow an aggressive pricing policy to overcome company- or country-specific standards which act as a barrier to entry. However, as mentioned above, the equipment markets have opened up considerably after the vertical links between service providers and equipment suppliers were broken down. This globalized market of today is very different from that of the 'closed' national markets of the past, which were characterized by selective procurement and certification policy, incompatible standards between markets and 'input specificity'.

With the vertical forward linkage broken, other elements of competition in addition to those mentioned above are becoming important. One of them is the chance to offer full line services across a range of products like those provided by some of the large equipment suppliers. Thus, rather than relying on a number of different specialist suppliers for their network equipment, customers can now rely on one that offers one-stop shopping all the way to the provision of turnkey networks. Also important were supplier credits in markets where the service provider lacked access to financial resources or capital markets. Other instruments are after-sales service and the build-up of reputation and trademarks, especially in the mass market for terminal equipment.

In some countries, production location remains an important determinant of the current market structure, given the insistence of national governments on maintaining at least some technology base in such an advanced manufacturing sector as telecommunications equipment. For a long time we observed this not only in the form of high barriers to entry but also in high barriers to exit. But even as the economies of scale in the industry increased, it took a long time before national or multinational manufacturers were allowed to rationalize their production and to close some plants which could not provide all the necessary economies of scale and specialization in a given national market. Even today, some companies are forced to maintain a local production site in a given national market in order to supply it, even if it means higher production costs. This is also becoming the case in CEE countries, despite the fact that their markets are even smaller.

2.5 Sources of Innovation and the Role of S&TS Policies

In the past, the equipment producers and some of the central research laboratories of the network service providers, such as Bell Laboratories in the USA, CNET in France or FTZ in Germany, have provided the bulk of innovation in the national industry. Some new concepts came from universities as well, especially where these institutions are now becoming competitive in product-related R&D services to equipment suppliers. Also of increasing importance in R&D is the role of the upstream component providers, especially from the related fields of data processing and computer production.

The sources of innovation from the equipment industry have changed with the emergence of the global equipment market and the trend towards service competition. The backward linkage of the national service providers to the national manufacturers that has been so important in the past, through either vertical relations or quasi-vertical relationships through chosen national suppliers, has been drastically reduced. As a consequence, there is a greater *international* division of labor in R&D taking place. But the role of manufacturers and specialist component suppliers is stronger than before. They have become the driving force for technical change in the sector. Much of the product-related R&D is in-house and financed directly by the enterprises. Some more risky projects are developed on a joint-venture basis. There may also be some subcontracting for certain aspects (for example, in the software area, for the local systems adaptation of switching equipment from one country to the next and so on) so that access to a network of national specialist suppliers is crucial as well. This leaves the traditional governmental policy towards national-oriented S&TS linkages in a dilemma. Strong national telecommunications research centers that have supported a number of national suppliers, as for example, CNET in France, have become fully integrated into the service provider France Telecom. Now its output is mainly proprietary and its traditional focus on the switching industry has shifted to more network-based products.

Governments have therefore had to switch to other supply-side instruments, such as sector-specific subsidy schemes, or support for special research topics. Funding of new service applications has also served as a demand pull instrument. But liberalization and deregulation policies have also been crucial in encouraging technical change, as have been the standardization issues.[120] Where the link to the S&TS establishment becomes

---

[120] These factors can all be seen at work if we analyze, for example, the rapid spread of mobile services in Europe, as a consequence of liberalization and the spread of the Global System Mobile (GSM) standard.

important for both service and equipment suppliers is for access to basic technology, for example, in specialized opto-electronics or component production, or where it emerges from military applications, for example, in satellites and packet switching. Given that the use of electronics has revolutionized the way that telecommunication systems work, the S&TS links of the electronics industry will in the future also have a strong bearing on the development of the manufacturer's technology base. If we take this wider view, we must also look at the national government's S&TS policy in this broader sense, or multinational efforts, as encouraged by the EU, to strengthen this sector.

2.6 Implications of the Changing Axis of Competition and the Infrastructure Gap for Post-socialist Economies

The convergence between telecommunications and data processing, the associated digitalization of services and the rapid globalization of the sector, first for equipment and more recently for services, has accelerated the speed of technical change in the industry. The competitive environment in which the industry operates, and the associated legal and regulatory structure are crucial for the realization of this growing technology potential, as is the overall macroeconomic environment.

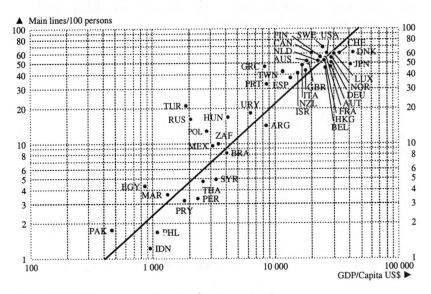

Figure 8.2 GDP v. penetration in telecommunications

However, this leads to a growing *technology gap vis-à-vis* countries that are still trying to complete this transformation process. Their difficult macroeconomic conditions increase the already large capacity gap with respect to their telecommunications infrastructure. As a consequence, *financing policies* and *technology transfer*, in addition to a liberal regulatory environment, become more crucial than S&TS policies.

Keeping these points in mind when considering the ongoing sectoral transformation in the post-socialist countries, we therefore start with a look at the aggregate demand for services as one of the major variables that drives technical change before seeing how firms and scientific institutions have behaved in this changing framework and what role R&D policy plays. In the discussion of the hierarchical production chain above we saw that with the digitalization of telephone services and its convergence with the computer sector, telephony *applications* in the Western economies are increasing enormously. An analysis of telephone penetration as an indicator of network access (measured in connections per 100 persons in relation to GNP) in Figure 8.2 helps to identify the current capacity *gap*, in terms of network infrastructure, which the post-socialist economies still have to close in order to catch up.[121]

Table 8.1 Annual telecommunication revenues: selected country markets

Country	Total telecom revenues (USD billions)	Telecom revenues per line (USD)	Telecom revenues (percent of GDP)
Russia	2.5	104	0.6
Czech Republic	0.8	361	1.9
Hungary	0.7	384	1.5
Poland	1.6	322	1.8
USA	178	1,193	2.8

Source: International Telecommunication Union (ITU), International Telecommunication Company (ITC).

Given the continuing decline in GNP per head in Russia, the figure also indicates that it will require a larger proportion of investment, given their GNP, in order to catch up, especially given the low levels of telephone revenue per line (Table 8.1). Foreign investment may therefore be required to

---

[121] In the figure one finds find Russia, Hungary and Poland with a telephone penetration of around 20 compared to 50–70 in the more developed OECD countries.

bridge the investment gap and to accelerate the necessary technology transfer.[122]

3. TRANSFORMING THE TELECOMMUNICATIONS INDUSTRY IN EASTERN EUROPE

3.1 The Old Regime

The socialist regime in the former USSR (and to some extent in the CMEA – or COMECON – states) gave a very low priority to the telecommunications sector. The situation in the other CMEA countries was somewhat better, with a higher density in Bulgaria and Poland, but compared to OECD countries they also had a considerably underdeveloped telecommunications infrastructure. Most of the telecommunications equipment produced (about 80 percent) was for *military* use; which went into the private, that is, non-military sector, was mainly for the government and commercial users. This policy resulted in a lack of adequate telecommunications infrastructure and an outdated technology with the subsequent technology gap in the equipment sector in most CEE countries, as is apparent from Table 8.2 (and Figure 8.1 above). As a consequence there was a considerable demand, with long waiting lists and also very few public pay phones.

The system was old-fashioned and of low technical quality, the degree of network automation was limited and many inter-city calls still had to go via the operator.[123] There was considerable reliance for equipment production on CMEA partners such as East Germany, Bulgaria, Hungary and Poland.[124]

---

[122] A more detailed analysis of telephone demand, which also considers the industrial composition in each country and the geographic distribution of population and industry, would provide a more exact measure of the existing capacity gap in the post-socialist countries. Russia, with its large rural population, would have a different investment need than, for example, Estonia.

[123] Campbell (1995, p. 21) mentions that in the mid-1980s probably nearly half of all telephone lines in the former Soviet Union were still connected to the old Strowger step-by-step mechanical exchanges. The rest of the equipment was mostly second-generation crossbar equipment. There were few possibilities for making international calls. Compared to the United States' 410 million calls in 1985, the USSR originated only 1.8 million calls (ibid. p.15).

[124] Campbell quotes a source which reported that 'before 1991 the share of imports in total supply available to the Soviet Union amounted to 40 percent of urban switches, 80 percent of rural switches and 30 percent of all radio and TV broadcasting equipment' (Campbell 1995, p. 71). The East German production of the ATSK exchange alone accounted for a total of 6 million lines. Also of importance was the old Ericsson plant of VEF in Latvia. In particular, the more modern digital equipment came almost exclusively from these sources. For the Soviet 12th 5-year plan 1986–90, the reliance on Eastern Europe in the mid-1960s was even higher, but was most crucial in the 1980s when modern digital exchanges could be

Given the bureaucratic nature of the system, it was difficult to bring new technology into the telecommunications network. As a consequence, until the breakdown of the Soviet Union there was very little use of fiber optic cables, which had been introduced commercially in the West ten years earlier, digital switching technology was lagging behind more than a decade and equipment producers had difficulty obtaining reliable components. In the end even the former Soviet Union had to rely on the import of equipment to fill some of the technology gap to the extent that this was permitted under CMEA trade restrictions.

Table 8.2 Telecommunication indicators: selected country markets, 1994

Country	Lines (m)	Population (m)	Teledensity (lines per 100 pop.)	Digitization (%)	Waiting list (yrs)	Population density (/sq. km)
Russia	24.1	148	16	12	>10	9
Poland	5.0	38	13	18	4.9	123
Bulgaria	3.0	9	34	1	2.4	80
Romania	2.8	23	12	7	>10	96
Czech Rep.	2.2	10	21	15	4.3	131
Hungary	1.7	10	17	41	3.4	109
Slovakia	1.0	5	19	15	2.3	109
China	27.2	1,191	2	90	>10	124
USA	156.8	261	60	65	0	28

Source: International Telecommunication Union (ITU).

3.2 Few New Services

In comparison with Western telecommunications systems, there was a great reliance on telegraph and telex services, which accounted for the relatively high importance of data transmission.[125] Fax services were introduced in the Soviet Union in the 1960s mainly to expedite the distribution of images for

produced only in the CMEA countries, some of them such as Hungary and Poland relying on imported components from the West.

[125] The telex system was also used as a pilot for the early e-mail system 'teletex' but which never really worked properly.

the press (Campbell 1995, p. 95).[126] Communication satellites started to become important in the 1970s, but mainly for broadcasting and originally with little use for telephony. While the technical achievements in the Soviet space program have been impressive, its commercial utilization, especially for telecommunications, has been minimal. Of the 21 satellite ground stations, only three were located at territory switching centers and could easily be integrated into the long-distance telephone network. The others were costly ways of serving a number of remote primary centers such as Siberia. Satellite transmission was also used to distribute newspaper images for decentralized printing, but access for data transfer to the telephone network was given only to enterprises and institutions, not to individuals. As a consequence the USSR had only a very rudimentary system for new services in place. Some new services were available (mainly to corporate customers and perhaps to the military), but the system used was so backward that in order to adapt the network to modern application, it was necessary to begin again with a more specialized overlay network.

Given the excellent survey by Campbell (1995) we shall list here some of his central observations as a conclusion for this section:

- very low priority for telecommunications, especially for private households, with adequate systems only for the military, the government and business (p. 23);
- little international use (p. 15);
- few economic incentives for pricing of the network use and its investment (p. 57);
- significant reliance on CMEA partners (mainly East Germany, Hungary and Bulgaria) for equipment production (p. 69);
- outdated technology, also as a result of COCOM (Coordinating Committee for Multinational Export Controls) restrictions (p. 75);
- high priority for military applications, but very weak leverage by the network operators to obtain more modern equipment for civilian use (p. 113); and
- inability to bring new technology to the sector (no use of fiber optics or cellular mobile technology (p. 23), no digital switching technology or reliable components (p. 77). The exceptions were uses for the broadcasting sector, including the use of satellites.

---

[126] These services were only for very specialized applications and could therefore rely on equipment imported from England, Japan and West Germany. But eventually the fax systems allowed private customers to bring a written message or a paper tape to a ministerial 'Minsviazi' office to have it transmitted.

3.3 The Science and Technology Link in the Socialist System of the COCOM States

The Soviet Ministry of Communications (MOC or Minsviazi) had difficulty in implementing new technology or getting prototypes built by the industry. The MOC itself had a weak R&D base in-house, with most Soviet R&D capabilities in this field subordinated to equipment producers outside. Minsviazi had under its control only two significant research institutes, namely, the Central Scientific Research Institute for Communications (NTsNIIS) and the Scientific Research Institute for Radio (NIIR). The equipment was designed mostly by laboratories external to the MOC or in collaboration with CMEA suppliers. Once a prototype had been approved and worked successfully in an experimental system, a suitable manufacturer had to be found, mainly from the factories under the responsibility of the Ministry of Defense (MPSS).

The role of the CMEA countries was to act as a conduit for Western technology of an earlier technology generation, which could then be transferred to the USSR under COCOM restrictions. For example, imports from Yugoslavia for computer-controlled PABX systems came from the joint venture between GTE and the Pupin factory in Nis. The Hungarians also had access to imported components and were able to produce some telephone exchanges based on an Ericsson license. The Yugoslav Iskra plant in Slovenia also had technology transfer agreements with Western firms, specifically with IT&T (then owner of Alcatel). In the 1970s, Poland produced the Pentaconta automatic exchange under license from the French firm Alcatel. The MOC also tried to enlist the help of foreign firms, for example, to produce the French MT-20 exchange in a technology transfer package to the UFA plant in Leningrad or a joint venture with Telefonica (Spain) to produce advanced handsets. This policy was also pursued with respect to the production of fiber optic equipment, with the MOC eventually turning to Western companies for help in all phases, providing cable, equipment for cable construction and the construction of turnkey fiber optic plants.

In the 1970s and 1980s the East European equipment producers were heavily involved in the R&D process in the Soviet Union as well. In 1971 the Soviets signed an agreement with East Germany to develop a unified analogue digital communications system which later became known as ISTOK (a combined digital and analogue exchange).[127] Much of the simple

---

[127] This exchange was produced by Robotron and the Soviet version under the auspices of the Ministry of Electrical Equipment Industry, which according to Campbell (1995, p. 78) had no experience or qualification for this kind of work, so that in 1987 production was shifted to plants of the MPSS. However, the MOC was so weakened in its bargaining positions that

terminal equipment also came from the CMEA areas. Campbell (1995, p. 72) mentions that in 1985, 54 percent of Bulgarian annual production (1.15 million units) was exported to the Soviet Union. Other important suppliers were the Czechs and the Hungarians.

The Soviet Union was more successful with satellites, which may be explained by the fact that their development was under the direct control of the USSR Ministry of Defense. Satellites were all produced in the Science Production Association of Applied Mechanics in the secret city of Krasnoiarsk-26. Even the satellites used for Intersputnik, the CMEA versions of Intelsat, were operated by SSSR, an arm of the MPSS. This program and some of the equipment development and production was eventually separated out institutionally and increasingly commercialized in the form of the Soviet space agency, thus the MOC actually had little control over communication satellites both in terms of their design and in terms of controlling their use, as outlined in the ministry's space doctrine of 1992. Production of switching equipment in the former Soviet Union was limited, and most of it came from the CMEA countries. Because of the complex nature of the product, the link between R&D, testing and series production was poor. The MOC had difficulty obtaining access to high-quality production facilities and the incentive system resulted in much faulty equipment being produced that could not deliver up to the expected levels.

3.4 The Transformation Process

With the breakup of the USSR and the breakdown of the old CMEA supply channels, network expansion plans suffered, especially as investment funds were also reduced. Keeping in mind our first hypothesis, this had disastrous consequences for technical change. However, one important change in Russia was the increased political and administrative support given to the telecommunications sector, as resources were shifted from military to civilian production. Firms from the military industrial complex started to look for civilian markets, including telecommunications. This new emphasis was even greater in Latvia and Hungary.

---

it was never able to get the MPSS to produce these exchanges. Campbell (ibid. p.72) also cites L. Misulovins, chief of the Riga division of NTsNIIS (which worked on the development of the ISTOK telephone exchange) that 'without the participation of East German industry it would have been impossible to bring the ISTOK system to successful commercialization within any realistic time'. This exchange, which took ten years to develop (1975–85) and was put into production in the mid-1980s in Russia and East Germany, never had a high output (in 1987, 35 exchanges – with an average capacity of about 100,000 numbers – were produced).

The other crucial change was the opening up of the national equipment market to the world economy. Direct contact with foreign manufacturers and joint ventures became possible. The disappearance of the COCOM trade restrictions allowed foreign equipment manufacturers almost unrestricted entry to the Commonwealth of Independent States (CIS) market. As a consequence of reduced demand and sudden globalization, the former East European suppliers ceased to be a competitive alternative and had to wind down their equipment production significantly. The national telephone companies in most CIS countries remained under state control, but they underwent a gradual process of commercialization. Since most of their markets continued to be protected, the subsequent restructuring was less radical, but still very dramatic, especially in Russia.

What had once been a unified communication monopoly across the Soviet Union became a decentralized one, initially under Mikhail Gorbachev, but especially after the breakup of the USSR at the end of 1991. It resulted in a variety of new entities. The national USSR ministries disappeared and were replaced by independent republican telecommunication administrations. The regional telephone companies at the oblast level, especially as most of them were partly privatized, had much more autonomy, not only in tariff setting but also in equipment procurement and network development. The result was a much more decentralized institutional system, especially as privatization and network entry was encouraged by the Ministry of Communications.

In other post-socialist states, the national telephone companies were sold off to foreign service providers, as in Latvia or Hungary, or looked for strategic investors, as in the Czech Republic. This resulted in a very different network expansion strategy, given their easier access to finance and internationally oriented procurement policy. While some of the post-socialist countries, especially among the newly industrialized states (NIS) and Russia, are still far behind, others are quickly catching up and will soon have an infrastructure as advanced and widely accessible as in the West.

This new decentralized and globalized environment is making it very difficult for local equipment manufacturers to survive. Producers were completely unprepared for outside competition. Lack of capital and commercial management has hindered efforts to develop modern telecommunications equipment. The Pyramid Research report (1995, p. 234) mentions that 'producers were completely unprepared for outside competition while a lack of capital and commercial management has hindered efforts to develop modern telecommunication equipment locally'. While much analogue switching and transmission equipment is still being produced in the NIS, few national or local operators are installing locally produced equipment, much of which is simply languishing in warehouses locally. On the other hand, the opening up of the CIS market to foreign trade created huge potentials for foreign equipment manufacturers: 'foreign suppliers have largely supplanted local manufacturers in the regions switching, trunk transmission and PABX market' (ibid., p. 1). The situation is not much different in the Baltic countries and the NIS, in Bulgaria, Romania and the states of former Yugoslavia. Only in countries where FDI and joint ventures have been able to benefit from technology transfer and significant domestic demand (such as Poland and Hungary) are there signs of an emergence of a viable equipment production sector, but on a much smaller scale than before.

3.5 The Role of FDI and Initial Assessment

Foreign direct investment will therefore be an important instrument to bridge the current investment gap and to finance the level of investment needed to upgrade fully the Russian network in the post-socialist states. Table 8.3 shows the calculations for achieving an average density of 35/100 population over a ten-year period for a number of CEE countries, including Russia. While these calculations may be a bit theoretical, they nevertheless show the difficulty of reaching higher infrastructure levels in the foreseeable future. FDI would allow direct strategic investment in some of the network operators. At the same time, the involvement of foreign equipment manufacturers in joint ventures with local producers will not only help financially, but also influence the transformation and restructuring process considerably.

We thus need to look at the role of joint ventures both for service provision and equipment production. In service provision their most likely role is for the construction and operation of overlay networks, often linked to international networks. Cellular joint venture systems have also been successful. Their main advantage is that given the lack of adequate modern infrastructure, they can be put into use very quickly as an overlay network, which already includes some advanced services plus links to international networks. The question to be explored is to what extent such joint ventures can help to jump-start the modernization of the network, especially when linked to other wireless telephone technologies and to what extent they can, as a competitive element, also stimulate the ordinary terrestrial network operators into more effective and efficient service provision.

The transformation process has opened up the markets (especially for equipment) to international trade, thereby putting national producers at a considerable disadvantage (given the existing technology gap, lack of marketing experience, no availability of supplier credit and so on) and made the old S&TS links useless. The reemergence of the sector will depend largely on the overall economic performance and the associated legal and regulatory environment, preconditions which are necessary to permit increased investment in the service sector.

Table 8.3 Cost to achieve 35 percent CEE teledensity, 1991–2000

Country	Population* 2000 (m)	Lines needed (000)	Lines 1991 (000)	Lines gap (000)	Cost ($ million)	Cost per annum ($ million)
Baltics						
Estonia	1.67	584	340	244	0.7	80
Latvia	2.81	984	640	344	1.1	120
Lithuania	4.01	1,402	820	582	1.7	190
Central Europe						
Czech Rep. and Slovakia	16.30	5,706	2,500	3,206	7.9	880
Hungary	10.60	3,711	1,100	2,611	5.9	660
Poland	38.89	13,611	3,600	10,011	22.2	2,470
Eastern Europe						
Bulgaria	9.00	3,151	2,250	901	3.2	360
Romania	24.53	8,587	2,400	6,187	13.8	1,530
CIS						
Russia	162.00	53,700	22,000	34,700	82.6	9,180
Ukraine	57.30	20,055	8,000	12,055	28.9	3,210
Total	327.11	111,491	43,650	70,841	168.0	18,680

Note: * Estimated.

Sources: Communication and Information Technology Research, London, Ameritech, US Department of Commerce, Bank of America, World Bank, Financial Times Conferences.

4. RESULTS FROM THE CASE STUDIES

If we assume that because of this process of opening up, the market forces are becoming more and more globalized and will also be shaping these markets, then the same industry determinants and competitive axis that we have seen in Section 2 should also play a similar role in the post-socialist economies. However, in these case studies, we find a significant contrast between Russia and the CIS countries on the one hand and some of the smaller East European states on the other hand, that is, related to their size and the quicker link into Western technology and trade flows. This is especially apparent with respect to FDI, which was very crucial in Hungary and to some extent in the Baltics, but which has played a much less significant role in Russia.

4.1 Restructuring of the Russian Telecommunications Industry

Today Russia has a highly decentralized and still very underdeveloped telephone system with by and large a very old infrastructure. In 1997, it had a fixed line teledensity of 18.5 access lines per 100 population, altogether a total of about 27.6 million access lines. Given the difficult macroeconomic situation, network and traffic growth has been slow.[128] Investment to upgrade the network continues to be at a very low level (about 0.3 percent of GNP, less than USD 1 billion per annum), given the limited access to foreign or domestic finance. Some experts anticipate that it would take between 15 and 20 years to clear Russia's waiting list. If one uses some of the old network expansion plans that were made during the Gorbachev period, which was to provide 90 percent of urban families and half of all rural families with residential telephones by the year 2000, then the total number of telephone connections needed would come to about 80 million, compared to the 27 million actually connected by the end of 1997 or the recent annual investment figures of less than one million access lines.

The situation is especially difficult for the regional operators who bear the responsibility for most of the basic network. With low and widely diverging incomes per line (in 1997 on average USD 100 per annum), growth in most regional companies is difficult to finance internally, since economic activity is concentrated mainly around the big centers and a few resource-rich regions. The result will be a much more regionally segmented market for telecommunications.

This lack of aggregate demand has repercussions for the derived demand for equipment and the associated S&TS links, especially as most of the equipment is imported. It implies even harsher conditions for the domestic R&D establishment. To serve this emerging market, all the major international equipment suppliers are now present in Russia and in some of the CIS states. Some have formed joint ventures with domestic equipment manufacturers, but the production of modern switching and transmission

---

[128] In 1993–96 1.7 percent per annum for long-distance traffic, with higher growth rates (6 percent per annum) for outgoing and still higher rates for incoming international calls (18 percent per annum), with severe congestion of the trunk network (with call completion rates between 80 and 90 percent per annum) and a limited ability to utilize automatic long-distance dialing (LDD).

equipment is still very limited (see below). Since Communication Premises Equipment (CPE, for example, terminal) can now be imported quite freely, even fewer incentives for domestic production exist, with the bulk of the equipment coming from Far Eastern suppliers. We thus find a fairly decentralized system, with large regional differences in infrastructure availability (in terms of volume, quality and modern technology) and tariffs. There is some emergence of competition in the form of alternative networks and mobile operators, but no sign of a return to the centralized monopoly structures of the past. The equipment sector is backward and underdeveloped, and was completely unprepared for the onset of globalization. The S&TS links to its old CMEA partners have been broken, and the continuing links to the domestic R&D base are only of marginal significance.

4.1.1 Limited role of FDI

Given the large capacity gap in telecommunications infrastructure and the sheer size of the country, foreign direct equity investment alone is *not* an option for a quick capacity buildup and the associated need of technology transfer.[129] There is also the associated political problem related to the fear of foreign dominance in certain sectors, partly supported by the political left and the administration, which is losing its influence.[130] FDI will still play a role in this process, but on a much smaller scale. For example, Rostelecom (with sales of about USD 1.1 billion in 1996 and 1997 and a pre-tax margin of around 25 percent) was also the largest investor in the sector (1997: USD 400 million), thanks to own and foreign financial sources. While it could not implement anything as grandiose as the 50 x 50 project, it has managed to implement an ambitious project of digitalization for its international and overlay network. However, given the lack of modern local equipment, these orders mostly went abroad.

---

[129] A look at the amount of yearly FDI per capita, (assembled by UNCTAD (United Nations Conference on Trade and Development) and reported in *The Economist*, July 11, 1998, p. 18) shows how far Russia (with 10 dollars per person) ranks behind such favorites as Hungary, Poland and Estonia (with between 80–140 dollars per person).

[130] However, around 1995, FDI was considered by the Russian government for the creation of an overlay network to give advanced customers and large enterprises access to modern telecommunications infrastructure. This so-called '50 × 50 project', called for the connection of 50 digital exchanges in the top 50 Russian cities, with 50,000 kilometers of fiber optical links, and 20 million new lines to be installed over a period of ten years, starting in 1996. Given the political and economic environment, this project proved to be overly ambitious and was never implemented. But the cost of the project (USD 40 billion for just an overlay network) shows the dimensions of the capacity and technology gap in Russia's telecommunications infrastructure. Most observers believe that instead of a unified modern fiber optical overlay network, the Russian long-distance infrastructure will evolve as a hybrid of terrestrial and satellite systems with multiple owners and operators (Public Network Europe (PNE) yearbook 1997, p. 89).

The situation is more difficult for the regional operators. The local and regional networks have been decentralized into 85 telephone companies, but are jointly owned (38 percent equity, 51 percent voting rights) by Swjasinvest (responsible for most of Russia's domestic traffic).[131] This leaves the regional operators, whose need for investment is most urgent, in a dilemma. Many are unable to obtain any outside funds at all, while others are able to secure only piecemeal domestic or foreign investment in specific local projects. Still others have managed to go directly to international stock markets, raising small, but for them still sizable, investment funds. As a consequence we observe a very decentralized decision-making process, with negotiation between regions or individual enterprises and foreign investors, often in the face of central bureaucratic pressures, to reduce the risk for the foreign investor.

Some recent estimates of FDI in the Russian telecommunications sector show them at a low level, but with an increase from USD 143 million in 1992 to USD 295 million in 1993 and USD 500 million in 1995 and 1996 (USD 200 million was by USWest for regional mobile projects, USD 70 million by AT&T). In 1997 the estimate was as high as USD 700–800 million, according to EI (1998, p. 13). If one compares these numbers with the investment figures reported by Goskomstat in Figure 8.3, the contribution of FDI is nevertheless very significant. But the FDI contribution appears so high only because of the very low domestic contribution to investment.

Given this lack of FDI and the inability to adjust tariffs on some parts of the network, the existing capacity and technology gap will remain for some time. As a consequence, telephone density is still very low (18.5 percent in 1997), but with much greater network variety and a strong private interest in the mobile sector in the urban centers, especially Moscow and St. Petersburg. As of May 1997, the MOC had issued more then 150 licenses in the mobile sector, that is, almost two per region, with some flexibility for the technology to be used. The actual buildup of the system proceeded slowly, however. There is considerable market fragmentation, with little critical mass and few countrywide or international roaming facilities.[132]

---

[131] This company was formed in 1995, to re-create a more centralized structure. It was also created partly as a potential FDI vehicle, to attract equity and to facilitate access to credit. In 1997, 25 percent of Swjasinvest was privatized at a cost of USD 1.9 billion. Only 15–30 percent of these proceeds are to be used for investment purposes in the telecommunications sector, however. The rest will be used to finance the budget deficit (EI 1998, p. 13). A further tranche of 24 percent was to be privatized in 1998, but this was postponed following the August 1998 devaluation.

[132] By mid-1997, only 93 systems had been launched, with about 209,000 subscribers, (that is, a penetration of 0.16 percent), with fast progress only in the most lucrative cities. The remaining systems are very small (1–2,000 subscribers per network), if at all built up, given the still-low profitability and penetration rates.

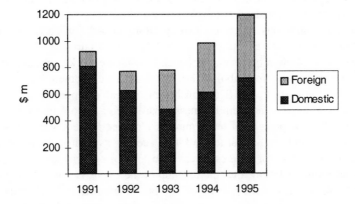

Source: Goskomstat.

Figure 8.3 Total telecommunications investment in Russia, 1991–1995

Today there exist large regional differences between the different regional operators of the Swjasinvest network, given the availability of local hard currency and supplier credit. Some local networks have been upgraded and expanded with proven Russian technology, but most have imported modern switching equipment. Similar developments are taking place for the long-distance network. Instead of a unified modern fiber optical overlay network, the Russian long-distance infrastructure will evolve as a hybrid of terrestrial and satellite systems with multiple owners and operators (Public Network Europe Yearbook 1997, p. 89).

4.1.2 Implications for the equipment market
The main constraint for network expansion is the lack of investment. Given that Russia is a highly rural society and the problem that providing services to the rural population is expensive and probably not cost effective, to bring these networks up to size will be even more costly and therefore expansion and upgrading will proceed even more slowly. If one continues to assume a relatively low investment level for the foreseeable future, derived demand for equipment will also be curtailed, resulting in even lower demand for the related R&D services that form the crucial S&TS link that we are interested in.

With a small manufacturing base (given previous dependency on CMEA imports) and an outdated technology, the Russian equipment industry is now facing global competition in a very uncertain business environment. There was a large reduction in investment in the early 1990s, as reflected in the number of new residential telephones installed.[133] The move to modern switching technology, supplied mainly from abroad (or partly assembled locally in joint ventures, but financed largely in hard currency) is proceeding only slowly. Modern business overlay and mobile networks, too, are supplied almost exclusively from abroad. For the Russian equipment manufacturers and their supporting S&TS establishment, global competition is therefore emerging in a very uncertain business environment. According to a study by ITC (1998), 80 percent of telecommunications equipment was imported in recent years and the newest technologies such as asynchronous transmission mechanism (ATM) or wireless local loop (WLL) systems are all imported. The early import frenzy after the breakup of the USSR is now slowing down. The MOC also limits the number of equipment suppliers in each market and sometimes requires some local production. Consequently, foreign suppliers have teamed up with local producers, but the lack of central regulatory authority (and finance) often produces a different picture.

Russian manufacturers' only chance of survival is in joint ventures with the established international manufacturers and with some financing arrangements which allows them to compete with international suppliers. Otherwise, the old equipment plants and R&D institutions (given lack of funds, broken linkages, and so on) face an uncertain future. Without a close link to manufacturing units (which had been missing in the past) they have only a limited chance to develop commercially successful products, even if the government tries to protect them with import restrictions for foreign suppliers and in its insistence on keeping to Russian standards.[134]

Most active among the large equipment manufactures are Alcatel, Siemens (together with its subsidiary ITALTEL), ISKRATEL (which served as an important technology conduit under the COCOM regime); Samsung and NEC for the production of switches for the fixed link networks, and Ericsson and Nokia for equipment to support cellular services, along with Motorola. But generally we find very low output levels at any of these joint ventures.[135] For other local manufacturers not involved in a joint venture, only a few of their

---

[133] In 1990, 1.202 million (all USSR), 1991 0.855 million, 1992 0.661 million (see Campbell 1995, p. 197).

[134] The government required the use of the Russian transmission standard C7 instead of the international standard CCITT-SS No. 7. This means that international compatible SS7 switching equipment from abroad has to be modified first.

[135] In personal interviews, Western equipment manufacturers complained about bureaucratic difficulties (slow, unpredictable); high taxes (often on sales and not profits); difficult and illogical custom procedures (that is, higher tariffs on parts than on finished products); and an unwillingness of Russian partners to contribute equally to the development. Indeed, the requirement for local manufacturing and the associated FDI could better be seen as an entry tax for those wishing to establish a longer-term presence in that market.

product lines are holding their own.[136] Thus, we find that the outlook for most local equipment suppliers is dim, as spiraling inflation has pushed local manufacturing costs close to Western levels, but few produce a high enough quality to command Western prices.

As for the military supply sector, in addition to technology (and management), transfer via joint ventures from abroad was the other option. Defense customers accounted for 80 percent of telecommunication orders in 1992. In 1994, the Russian Federation Organization of Defense Industries announced a two-year modernization and conversion plan, with investment of 400 billion rubles (USD 580 million) but the results are uncertain. However, the conversion of the military satellite system GLONASS to civilian use, and access to the Khrnichev Space Center at Baikonur (Kazakstan) have now taken place.

There have also been a few successful spin-offs, mainly for the installation of internal networks or as partners in joint ventures (for example, in Telesoft Russia, a Russian–Italian joint venture for a digital network management system). Those that are successful, especially in the satellite area, had this link in the past, and did not have the same technology gap. While satellite systems, too, used to rely entirely on domestically produced equipment, that equipment was more modern and reliable than the equipment produced for the regular services. Consequently it was easier for these suppliers to participate in a joint venture with Hughes or for Intersputnik and Lockheed to work together (EI 1998, p. 47).

There are also some successful spin-offs in the software sector, because these tools could easily be transferred or acquired and needed only a small capital base, compared to the requirements of hardware production.[137] This development, too, shows that there are some markets where the local firms could successfully enter and thrive, thus providing an outlet for some of the many telecommunication experts who lost their jobs because of the radical restructuring of the equipment sector. But few of these developments are a result of governmental initiative or the strengthening of S&TS links.

---

[136] No local manufacturer has successfully produced a digital exchange even though a joint venture made up of NPO, Impulse, Saturn and Kwant claims to have developed one (Pyramid Research 1995, p. 239).

[137] This trend is also indicated by the small, but continuously evolving Internet services. Estimates for this segment are difficult to obtain, however. In 1997 there were 220,000 subscribers and 2,200 sites, growing at about 60–80 percent per annum. Some of the major players for service provision are Sovam Teleport, Demos and Relcom (which is using satellite linkages set up by the Radiotechnical Institute). On the other hand, America Online (AOL) and CompuServe left Russia because of problems with fraud.

4.1.3 S&TS links

The macroeconomic and institutional adjustment problems of the transformation process have reduced the overall demand for investment. But the process has at the same time opened up the national markets (especially for equipment) to international trade, thereby putting national producers at a considerable disadvantage (given their technology gap, lack of marketing experience, no availability of supplier credit and so on). It also has rendered useless the old S&TS links. With the backwardness of the equipment industry and the past reliance on CMEA specialists, the crucial task was to assist the domestic equipment manufacturers to regain some market share, so that local R&D could be used as an input. In addition, local services also want to rely on local know-how.

At the moment, given the lack of finance for upgrading the overall infrastructure, investment is very much tilted towards the construction of overlay and backbone networks, which rely heavily on foreign-produced equipment and know-how. This is also true for mobile networks, given the needs of the emerging entrepreneurial firms, with some of them looking for external market links with foreign businesses and institutions, the increasing needs of tourism and the data needs of the financial sector. These customers will be able to pay and use modern (imported) equipment and are therefore prime candidates for modern business overlay networks. On the other hand, most households are likely to continue to afford only simple telephone services. But given their low- or medium-income levels, which are resulting in an average yearly telephone income of less than USD 100 per line (compared to the USD 340 reached in Hungary or Poland, as shown in Table 8.3 above), little derived demand is arriving from that end, even though domestic equipment may be more competitive in that sector of the market.

As a consequence, the market for local R&D has dried up almost completely, except for those firms who were able to upgrade their system (as in the satellite sector) or those who participated in a joint venture which included an explicit transfer of know-how from abroad (both for service provision and equipment production). The reemergence of the sector will therefore largely depend on the overall economic performance and the associated legal and regulatory environment, since both factors greatly influence derived demand and sectoral investment.

4.2 Radical Restructuring in Latvia

4.2.1 Overview

Within the system of the Soviet republics, the telecommunication networks in the Baltic states of Lithuania, Latvia and Estonia were more advanced than in most other republics and had a higher telephone penetration.[138] As a consequence, the production facilities and knowledge base located in Latvia (and in Riga in particular) was disproportionately large. There were 64,000 employees working in the electrical electronic and telecommunications sector in 1991. Of these, 25 percent were highly educated engineers and technicians. The leading Latvian manufacturers were VEF in the telecommunications sector and ALFA in components and microelectronics.[139] In addition, there was the central research laboratory for telecommunications (RUNIS) which was important in the Soviet R&D scene (in addition to those of the Academy of Science in Kiev, St. Petersburg and Moscow, TsNiRS).

After the collapse of the Soviet Union and the restoration of Latvian independence, the links to the old equipment markets, the CIS countries, were cut. Trade with Russia was made even more difficult because of ongoing political disputes, trade restrictions by both sides and an attempt by Russia to reduce its dependency on technology centers in the Baltic states. At the same time, the telephone system left behind by the Soviet authorities had to be restructured and the service company commercialized. The framework chosen for this transformation was that of a free-market economy. As a consequence, a strategic investor was sought for the national telephone company, just as in Estonia.[140] Only Lithuania tried to make transformation initially within a commercialized state-owned company.

This is why Latvia represents a particularly interesting case study within our project. On the one hand, it was a regional center of technical excellence and an agglomeration of manufacturing know-how in the sector. On the other, the foreign direct investment of Cable & Wireless (C&W) and Telecom Finland (today Sonora) in the national telephone company Lattelkom, where the role of the strategic investor is particularly pronounced, is an interesting experiment in FDI.

---

[138] According to Campbell (1995, p. 136) the republic ministries in the Baltic region had enough freedom and resources to create telecommunication systems that were much better than the Soviet average (in terms of density, connectivity, variety, quality of service offered, injection of new technology such as data transfer, direct dialing of long-distance calls and digitalization).

[139] The Latvian equipment supplier VEF had been an important production center for telecommunications. It even gained considerable experience in the production of digital long-distance and business exchanges (the Kwarts and the Kvant) under license from Nokia (in a barter-type joint venture) during 1983–1991.

[140] A similar strategy was pursued by Estonia Telecom (ETC), the state holding company, in which a 49 percent FDI took place in the form of Baltic Tele, a joint venture set up by Telecom Finland and Telia of Sweden.

4.2.2 Reorganizing with a strategic investor
In the smaller CEE countries, especially the Baltics, the potential of FDI as an instrument of transformation is much greater than in Russia.[141] In Latvia, the public telephone operation was taken over by a strategic investor (with an equity stake of 49 percent, but also a management contract),[142] with a long monopoly period (until 2013) envisaged. This provided a fairly secure market framework in which access to foreign capital could be used to upgrade the network. Similar FDI took place in the mobile sector, with the first analogue license already awarded in 1992 to a consortium with Telia of Sweden and Sonora of Finland, and two additional GSM licenses being awarded in 1994 and 1996.

While most of the investment plans under the privatization scheme seem to have been achieved (with very high investment levels), there was nevertheless some dissatisfaction on both sides. The network which was inherited by Tilts was in far worse shape than originally anticipated so that modernization and upgrading became much more expensive. At the same time, the promised tariff increases, which were necessary to cover this level of investment, were not politically (and perhaps economically) sustainable. The question remains, whether the network upgrading envisaged in the initial privatization agreement was not overoptimistic, since the country could not afford it.

4.2.3 Collapse of the equipment sector
With the breakup of the Soviet Union in 1992, the telecommunications equipment markets were quickly lost to Western equipment suppliers, who could also provide service functions and finance (often at subsidized rates). It thus became impossible for Latvian manufacturers to compete in their old home markets. At the same time, domestic demand (with only 2.5 million inhabitants in Latvia) could not compensate for the previous Soviet Union market, even if modern technology had been available. In the market for mobile equipment, which was picking up rapidly as well, most products were also being imported. The existing technology gap was too large and the lack of organizational know-how (how to deal with competitive markets) meant that Western markets were not accessible, either. Their only chance was to find foreign partners, both to provide the necessary funds for the reorganization (and to help with supplier credits), but also to help in the transfer of know-how to overcome the technology and reputation gap.

---

[141] This was also shown in Hungary, where the national telephone company Matav was partly privatized in 1993 to a consortium of Deutsche Telekom and Ameritech International.
[142] In the form of the TILTS consortium (63 percent Cable & Wireless, UK, 27 percent Telecom Finland and 10 percent International Finance Corporation – ISC) in 1993.

The procurement policy of Lattelkom, which relied on the worldwide (C&W) procurement network was also a cause for the sector's decline. Given C&W's worldwide purchasing power and the remaining technology gap faced by the domestic suppliers, it was difficult to use much of the local equipment, especially if modern equipment could be bought more cheaply on the world market. The management of Lattelkom argued that it could not afford to subsidize the domestic industry as well. On the other hand, given the size of the investment and the associated multipliers, some positive externalities for the local manufacturing sector (and the associated R&D base) could perhaps have justified such a policy.

In this transformation process the role of the Latvian Privatization Agency was actually more crucial than the procurement offers that could be provided for by Lattelkom. The transformation and privatization process took a long time and it started from unrealistic expectations. As a consequence any remaining funds within VEF or other equipment manufacturers were quickly eaten up by maintaining the status quo, especially with respect to employment. As of 1997, VEF had not been privatized, but it is a shadow of its former self with only about 400 engineers remaining.[143]

One alternative could have been to follow the more domestically oriented procurement policies in Lithuania and Poland. They have produced a slightly different demand structure for the local equipment industry and as a consequence greater derived demand for S&T developments than that observed in Latvia. In other words, parts of the network could have been upgraded with local technology at close to competitive costs, given the willingness to provide some start-up help.

More success can be reported from the software and service support front. For example, an early and successful spin-off from VEF (actually from its research institute) is Kvant-Interkom, which employees about 200 engineers. It is also involved in planning and upgrading corporate networks and security systems in the Baltics and former CIS markets, as are the other spin-offs such as AND-Electronica and Telesoft. Similarly, LATI has been developed by its founder Lachenbach into an important software company, whose services are increasingly being sought by Western computer and software companies. These examples make clear that the sheer magnitude of expertise that existed there in the form of human capital has not all been made redundant and unemployable, despite the almost complete write-off of physical capital, the radical change of markets and the need to overcome the technology and

---

[143] The production for radio receivers (employing at one time 4,000 workers) was closed down in 1992. In 1998, the section producing customer premises equipment (2–3 million telephone sets per annum) was put into liquidation and the VEF transistor company was reduced to refurbishing used telephone sets imported from Germany.

organization gap as a result of globalization. Even though the local market is small, and the macroeconomic conditions remain difficult, Latvia remains an important transit region that benefits by serving surrounding markets.

4.2.4 Science and technology links

In the old days, with Riga being an important research and development network within the Soviet Union, scientific links to the other research centers in the Soviet Union were excellent, but to the outside world they were limited. With the newly gained independence, links to the West have improved, while those to the old Soviet research centers in St. Petersburg, Moscow and Kiev are still more or less maintained. To what extent Riga can claim to have a comparative network advantage in the future is difficult to assess. Its technology base has been severely weakened by globalization and the severing of important trade links. But the potential to reestablish itself to some extent is certainly there, given the large science and educational base.

Its major institutions of higher learning, such as the Technical University, Riga Aviation University, Latvia University and several smaller institutions, which were responsible for much of the ongoing training and research during the Soviet era, remain important centers of excellence, especially after experiencing a period of refocussing, coupled with the establishment of new scientific linkages. However, the telecommunications research center RUNIS was closed down and there has been no replacement.

Attempts have also been made to use the technology potential in the old manufacturing units of VEF, ALFA and so on as a basis to create technology parks.[144] Similar proposals have also been made to set up supporting training infrastructure, such as business schools, and to create a more favorable commercial environment. Much of this is under way, but it remains to be seen to what extent Latvia can be developed as a favorable location in this area, rather than only as a small market to serve its own limited needs.

In summary, we observed a radical reduction in aggregate demand for traditional equipment suppliers (much more radical than the gradual commercialization observed in Lattelkom), coupled with a major upgrading of infrastructure and services. Domestically, the derived demand for S&TS links could therefore only come from that side, that is, from within Lattelkom and the mobile service providers, as they learned how to act in a commercial environment and with the slow emergence of competition, and from new network services and private, corporate networks. In addition there remained a very small demand on the equipment side, on the one hand to serve an old network base, and on the other to find new niche markets, also internationally,

---

[144] See the plan for setting up the business innovation center of Latvian electronics industry of December 1996.

but with limited financial potential to support major S&TS links. Internationally, links to the West are gradually being established, but derived demand is too small to allow the reestablishment of S&TS links on the former substantial basis. The government itself has so far done little to reestablish this link by developing other projects.

4.3 Restructuring in Hungary: A Success Story?

4.3.1 Restructuring and privatization

Hungary, a country with 10.2 million inhabitants and a GNP per head of USD 3,300 (in 1996) represents a very unusual form of transformation in the telecommunications sector. It had a very low network penetration in 1990 (9.6 lines/100 population), but the effective privatization of Matav, its dominant telephone company, to a group of strategic investors, and the stable business environment following its transition have brought Hungary's level of telephone infrastructure close to that of the other EU countries.

Already in 1988 it was decided to restructure the traditional state telephone monopoly into a limited company, in order to open up the sector to FDI. The independent operator Matav was formed, separate from broadcasting and postal services. It was established as a joint-stock company in July 1991 and privatized in 1993 (a 30 percent stake was sold to Deutsche Telekom AG (DTAG) and Ameritech, later increased to 60 percent). DTAG has made Hungary, through its investment in Matav, its Eastern European center, which has further strengthened Matav's importance. It is therefore a role model for the development of other post-socialist economies.

The restructuring and privatization of Matav also had to bear in mind the national telecommunications development plan. In the tradition of centralized planning, a ten-year national plan (1990–2000), envisaged:

- first, the creation of a backbone digital network;
- then a modernization and upgrading of the rest of the system ('national infrastructure buildup');
- to be followed by the phase 'elaboration of services', that is, better business services and so on. The whole investment cost was estimated to be USD 7.2 billion in 1990 prices;
- this plan was modified to a three-year planning framework, when the reformist government came to power. All concession contracts (that is, of Matav and the local telephone operators, (LTOs, see below)) had to fulfill most of the elements of this plan by:
- increasing the available access lines by 15.5 percent per annum,

- installing, from 1997 on, within six months, 90 percent of all telephone requests; and
- setting prices on the basis of a price cap model.

The provision to establish, for political rather than for strategic reasons, separate LTOs in one-third of the country was somewhat controversial. While Matav maintains monopoly rights for long-distance and international calls, local concessions to provide basic telephony were to be awarded to LTOs as well. These took a long time to get established, again due to regulatory problems (Public Network Europe Yearbook 1997, p. 68).

Also crucial for the network development was the licensing process for mobile services. Westel Radio Telephone, the first Hungarian analogue mobile network licensed in 1990, already had 70,000 subscribers by August 1996 and covered 100 percent of the population. But the market really took off with the introduction of a GSM license in 1994. The two GSM operators (Westel 900 GSM and Panon) are now larger than the analogue mobile network.[145] As a consequence, the telecommunication penetration increased significantly and is now, with a penetration of over 6 percent in October 1997, in line with some of the EU countries. Compare this with the high-price, slow penetration policy for mobile services in Russia.[146] The Hungarian government is also following European policy by moving towards some network liberalization before 2003.[147] This means that further direct investment in networks is likely to take place. Already foreign operators have set up network nodes in Budapest (such as France Telecom, British Telecom and the Dutch operator KPN).

4.3.2 The role of strategic investors

The privatization of Matav was a key development. Along with the first partial privatization (30.5 percent)[148] came the management right for 25 years. This privatization therefore implied not only access to foreign capital, and access to cheaper sources of investment funds (cheaper than could be borrowed by the Hungarian government), but also access to management and

---

[145] Given the success in this field, the government considered issuing further licenses for the DCS 1800 standard.

[146] That speed can be important for rentability, even when coupled with network competition, was shown by the financial success of the two players in the GSM network, which with 0.5 million subscribers is as great as that of the 2.8 million subscribers of Matav in the fixed network.

[147] The Telecommunication Act of 1992 followed the EU's overall policies closely, with a liberalization of most services, except for a continued monopoly on basic voice services until 2003.

[148] In November 1995, a further 35 percent of Matav was sold to the two Western investors, with the promise of reducing their stake at a later flotation (in 1997) to 51 percent.

operational know-how. The result of this process was not only a fast upgrading and expansion of the system (Matav doubled its installed line base between 1992 and 1997), but also very effective implementation in terms of productive efficiency and innovative services (labor productivity increased from 79 to 137 lines per employee). In addition, the state had access to large privatization proceeds:[149]

- USD 0.875 billion in 1993 for 30.3 percent equity (a record price of USD 2,600 per line, compared to an average price of USD 1,600 in Western Europe);
- USD 1.1 billion for a further transfer of 37.1 percent in 1995; and a further
- USD 1.2 billion for around 25 percent in 1997 during the successful flotation on the New York Stock Exchange.

FDI will also be crucial for the development of the competitive network provider MKM-Tel, which was formed in 1997 from the networks of MAV, the state railway, MOL, the largest oil company and the IT research company, KFKI. The selected investor UNISOURCE had also concluded an agreement with MVM, the electricity grid operator, to give it a better opportunity to gain market share after the expected network liberalization in 1999.

The concept of separate LTOs also allowed for some interesting test beds for FDI.[150] Finally, FDI was crucial for the development of the mobile sector. Foreign specialists provided know-how and finance and a fast roll-out plan, with significant price and service competition. In addition, the state received over USD 90 million for the sale of the two GSM licenses in 1993.

4.3.3 Restructuring the equipment sector through FDI
In the old CMEA days, Hungary was a major supplier for telecommunications equipment (with companies such as Telefongyar, BHG, Budavox and Videoton). Up to 50 percent of the output was exported. Its equipment supplier had access to some Western know-how through limited licensing agreements. However, with the breakdown of the old trading order and the loss of markets in other neighboring countries, mainly the Czech Republic and the CIS countries, and the increased competition for the market at home, the sector had to retract. Much depended now on the ambitious modernization

---

[149] FDI was also crucial for the development of LTOs. The state received USD 80 million for the sale of these 25 LTO licenses. The results on this front were less successful, however. With hindsight, it would probably have been better to have left them with Matav in the original privatization concept.

[150] For example, the French company Cegetel in the south of Hungary experimented in one of the local LTOs with the new WLL technology as a test bed for later expansion both in Hungary and in France.

and expansion plan in Hungary itself and the possibility of redirecting exports to the world market.

Matav issued international tenders for modern switching equipment in 1990, which were won by Siemens and Ericsson, with an obligation to produce locally. The local 'Telephone Factory' was then taken over in 1991 by Siemens Austria, linking the Hungarian experts to those in Vienna, Graz, Salzburg, Bratislava and Prague. The main task was to adapt and 'Hungarianize' the Siemens products. Ericsson, the other winner of the 1990 bid, took over the computer company Müszertechnica RT, first setting up a joint venture, Ericsson Technika, which later became a wholly owned subsidiary. Meanwhile, Ericsson Hungary had become an established center of excellence within the Ericsson network.[151] However, over the years hardware production has decreased, given the large economies of scale, so that much of the assembling is carried out abroad.[152] Today both companies produce only some switching equipment and make the final tests and installation to assist inbound trade. Given that the market for components is worldwide, it seems a fairly logical division of labor. Components are almost exclusively imported. The market is too small to engage in local assembly of complex systems, which are produced in much greater quantities at globally oriented manufacturing sites. Instead, both firms have been investing much more in the development of a local software capability, where they seem to have a comparative advantage.[153]

Also important for the development of the Hungarian market was the early introduction of a *GSM license* in 1992 and 1993, only one year behind Western European developments. This gave the Hungarian management and key personnel a chance to learn how to work with modern equipment,

---

[151] In 1993 it received worldwide product responsibility for one of the Ericsson products and also received special responsibility for regional product support for its neighboring markets such as in Poland, the Czech and Slovak Republics, Croatia and so on.

[152] For example, Ericsson today concentrates mostly on software production (roughly 50 percent of value added, with around 10 percent for hardware design and implementation and 40 percent for after-sales and customer services).

[153] Ericsson's buildup of technology transfer and own R&D was further strengthened through cooperation with the Technical University of Budapest by setting up a joint research lab with the Department of Electrical Engineering in 1996. This episode shows that the successful companies had to adapt their product line in order to survive. Müszertechnika came from the PC sector and assembled switching equipment and supported its software, while the Hungarian Telephone Factory, which came from the transmission side, had to learn the manufacturing of switching equipment. Initially Siemens also used the Hungarian plant to supply components and to assemble for Austrian and German markets, given the initial procurement preference for local production. For some of the newer products, such as for mobile services, no such policies were pursued. As a consequence, the Hungarian equipment manufacturers could barely play a role in the supply of these newer network products.

experience new marketing and distribution techniques and learn how to survive successfully in a competitive environment.

4.3.4 S&TS links

The loss of traditional CMEA export markets and the effects of globalization left technology transfer via FDI and joint ventures as the only option, given that there was only a temporary restraint on imports due to the initial insistence on domestic manufacturing for switching. This policy of encouraging FDI was very successful in the service sector, mainly because of the associated increase in network size and quality and technology improvements (including a successful launch of integrated services digital network (ISDN) and ATM and WLL technology) and the very cautious restructuring of Matav. FDI was also successful in the equipment sector, as we have seen, but against the background of a much more dramatic sectoral restructuring. To some extent, FDI was helped by a favorable legal environment and a stable procurement framework, since Matav had meanwhile become privatized and purchased its equipment on the open market. Also important for the development of the new operating concepts was the early introduction of a competitive cellular market.

Today, because of the success of the initial round of investment by Siemens and Ericsson in software and electronics, other companies are following, such as IBM, Motorola and Nokia. What seems to be important is to look at these foreign investments not only as investments in a *market* (to capture the available local demand and to influence the customers), but also as an investment in a *location* in which one can benefit from its comparative advantage by developing local centers of competence. Such an FDI strategy was helped by a favorable legal environment (the Telecommunications Act of 1992) which made Hungary a low-risk area for FDI. Furthermore, the fact that Matav had meanwhile become privatized and purchased on the open market also made it a more stable environment in which to work, even though the purchasing conditions were quite tough. It was these policies, rather than specific S&TS policies which have brought about a change.

5. LESSONS

5.1 Globalization of R&D

The sources of innovation from the equipment industry have changed with the emergence of the global equipment market and the trend towards service competition. In the past, the equipment producers and some of the central research laboratories of the national network service providers had provided the bulk of innovation in the industry. Also of increasing importance in R&D is the role of the upstream component providers, especially from the related fields of data processing and computer production. Much of the product-related R&D is in-house and financed directly by the enterprises. Some more risky projects are developed on a joint-venture basis. There may also be some subcontracting in certain areas (for example, for the local software adaptation of switching equipment from one country to another) so that access to a network of national specialist suppliers is crucial as well. As a consequence of this globalization of R&D, the backward linkage of the national service providers to the national manufacturers which has been so important in the past, either through vertical or quasi-vertical relationships through chosen national suppliers, has been drastically reduced.

Today, a greater international division of labor in R&D is taking place, with the role of manufacturers and specialist component suppliers stronger than before. They have become the driving force for technical change in the sector, with its traditional focus shifting from the switching and transmission sector to more network-based products. This leaves in a dilemma the traditional governmental policy towards nationally oriented S&TS linkages. Strong national telecommunication research centers that have supported a number of national suppliers, as for example, CNET in France, have now become fully integrated into the service provider France Telecom. Now their output is mainly proprietary, serving only one service supplier. Governments have therefore had to switch to other supply-side instruments, such as sector-specific subsidy schemes, or support for special research topics. Funding of new service applications has also served as a demand pull instrument.

But liberalization and deregulation policies have also been crucial in encouraging technical change, as have been the standardization issues. These factors can all be seen at work if we analyze, for example, the rapid spread of mobile services in Europe, as a consequence of liberalization and the spread of the GSM mobile standard. Where the link to the S&TS establishment becomes important for both service and equipment suppliers, is for access to basic technology.

5.2 Implications for Post-socialist Economies

The convergence between telecommunications and data processing, the associated digitalization of services and the rapid globalization of the sector, first for equipment and more recently for services, has accelerated the speed of technical change in the industry. The competitive environment, in which the industry operates, and the associated legal and regulatory structure (not only for the service sector, but also for the commercialization and privatization of the equipment sector), are today crucial for the realization of this growing technology potential, as is the overall macroeconomic environment. But given the weakness of the post-socialist countries on these issues, this has led to a growing technology gap *vis-à-vis* the more advanced countries. In addition, their difficult macroeconomic conditions, especially in the CIS and some of the CEE countries, have increased the already large capacity gap with respect to their telecommunications infrastructure. As a consequence, financing policies and technology transfer in relation to enterprise restructuring, in addition to a liberal regulatory environment for the development of a competitive service market, become more crucial than S&TS policies.

There is evidence that limited growth and investment restricts the role of S&T policies, since the sector uses up only its current stock of network equipment. As a consequence, we have concentrated on aggregate demand for services as one of the major variables that drives technical change. This was especially obvious in the comparison between Russia and Hungary (and to some extent Latvia). The case study of Russia showed clearly that the potential for technical change is limited, if aggregate demand in the service sector is more or less stagnant and services operate mainly on the basis of outdated capital stock and technology. As a consequence, derived demand for the equipment sector, in which much of the drive for technical change is taking place, was almost completely absent, especially as much of this demand was satisfied from imports.

Since the form and product distribution of aggregate demand changed, as large state enterprises were replaced by more decentralized decision making and a stronger influence of demand from private households, their derived demand has also changed. We have shown that skewed demand for modern telecommunication services is oriented mostly towards imported technology from the West. This was evident in all country studies, but particularly in Russia (given the emphasis in building up overlay and mobile networks, while the upgrading and modernization of basic network lags hopelessly behind).

In the process of analyzing these overall market trends and observing how firms and scientific institutions have behaved in this changing framework, we also noted a further institutional theme, which became central to our analysis: the breakdown of the old scientific linkages and supply networks has dramatic implications on the role played by S&TS policies. In the old Soviet system, there had been a major reliance on the CMEA partner countries such as East Germany, Bulgaria, Hungary, Yugoslavia and Poland for equipment production and the associated R&D processes. In addition to collaborating with the Soviet research centers, the S&TS role of the CMEA countries was to act as a conduit for Western technology. This whole network of CMEA countries become almost completely irrelevant with the end of the Cold War and the opening up of their national equipment market to the world economy. Direct contact with foreign manufacturers and joint ventures became possible. The disappearance of the trade restrictions under COCOM allowed foreign equipment manufacturers almost unrestricted entry into the CIS market. As a consequence of reduced demand and sudden globalization, the former East European suppliers ceased to be a competitive alternative and had to radically wind down their equipment production. This led to a very dramatic downsizing of the old R&D establishments. If one ignores the stimulus in increased demand, which took place in some of the CMEA countries as a process of transformation and protective procurement policies, their downsizing was even more pronounced, as they lost their foreign market as well as their domestic market (especially in the case of Latvia).

Furthermore, the transformation process has reduced the overall demand for investment substantially, especially in the CIS. The end of trade restrictions has at the same time opened up their national markets (especially for equipment) to international trade, thereby putting national producers at a very large disadvantage (given the existing technology gap, lack of marketing experience, no availability of supplier credit and so on). The case studies have also shown that the reemergence of the sector will largely depend on the overall economic performance and the associated legal and regulatory environment, preconditions which are necessary to permit increased investment in the service sector. There has been good progress in Hungary and Latvia, but patchy progress in Russia, with the exceptions of St. Petersburg and Moscow and resource-rich regions and the overlay network created by Rostelecom. There has been little progress in the equipment sector except where FDI could play a role or where the technology gap was not as large (as in the case for satellites and supporting space infrastructure in Russia). New S&TS links are developing only slowly, even when supported by tentative governmental policies (trade restrictions, local content rules).

The loss of traditional CMEA export markets and the effects of globalization left technology transfer via FDI and joint ventures as the only option, given that there was only a temporary restraint on imports due to the initial insistence on domestic manufacturing for switching. We saw that this policy of encouraging FDI was very successful in the service sector in Latvia and Hungary, mainly because of the associated increase in network size and quality and technology improvements. FDI was also successful in the equipment sector, as we have seen, but against the background of a much more dramatic sectoral restructuring.

5.3 The Limited Role of S&TS Links During Transformation

If we approach the market from the view of demand-led growth (hypothesis 1), then it becomes clear that the overall macroeconomic framework on the one hand and sector-specific conditions, such as the regulatory framework and treatment of FDI on the other, or the effectiveness of the commercialization and privatization process, have tremendous consequences for the development of both the basic access networks and the related services. Of course, this then also has an indirect impact on the telephone equipment market in the form of derived demand and the associated S&TS linkage. The smaller markets, for example, of the Baltics and Hungary, show that given the larger weight of telephone users, the forces protecting the equipment manufacturers and their technology links were quickly pushed aside in favor of a fast technology transfer from abroad (in the form of imported equipment and the associated joint venture to restructure the equipment sector). This process was probably most extreme for the S&TS establishments in Latvia, since demand for indigenous equipment disappeared overnight, while the links to the old Soviet research establishment were quickly broken and are now of little significance in any case. However, in Hungary, too, a significant reorganization of the equipment sector took place, again with not enough time to adapt sufficiently to international competition. The adjustment was sheltered to some extent by initial domestic procurement rules and the requirements for joint ventures. But already in the last few years, the level of domestic equipment production has been linked to a greater extent to local production cost and its link to the international manufacturing process than to domestic demand.

While there will always be some local needs to adapt global products to national conditions, given the specifics of national telephone networks, the amount of science and technology needed for these adaptations or localization of products is not too high. A full integration into the international division of labor is therefore the only viable solution for these smaller countries, keeping in mind their comparative advantages. The government can only guide this process along, including some support for S&TS, but not stand in its way.

For Russia, on the other hand, the lack of a clear macroeconomic and regulatory strategy and the subsequent lack of foreign direct investment has also led to much less derived demand for indigenous equipment (also for imported equipment) and the associated S&TS links. As a consequence, the implications for the upgrading of the overlay network are similar to those just discussed for the basic networks in Hungary and Latvia, with much of the derived demand going outside the national market. The main reasons are a lack in aggregate and therefore in derived demand (given the sharp drop in national income) and the strong tilt in equipment demand for overlay and mobile networks towards imported products.

It is difficult to evaluate to what extent upgrading of domestic networks could have been feasible without significant know-how transfer. Likewise, one can only hypothesize as to what extent local equipment manufacturers and service suppliers would have been able to have access to both the technology base and the expertise of foreign manufacturers without their significant involvement, relying instead on a more concerted coordination of equipment demand and access to foreign finance. This leaves the S&TS links very much hanging in the air, except where they are directly involved in commercial product support. The same question of technology transfer arises with respect to service networks, both for overlay and national regional networks as well as for mobile and data networks.

BIBLIOGRAPHY

Adam Smith Institute (1998), 'Telecommunications in the Russian Federation', Conference Documentation, Vienna, March 4–5.

Campbell, Robert W. (1995), *Soviet and Post Soviet Telecommunications: An Industry Under Reform*, Boulder, CO: Westview Press.

Davies, G. et al. (1995), *Key Technological and Policy Options for the Telecommunications Sector in Central and Eastern Europe and the Former Soviet Union*, London: European Bank for Reconstruction and Development, March.

Deutsche Morgan Grenfell (1997a), *Russia: The Bear Facts, Emerging Europe Telecommunication*, Moscow. Deutsche Bank.

Deutsche Morgan Grenfell (1997b), *Emerging Europe Telecommunication*, Moscow: Svyazinvest.

Electronics International (EI) (1998), *Telecommunications in Europe*, Chichester.

Elixmann, D. (1996), 'Globalization of the Telecommunications Sector', *DIW Quarterly Journal of Economic Research*, **65** (4), Berlin, pp. 464–58.

Iván, Mayor (1992), *Telcommunications Investment and Tariff Policy in Hungary*, Budapest.

Kessidis, Ioannis N. (1996), *The Russian Telecommunications Industry: Policy Issues and Options*, Washington, DC: World Bank.

Kubasik, Jerzy (1996), *Integration Objectives, Current Status and Abilities of the Central European Telecommunications Network*, Poznan.

Law, Carl Edgar (1995), 'Telecommunications in Eastern Europe and the GUS, Prospects and Markets to 2000', *Financial Times*, Management Reports, London.

Lowry, Tim (1997), 'The Baltic Experience: Case Study Latvia', Conference Documentation, IBC UK Conferences Ltd.: Privatization and Foreign Investment in Central and East European Telecommunications, Sheraton, Warsaw.

Pitelis, C.N. (1997), *Economic Integration Through Foreign Direct Investment in (the Less Favoured Countries of) Central and Eastern Europe and Impact on the (Less Favoured Countries of the) European Union*, Cambridge.

Public Network Europe Yearbook (1998), *Yearbook*. London: The Economist Newspaper Ltd..

Pyramid Research Inc. (1995), *Telecom Markets in the Newly Independent States*, Cambridge, UK and Boston, USA.

Rudaka, Inara (1997), 'Privatization Results in Latvian Telecommunications', Conference Documentation, IBC UK Conferences Ltd.: Privatization and Foreign Investment in Central and East European Telecommunications, Sheraton, Warsaw.

Rus, Marco (1998), 'Russian Telecommunication: Development and Problems, Telecommunications in the Russian Federation', Conference Documentation, Price Waterhouse, Vienna–Moscow, March 4.

Siemens AG (1997), *Daten zur Telekommunikation in russischen Regionen*, Berlin.

Sudol, Y. (1997), *Russian Regional Telcos*, London: Merrill Lynch.

Sudol, Y. (1998), 'Growth Prospects of Russian Telecommunications, Telecommunications in the Russian Federation', Conference Documentation, Merrill Lynch, Vienna–London, March 4.

9 Software: New Industries and New Enterprises in Eastern Europe

Jürgen Bitzer[154]

---

1. INTRODUCTION

The software sector plays an important role in every industrialized economy because software is almost omnipresent. The application fields extend from clock radios to automated production processes. Software makes a microwave oven function, monitors the fuel injection in a car, or replaces the typewriter with a word processing program.[155] In contrast to capitalist market economies, the application of computer technology in the socialist countries was used mainly to support central planning (for example, economic modeling, statistical analysis and data base services for collecting data). Despite the more limited fields of application, the outstanding software development skills of Eastern European experts, based on fundamental research in mathematics, have been widely recognized.

This chapter aims to analyze the emergence of the East European software industry in the light of international developments in this sector. Our first hypothesis is that neither a software sector nor a software market existed in the socialist period. Second, human capital in software development – despite its devaluation in the post-socialist period – became the base for the

---

[154] The author would like to thank Eduard Steinmueller, David Dyker and Christian von Hirschhausen for comments and Michael Jahn for proofreading the chapter. The usual disclaimer applies.

[155] This chapter is concerned only with computer software and not the software embedded in electronic systems, because a market for this does not exist. The software needed in these electronic systems is developed mostly in-house by the producers of electronic products themselves. There are two reasons for this. The first is that they do not want to give away their own company's knowledge. The second reason is the high cost of knowledge transfer which would be needed. So the make-or-buy question is frequently answered with in-house development.

emergence of the new Eastern European software sector. Third, although sectoral innovation systems for software development did still exist after the collapse of socialism, completely new and international innovation structures emerged and replaced the former national structures. Fourth, the process of catching-up technologically is based on international cooperation networks and is not influenced by institutional leftovers from socialism.

The second section of this chapter discusses the particularities of sources of innovation in software production; examines the structure of the EU software market; and analyzes the conditions in the different market segments. Section 3 examines the socialist organization of software development and the changes in the structure of this sector from the transformation period up to the present day. Section 4 summarizes the case studies of the Baltic countries Lithuania, Latvia and Estonia, and the Czech Republic. Section 5 concludes with the main results of the sector study of the software sector in Eastern Europe.

2. ANALYSIS OF THE INTERNATIONAL SOFTWARE MARKET

When IBM started to sell computer hardware and software separately in 1969, the computer software market was born. Since then, both this market and the market for related computer services have grown rapidly. In its early years, the software sector was a heterogeneous, fast-changing and small-business-dominated sector. Since then the sector has grown up, and its structure as well as its software creation procedures have changed. Whereas the size of enterprises in this business range from one-man enterprises to huge firms with several thousand employees, the software development methods do not differ significantly. This chapter analyzes the particularities of the software sector and the software market, because they are the background for the emergence of the East European software sectors.

2.1 Software as Product and Service: Peculiarities of Software Creation

A closer analysis of the development process of software shows that two completely different types can be identified. Depending on the number of potential customers, we can distinguish between the development of *custom* and *standard*[156] software. A decisive factor in the development strategy used

---

[156] The author's concept of standard software includes all kinds of software which, in contrast to packaged software, are not produced in single-unit production within a software development project.

is the degree of standardization of the software. The degree of standardization (DS) is the relation between users with tasks in the same application field (B) and those users who can solve their problems with the same software (A) (DS $\equiv$ A/B). Logically, the degree of standardization increases with the growing number of users who are able to carry out their tasks with this software. Therefore the degree of standardization is influenced not only by the complexity of the application field but also by other factors such as international standardization (for example, international accounting rules) and the strategy of the software-producing enterprises (for example, extension of the function of products).

The development of *custom software* is characterized by its *service character*, which is reflected in the individualized, customer- and order-oriented, single-unit production. The software is developed within a single project and its use for other projects is limited. Customized software is heterogeneous, corresponding to the character of a service. The customer has the opportunity to bring his or her requirements into the software development process. Because of the *project character* of this process, the risks associated with financing, faulty development and delayed completion are borne by the customer (Baaken and Launen 1993, p. 5). The customer carries all the development costs because the software is a single unit production and can usually be sold only once. Single-unit production leads to high prices because of the high fixed costs which are not shared by several customers. Additionally, custom software has to be developed from the ground up, and is therefore not immediately available. For the development process of such software, a close proximity between supplier and customer is needed. Thus, a distribution network does not exist.

In the segment for *standard software*, development is geared towards selling it several times, in fact, as often as possible. Potential customers have virtually no influence on the development of the software. This shows that in contrast to custom software, standard software has a *product character*. The condition for the development of standard software is that standardization is possible: the software must be able to meet the needs of potential customers with standardized functions. The risks associated with the financing, development and sale of the software are carried by the developing enterprise. The price is lower than that of custom software because development costs are shared by several customers. The advantages of standard software are its immediate availability, the guarantee of its further development and the elimination of bugs in future software generations. Because of the advantages of standard software on the one hand and the high development costs of custom software on the other hand, the market share of the latter is falling, while that of the former is rising. But with this development, the importance of the individual adaptation of standardized software is increasing as well (Deppe 1994, pp. 52–7). The suppliers of standardized software often use the same distribution networks as the producers of computer hardware: computer and software products can frequently be bought in the same store.

The *sources of innovation* do not differ depending on whether software is developed as a product or as a service: the main source of innovation in the software sector is in-house R&D capacities. Whereas the use of R&D capacities does not differ between these two kinds of software development, the organization of R&D locations does. Because of the service characteristic of custom software, the R&D capacities are located in every regional market in which the enterprises are present. In contrast, enterprises that develop standard software have mainly home-based R&D capacities, the result of the almost-identical development process for software products (Baaken and Launen 1993, p. 11). In both cases, there is usually no significant external innovation procedure.[157] The reason for this can also be seen in the process of software development. If an enterprise were to outsource the development of software, the external partner would be able to reproduce this product for him- or herself: perhaps, with some modifications, even as a competing product. The normal way of getting access to required components, products or knowledge is to take over the enterprise in question. This lowers the risk of potential competition and furthermore lowers the costs and the time needed for in-house development.[158] Furthermore, the external development of a component would cause enormous extra costs because the component would have to be integrated into the complete software package. This is far more complicated than assembling a car from several parts which have been produced externally.

2.2 Different Types of Software

Besides these different kinds of software development, the intended use for which the software has been designed enables further distinctions to be made among software types. One can distinguish between user-oriented software (application software) and hardware-oriented software (system programs). A

---

[157] Cooperation in software development between different software enterprises exists only between different segments; for example, between operating systems and application software producers. Here, the cooperating enterprises do not develop one product together; they each develop a particular component of their own (for example, IBM develops the operating system OS/2 and Microsoft develops the application software Microsoft Office for this operating system). But even these attempts at cooperation between software enterprises often fail (for example, Microsoft and IBM).

[158] IBM, for example, bought Lotus because it needed application software for its operating system OS/2. See Benedikter (1993).

third segment should be added: entertainment software, which has special characteristics.

The application software segment includes software programs oriented towards the solution of users' problems.[159] This corresponds to the OECD definition, which states that the concept of 'application software' covers all programs whose purpose is to solve the computer user's problems.[160] Examples of such problem-oriented software are word-processing programs, calculation software, presentation software, process-controlling software, software for stock control, accounting software and so on.

The segment for standardized system software contains software programs which are oriented towards problems with hardware operation.[161] These programs make the use of a computer possible: they are the link between the hardware and the user. System software is hardware-oriented and is required for the operation of data-processing systems. Therefore the entire development process is oriented towards the attributes of the computer hardware. Examples of such programs are operating systems, programming tools, security utilities and so on.

The entertainment software segment has its own rules. The term 'entertainment software' covers programs such as computer games, multimedia CD-ROM programs, and reference work programs. The customers of enterprises in this market segment are private households. Private sector demand is growing, particularly in Western countries: more and more private households own computers and the younger generations are becoming an important customer group for this market segment. The products are highly standardized so that they can be sold often.

Theoretically all of these software types can be developed both as standard and as custom software. In reality however, both system and entertainment software are developed nearly exclusively as standardized software. Only in the case of application software are both kinds of development observable. Correspondingly, various market segments can be identified (see Figure 9.1).

---

[159] The value of this market segment in the EU in 1996 was ECU 14,732 million which correspond to a market share of 49 percent of the standard software market.

[160] OECD (1985, p. 23).

[161] The value of this market segment in the EU in 1996 was ECU 14,134 million, which corresponds to a market share of 51 percent of the standard software market.

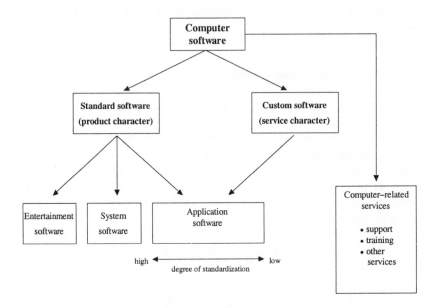

Figure 9.1 Segments of the computer software market

2.2.1 Competition and status quo in the market segment for standard software

Application software: Because of the overwhelming share of business customers, the downstream competition in the market segment for application software is carried out mainly on the following competition axes: quality of the product, reputation of the enterprise, compatibility with other programs or the data format of former program generations, installations (number of users) and price.[162] In particular the network effects, which exist in the application market segment, represent a high entry barrier to new competitors.

The degree of standardization strongly influences the competition intensity in this market segment. The global software market for highly standardized application software is characterized by an increase in competition and concentration. Reasons for this are the high transparency of the market and the immense development costs. The number of potential competitors rises with the degree of standardization. The increasing competition of recent years, however, has led to a strong concentration on the market for highly standardized software. The current situation is that this market is dominated

---

[162] See Bitzer (1998b, pp.14–18) or Bitzer (1997, pp.15–19) for detailed competition analysis in this market segment.

by a small number of enterprises: for example, Microsoft for office application software.[163] The position of the market leader in such segments is very strong due to existing/created network effects, acquired reputation, quality advantages through experience gained and presence on the market, and the existing number of installations.[164] The substantial expenditures of money and labor for development are the reason why only large enterprises are present here. The market segment for highly standardized application software is protected by high entry barriers. To enter this market, a potential competitor must be able to offer products of equally high quality to be an alternative to the enterprises which are already present. Furthermore, the competitor has to offer a lower price and have a good reputation. But even given such near-perfect conditions it would take a number of years to capture a market share. A successful market entry for highly standardized application software requires considerable financial resources. A 'hit-and-run' strategy is, due to existing network effects, not possible in this market segment.

In market segments with a lower degree of standardization, the intensity of competition drops, and with it, the concentration. Market transparency is much lower than with highly standardized software products. Such market segments are usually dominated by domestic enterprises, because they have competition advantages over international companies. Such competition advantages are higher flexibility, a lower break-even point in terms of customers, personal contacts, knowledge of language, mentality, culture, laws, national procedures and so on. With a decreasing degree of standardization, the number of small and medium enterprises on the market increases because their proximity to their customers, their flexibility and their lower break-even point in terms of customers are paying off.

System software: In the case of standard system software, downstream competition takes place on the competition axes of quality, which is crucial for the smooth functioning of the computer system; reputation of the enterprise, which 'proves' the firm's reliability; and available application software, which makes the use of the system software sensible. In particular the quality of the system software is of crucial importance: only with it is the hardware usable, and a malfunction could cause serious consequences for the applying enterprise (for example, significant losses in the case of the breakdown of a production process).

Because of the hardware-orientation of the system software market segment, hardware producers play the dominant role due to their knowledge of the hardware. Most system software is developed by hardware producers

---

[163] Other examples of leading software enterprises are: IBM, Oracle, SAP, Adabas and so on.
[164] See Bitzer (1998b) for detailed competition analysis in this market segment.

themselves;[165] only Microsoft was able to introduce an operating system successfully without being a hardware producer.[166] In higher computer classes (workstations, mainframe computers and supercomputers) such development is hampered by the proprietary architecture of the computers. As one leaves the area of the operating system, the importance of hardware producers falls because the software loses its hardware (system) orientation.

Because of the special knowledge and the high quality necessary, the number of suppliers on the system software market is small. System software is mostly developed for a special computer platform because its instructions directly address the hardware. Only some system software is created to deal with different systems, for example, some variants of UNIX and Windows NT. Network effects play a lesser role here than on the market for application software, because no data is accumulated with this kind of software. As a rule of thumb, with increasing computer size, the importance of hardware producers in the system software segment increases as well. The reason for this is that the knowledge of hardware technology is needed to put an enterprise in a position to develop system software. Another reason is that know-how accumulated over a period of time in this field works as competition disadvantage for potential newcomers.

Entertainment software: A small but steadily growing segment of the software market is that of entertainment software.[167] This market segment is characterized by an absence of network effects, compatibility requirements and a dominating market leader, and by a lack of saturation. Because the users of this kind of software do not accumulate data, network effects and compatibility requirements are of no importance. Furthermore, the importance of correct functioning of the software is not critical. Quality has another meaning in this market segment: it means 'more fun'; thus, improved graphics or sound design are perceived as an increase in quality. With this, the main arguments for the necessity of a good reputation – crucial in the application, system and custom software market segments – disappear. Nevertheless, quality (in the sense mentioned above) is an important competition factor among enterprises here. Therefore an important competition axis is a knowledge of changing customer preferences and good timing in bringing new computer games onto the market.[168] The development of the

---

[165] IBM was by far the largest software supplier in 1995. In the same year, six of the top ten software suppliers were hardware producers. See Petska-Juliussen and Juliussen (1996, p. 34).

[166] Another attempt was made by Novell with Novell Dos 7.0, but this failed.

[167] The value of this market was not available because statistically it is attached to the toy industry.

[168] For example, several years ago, flight simulations were very popular; today simulations of

entertainment software market, such as the fashion market, follows customer tastes. Thus the 'normal' competition instruments have no importance in this market segment. Competition is nevertheless low because the numerous products are not substitutes for each other: every game has its own concept or background. With every new game developed, the fight for customers starts at zero. Furthermore, no saturation is currently observable.

In this segment, small and medium enterprises have good opportunities because market barriers do not exist. A hit-and-run strategy works in this market segment, because continuity is not needed. An important factor for the growth rates in this market segment are computer installations in private households, which increase with the standard of living. But this shows that today, the potential markets for entertainment software are mainly the industrialized Western countries.

2.2.2 Competition and status quo in the market segment for custom software

The competition on the market for *custom application software* takes place along the axes quality, possibility of offering a complete solution (only in the case of large projects), reputation of the enterprise, and personal contacts.

Large international enterprises dominate the market segment for large, high-complexity custom software projects. This is usually the case when state administrations, large insurance companies or banks are searching for complete solutions. Only large enterprises have the capacity and capabilities to handle such projects. Their disadvantages compared with domestic enterprises are generally low because such customers usually act according to international procedures.[169] The number of potential suppliers diminishes with the capacities required to handle such projects. Thus, this market segment is also dominated by large international software enterprises and system houses that can offer hardware solutions.

With a decrease in the size and complexity of software projects, entry barriers are lowered as well and the competitiveness of small and medium domestic enterprises rises. Such market segments are dominated by domestic enterprises because they have competition advantages over international companies, such as higher flexibility; lower costs; personal contacts; and knowledge of language, mentality, culture, laws and national procedures. The domestic software enterprises' flexibility, lower costs, and proximity to their customers pay off.

---

the development of societies are popular.
[169] For example, enterprise groups such as Daimler/Chrysler use an international accounting system, because they are also present on international stock exchanges.

2.3 The Software Market in the European Union

In the 1990s, the market for computer software is still growing at two-digit rates in Western countries. Even this volume is underestimated: most in-house software development is not included because enterprises generally do not give separate figures on it.

Why are there such continually high growth rates on the computer software market even in times of recession? The answer can be found in the field of computer software applications. Software is usable where processes can be automated or rationalized, which is true for most parts of the economy. Automation and rationalization in Western countries has increased in recent years and with it, significance and sales of computer software – even in times of depression. Nevertheless, in recent years a gradual saturation of the market for computer software in Western countries has been noticeable. In CEE and CIS countries, the level of automation is still low; this means that the software sector in these countries will grow quickly in the years to come.

Table 9.1 The software market of the EU, 1994–1998

Years	1994	1995	1996	1997[a]	1998[a]
Value of the EU computer software market (million ECU)					
Type of software					
– System software	12,051	13,047	14,134	15,414	16,821
– Application software	12,149	13,460	14,732	16,108	17,670
Standard software[b]	24,200	26,507	28,866	31,522	34,491
Custom software	20,555	22,360	24,086	25,955	28,213
Computer software	44,755	48,867	52,952	57,477	62,704
Shares of different kinds of software in the EU (in %)					
Type of software					
– System software	27	27	27	27	27
– Application software	27	28	28	28	28
Standard software[b]	54	54	55	55	55
Custom software	46	46	45	45	45
Total	100	100	100	100	100

Notes:
[a] Estimated by EITO.
[b] Sum of system and application software.

Source: EITO (1997).

The market segment for standard software in the EU had a value of ECU 29 billion in 1996 which corresponds to a share of 55 percent of the overall software market. Table 9.1 shows the value of the different software market segments in the EU between 1994 and 1998. Unfortunately, figures on the market volume for entertainment software are not available, because statistically they are connected to the toy sector and usually not revealed separately. On average, the market for computer software grew by 9 percent per year which is far above the growth rates of the overall EU economy. In 1996, more money was spent on software (ECU 53 billion) than on computers (ECU 44 billion). This shows the importance of software in the computer industry. Fifty-five percent of the software market was accounted for by software products and the remaining 45 percent by custom software solutions (EITO 1997, p. 279).

3. THE SOFTWARE SECTOR IN EASTERN EUROPEAN COUNTRIES

3.1 Software Development under Socialism

In the socialist period, software development took place mainly in industry and in government ministries. Application software was developed largely for the needs of the military–industrial complex and the institutions of central planning and scientific and technical computing. Software development was seen as a supporting service and not as a producing sector in its own right. Therefore units for the development of software solutions were created only as internal departments in the core areas of computer use. Cooperation between the software developing units was weak and therefore each institution provided itself with the required software.[170] Nearly all software used was produced as single-unit developments. Software products were not commodities for sale and therefore, a software market where software was traded did not exist: hence no software sector existed.

Apart from these organizational issues, the isolation of the socialist East European countries from the Western world was another reason for the backwardness of East European software. The lack of hardware was a serious obstacle to software development in socialist countries. Because of the COCOM list, the newest computer technology was not available in socialist countries. This was a particularly decisive factor in the field of supercomputing. Without a large amount of the required hardware, the

---

[170] Thus the military–industrial complex prevented the extensive use of military R&D as a source of civilian software innovation.

development of modern software is impossible. The restrictions of the socialist countries further hampered the exchange of ideas between software experts of East and West. Having no access to leading trends, information and modern computer technology, the software institutions produced software far below the level of Western enterprises (Burghart 1992, p. 131). The population of experienced programmers remained small in socialist countries, and there was a critical shortage of programmers with experience on large modern computer systems.

Government policy-makers, who wanted to develop computer and software technology without high R&D costs and the uncertainty of R&D processes, decided to catch up in computer and software technology through imitation rather than through innovation (Katkalo and Mowery 1996, pp. 241–2). Often, Western software products were bought, illegally copied and distributed at low cost. The situation changed only in the 1980s when the priority of information technology rose. This was due to the socialist party's decision to identify information technology as a 'future technology'. With this decision, the significance of software development rose as well.[171] But this change in the opinion of policy-makers was not supported by policies. The funding of R&D, personnel training and equipment did not rise. As a result, efforts to catch up in computer and software technology did not succeed, and governments permitted other means of attaining a supply of modern technology.[172]

In conclusion, the situation of software development under socialism was characterized by:

- single-unit software developed in-house,
- strongly limited spillover effects between software-developing institutions,
- restrictions in terms of hardware,
- a lack of exchange of knowledge on modern computer technology, and
- an absence of trade in software accompanied by the absence of a software market and a software sector.

3.2 The Emergence of a Software Sector

With the collapse of socialism, the situation in software development and trade changed completely. Software products from the West as well as from the East became available for purchase. This was the *birth of software*

---

[171] See the changes in the Russian software industry throughout the Gorbachev period.
[172] Poland, for example, turned a blind eye to the organized, but unofficial, importation of computers, computer components and software via tourists in the 1980s. See Dyker (1996, p. 2).

markets in Eastern Europe. The rapid introduction and absorption of new international hardware technologies required a completely different kind of software, not only in terms of the software technology used, but also in terms of the areas of application. The competition axes, competitors, human capital, quality and application fields of the software in demand, and other internal factors have changed, and now these factors serve as entry barriers to new software enterprises. The demands on software enterprises have expanded: while the knowledge of how to program software was once the main requirement, now knowledge of what customers need is necessary. Thus a detailed knowledge of software application fields is essential. But with the introduction of a capitalist market economy, the forms of organization, strategies and technologies of the potential customers have changed. The software-developing enterprises had to acquire new knowledge because every competitor is able to program. Therefore, the ability to fulfill the requirements of the customers has become a very important competition factor on the software market. A part of the human capital of the Eastern European countries in software technology was consequently devalued by these developments.

The lack of competitiveness led to a rapid penetration of the market with standard Western software, causing the shutdown of internal software development departments, the former centers of software development. Former employees of the specialized software departments left their positions or lost their jobs through these closures and entered the emerging software sector. New enterprises were set up which started to trade with Western computer and software products. From this point on, enterprises undertook to become integrated into international networks through contracts and agreements for cooperation with international software suppliers. With the development of the computer market, the demand for more complex software solutions increased and led to more sophisticated activities of the East European software enterprises. At the local level, domestic enterprises started to develop software with a low level of standardization, as well as custom software, and to offer services such as implementation, installation, adaptation and training. The further development of Eastern European software enterprises in these more sophisticated activities was and still is based on the technology transfer of their contractual or cooperation partners. In this context, relations between the Eastern European and Western software enterprises intensified quickly. Eastern European enterprises were established as simple resellers, but with increasing experience in business and new technologies, they were able to establish closer relations to international software suppliers, and some were even integrated into the innovation networks as adaptation and implementation partners. With the development of the East European markets they also became attractive for international competitors. Whereas in the initial years following the collapse of socialism, Western software companies sold their products through domestic distributors or other trading partners, several years later they opened their own subsidiaries in each of the CEE and CIS countries.[173]

Today, the new Eastern European software enterprises dominate the market segments for software with low standardization, adapted software and small-scale custom software projects. Furthermore, the segment for computer-connected services such as installation, implementation and training is also dominated by domestic enterprises. The remaining segments are dominated by well-known Western software companies. The market segments in which Eastern European domestic enterprises are active are similar to those of Western countries: in these segments, the competition advantages of domestic enterprises (knowledge of language and culture, personal contacts) come into play. On international software markets, Eastern European software enterprises have no significance, although a handful of enterprises have been able to sell their specific knowledge.

3.3 The Current Software Market Structure in Eastern Europe

Like the computer hardware market, the Eastern European software market is still small. In comparison to the EU software market, East European software markets are insignificant: they are only a fraction of the size of the Spanish software market. In particular, the software markets of Russia and Poland are very small by comparison and rank only second and third, although they have the largest and second-largest GDP, respectively, of the four countries compared (see Table 9.2).

Table 9.2 Value of software markets of several Eastern European countries

Countries	Population 1996 (m)	GDP ($ bn)	Market value 1996 (ECU m)	Spanish soft-ware market (%)	EU software market (%)
EU	366.8	7,635.0	52,952	–	100
Czech Republic	10.3	52.1	353	19.5	0.66
Russia	147.5	440.0	338	18.6	0.63
Poland	38.6	130.7	216	12.0	0.40
Hungary	10.2	43.9	205	11.3	0.38

Sources: EITO (1997); BMWI (1997).

---

[173] Examples: Microsoft Hungary 1992, Oracle Hungary 1993, Novell Hungary 1994, Budapest Business Journal (1997, pp. 104–6).

The computer software markets in Eastern Europe are underdeveloped in comparison to the computer hardware markets. There are several reasons for this: first, the large extent of software piracy reduces the value of the software market considerably and with it, the turnover of software enterprises on these markets. Table 9.3 shows that expenditures for computer hardware are much higher than for software. This itself suggests that expenditures on software are so low because it can be copied illegally.

Table 9.3 Relation between expenditures for computers and software, 1996 (%)

Countries	Software	Computers	Total
EU	50	50	100
Czech Republic	42	58	100
Russia	19	81	100
Poland	29	71	100
Hungary	46	54	100

Source: EITO (1997); author's calculations.

Table 9.4 Relation between standard and custom software in different countries, 1996 (%)

Countries	Standardized software	Custom software	Total
EU	55	45	100
Spain	62	38	100
Russia	45	55	100
Poland	53	47	100
Czech Republic	37	63	100
Hungary	48	52	100

Source: EITO (1997), author's calculations.

A second reason for the underdevelopment of Eastern European software markets is the prevailing importance of custom software solutions, which are developed by domestic enterprises at low prices. This keeps the expenditure on software low and therefore, the value of the market remains small. Only the Polish software market has a similar structure to that of the EU in terms of the relation between standard and custom software. In all other Eastern

European countries, the custom software segment is dominant. It should be mentioned again, however, that these figures present a distorted picture because of the high share of software piracy (see Table 9.4).

In the market segments for small custom software projects and for software products with a low level of standardization, domestic enterprises dominate the market. One can assume, however, that with a stabilization of the economic and political situation, the importance of custom software will shift to standard software because this will enable the standardization of several application fields. This will lead to domestic enterprises losing part of their competitive advantage and international enterprises entering the markets.

3.4. Prospects for Software Enterprises from Eastern European Countries

In the early years of post-socialism it was often stated that the software enterprises of CEE and CIS countries had 'glorious' times ahead of them and that they would play an important role in the global software market of the future due to their 'outstanding' skills, based on fundamental research in mathematics (Katkalo and Mowery 1996). But developments in recent years have shown that fundamental changes in the software business hit Eastern European software developers, who were completely unprepared and unable to compete under these new conditions. The catching-up process was and still is based on foreign technology transfers. What are the future prospects for the Eastern European software enterprises?

As mentioned above, Eastern European software enterprises dominate domestic market segments for software with a low degree of standardization, adapted software and small-scale custom software projects. Based on a comparison of this situation and Western structures, it can be expected that domestic enterprises will be able to defend their domination in those market segments due to existing competition advantages, especially because of their knowledge of the market conditions. But it should be mentioned that the market segments for software with a low degree of standardization and custom software will shrink in the following years, and the domestic software enterprises active in these segments will face growing competition from domestic competitors. This tendency can be explained by an increasing standardization of business and production practices which will enable the software producer to increase the standardization degree of software applications. Consequently Western enterprises, too, will enter into competition or offer already-available standardized software.

It is unlikely that those Eastern European software products which are almost completely absent on the international software market will gain an increasing role. The domination of Western software enterprises in the segments for standard application and system software will, in the short and the medium term, prevent the successful establishment of Eastern European software products. An exogenous limiting factor is the small size of domestic markets, which are therefore unable to provide a platform for the development of complex and costly products. The same is true for large-scale custom software: experience in the business for which the software is providing a service is required, and so is the possibility of offering complete solutions. Both will remain competition disadvantages for Eastern European software enterprises in the short run. Another reason for the problems of East European enterprises in entering international markets is their small size. The lack of the domestic enterprises' financial resources also presents a competition disadvantage when compared with international enterprises, particularly in the case of large projects. Nevertheless, some Eastern European enterprises have been able to enter the international market with good strategies and establish themselves successfully in small and very specific market segments (for example, handwriting recognition software). The entertainment software market offers promising opportunities for the entry of the international market, due to the characteristics mentioned in Section 2.

The development of East European enterprises will continue to depend heavily on the development of their domestic markets, the basis for their further development towards which they are oriented almost exclusively. In this regard, the removal of bottlenecks in infrastructure and legislation will be a crucial prerequisite. This includes the introduction of standardization procedures and patent legislation (and its enforcement) as well as the improvement of telecommunications (Correa 1993b). The lack of enforcement of patent legislation is a significant hindrance to the development of the software sector and of software enterprises: without enforcement, price is excluded as an axis for competition. This is a great disadvantage for small and medium-sized domestic enterprises, because even with the cheapest software they are unable to compete. A further result of illegal software copying is that Eastern European software enterprises are not paid for their products. The international enterprises are able to make profits on other (Western) markets and to simultaneously create network effects through the dissemination of their software products, which will work in the future as an entry barrier on those markets (Correa 1993a, pp. 5–7; 1996, pp. 173–4).

Often the example of India is cited as promising strategy for Eastern European countries. Indeed, the idea of carrying out programming work with cheap labor is a possible strategy. However, it has to be taken into account that India itself will be the main competitor, because of its low labor costs and, in contrast to East European countries, stable economic and political conditions, as well as huge public support. Nevertheless, some successful examples can be found in Central European countries such as Hungary and Poland, where Western enterprises outsource the programming of software modules.[174]

4. CASE STUDIES: THE BALTIC COUNTRIES AND THE CZECH REPUBLIC

4.1 Baltic Countries: Lithuania, Latvia and Estonia

4.1.1 Socialist software development and the emergence of a Baltic software sector

The development of software in the Baltic Soviet republics started with the introduction of the first mainframe computer in the mid-1960s. The development of software was decentralized and established at the most important locations of computer use: institutions of central planning such as ministries; the (military) industrial complex; and science and research institutions. According to socialist practice, institutions and budgets for this development were provided by the government which, in the case of the Baltics, was located in Moscow. University courses for the education of programmers and computer engineers were established in all of the Baltic republics' universities.[175] Furthermore, specific educational institutions were established which trained specialists for specific tasks in the economy, for example, the Agriculture Academy of Latvia and Riga's Aviation Institute. Research in software technology was organized as in other fields of the economy and was carried out in the academies of science, where corresponding institutes were established.[176] Major application fields for

---

[174] For example, Ericsson outsource the programming of software for their cellular phones to Hungary.

[175] In Lithuania, for example, courses were available at Vilnius University and Kaunas Polytechnical Institute. The corresponding education institutions in Latvia and Estonia were the University of Latvia, Riga's Polytechnical Institute, Tallinn Technical University and Tartu University.

[176] Lithuania's main research institution in hardware and software technology was the Institute of Mathematics and Informatics of the Lithuanian Academy of Sciences. The Institute was founded in 1977. In Latvia, the Institute of Electronics and Computation Science of the Latvian Academy of Sciences was responsible for basic research. The basic research in software technology for Estonia was carried out by the Institute of Cybernetics of the Estonian Academy of Sciences.

computers and therefore also a major part of the developed software was used for:

- data processing of state statistics,
- data processing and management support in enterprises, and
- statistical analysis, modeling and forecasting.

The main task of computer and software technology was the support of central planning. Data processing, modeling and forecasting were established at all levels of the economy. The result was a huge number of institutions which participated in the registration, processing and analysis of data.[177] Cooperation between those institutions was weak and therefore each institution provided itself with the required software programs. Spillover effects remained small and the development of software was characterized by single-unit production with no standardization. As in the other socialist countries, software was not a commodity for sale and therefore a market for software did not exist. This absence of a software market shows that effectively no software enterprises and no software sector existed in the socialist period.

The situation changed dramatically with the collapse of socialism and the restoration of independence in 1991. With the opening of Baltic markets, Western products became available immediately. This led to a rapid penetration with Western computer technology and suitable software. For the first time, software was traded freely and available to everybody. The Baltic software market was born.

The former centers of software development underwent a dramatic change. With the introduction of a market economy, the main task of the computer and software institutions – supporting central planning – vanished from one day to the next. Most of the institutions were shut down or had to re-focus their activities. The computation centers in the ministries and the enterprises were shut down, because of either the shutdown of the host institution or the inability to compete against Western software products. The former employees of the computation centers entered the newly emerging computer and software sectors.

With the newly emerging private sector, the demand for information technology increased sharply. However, the software in demand today differs

---

[177] One-hundred and twenty 'automatic management and data-processing systems' were in operation in Latvia in 1996. Forty-three of them were used for enterprise management, 16 for the management of technical processes, 14 for regional planning, 28 for planning issues at the ministerial level and 19 for other data-processing issues (for example, at universities). See Karnite and Karnitis (1998, pp. 693–4).

immensely in its application fields from that in the socialist period. The numerous small businesses require only small-scale computer capacities and suitable software. Both could be provided immediately by Western computer manufacturers. New enterprises, founded mainly by the former employees of the computing centers, took over the trade and distribution of Western software. They also offered installation and support services to their customers. After some time in this business and having acquired the necessary knowledge, local enterprises also started to offer specific solutions with a low degree of standardization. In particular, in the field of business management software (that is, accounting software, storage management software and cost calculating programs) the Baltic software enterprises were able to establish themselves successfully on the market. A further step in the development of the Baltic software sector was the adaptation of Western standard software to local requirements.

4.1.2 Market situation today and sources of innovation

The software market in the Baltic countries is characterized by small computer/software enterprises. They trade in computers, computer components and software, assemble PCs and offer related services such as installation, support, programming, training and implementation. Pure software enterprises are very rare because the computer and software markets are not highly specialized.[178] The predominant activity of Baltic software enterprises is still trade with standard Western software. Software developed in the Baltic countries is limited to the segments of software with a low level of standardization and custom software. Because of this limited product range, the Baltic software enterprises are active mainly on their own domestic markets. The development of custom software and software with a low level of standardization is closely connected to the local environment: thus, the export of these products is not easy. On foreign markets they lose the competition advantage presented by a knowledge of the particularities of the country. Exports to other countries are therefore very rare.

The high share of software piracy hampers the development of domestic enterprises through lost revenues and the exclusion of price as an axis of competition. Whereas international enterprises are able to cope with this loss more easily, domestic enterprises with their small financial resources are affected heavily by the illegal copying of their software. Furthermore, the Baltic software enterprises are often still unable to provide the quality

---

[178] For 1997, the official statistics list the following number of enterprises active in these businesses: Lithuania: 700; Latvia: 321; and Estonia: 260. The overwhelming number of these enterprises have fewer than ten employees and about 98 percent of them are privately owned. See Morkūnaite (1998), Karnite and Karnitis (1998), Kilvits (1998).

required to satisfy their customers, especially when illegal versions of Western products can be purchased at a very low price, resulting in most customers choosing the latter. All Baltic countries recognized the problem of illegal software markets and passed patent and copyright legislation.[179] Nevertheless, because these laws are not enforced, the share of illegal software is still estimated to be around 90 percent.

Despite these disadvantages, some Baltic software enterprises were able to obtain orders from the local public sector, which introduced information technology on a large scale. The development of custom software solutions for state administration and the domestic banking sector was often carried out by domestic enterprises because of their specific knowledge of the existing conditions (for example, culture and language). The state therefore still accounts for a significant part of the Baltic software market. In a survey carried out in Lithuania, the participating enterprises reported that in 1996 about 39 percent of their turnover depended on the public sector (Morkûnaite 1998, pp. 675–6).

The main sources of innovation are the well-known Western software enterprises for which the Baltic enterprises act as distributors, cooperation partners or representatives. Nearly every enterprise active in the software business – whether in trade only or in adapting software to local needs – enters into contractual agreements or cooperation with international software enterprises such as Microsoft and Oracle. These agreements provide the enterprises with access to the required technological information for the supported software products. If these products are to be adapted to the local environment, this information is crucial. It is also required for support services such as installation, training and technical support.

In the case of the development of custom software, the sources are mainly internal, that is, the employees. The educational level of the employees in Baltic software enterprises is very high. About 80 percent have a degree from a university or academy (Morkûnaite 1998; Karnite and Karnitis 1998). This well-educated workforce was the basis for the emerging computer and software sectors. Without this human capital, the application of state-of-the-art information technology in the economy would have been impossible.

4.1.3 Enterprise case study: Fortech Ltd., Latvia

Fortech Ltd. was founded in 1991 following a strategy designed to enable it

---

[179] In 1996, the Lithuanian government passed the 'Law on legal protection of computer programs and data bases' and a second 'Law on authors' and adjacent rights' was prepared in 1997. See Morkûnaite (1998, p. 686). Similarly, the Latvian government passed the 'Law on copyrights and neighboring rights' and also established several regulations for licensed software. See Karnite and Karnitis (1998, p. 703).

to become an IT integrator: consequently it started by trading with computers, computer components and software products, which were adapted to meet local requirements. Fortech also offers a complete range of support services for its products, including installation, implementation, training and technical support. Furthermore, the enterprise was engaged in the development of software for the local market. This combination of services enabled Fortech to become the largest IT system integrator in Latvia with more than 200 employees in 1998 and a subsidiary in Lithuania. The staff of the company is well educated, with more than the half of the employees having a university degree. Table 9.5 shows the specific skills of the employees of Fortech.

The average age of Fortech's employees is 27, which shows that the overwhelming majority of the employees did not come from former socialist institutions.

Table 9.5 Number and characteristics of Fortech experts

Group	Subgroup	Number of certified experts
Operating systems	MS DOS	18
	WINDOWS and	12
	Unix	2
	Novell Netware	5
	OS/2	4
Application development tools	MS VISUAL BASIC	4
	BORLAND DELPHI	8
	GUPTA SOL WINDOWS	7
	C++	4
DB/DBMS	ORACLE	7
	MS FOXPRO	15
	MS SOL SERVER	4
	GUPTA SOL BASE	3
	DB2	3

Source: Taken from Karnite and Karnitis (1998, p. 646).

Fortech is among the top 150 Latvian enterprises with a turnover of LVL 3.4 million in 1996 and LVL 5.9 million in 1997. Besides various agreements with Western hardware producers (for example, Dell computers, Hewlett Packard and Sony) it also entered into cooperation with the most important software producers. Table 9.6 shows Fortech's most important cooperation partners.

Table 9.6 Fortech's most important cooperation partners

Cooperation partner	Fortech's status
Microsoft	Microsoft qualified solution provider, Microsoft Qualified dealer
Novell	Authorized reseller
Oracle	Application developer
SAP	Implementation partner
Dell Computers	Authorized distributor in Latvia and Lithuania
Hewlett Packard	Authorized reseller, service center
Sony	Service partner
Madge Networks	Authorized reseller
Lucent (AT&T) Technologies	Authorized reseller
NEC	Authorized reseller
CTX	Authorized distributor
Fujitsu	Authorized reseller

Source: Taken from Karnite and Karnitis (1998, p. 644).

Fortech operates in several market segments; their customers range from small and medium-sized enterprises to large industrial companies and government institutions. Among these are the industrial companies Nafta in Ventspils, and Gaze and Siltums in Riga; the government Customs Department and Committee of Statistics; several government ministries; and the Riga City Council. Furthermore, Fortech has participated in several PHARE projects in which it was responsible for the implementation of information technology.

Key factors in Fortech's success have been the modern structure of the company, enabling it to offer complete solutions; cooperation at an early phase with other enterprises; and its well-educated staff (see Karnite and Karnitis 1998).

4.2 The Software Industry in the Czech Republic

4.2.1 Starting point and the emergence of a new software sector

The structures for software development in Czechoslovakia were created in the 1980s. Within the 'State Program of Computerization' a massive top-down promotion of information technology took place. In the framework of the program, new professions were defined and the corresponding education opportunities were created. Furthermore, the implementation of information technologies in enterprises was carried out extensively. For the support of the computer systems (for example, software development and hardware maintenance), corresponding in-house departments were established in the applying institutions. In these programming centers, about 100 thousand IT professionals were employed. In addition, large complementary institutions[180] were created to develop system software for Czech-made computer systems.[181] They employed a total staff of several thousand professionals. But despite these efforts, the diffusion of computer technology progressed only very slowly because of resistance in the management of the socialist production units. The reason for this resistance was that the installation of the computer systems represented an instrument of state control.

As in other Eastern European countries, software-developing institutions were not prepared for the competition which started with the end of socialism. The orientation towards large computer systems and the lack of technological compatibility to newly-available and quickly-diffusing hardware led to a collapse of most of the software development institutions. Further, the privatization of state enterprises led to the release of IT experts into the newly emerging software sector. The former employees of these institutions set up new small enterprises and started to trade and adapt Western software. The new software sector emerged in two waves: in 1990–91 as result of the collapse of socialism and in 1995–96 after the period of mass privatization. The number of greenfield creations increased abruptly. These new enterprises, along with international firms which entered the newly opened markets, today shape the structure of the Czech software sector. Together they have become the key challengers of the still-remaining software development institutions. Of the latter, only PVT was able to survive and establish itself successfully in the custom software segment, where it supplied software mainly to state administrations and state companies (for example, registration software for privatization coupons).

4.2.2 Market situation today

The current sector structure is characterized by individual entrepreneurs, who account for as much as 85 percent of all software enterprises in the Czech Republic. Only 11 firms have more than 100 employees. In recent years, a concentration process can be observed which is characterized by an increase in enterprises with more than one employee and a decrease in the number of individual entrepreneurs (Müller and Vorisek 1998). The Czech software enterprises are active mainly in trade, adaptation and implementation of Western software packages. Some of them have preserved their programming

---

[180] For example, Office machines, Datasystem and PVT (Enterprise for Computer Technology).
[181] Examples of established enterprises at this time are office machines, data systems and PVT.

capacities and now develop small-scale custom software or software with a low level of standardization for small domestic enterprises. Nonetheless, Western software enterprises control large parts of the software market (market leader is IBM). They are well-positioned in highly standardized software, application tools, especially for relational database management systems, and large-scale custom software (EITO 1994, p. 162). Whereas the largest Czech software house, PVT, was able to become the second-largest software enterprise in 1995, it dropped dramatically to sixth place in 1996, with a fall in its turnover of 51 percent (see Table 9.3).

Table 9.7 Largest firms in the software market by sales

Company / sales (million CZK)		1994	1995	1996
1	IBM CR	2,600	3,570 (1)	4,106 (1)
2	Hewlett Packard CR	2,380	3,500 (3)	4,030 (2)
3	PVT	2,263	3,645 (2)	1,790 (6)
4	Elko Computers	1,848	3,105 (4)	2,660 (3)
5	TH'system	1,640	1,905 (5)	2,480 (4)
6	Digital Equipment	1,215	1,690 (7)	1,411 (7)
7	Vikomt	1,190	890 (9)	1,050 (9)
8	Autocont	1,080	1,800 (6)	2,300 (5)
9	Escom CS	966	876 (10)	835 (10)
10	Siemens Nixdorf	925	665 (11)	737 (11)
11	Microsoft	532	1,053 (8)	1,275 (8)

Note: Differentiation follows: OKEC 72 10, 72 20, ranked for 1994.

Source: ComputerWorld (various issues).

The main sources for the Czech software enterprises are the international software producers from whom the Czech software enterprises benefit through cooperation agreements. The Czech software market is among the most dynamic in Eastern Europe: in 1996, it was the largest (ECU 353 million), even larger than the Russian software market. The most solvent customers in the Czech Republic are banking and financial services, government administrations, insurance, industry and manufacturing, telecommunications, health services, transport and small private firms (ibid., p. 60).

4.2.3 Enterprise case study: FCC Folprecht GmbH

The development of FCC Folprecht GmbH is a representative case for the emergence of a mixed IT company in Eastern Europe with a growing specialization in software. When FCC Folprecht was founded in 1990, it started business with the sale of computer hardware. By 1992 it already employed a staff of 54, and 90 percent of its turnover still came from hardware sales. Based on these capabilities, the enterprise became one of the most important system integrators, the producer of its own applied software and the leading partner of the German company SAP in the implementation of system SAP R/3. Its growth was exponential, in terms of both employment (from 54 in 1992 to 230 in 1996) and sales (from 130 million Czech crowns in 1992 to 480 million Czech crowns in 1996).

By 1996, FCC Folprecht had become an IT consortium including the enterprises FCC Industrial Systems, FCC Public and FCC Folprecht System. The share of hardware sales decreased in the same period to about 50 percent. The consortium developed applied software for monitoring and dispatching systems in energy and gas production and distribution, water supply systems, hydroecological systems, industrial and trade companies, geoinformation systems, and the formation and collection of multimedia information. The share of software production grew steadily – from about 10 percent in 1992 to about 45 percent in 1996. Folprecht had built up a network of subsidiaries and is now operating in all regions of the domestic market.

5. CONCLUSIONS

In contrast to the production of other goods, software development was not highly centralized in socialist times. It was carried out at the core locations of computer use because it was seen as an auxiliary service for other tasks and not as a commodity good in itself. Therefore, software development was carried out within ministerial departments, industrial combines, the military–industrial complex and institutions of R&D and education, which provided their 'host institutions' with the required application software. The required education and research institutions for software development were established around these 'host institutions'. Due to the absence of the common division of labor which had spread production over several socialist countries, every country owned a complete innovation system for the development of software. This situation remained even after the collapse of socialism. Thus, the software sector differs from those sectors in which the intra-socialist innovation and production networks collapsed simultaneously with socialism.

Nonetheless, the lack of competitiveness in relation to the newly emerging products, which were mainly imported, resulted in the collapse of the national innovation systems and the emergence of international structures. One of the main reasons for this was the focus of the innovation networks on single-unit mainframe software production and the application fields of central planning. The rapid introduction and absorption of new Western hardware technologies after the collapse of socialism required a completely different kind of software, not only in terms of the software technology used, but also in terms of the areas of application. The human capital of the Eastern European countries in software technology was partly devalued by this development. The required software products were immediately available from Western companies, in highly standardized form, containing 100 percent codified knowledge. Employees of the specialized software departments left their positions or lost their jobs through department or host institution shut-downs and moved into the newly emerging software sector. New enterprises were set up and started to trade in the new computer and software technologies.

With the development of the computer market, the demand for more complex software solutions increased and led to more sophisticated activities on the part of Eastern European software enterprises. These enterprises started, at the local level, developing software with a low level of standardization and custom software; and began offering services such as implementation, installation, adaptation and training. The further development of the Eastern European software enterprises into these more sophisticated activities was based on the technology transfer of their agreement or cooperation partners. Western software enterprises remain the main sources of innovation, while the conditions for the absorption of the new technologies are the already-existing, though devalued, human capital.

The new Eastern European software enterprises – the overwhelming part of which are greenfield creations – now dominate the market segments for low standardized software, adapted software and small-scale custom software projects. Furthermore, the segment for computer-connected services such as installation, implementation, training and so on is dominated by domestic enterprises. The remaining segments are dominated by the well-known Western software companies. The market segments in which the domestic enterprises are active are similar to those of Western countries because in these segments, the competition advantages of domestic enterprises come into play (for example, knowledge of language and culture, personal contacts).

The development of the software sector was not actively supported by any of the Central and Eastern European governments. The only political measures were the introduction of patent-protection laws, which lack rigorous enforcement. Perhaps this strategy was designed to promote the quick penetration of the market with state-of-the-art software technologies. A possible starting point for public policy could be the provision of specific parts of the infrastructure: for example, the introduction of standardization procedures and quality standards, the improvement and enforcement of telecommunication and patent-protection laws. Another important element of public policy is the modernization of education in imparting knowledge of modern computer technology. The partial devaluation of human capital should be balanced by education measures.

Economic and political stability is an essential aid to the software market and the software industry as a whole: it grants customers planning security for the purchase of software. Instability in legislation leads to the postponement of investments in computer software because either adaptation creates immense costs, or the software becomes completely useless. Because of the financial situation of the enterprises seeking new computer technologies, they are not willing to risk a worthless investment.

BIBLIOGRAPHY

Baaken, Thomas and Michael Launen (1993), *Software-Marketing*, München: Vahlen.

Benedikter, Walter (1993), 'Strategische Allianzen im Softwaremarkt', in Frank Wimmer and Lothar Bittner (eds), *Software-Marketing, Grundlagen, Konzepte, Hintergründe*, Wiesbaden: Gabler, pp. 71–9.

Bitzer, Jürgen (1997), 'The Computer Software Industry in East and West: Do Eastern Countries Need a Specific Science and Technology Policy?', DIW Discussion Paper (149), Berlin.

Bitzer, Jürgen (ed.) (1998a), *Final Report – Work Package C 'Industrial Restructuring' Part C.4 Sector Study: Software*, TSER Project: 'Restructuring and Re-integration of Science & Technology Systems in Economies in Transition', Berlin: DIW.

Bitzer, Jürgen (1998b), 'Restructuring in the Software Industry in West and East – Industrial Economic Analysis and Special Reference to the Role of S&T Policy', in Bitzer (ed.) (1998a).

BMWI (1997), Bundesministerium für Wirtschaft (ed.), *Wirtschaftslage und Reformprozesse in Mittel- und Osteuropa*, Bonn.

Budapest Business Journal (1997), *Book of Lists: The Guide to Business and Services in Hungary*, Budapest.

Burghart, Daniel L. (1992), *Red Microchip, Technology Transfer, Export Control, and Economic Restructuring in the Soviet Union*, Aldershot, UK and Brookfield, USA: Dartmouth.

Correa, Carlos M. (1993a), *Strategies for Software Exports in Developing Countries*, Vienna: United Nations Industrial Development Organization (UNIDO).

Correa, Carlos M. (1993b), *Legal Protection and Innovation in the Software Industry*, Vienna: United Nations Industrial Development Organization (UNIDO).

Correa, Carlos M. (1996), 'Strategies for Software Exports from Developing Countries', *World Development*, **24** (1), pp. 171–82.

Deppe, Markus (1994), *Software-Service: Servicepolitik von Software-Herstellern*, Europäische Hochschulschriften: Reihe 5, Volks- und Betriebswirtschaft, no. 1515, Frankfurt am Main: Peter Lang.

Dyker, David (1993), 'Russia and Eastern Europe Technology, Trade and Transformation', *ESRC Centre for Science, Technology, Energy and Environment Policy (STEEP) Discussion Paper*, (10), Sussex: STEEP.

Dyker, David (1996), 'The Computer and Software Industries in the East European Economics – A Bridgehead to the Global Economy?', *ESRC Centre for Science, Technology, Energy and Environment Policy (STEEP) Discussion Paper*, (27), February, Sussex: STEEP.

EITO *European Information Technology Observatory*, (various issues).

Gerhardt, Tilman (1992), 'Strategie und Struktur in der deutschen Softwareindustrie: Eine Industrieökonomische Untersuchung der Unternehmensentwicklung in der Softwarebranche', in Arnold Picot and Ralf Reichwald (eds), *Unternehmensentwicklung* (13), München: VVF.

Karnite, Raita and Kriss Karnitis (1998), 'Software Industry in Latvia', in Jürgen Bitzer and Christian von Hirschhausen (eds), *Industrial Restructuring and Economic Recovery in the Baltic Countries – Lithuania, Latvia, Estonia: Infrastructure Policies for Sustained Growth in the Baltic Countries*, Berlin: DIW, pp. 691–720.

Katkalo, Valery and David C. Mowery (1996), 'Institutional Structure and Innovation in the Emerging Russian Software Industry', in David C. Mowery (ed.), *The International Computer Software Industry*, New York, Oxford: Oxford University Press, pp. 240–71.

Kilvits, Kaarel (1998), 'Software in Estonia', in Jürgen Bitzer and Christian von Hirschhausen (eds), *Industrial Restructuring and Economic Recovery in the Baltic Countries – Lithuania, Latvia, Estonia: Infrastructure Policies for Sustained Growth in the Baltic Countries*, Berlin: DIW, pp. 721–40.

Kubielas, Stanislaw (1996), *International Co-operative Agreements in Poland in the mid 1990s: Evolution, Organizational Forms and Industry Characteristics, Part I: Country Industrial Report*, Warsaw: Faculty of Economic Science Warsaw University.

Kubielas, Stanislaw (1998), 'The Software Industry in Poland', in Bitzer (ed.) (1998a).

Morkûnaite, Rasa (1998), 'Software Sector in Lithuania', in Jürgen Bitzer and Christian von Hirschhausen (eds), *Industrial Restructuring and Economic Recovery in the Baltic Countries – Lithuania, Latvia, Estonia: Infrastructure Policies for Sustained Growth in the Baltic Countries*, Berlin: DIW, pp. 670–90.

Mowery, David C. (ed.) (1996), *The International Computer Software Industry, A Comparative Study of Industry Evolution and Structure*, New York: Oxford University Press.

Müller, Karel and Jiri Vorisek (1998), 'Case Study: Restructuring of the Czech Software Industry (special reference to S&T policy)', in Bitzer (ed.) (1998a).

Organization for Economic Cooperation and Development (OECD) (1985), *Software: An Emerging Industry*, Paris: OECD.

Petska-Juliussen, Karen and Egil Juliussen (1996), *The 8th Annual Computer Industry Almanac*, Florence, Kentucky: International Thomson Publishing.

10 The Eastern European Computer Industry: National Champions with a Screwdriver

Jürgen Bitzer[182]

1. INTRODUCTION

The importance of computer technology in industrial countries is increasing steadily. In the last few decades the development thereof has resulted in large increases in the productivity of industrial countries. In many cases, special production processes were not possible before the introduction of modern computer technology (for example, modeling in industries such as chemistry, aerospace, car manufacturing). In Western industrial economies, the penetration of computers into industry and society is well advanced. Experts forecast above-average growth rates well into the next century, based on predictable developments in Western economies (for example, production processes and organization types).

In the early phase of transformation, Eastern European countries believed that a gradual restructuring of domestic computer industries would be possible and that the existing innovation and production structures could serve as springboards for the catching-up process in computer technology. Today, considering the actual development of the Eastern European computer industry in recent years, these expectations have to be revised and replaced with realistic estimates. Often a lack of money is cited as a reason for the disappointing development of the computer industry in Central and Eastern Europe. Governments in particular believe that a science and technology

[182] The author would like to thank Eduard Steinmueller, David Dyker and Christian von Hirschhausen for comments and Deborah Anne Bowen and Michael Jahn for proofreading the chapter. The usual disclaimer applies.

(S&T) policy with large financial means could fix the problems of domestic computer enterprises in competition against large international computer manufacturers. We do not agree with this assessment; by contrast, our main hypothesis is that the 'socialist technological paradigm' in computer technology came to a sudden end with the collapse of socialism. The development of the Eastern European computer industry during the post-socialist period was not influenced significantly by the former socialist computer industry structures. As a result, the innovation process of the Eastern European computer industry is at present based exclusively on foreign (Western) suppliers and their innovation systems. The existing (socialist) knowledge base was not competitive and compatible with Western technologies. There is little room for Eastern European governments to support the development of the domestic computer industry.

To test this hypothesis, this chapter is structured as follows. Section 2 gives a brief historical outline and short description of the computer market, followed by an analysis of the competition and production structures in the European personal computer (PC) business. This provides an international background for an assessment of the developments in the Eastern European computer industries. Section 3 gives a general picture of the initial state and subsequent restructuring of the socialist computer-producing sector. Following this, the computer market in Central and Eastern Europe is analyzed with particular attention to Poland, Hungary, the Czech Republic and Russia. Section 4 provides a summary of the two case studies in the Czech Republic and the Baltic countries. Section 5 concludes with a focus on possible policy strategies for supporting the development of the domestic computer sectors in the Eastern European countries.

2. THE INTERNATIONAL PERSONAL COMPUTER BUSINESS

2.1 Significance and Development of the PC Market Segment

When discussing computer industries, we have to distinguish between three different segments which are closely linked, but characterized by individual features and conditions: the *hardware* industry, the *software* industry and the *service* industry. Because of the increasing complexity of products in Western countries, an increasing number of highly specialized enterprises have emerged, whose focus is on a product range within one of these segments. This chapter deals with the production of PCs particularly on the last level of the value-added chain, the computer-assembling industry. Computer component producers are treated only as suppliers and not as an industry and as actors in their own right. Therefore neither the competition between component producers nor their production structure will be analyzed. Nevertheless the relations between component producers and computer manufacturers will be analyzed because of their crucial role in the innovation process of the PC manufacturing industry. The computer software industry, which is the subject of Chapter 9 of this book, and the service industry will be mentioned only where necessary for the analysis of the PC manufacturing industry.

The history of the computer manufacturing industry goes back to the year 1951, when the company Remington Rand installed the first commercially viable electronic computer system called UNIVAC. Since then, the computer market has changed fundamentally. Today the following segments can be distinguished: PCs, workstations, servers and supercomputers. In the following, the last two segments will be treated together under the label 'servers'.[183] The computers in these segments differ in their calculating power, price and realm of application.[184] The PC segment differs from the other three, in particular in terms of competition axes, potential customers, R&D intensity and market barriers.

PCs are the least powerful and least expensive computers of the three market segments and are used mostly for desktop applications such as word-processing, spreadsheets and small databases (US International Trade Commission 1993, pp. 68–71). In 1977, Apple introduced the first commercial PC. Until 1981, when IBM introduced its first PC, Apple held a monopoly based on proprietary technology. The birth of the PC computer market as we know it today was 12 August 1981, when IBM put their first PC model on the market. It was designed as an open system: instead of using a proprietary technology, they incorporated off-the-shelf components such as Intel's microprocessor 8088 and Microsoft's operating system MS-DOS. IBM's use of mass-produced components combined with the widespread dissemination of its PC technology led to the emergence of IBM-compatible machines and clone-makers.

---

[183] In statistics, supercomputers are often added to the server market segment. Even though the author does not support this classification, the available statistics offer data only for the market segments PCs, workstations and servers. For an analysis of the supercomputer market segment, see Bitzer (1997).

[184] Nevertheless, with the rapid development of computer technology, the borders between the different segments have become less clear-cut. The processing power of PCs today has almost reached that of workstations. Workstations are nearly as powerful as mainframe computers.

Table 10.1 The computer market in the EU, 1994–1999

		PCs	Work-stations	Servers	Total computer market
1994	ECU (m)	19,515	2,435	12,207	34,157
	market share in %	57.1	7.1	35.7	100*
1995	ECU (m)	22,956	2,717	12,207	37,880
	market share in %	60.6	7.2	32.2	100
1996	ECU (m)	25,188	2,674	12,418	40,280
	market share in %	62.5	6.6	30.8	100*
1997	ECU (m)	27,250	2,370	13,587	43,207
	market share in %	63.1	5.5	31.5	100*
1998[a]	ECU (m)	29,256	2,195	14,763	46,214
	market share in %	63.3	4.8	31.9	100
1999[b]	ECU (m)	31,178	2,131	15,809	49,118
	market share in %	63.5	4.3	32.2	100

Notes:
* Rounded to 100.
[a] Without add-ons and printers.
[b] Estimated by EITO.

Sources: EITO (1998, p. 349); author's calculations.

In 1997, the market for PCs in the European Union had a value of about ECU 27 billion (63 percent of the computer market in terms of value in the EU, see Table 10.1) and was the largest of the four segments of the computer market. Over 17 million PCs were sold in the EU in 1997, and the growth rate was 11.1 percent in terms of units (EITO 1998, pp. 349, 359).

In recent years, a saturation of the PC market has occurred (see Table 10.2). The demand by private households, however, has increased and partly compensates for the decrease in the professional market segment (Drüke 1993, p. 3).

Because of the openness of PC technology, the sources of innovation, the system of production, the competition axes used and the market structure in the PC market segment are fundamentally different from those in the other computer segments (Kauffmann 1993, p. 5).

Table 10.2 Growth rates of different computer market segments in the EU

in %	1995	1996	1997	1998[a]	1999[a]
PCs	17.6	9.7	8.2	7.4	6.6
Servers	0.0	1.7	9.4	8.7	7.1
Workstations	11.6	−1.6	−11.4	−7.4	−2.9
Total computer market	10.9	6.3	7.3	7.0	6.3

Notes:
Without add-ons and printers.
[a] Estimated by EITO.

Sources: EITO (1998, p. 349); our calculations.

2.2 Production and Innovation in the PC Business

The production of PCs is characterized by the open standards of PC technology interfaces, which ensure the mechanical connection as well as the data transfer through standardized hardware.[185] This enables enterprises to produce components for PCs without a license or direct cooperation with a PC manufacturer. The result of this characteristic of personal computer design is that a large number of highly-specialized component producers exists, which develop and produce such components independently of PC manufacturers.[186] Such enterprises produce the components in mass production, efficiently and therefore cheaply. The result has been a massive price drop for the main components in recent years (for example, microprocessors, memory chips, graphic devices and hard drives).[187] Therefore only a few of the largest PC manufacturers continue to depend heavily on internal sources of components.

It is evident that this has also affected the organization of PC production.

---

[185] See Meffert (1993) for a detailed discussion of computer standards.
[186] Conversely, in recent years several component suppliers have tried to establish proprietary technologies as industry standards, for example, Intel with its SLOT 1 CPU interface technology.
[187] Examples of such component manufacturers are: Intel for its microprocessors; Microsoft for its operating system and application software; Diamond, Elsa and Miro for graphic devices; and Seagate and Western Digital for hard drives and other components.

Because all components are highly standardized, PC assembly is, without differences in the size and location of enterprises, typically carried out with simple conveyor belts and hand-held screwdrivers. Compaq, for example, produces its PCs in a single conveyor belt process. Thus the entire PC is assembled at one location (US International Trade Commission 1993, p. 113). The same is true for Vobis, one of the largest German PC manufacturers. Because of the module architecture and the highly standardized components, large productivity differences do not exist in the PC manufacturing industry. The main differences among enterprises can be found in logistics as well as in the economies of scale which play a crucial role in the purchase of components.

As a consequence of the design of the PC and the organization of production, the component suppliers are the main source of innovation in the PC market segment. New processors, graphic devices, motherboards, disk drives and similar components are developed and produced mainly by highly specialized component suppliers. Only a few large PC producers still have internal capacities for the development and production of components. For example, IBM still has large capacities devoted to chip production but this is also the result of activities in other computer segments.[188] PC clone-makers as well as PC brand-name manufacturers benefit from the innovations of their highly specialized component suppliers. Only a few large PC brand-name manufacturers have their own R&D capacities for the development of PC components. The most important components in PC technology, the processor and the operating system, are dominated worldwide by the American enterprises Intel (about 85 percent market share) and Microsoft (90 percent). The sources of innovation are therefore mainly external. Thus the innovation system from which the PC manufacturers benefit depends upon the origin of their suppliers and the innovation sources used by them (for example, in the case of Intel, innovations would originate from the American innovation system).

2.3 Competition in the PC Market Segment

In contrast to the segments in which proprietary technologies dominate the market, the entry barriers to the PC market are low. The reason for this is that enterprises wanting to enter the market do not have to build up any R&D facilities (Denger 1997, p. 26). They can buy any component on the market and with it 100 percent codified knowledge. Furthermore, capital intensity for production is low, so that large financial means are not needed to enter the PC

---

[188] For example, in 1995, IBM ranked 8th among worldwide semiconductor suppliers.

market. Competition is therefore intense; international enterprises must compete on regional markets with small regional clone-makers who are serious competitors especially in the home-user market[189] (Kauffmann 1993, p. 18).

Only on the PC market do private households represent an important part of total demand. In 1993, 2.7 million PCs were sold to EU households (home users) with a value of ECU 2.4 billion, which corresponds to a market share of 15 percent in terms of value. On the other hand, in 1993, 6 million PCs with a value of ECU 13 billion were sold to professional users, which corresponds to a market share of 85 percent in terms of value (EITO 1993, p. 233). Home users and professional users make different demands on PCs. Therefore the competitors use different *downstream* competition axes on the home-user market than they do on the professional market in their attempt to attain a temporary monopoly. Whereas on the home-user market the price, the offer to assemble custom PCs, advertising and warranty conditions are used as active downstream competition axes, on the professional market, the price is currently the only remaining active downstream competition axis, along with the passive competition axes quality/support, integration/installation competence and complete system supply.[190]

In contrast to downstream competition, the *upstream* competition axes of manufacturers for the home-user market do not differ from those of manufacturers for the professional market. With the emergence of independent component suppliers and the reduction of internal R&D and production capacities, the importance of relations to component manufacturers has increased. Because of this, PC assemblers compete for the best purchase conditions for required components because smooth production depends not only on price, but on the delivery conditions, and on receiving the right number of high-quality components at the right time (US International Trade Commission 1993, pp. 112–13). Relations with component suppliers also determine the 'time to market'. For this, it is crucial to produce single units during the development period so that the manufacturer can test the new component with other components of his or her PC product. This helps to reduce the time to market.

Currently, two strategies for attaining advantages over competitors are prevalent: *exclusive contracts* and *increase of purchasing power through growth*. One example of the first strategy is the contract between Compaq, Intel and Microsoft. For Compaq, the contract ensures the best conditions for

---

[189] The market segment Small Office/Home Office (SOHO) is included in the home-user market due to the similar requirements for PCs which differ from those of professional users (Petska-Juliussen and Juliussen 1996).

[190] See Bitzer (1997, 1998), for detailed analysis of the competition axes.

the delivery of processors and operating systems. Intel and Microsoft, on the other hand, bind the largest PC manufacturer in the world to their products. Furthermore, economies of scale in purchasing play an important role in competition. Examples of such a competition strategy are the mergers of recent years. For example, Siemens tried to sell its PC production to ACER, where a declared aim of the merger was to improve the purchasing conditions for components.[191]

3. THE COLLAPSE AND REEMERGENCE OF THE EASTERN EUROPEAN COMPUTER INDUSTRY

3.1 Starting Point and Transformation

In the socialist period, because of its importance for the military–industrial complex and state institutions, the production of computers and required components was strictly controlled by the state. Not only was production organized nation-wide by the state; even the division of labor all over the Eastern bloc was determined by the socialist party. The institutional framework established in the CMEA countries was the program of 'Unified System of Electronic Computers' which was introduced in the mid-1970s. It determined the division of labor among the participating countries, which effectively meant that the development and production of required products was allotted to different countries. This happened without taking account of already-existing structures.[192] The largest and most important capacities (for example, microprocessor design) were located mainly in the Soviet Union. Individual countries had corresponding programs implementing the development and production of the allotted computer products. Within these programs, activities were coordinated, required funds were provided and relevant policies for development in particular fields were formulated. According to general socialist practice, the innovation system was organized in a linear way with strictly separated tasks. Research was carried out in specialized institutes of the Academy of Sciences while product development was carried out in specialized branch research institutes. The production units had only very small R&D departments at their disposal because their main task was seen to be in production only (Bitzer and Hirschhausen 1998a).

With the collapse of socialism, the established division of labor collapsed, and with it the innovation and production networks. The entry of international

---

[191] ACER drew back from the merger because of problems resulting from the Asia crisis.

[192] In the case of Poland, for example, this destroyed the promising production of mainframes which had been successfully under way.

computer enterprises with their superior technology quickly showed that the existing technology was neither competitive nor compatible. The former computer producers collapsed, or switched to other activities or started assembling PCs. The collapse of obsolete capacities released personnel into the newly emerging private computer industry. The development of the emerging computer-assembling industry was dominated by the emerging greenfield creations which quickly took the lead in this 'new' business. Initially, the newly founded and exclusively private enterprises started to trade in Western computers, computer components and suitable software. After having gained experience in this business, they started assembling PCs where the required components were imported from the Far East or the USA. The trade activity remained a very important part of the domestic business, but with the development of the computer markets, services gained increasingly in importance. A division of labor among the computer, software and services sectors as in Western countries has not yet occurred. The overwhelming majority of Eastern European enterprises are engaged in all three segments of the computer industry (hardware, software and services). One reason for this is that the IT markets in Eastern Europe are still in their infancy.

3.2 Production and Sources of Innovation in the 'New' Eastern European PC Business

The rapid collapse of the socialist computer industry and the emergence of a new, completely differently-structured computer (assembling) industry shows that the socialist technological paradigm was not competitive and compatible with globally predominant computer technology. The new production and innovation networks have nothing in common with the former socialist structures; thus, the socialist technological trajectory ended with the collapse of socialism. The new technological trajectory is determined by worldwide technological trends and does not represent a different 'post-socialist' trajectory.

In the higher market segments (workstations and servers), domestic industry was shut down completely and no new industry emerged. The usable remnants of the industry were acquired by international manufacturers to serve as local bases for distribution and support. In the years that followed, the major players in those segments opened subsidiaries owned entirely by them in nearly all of the CEE and CIS countries. The complete disappearance of socialist mainframe production and the fact that nothing new emerged were the results of the huge technological gap (Adirim 1991) between Eastern European and Western computer technology, and of the predominance of proprietary computer technology in these segments. A direct comparison of socialist and capitalist technologies on the computer market reveals the fact that even with immense efforts in the medium term, catching up with Western technology would not have been possible. In particular the dominance of proprietary technologies in these market segments left Eastern producers with only one possible means of catching up: their own innovations.[193]

The situation in the PC business was completely different. Although the socialist production units also collapsed, they were quickly replaced by new and competitive PC-assembling enterprises which took over Western production and innovation structures. Because of the special production and innovation conditions in the PC business, the entry barriers for newcomers are low. The required components are freely available on international markets. Because of their high standardization, they are easy to assemble and contain the required knowledge in 100 percent codified form. The production and innovation process is therefore not capital intensive. PC assembly is normally carried out with simple screwdrivers; R&D capacities are not needed. This explains the success of domestic assemblers on Eastern European markets, as the next section shows. The sources of innovation are exclusively foreign suppliers and therefore the Eastern European PC industry is a classic supplier-dominated sector (Pavitt 1984). At present, there is no observable emergence of an Eastern European computer supplier industry. The innovation process in the Eastern European PC industry is therefore based exclusively on foreign innovation systems.

3.3 The Computer Market in Central and Eastern Europe

In the socialist period, the use of computer technology in Eastern European countries was characterized by low penetration of the economy, a strong orientation towards mainframe computers and limited application fields, the main task being the support of central planning. Through the introduction of Western computers on Eastern European markets after the collapse of socialism, computer technology was available as a commodity good for the first time. Newly emerging private businesses wanted to utilize the relatively cheap computer technology of PCs, resulting in a dramatic rise in demand. The market for larger computers collapsed because of the unstable financial situation of potential private customers. This lack of financial demand for larger computer systems led to the dominance of PCs on the CEE and CIS computer markets. The main customers remain the government agencies and administrations, agricultural cooperatives and state enterprises which were

---

[193] See Bitzer (1997) for an analysis of production and innovation process in the higher computer classes.

often supported financially by the World Bank, the European Bank for Reconstruction and Development (EBRD) and the European Union (EITO 1993, p. 153). Only in recent years has the banking sector developed into a potential customer for information technologies. When the economic situation stabilized after its initial turbulent years, the strong competition had left only a few very successful domestic private assemblers on the PC market (ibid., pp. 166–7).

The computer market in Eastern European countries is at an early stage, and the main competition axes are still price and availability. The home-user markets, corresponding to the low standard of living, are insignificant in all Eastern European countries. Axes of competition such as quality and support grow with the saturation of the backlog demand. Thus, particularly in the Central European countries, a shift to quality and support as the decisive buying factors can already be observed. The situation on the Eastern European computer markets is summarized in Table 10.3.

Table 10.3 Situation on the Eastern European computer markets, 1996

Countries	Russia	Poland	Czech Republic	Hungary	EU
Population 1996 in millions	147.5	38.6	10.3	10.2	373.3
GDP in billion USD	440.0	130.7	52.1	43.9	8,601
Market Value 1996 in million ECU	1,489	523	483	239	44,062
Percent of Spanish computer market	76	25	25	12	–
Percent of EU computer market	3	1	1	1	–
Penetration with computer technology (PCs per 100 white-collar workers)	6	19	26	34	88
Share of PC market segment in terms of value in percent	88	85	80	78	53
Market leader in the PC segment January–June 1996	VIST (domestic)	Optimus (domestic)	IBM	Albacomp (domestic)	n.a.

Sources: EITO (1997); BMWI (1997); Business Central Europe (1996).

As mentioned above, the PC market segment is by far the dominant one in Eastern European countries. At the same time, it is the only segment in which domestic enterprises were able to compete with international computer enterprises. Often the market leader is a domestic PC manufacturer. The other computer market segments are controlled by well-known, large international computer companies. The comparison between the expenditures on computers in Spain and in the Eastern European countries shows that hardware spending in Eastern Europe remains much lower than the average spending in Western Europe, despite large financial programs supporting the computerization of those economies. The result is still a relatively low penetration of the economy with computer technology, as Table 10.4 shows.

Table 10.4 Computer base in Eastern European countries

	1991	1992	1993	1994	1995	2000*
Czech Republic						
Computers in use (m)	0.16	0.23	0.30	0.38	0.50	1.40
Change in %	–	43.8	30.4	26.7	31.6	180.0
Computers/ 1000 people	15.50	21.70	28.60	36.00	47.70	131.10
Hungary						
Computers in use (m)	0.18	0.25	0.34	0.44	0.56	1.60
Change in %	–	38.9	36.0	29.4	27.3	185.7
Computers/ 1,000 people	17.30	23.80	32.60	42.70	54.40	153.30
Poland						
Computers in use (m)	0.44	0.59	0.76	0.97	1.20	3.80
Change in %	–	34.1	28.8	27.6	23.7	216.7
Computers/ 1,000 people	11.70	15.40	19.80	25.10	31.70	95.20
Russia						
Computers in use (m)	0.65	0.93	1.40	1.90	2.70	9.20
Change in %	–	43.1	50.5	35.7	42.1	240.7
Computers/ 1,000 people	4.40	6.30	9.10	12.90	18.00	60.60
Spain						
Computers in use (m)	1.40	1.80	2.30	2.90	3.50	8.10
Change in %	–	28.6	27.8	26.1	20.7	131.4
Computers/ 1,000 people	36.40	47.20	59.10	72.60	88.00	201.70

Note: * Estimate.

Source: Petska-Juliussen and Juliussen (1996).

4. CASE STUDIES ON THE COMPUTER INDUSTRY IN EASTERN EUROPE

4.1 Case Study: Czech Republic[194]

4.1.1 Point of departure, collapse of the computer production units and emergence of greenfield enterprises

As in all Eastern European countries, the development and production of computer technology in the Czech Republic was organized as part of a steeply hierarchical process. The responsibility for the development of new technologies and products was located in the Institute for Technical Information and Automation and the Institute of Radioelectronics of the academies of sciences; in the technical universities; and in the two leading branch research institutes Research Institute for Communications Technology – VUST A.S. Popova and the Research Institute of Mathematical Machines (VUMS), which were the centers of technological competence in the Czech Republic. VUMS, for example, carried out the complete development and design of the mainframe computers produced in Czechoslovakia. Computer manufacturing was concentrated in the three large electro-engineering 'production economic units' – TESLA, ZPA (Industrial Automation) and Datasystem – which have only very limited R&D capacities. Only capacities closely connected to manufacturing, such as testing and services, were located at the production locations.

The regulatory framework for the innovation and production process was provided by the program of 'Informatization of the National Economy'. This entailed the coordination of activities within the field, provision of required funds and formulation of relevant policies for development. Furthermore, all institutions took part in the CMEA program of 'Unified System of Electronic Computers' which resulted in the development and production of specific types of computers in Czechoslovakia. Whereas the development and production of mainframe units (re-engineered IBM 370) were located in the Czech part of the country, the Slovak part carried out the development and production of small computer units (re-engineered PDP 11).

The main application fields for computers were the (military) industrial complex, and the institutions of central planning and scientific and technical computing. Production was exclusively for the use of these institutions – private computer use was virtually non-existent. In industry, computer technology was used less for production reasons than for the tasks of planning. It was expected that the improved connection between central

---

[194] This section is based on Müller and Vorisek (1998).

authorities and supervised companies by means of advanced communication and data-processing technologies would, in turn, radically improve central planning as a whole.

Summarizing the point of departure of the Czech computer industry, computer production in Czechoslovakia was characterized by (i) separation of R&D and production locations, (ii) large-scale production with high vertical and horizontal integration, and (iii) the international CMEA agreements on specialization which located the production of mainframe computers in the Czech part and the production of smaller computers in the Slovak part.

With the collapse of socialism, the formerly closed markets were now opened for international enterprises. The entry of international computer enterprises and computer component suppliers onto the Czech market resulted in the emergence of stiff competition. As in all Eastern European countries, computer production in Czechoslovakia decreased markedly. A lengthy process began, from 1988 to 1995, in which the state privatized the main parts of the state-owned enterprises, including the electric-engineering industry with its production units for computers.[195]

During this period, developments similar to those in other Eastern European countries could be observed in the Czech Republic. The production of higher computer classes (workstations, mainframe and supercomputer) collapsed totally and today, all of these computers are imported.[196] Currently, the only computer production carried out in the Czech Republic is the assembly of PCs from imported computer components. As in other East European countries, foreign suppliers became the main sources of innovation in the computer industry. Some university and academy staff are still doing research in information technology and information systems (IT/IS), but they play no significant role as sources of innovation for the commercial enterprises. This drop in the importance of the domestic innovation system also results in a drastic decrease in research personnel. The R&D personnel employed in electrical engineering dropped from 9,451 in 1990 to 846 in 1995. Furthermore, industrial research institutes were privatized and left to market forces. For example, the VUMS, the former center of competence, was privatized and the overwhelming majority of its employees moved into business. The chairs at the universities were maintained and other universities produced studies on IT/IS. Only basic research is still publicly funded. Today the relevant research is carried out at the Technical University of Prague, the Charles University in Prague, the Economic University in Prague and the Technical University in Brno.

As a result of the specific production and innovation patterns of PC

---

[195] See Müller and Vorisek (1998) for a detailed description of this process.
[196] Müller and Vorisek (1998, p. 12).

manufacturing, the computer business in the Czech Republic is currently dominated by small and medium-sized enterprises, which account for about 94 percent of the Czech computer output. These new enterprises were founded mainly by former employees of the research institutes (for example, VUMS), university members or former employees of the computation departments of large enterprises.

4.2.2 Current market structure

In 1996, the Czech computer market had a value of ECU 483 million which corresponded to 1 percent of the EU and 25 percent of the Spanish computer market. As in the other Eastern European countries, the PC market segment is largely dominant, with a share of 80 percent of the whole computer market value (see Table 10.4). In the Czech Republic, 47 PCs are installed per 1,000 persons of the population. This is the second-highest penetration in the CEE and CIS countries.[197]

In contrast to all other CEE and CIS countries, a Western enterprise is the market leader in the Czech Republic's PC market segment. In 1996, IBM led with a market share of 10.4 percent of all units sold. The market position of the domestic enterprises is not as strong in the Czech Republic as in other CEE countries. In the same year, only four of the top ten PC manufacturers were domestic enterprises. This market segment has the highest share of Western penetration and the large Western brands together hold about one-third of the PC market. The market structure mirrors the trend in the Czech Republic that the importance for customers has been shifting increasingly in recent years from price as a decisive factor towards quality and support.[198]

The home-user market is insignificant in the Czech PC market. Only about 1 percent were sold to private home users. Thus, the professional application of PCs dominates in the competition of PC manufacturers.[199] In 1997, the PC market segment shrunk dramatically by 12.2 percent. The reason for this development can be found in three macroeconomic developments: first, the devaluation of the crown, which works as a price increase; second, a high account deficit; and third, a slowdown in economic growth. Private enterprises as well as state administrations cut their IT investments. A recovery and return to higher growth rates was being predicted for the year 1999.

---

[197] EITO (1997, p. 63).
[198] EITO (1994, p. 159).
[199] EITO (1993, pp. 200–75).

Table 10.5 Growth rates of the Czech PC market segment in terms of value

Year	1995	1996	1997	1998	1999*	2000*
Market segment PCs (growth rate in %)	+14	+15.3	−12.2	−5.2	+5.8	+8.1

Note: * Estimate by EITO.

Sources: EITO (1998, p. 344; 1999, p. 368).

4.1.3 Case Study: AutoCont plc

The company was founded in 1991 by a group of software experts. After an impressive growth period (see Table 10.6), the enterprise changed its organization form into a holding company in 1995. The parent company had its headquarters in Prague with subsidiaries in several regions, including one in Poland and one in the Slovak Republic.[200] In 1998, the organizational form was changed again. The regional form of organization was abandoned to a form based on division of functions. The wholesale part of AutoCont was therefore separated and transferred to the newly founded enterprise 'AT Computers'. AT Computers has, since then, taken on responsibility for production of the brand-name PC 'AutoCont', wholesale and distribution of HP products, and brand-name PC components, notebooks and peripherals. AutoCont carries out customer services (such as implementation), sales of AutoCont PCs, and recently also sales of HP products and after-sale services. The organizational division of business activities (production and services) realized here is still rare for East European enterprises.

Table 10.6 Turnover of AutoCont plc, 1991–1997

Year	1991	1992	1993	1994	1995	1996	1997
Turnover in (m) CZK	70	302	660	1,080	1,700	2,230	2,360

Source: Müller and Vorisek (1998, p. 23).

Since 1994, AutoCont plc (now known as AT Computers) has been producing PCs under the ISO 9000 and 9001 certification. Today, AT Computers is the largest PC manufacturer in the Czech Republic with a

---

[200] Internet site of AutoCont plc: 'www.autocont.cz'.

market share of more than 10 percent.[201] It employs about 100 employees and assembled 29,802 PCs in 1998. Table 10.7 shows the development of units produced.

Table 10.7 PCs produced by AutoCont plc, 1991–1997

Year	1991	1992	1993	1994	1995	1996	1997	1998*
Units produced	800	2,900	5,500	12,500	19,000	22,700	26,300	29,802

Note: * Figure for AT Computers.

Source: Müller and Vorisek (1998, p. 24), Internet site of AT Computers: 'www.atcomp.cz/profil/profilEnglish.htm'.

It is remarkable that this enterprise did not suffer from the strong drop in the Czech PC market from 1996 to 1997: this indicates the competitiveness of the enterprise. Effective as of September 1, 1998, the company AT Computers became a Certified HP Connect Wholesaler in the field of servers, workstations and personal computers. Furthermore, the company cooperates closely with the following suppliers for which it is an important customer in the region: ASUStek, ATI, Fujitsu, Hewlett Packard, Hitachi, Hyundai, Intel, KFC, Logitech, Microsoft, Seagate, Sony, ViewSonic, Western Digital and others. The list of suppliers shows the strong international orientation of the supplier and of the enterprise's innovation network.

AutoCont CZ, on the other hand, is focussed mainly on sales of computers, components and peripherals, and services connected to computer technology. These services include activities such as implementation of networks and software packages, development of custom software solutions, training and so on. The enterprise has 53 subsidies in the Czech Republic, with training centers in Prague, Brno, Ostrava and Karlovy Vary. AutoCont CZ employs a staff of 290, of whom 32 percent deal with sales activities, 13 percent are software experts, 13 percent are responsible for creation of networks and the other 42 percent deal with services and auxiliary activities. Even though one of the most important suppliers of AutoCont is the Czech enterprise AT Computers, which supplies the Czech brand 'AutoCont PC', the supplier and innovation network nevertheless has a strong international orientation. Thus, AutoCont CZ is also, for example, a Certified Microsoft Solution Provider, and has included the complete product range of Hewlett Packard in its hardware sale assortment.

---

[201] Internet site of AT Computers: 'www.atcomp.cz/profil/profilEnglish.htm'.

4.2 Case Study of the Baltic Countries: Lithuania, Latvia and Estonia

4.2.1 Starting point, collapse and reemergence of the Baltic computer industry

During the Soviet period, the Baltic countries' production of computers was brought into the electrical engineering sector, regarded as a center of competence, in which a huge range of electronic products for civil as well as military use were developed and engineered. Production ranged from computers to circuit boards and from television tuners to compressors for automobiles. For each of the three countries, the electronic industry provided a significant amount of employment.[202] As part of the Soviet Union, the Baltic countries participated in the CMEA program 'Unified System of Electronic Computers'. According to this program and normal socialist practice, R&D and production were divided among different locations. Whereas production was located mainly in Belarus,[203] a significant share of R&D, as well as some production was carried out in the Baltic countries.[204] The collapse of socialism and the restoration of independence in 1991 affected the computer industry in the Baltic countries profoundly, and caused far-reaching changes: the collapse of the innovation and production networks as well as of the trade relations established in Soviet times. What remained was a deeply fragmented innovation and production network. Former inputs, material or non-material (such as research results), were no longer available. Furthermore, the demand for computers produced in the Baltic countries dropped dramatically. Their small and underdeveloped markets could not compensate for this drop in demand. In addition, Western computer enterprises entered the market with their technologically advanced products.

As a result, most of the former electronics industry collapsed. The former production units could not keep up with foreign competition and were unable to reorient their products and markets to the new demand. They quickly lost their markets and most were shut down. Only some received state support during this difficult restructuring phase (for example, Sigma in Lithuania). At the same time, small computer companies were established, usually starting

---

[202] In Estonia, for example, 13 percent of the workforce was employed in the electronic industry and 10,000 specialists in the Lithuanian computer industry, (see Kilvits 1998, p. 651; Morkûnaite 1998, p. 599).

[203] Among the Baltic research institutes participating in R&D of computer technology were the Institute of Electronics of the Latvian Academy of Sciences, Riga's Polytechnical Institute (Latvia), Kaunas Polytechnical Institute (Lithuania), and the Institute of Cybernetics of the Estonian Academy of Sciences.

[204] Significant production units engaged in the production of computers or computer components were: Sigma Computer Plant (Lithuania), Vilnius Vingis (Lithuania), Venta State Micro-Electronic Enterprise (Lithuania), ALFA (Latvia) and VEF (Latvia), (see Karnite 1998; Kilvits 1998; Morkûnaite 1998).

by re-selling imported Western computers, computer components and suitable software. The availability of computer technology to private users resulted in the emergence of a computer market on which computer technology was traded freely for the first time. With the computer market, a computer sector characterized by small enterprises, was born as well.[205] After a short period in this computer trade business, domestic enterprises started to assemble PCs themselves. Without any state support, these enterprises were able to take the lead in the newly emerging Baltic computer markets. As in other Eastern European countries, domestic enterprises were active exclusively in the assembling of PCs, and the former mainframe computer producers as well as the R&D institutions were either shut down or switched their activities to other businesses. In contrast to the PC market, new enterprises did not emerge.

4.2.2 The current market situation, sources of innovation and public policies

The PC market segment is by far the dominant one in the Baltic computer market. Experts estimate that 85 percent of computers sold in Lithuania are PCs. The penetration with computers is still low in all Baltic countries.[206] After the collapse of socialism and the simultaneous emergence of private enterprises, the application fields for computer technology expanded dramatically. This led to a large and unfulfilled demand for computer technology. Therefore the Baltic computer markets have two-digit growth rates (for example, Latvia 35 percent in 1996). Nevertheless, the size and future development of the Baltic computer markets should not be overestimated.[207] Baltic computer enterprises are generally bound to their domestic markets and only larger enterprises export their PCs. Those exports are directed mainly towards the two other Baltic countries, while only an insignificant number of the PCs were sold to other countries such as Russia, Poland and Germany.

The *downstream* competition on the Baltic computer markets is carried out mainly along the price axis, although quality is becoming more and more important, as is demonstrated by the increasing number of computer manufacturers trying to obtain the ISO 9000, 9001 and 9002 certification. Another important element of downstream competition on Baltic computer markets is the ability to offer support, maintenance and installation. This can

---

[205] In Lithuania, 42 percent of all computer enterprises have less than 20 employees (see Morkûnaite 1998, p. 606).

[206] In Lithuania, for example, 16 PCs per 100 white-collar workers (see ibid., p. 603).

[207] In Lithuania, the largest of the three Baltic countries, 28,000 computers were sold in 1996. The base of installed computers is roughly 120,000 and experts believe that it could grow to between 400 and 700 thousand, (see ibid., p. 602).

be explained by the fact that have been the main customers of the computer industry were the newly emerging enterprises and state institutions. Private customers have appeared only recently on the computer market. The demand of private households will develop in conjunction with the rising standard of living.

On the *upstream* side, enterprises cite the relation to component suppliers, cooperation agreements and financial resources as the main competition axes. The relation to component suppliers is the crucial condition for assembling PCs, as is the case all over the world. Cooperation agreements, another competition axis, represent a deeper relationship to suppliers. In order to obtain permission to act as the official supporting enterprise or to become a representative of a foreign enterprise, it is necessary that the enterprise's technological capabilities be approved by the awarding enterprise. Certification is therefore a factor of competition in that officially certified enterprises can prove their specific knowledge of the products they sell, maintain, install or support. Furthermore, when such cooperation agreements exist, the awarding enterprise provides better support with information and technological know-how, thereby improving the capabilities of the recipient. The last significant upstream competition axis is financial resources, which do not play an important role as an investment source for equipment, but are important for the purchase of components. Often, Eastern European enterprises still have to pay in advance and therefore require adequate financial resources.

Although R&D capacities in the Baltic countries existed in 1991, they completely lost their function in the innovation process of the post-socialist Baltic computer enterprises. The newly founded enterprises started to organize production of computers according to the practice which had been established in the rest of the world. Traditional relations or close links between the former R&D centers and the new computer enterprises did not exist and new ones were not created because all required knowledge was available through the purchase of components. The computer enterprises obtain access to new technologies through the computer components, which contain 100 percent codified knowledge. Therefore the exclusive sources of innovation for the Baltic computer manufacturers are the component suppliers.

The involvement of the Baltic governments in the domestic computer sectors was limited mainly to their role as a customer of computer technology. Only during the initial years following independence in 1991 did Lithuania and Latvia play a significant role in the restructuring process of the electrical engineering industry. Whereas Lithuania actively supported the restructuring process of Sigma, Latvia divided its remaining enterprises into parts and privatized them. Estonia decided to leave its enterprises to market forces and did not support the restructuring process. Today, none of the three Baltic governments play an active role in the computer industry.

4.2.3 Case study: Sigma computer enterprise

During the Soviet period, the Sigma Computer Plant was one of the main computer producers in Lithuania and contributed 3–4 percent to the entire Soviet computer production. In the period between 1990 and 1992, the demand for Lithuanian-made computers dropped dramatically and Western computer enterprises were able to increase their market shares rapidly. In 1991, Sigma had a production capacity of 600 SM1600 and SM1700 mainframe computers, but only 141 were sold. The production profile of Sigma was broadly diversified and included machine and assembly workshops, maintenance and power engineering, civil engineering and transport capabilities. In connection with the drop in demand for Sigma computers, the enterprise shifted its output mix, and the share of the computer business declined from 80 to 12 percent (World Bank 1993, p. 147). Sigma then entered into a joint venture with an American computer enterprise, with Sigma contributing 25 percent of the capital. This joint venture started the development of an IBM compatible prototype based on an Intel 8088 processor. This computer, which was similar to an IBM XT, never entered the production phase.

In mid-1992 the first step towards privatization was taken. Two percent of the capital was sold to Sigma's employees. But these changes did not improve the situation of the enterprise. In 1994 the Lithuanian government tried to prevent the shutdown of the Sigma Computer Plant by providing public support. It reorganized the plant into a new company called Sigmanta (77 percent private ownership, 23 percent state ownership), supported by the Ministry of Communication and Information Technology. The 'National Program for the Development of Communication and Informatics' defined the strategy of Sigmanta: the production of RISC Power PC workstations and servers, despite the insignificant and slowly developing demand for computers of the higher classes. Sigmanta was to be financed by the Public Investment Program of Lithuania, which provided a financial investment volume of USD 7,136 million, USD 6,468 million of which was to come from public investment programs.

Despite this public support, the situation of the enterprise did not improve, and in September 1997, it switched to the assembling of PC clones. Sigmanta introduced a new Lithuanian model called Bildukas. Today Sigmanta employs 40 people (Morkûnaite 1998, p. 607).

5. CONCLUSIONS

The emergence and development of the new Eastern European computer industry was influenced decisively by Western technologies. The existing, freely available and highly standardized PC technology enabled entrepreneurs to start businesses without having specific knowledge as a prerequisite. The modular production in the PC-assembling business was introduced from scratch in the Eastern European countries and existing structures could therefore not be used. Existing socialist production and innovation structures were neither competitive nor compatible with this new production method. The result was that the overwhelming majority of the former computer production units collapsed or switched to other activities, for example, in the electrical engineering sector. Thus, with the collapse of socialism, the socialist technological trajectory came to a sudden end. The development of the new computer sector was influenced mainly by greenfield creations which determine the structure of the sector today. The structures of the former (socialist) computer industry had no significant impact on the development of the emerging computer industry. Common problems of the restructuring process such as privatization issues and restructuring of large production combines into capitalist enterprises could be overcome quickly. A completely new industry emerged which has no socialist connections. The present innovation networks of the Eastern European computer enterprises are international and exclusively based on foreign sources of innovation. Domestic sources have no importance in the current innovation process and there are no signs that this will change in the near future. Thus, nothing like a 'post-socialist' technological trajectory has emerged; in contrast, the new computer-assembling industry has adopted international procedures. The future development of the technological paradigms and trajectories of Eastern European computer industries will therefore be determined by worldwide technological trends.

The immediate availability of technology allowed new enterprises to catch up technologically through the innovation systems of their foreign suppliers. This gave both computer enterprises and their customers the opportunity to use state-of-the-art computer technology without delay. The fact that only PC assembly is carried out in Eastern European countries should not be seen as a negative development, because it corresponds to worldwide PC production structures. The tremendously fast and successful development of the sector also led to a situation in which governments saw no reason to intervene. With only a few exceptions, governments left the development of the computer sector to market forces and emerging computer enterprises. The influence of the state was limited mainly to the role of customer (for example, automation of administration, and introduction of IT in schools and universities) and provider of education opportunities.

In the case of the PC market, domestic enterprises were able to establish themselves successfully. In the market segments for higher-class computers, however, the existing production and R&D structures were not competitive and collapsed completely. This market is dominated by large international computer enterprises such as IBM, Siemens and Fujitsu.

The development of Eastern European computer enterprises will depend heavily on the growth of domestic computer markets, because of their strong orientation towards these markets.

BIBLIOGRAPHY

Adirim, Itzchock (1991), 'Current Development and Dissemination of Computer Technology in the Soviet Economy', *Soviet Studies*, **43** (4), pp. 651–67.

Bitzer, Jürgen (1997), 'The Computer Industry in East and West: Do Eastern European Countries Need a Specific Science and Technology Policy?', DIW Discussion Papers (148), Berlin.

Bitzer, Jürgen (ed.) (1998), *Final Report – Work Package C 'Industrial Restructuring' Part C.6 Sector Study: Computers*, TSER Project: Restructuring and Re-integration of Science & Technology Systems in Economies in Transition, Berlin: DIW.

Bitzer, Jürgen and Christian von Hirschhausen (1998a), 'Science and Technology Policy in Eastern Europe – a Demand-Oriented Approach', *DIW Quarterly Journal of Economic Research*, **67** (2), Berlin, pp. 139–48.

Bitzer, Jürgen and Christian von Hirschhausen (eds) (1998b), *Industrial Restructuring and Economic Recovery in the Baltic Countries – Lithuania, Latvia, Estonia: Infrastructure Policies for Sustained Growth in the Baltic Countries*, Berlin: DIW.

BMWI (1997), Bundesministerium für Wirtschaft (ed.), *Wirtschaftslage und Reformprozesse in Mittel- und Osteuropa*, Bonn.

Business Central Europe (1996), *Special Supplement: Information Technology*, November, pp. 1–15.

Denger, Katharina S. (1997), 'Wettbewerbsstrategien und Innovations- prozesse in der Computerindustrie', *Dortmunder Diskussionsbeiträge zur Wirtschaftspolitik* (81), Dortmund.

Drüke, Helmut (1993), 'Restructuring in the PC Industry: New Challenges, New Actors, New Strategies, a Study in Labor and Industrial Policy', *WZB Papers* (93/201), Berlin.

Dyker, David and Jacques Perrin (1997), 'Technology Policy and Industrial Objectives in the Context of Economic Transition', in David A. Dyker (ed.), *The Technology of Transition*, Budapest: Central European University Press, pp. 3–19.

EITO (various issues), *European Information Technology Observatory*.

Karnite, Raita (1998), 'The Computer Industry in Latvia', in Bitzer and Hirschhausen (eds) (1998b), pp. 618–49.

Kauffmann, Manfred (1993), *Marketing Analysen: Konzepte und Strategien im PC-Markt*, München, Wien: Profil Verlag.

Kilvits, Kaarel (1998), 'Hardware in Estonia', in Bitzer and Hirschhausen (eds) (1998b), pp. 650–64.

Kubielas, Stanislaw (1996), *International Co-operative Agreements in Poland in the mid 1990s: Evolution, Organizational Forms and Industry Characteristics, Part I: Country Industrial Report*, Warsaw: Faculty of Economic Science Warsaw University.

Kubielas, Stanislaw (1998), 'Restructuring of the Polish Computer Industry', in Bitzer (ed.) (1998).

Meffert, Jürgen P. (1993), 'Standards als Integrationsinstrument in der Computer- und Kommunikationsindustrie: Wettbewerbsstrategische Bedeutung und Durchsetzung', *Internationales Management* (9), Konstanz.

Morkûnaite, Rasa (1998), 'Hardware Sector in Lithuania', in Bitzer and Hirschhausen (eds) (1998b), pp. 598–617.

Müller, Karel and Jiri Vorisek (1998), 'Case Study: Restructuring of the Czech Computer Industry', in Bitzer (ed.) (1998).

Pavitt, Keith L.R. (1984), 'Sectoral Patterns of Technological Change: Towards a Taxonomy and a Theory', *Research Policy*, **13** (6), pp. 343–73.

Petska-Juliussen, Karen and Egil Juliussen (1996), *The 8th Annual Computer Industry Almanac*, Florence, Kentucky, USA: International Thomson Publishing.

US International Trade Commission (1993), 'Global Competitiveness of US Advanced-Technology Industries: Computers', *World Trade and Arbitration Materials*, **6** (2), pp. 55–141.

Vickery, Graham (1996), 'Globalisation in the Computer Industry', in Organization for Economic Cooperation and Development (OECD), *Globalisation of Industry: Overview and Sector Reports*, Paris: OECD, pp. 109–51.

World Bank (1993), 'Lithuania: The Transition to a Market Economy', *World Bank Country Study*, Washington, DC: World Bank.

11 Restructuring the Computer and Software Industries in Poland

Stanislaw Kubielas

1. INTRODUCTION

The evolution of computer and software industries in Poland can generally be divided into two periods: before and after the collapse of communism in 1989. In the first period, the development of the sector occurred under conditions of relative autarky with restricted access to world technology and markets. It resulted in persistent underinvestment and an increasing technological gap to world leaders in the industry, since the planning system was unable to absorb and assimilate emerging innovations in microelectronics. On the whole, the failure to come to terms with the microelectronic revolution was one of the biggest technological factors in the collapse of that system.[208] It is then no surprise that the transformation has brought about dramatic changes in the industrial landscape of the sector.

It should also be noted that the great transformation of the economic system coincided with radical shifts in the technological trajectory of the computer industry itself and its rapid globalization worldwide. It was only in the early 1980s that the emergence of personal computers paved the way for a new matured industry structure based on increasingly standardized inputs which embodied highly integrated and codified technological knowledge. An effective assimilation of this technological discontinuity might have been largely facilitated by the discontinuity and collapse of the old economic structure as well as the shock-therapy type of transition to a market economy. Equally surprising, then, was the rapid emergence of a modern domestic PC industry in a country such as Poland where obsolete technological trajectory of the industry was consistently cultivated through deliberate autarky policies

---

[208] See Dyker and Perrin (1997, p. 98).

and arbitrary non-market allocational decisions made by the state before 1989. This remarkable success of the new high-tech industry which implied accelerated absorption of the latest state-of-the-art technology was only possible because of vast market liberalization, an outburst of private entrepreneurship, and increased access to world markets and technology through cooperative strategic alliances. These were the main factors which led to the characteristic dominance of a few single local producers in the Polish computer market, which now seems to be quite competitive compared to Western standards. Additionally, a relatively large domestic market (as compared to other Central and Eastern European Countries – CEEC) eased the attainment of scale economies, which were also important for exploiting local comparative advantages. It must be noted that those market factors appeared crucial in the absence of any deliberate state science and technology policy, which simply did not exist.

On the other hand, the software industry in Poland was the sector that was least affected by the economic crisis and transition after 1989. This is not to say that the industry did not undergo some fundamental structural changes. It certainly did, but these were the changes that affected the whole IT industry worldwide, namely the disintegration of the former IT industry structure with the emergence of PCs. It was, nonetheless, the adjustment capability and viability of the software industry in Poland which is an interesting phenomenon that needs explanation.

The emergence of PC computer technology dramatically changed the structure of the hardware–software industry both in the West and in the East. The changes came to the CEEC, after some delay, generally after the opening-up of the Eastern economies in 1989, but had a roughly similar disintegration effect on the hitherto-prevailing vertical structure of the entire computer industry. It thus had an impact on the position of software services in the production chain and the implementation of computer technology. In the era of mainframes, all the production stages of a computer were usually vertically integrated within one big computer firm, such as IBM: manufacturing integrated circuits, assembling computers, producing system software, producing application software, and final implementation (distribution) of the computer system for the end-user. The introduction of PCs broke up this production cycle into segmented markets with horizontally integrated companies, specializing in: semiconductors, assembling, system software, general-purpose application software, customer-tailored application software, distribution, and finally integration of segmented highly specialized components into a useful computer system ready for operation by end-users.[209]

In the course of the rapid development of the industry, three of the niches became incredibly concentrated: semiconductors, system software and general-purpose software (word processing, spreadsheets, databases). To date, the situation on the market is such that practically the whole world is supplied by two giant companies: Intel for semiconductors, and Microsoft for system and general-purpose software. Even in the Western countries most advanced in computer technology, almost all local competitors in these niches failed to stand up to the competition from these two giants and dropped out. In the remaining market niches – assembling, customized application software, distribution and integration – local competitors flourish or even dominate the world leaders on local markets.

It should be no surprise that the lagging CEECs immediately abandoned any attempt to enter the market dominated by the two world leaders when confronted with open international competition. This happened in the semiconductor sector, while assembling personal computers appeared to be a prosperous business. The same occurred in software where standard software (system and general purpose) was simply imported and traded by so-called authorized dealers or value-adding resellers (usually domestic software houses or PC computer assemblers for system software). The immediate niche that opened up for domestic companies was distribution, and only later came their own production of customized application software and integration as the systems became more and more complex. On the whole, the fragmentation of the computer production cycle was another important factor for rapid restructuring and globalization of both the computer and the software industries in Poland.

This chapter is an attempt to take account of the radical restructuring that occurred in the Polish computer and software industries since the economic transformation began. In the first section the legacies of the past system will be presented. Then, the growth of the sector will be analyzed with special emphasis on the behavior of particular market segments in the process of technological adjustment to world market conditions. Finally, the sources of growth and innovation will be discussed with reference to the case studies of major market players, followed by an account of the possibilities for S&T policy in this particular industry.

---

[209] With regard to standardization, system software and general-purpose application software may be treated as one category of standard software, and customized application software as individual software (see Bitzer 1997, p. 14). The breakdown into system and application software refers instead to its functional characteristic.

2. COLLAPSE AND REEMERGENCE OF THE POLISH COMPUTER INDUSTRY

In the late 1950s and early 1960s, the first Polish computing machines were built on an experimental basis by the Polytechnic of Warsaw and the Institute for Mathematical Machines of the Polish Academy of Sciences. However, all demand for computers of higher capacity used for more sophisticated industrial applications was covered incidentally by imports. Serial manufacturing of computers began in the mid-1960s, when ODRA 1000–1200 was launched by ELWRO (Wroclaw), a state-owned company which later cooperated with the British mainframe producer ICT (later known as ICL).[210]

In 1964, the government decided to take control of the entire industry within one body. The state-administered conglomerate MERA was created, and this played a major role in the state policy designed for this branch until the end of 1980s. MERA was in charge of ELWRO (the main serial production unit), the Institute for Mathematical Machines (research and experimental prototypes), Blonie (peripheral devices – printers), MERAMAT (tape memories), ERA and ZSM (drum and disk memories), and Zabrze (perforated tape and monitors). However, no more active S&T policy emerged until the early 1970s when the new government began to modernize the economy using Western credit, and a first countrywide information program was launched, with a number of state committees and councils responsible for its implementation.

The heyday of the computer industry, combined with large hardware imports from major world manufacturers, was as short-lived as the money borrowed, and finished in about the mid-1970s when the CMEA imposed a specialization program for the computer industry in member states, the so-called 'unified system' (based on the RIAD model).[211] Whereas the Soviets achieved some progress in mainframe technology, any innovation in the field was kept top secret and never shared with allied countries. Nor were any of the more advanced Western computer technologies available to socialist

---

[210] As a result of that cooperation, the ODRA 1300 model series based on the ICL 1900 standard was introduced, and it became very popular by the mid-1970s. The ODRA 1305 model – entirely compatible with the ICL standard – was then regarded as the most advanced computer model produced in the Eastern bloc. The company produced up to 50 units per month.

[211] Actually, it was a copy of the IBM 360 standard, but ELWRO – then a major computer producer in Poland – was forced to convert to a new system, and to give up the ICL architecture which had been successfully developed so far. Furthermore, the COMECON program obliged Poland to specialize in peripheral devices, in particular in tape memories, while the Soviet Union was to monopolize production of mainframes and central processing units.

countries (including Poland), on account of the COCOM restrictions which imposed a total embargo during the late 1970s and 1980s. This was a sure way to technological stalemate, which forced ELWRO to continue producing RIAD models which became more and more obsolete. As the PC technology emerged in the 1980s, the state-owned computer firms were discouraged by the government from entering this field since the new technology was perceived as undermining the autocratic rule of the party (printers were particularly dangerous as they could be used to proliferate uncensored publications).[212]

On the whole, central planning, in particular coordinated under the COMECON program, proved unable to develop the infrastructure conducive to innovations or at least assimilation of the state-of-the-art technology into the computer industry. The entire sector was somewhat poorly developed, and the technology gap between state-administered domestic computer firms and their Western counterparts increased to such a degree that after the disintegration of the COMECON market in 1989, the home-grown hardware sector all but collapsed in the face of foreign competition. For example, ELWRO, once the biggest Polish mainframe manufacturer, since 1968 in cooperation with ICL and later within the COMECON program, switched to car alarms, and finally was acquired by Siemens in the telecommunications deal with the Polish government, later to be shut down and liquidated as a computer factory. Nor could the home-grown semiconductor industry survive the sudden exposure to foreign competition. The largest state-owned supplier CEMI almost closed down semiconductor production and turned to the real estate business; even new investment in an integrated circuit line of VLSI could not save the company from insolvency in 1994. The only Polish manufacturer of integrated circuits to survive is the Torun-based company, Toral. Alhough the first Polish PC, Masovia, could itself not withstand foreign competition, its producer Mikrokomputery survived as the only computer manufacturer of the former period (however, as a PC assembler and dealer).

As the state-owned mainframe and semiconductor industry was swept away totally by foreign competition, the new PC industry emerged as a horizontal structure of *de nuovo* private firms, focussed exclusively on assembling, and relying totally on foreign imports of components. Because of the technological gap to world leaders inherited from the central planning system, upstream levels of computer industry structure could not be

---

[212] The first Polish PC (Masovia 1016, a 16-bit-microprocessor K1810 WM86, similar to Intel 8086) was launched in 1986, by Mikrokomputery Ltd, a joint venture set up by state-owned companies manufacturing various computer parts and equipment (most of them formerly belonging to MERA).

maintained as economically and technologically viable.

Ironically, it was Poland, whose COMECON specialization lay firmly in the consumer electronics field and peripheral devices, rather than in mainframes or semiconductors, which found itself best suited to exploit the new opportunities in the PC assembly business. Primarily, this required extended cooperation with input suppliers rather than accumulation of proprietary technologies. A favorable condition for the emerging horizontal private computer industry occurred in the late 1980s when the government, under pressure from the military, abolished customs duties on, and turned a blind eye to, the 'shuttling' (unregistered 'suitcase' imports) of computers and computer components into Poland to supply the infant domestic computer assembly industry. This is how the sector actually emerged, since nearly all the private firms were boosted by suitcase imports of Western technology, while all state-owned computer companies, which were dependent on the Soviet márket, were made bankrupt. Between five and six thousand private companies mushroomed in the mid- and late 1980s. A strong impulse to growth came from the full trade liberalization and internal convertibility of the Polish currency, introduced in 1989.

3. RISE AND ENTERPRISATION OF THE POLISH SOFTWARE INDUSTRY

The first programming and computing centers in Poland came into being as soon as the first computers were constructed or imported. Originally they were individual ventures carried out either in research institutions or in public or industrial central administration units. As the demand for software and computing services grew in the mid-1960s, a network of computing centers, so called ZETOs (Center for Electronic Data Processing), was established on a regional basis. To serve local needs for programming and computing, a ZETO unit was set up in each voivodship and the Warsaw-based SOETO (Capital Center for Electronic Data Processing) was established. These two activities were usually carried out within the same facility because software services were tailored to specific computation tasks and were not tradable on the market; the market for software products did not exist as such. ZETOs were originally equipped with mainframe computers that were either manufactured domestically (ODRA, RIAD) or imported (ICL, IBM, NCR), and constituted the major client for the emerging computer industry. Apart from ZETOs there were also some industrial computing centers affiliated with the biggest state enterprises such as the shipyards, the coal mines, the steelworks, the railways, or with central institutions such as the Central

Statistical Office, the National Bank of Poland and so on.

This system of organization for domestic software industry survived basically unchanged until the end of the 1980s, with its heyday in the 1970s. Over time, ZETOs accumulated most of the indigenous human capital specialized in programming and computing services, which was a crucial production factor for this type of industry. The people employed were well acquainted with the state-of-the-art technology in their business although often could not utilize their capabilities because of the obsolete hardware equipment. As that sort of software services provision began to lessen in importance on account of the emergence of PC technology, the ZETOs were readily privatized at the beginning of 1980s and could withstand the competition from newly established software houses and companies surprisingly well. In late 1980s, some of the former ZETO employees set up a number of spin-offs, which were then privatized and became major software producers on the domestic market.

The old mainframe-era software industry organized in the ZETO network was typically vertically integrated. Opening up the Polish economy speeded up the process of disintegration and restructuring into horizontal structures adjusted to modern PC technology. However, the shock was not as severe as in computer manufacturing, because the basic input (human capital) was already there. ZETOs were simply privatized, or some of their former employees transferred to the newly established private companies which had adapted to the new competitive conditions. This was a clear *enterprization* process of the industry, with proper reorientation towards emerging market niches while the only missing factor was expansion capital to be raised during the period of general financial crisis. Twenty-one entities from former ZETOs survived, each now employing 50 persons on average, with average sales of USD 3–5 million (the entire ZETO market amounting to USD 600–800 million, which includes mainly distribution and integration, with its own software production constituting only a small fraction). Newly established software companies, mostly set up by former ZETO employees, succeeded in raising the necessary funds for expansion, and now dominate the market for application software and integration services.

4. GROWTH, MARKET STRUCTURE AND COMPETITION

The dramatic disappearance of the whole state-administered computer industry, poorly developed under conditions of technological autarky, and the instant emergence of a viable private high-tech sector totally dependent on leading world suppliers, which occurred in Poland in the wake of deep economic crisis, is a unique historical example of a burst of *entrepreneurship* rather than *enterprization* of old structures which simply ceased to exist. The newly established companies which now dominate the computer industry in Poland were built up from scratch, entirely on the principles of market economy, assuming all corporate governance functions of an ordinary enterprise.

Most of the newly established computer companies started by trading imported hardware, components and software, which for many of them still remains an important part of the business. Despite a large number of companies reported in the business press as operating in the computer industry, only a few actually dealt with manufacturing computer equipment, producing software or providing integration services, while most of them operated as dealers or distributors. This has always been the case with new entrants into an infant industry.

The emergence of PC technology, which entailed massive imports of either original PCs or clones from abroad, was necessarily accompanied by imports of related software. Two sorts of software were of immediate importance without which imported hardware would be useless – system software and general-purpose application software, that is, standard software. These products were primarily brought in by direct individual importers or distributed by authorized dealers and later on by so-called value-added resellers. The existing ZETOs as well as newly set up software and hardware distribution houses immediately entered the business. Some of the world software leaders (for example, Microsoft, Novell and Informix) set up representative offices for the distribution of their products and concluded a number of distribution agreements with Polish partners. However, it should be noted that apart from officially sold software, in the absence of appropriate protection laws there was a proliferation of illegal copies. The absence of such protection has been cited as an argument explaining the poor interest shown by world software vendors on the Polish market. But some of them did report substantial sales of their software products in Poland via their distributors or other trading partners even before they made a direct official appearance on the Polish market.[213] Among the best-selling system software products were PC operating systems by Novell, Microsoft and SCO; general-purpose software by Lotus, Borland, Word Perfect and Autodesk; or unix database management systems by Informix, Progress, Ingress and Oracle.

---

[213] The most spectacular success was achieved by Microsoft, who made USD 17 million from sales of its software products in the fiscal year 1994–95. The company arranged promotion campaigns while selling the Polish versions of its products at dumping prices (sometimes gratis) to inhibit any local competition. As a result, the market segment of standard software was soon completely dominated by foreign software.

4.1 Computer Industry

Table 11.1 provides industrial data on companies which were registered as computer equipment manufacturers, with more than five employees (thus obliged to report to the Central Statistical Office). The striking features of the trend in 1991–94 were dramatically declining employment (to about 40 percent), almost disappearing exports (from 25 to 3 percent of sales), radical decapitalization of industry (equity capital shrank by half in nominal terms), and huge financial losses (negative profitability of minus 15 percent). At the same time, total sales more than doubled and the FDI share in equity capital rose to more than 50 percent.

Table 11.1   Computer equipment manufacturing – industry data, 1991–1995

PLN (m)	1991	1992	1993	1994	1995
Number of companies (units)	69	99	106	100	99
Number employed	8,045	4,548	4,243	3,326	3,949
Total sales (PLN m)	150,390	196,392	267,645	349,716	904,651
Exports as percentage of sales	24.7	5.1	1.8	3.3	1.8
Equity capital (PLN m)	118,572	69,844	50,126	65,480	129,687
Foreign share					
as % of equity	3.1	15.6	26.1	57.7	69.2
Total assets (PLN m)	174,393	162,033	178,501	239,070	468,971
Intangibles					
as % of fixed assets	0.7	1.0	0.7	1.2	6.4
Pre-tax profits (PLN m)	(23,143)	(27,179)	(21,777)	(44,995)	50,868
Net profits (PLN m)	(25,256)	(29,700)	(28,354)	(49,775)	37,935
Productivity (sales/employee)					
(PLN m)	0.019	0.043	0.063	0.105	0.229
Profitability (net profit/sales)					
(%)	–16.79	–15.12	–10.59	–14.23	4.19

Note: Average annual exchange rates PLN/$: 1991: 1.05; 1992: 1.36; 1993: 1.81; 1994: 2.27; 1995: 2.39; 1996: 2.65. One 1991 new Polish zloty is approximately equal to one dollar.

Source: Central Statistical Office. Author's own calculations from balance sheet data.

The aggregate data of the industry is obviously a result of two opposite developments: a declining state-owned sector (obsolete mainframe and minicomputers, as well as semiconductor components), and a growing private PC industry. The latter concentrated on assembling rather than manufacturing components (imported mainly from the Far East), with minimum initial capital and a moderate scale of production. While state companies were running huge losses, the private ones improved productivity per employee, which increased six fold on average over the period.

The situation changed dramatically in 1995 when the new industry as a whole embarked on a path of fast growth. In nominal terms, equity capital almost doubled, sales rose by about 160 percent in one year, and the industry as a whole showed a profit (with a profitability rate of 4.2 percent), for the first time since the beginning of transformation. This was accompanied by a further increase of FDI share in equity capital to about 70 percent, and an increase of intangibles' share in assets from 1.2 to 6.4 percent. Also impressive was a doubling of productivity as measured by sales per employee.

The Polish computer market fields from five to six thousand firms, employing between one and 800 people, but only 18 of them employed more than a hundred at the end of 1994 and only six provided jobs for 200-plus employees. While supercomputers or large mainframes are marketed by a few foreign companies – IBM, Siemens Nixdorf and Unisys – a majority of Polish market players specialize in personal computer hardware and software with annual sales on the domestic market of approximately 500 thousand PCs and 300 thousand printers. From 1994 onwards, the structure of the market has become relatively stable and exhibited unruffled linear aggregate growth of sales by about 40–70 percent annually, in various market segments.

Table 11.2 presents the distribution of revenues by type of activity of the 200 largest IT companies on the Polish market (total turnover about 5.2 billion zlotys or 2 billion dollars in 1996). Software services provided by domestic companies can be found under the heading of software production and integration. Distribution and dealing of software and hardware are merged together, but it is estimated that two-thirds of revenue comes from hardware trading and one-third from software trading. As can be seen, the largest share of the market is captured by distributors and dealers (62 percent), while software services (software producers and integrators) receive no more than 22 percent of all revenue, and pure hardware manufacturers only 14 percent. However, integration is the most rapidly expanding activity of all, which certainly gave impetus to the growth of the domestic software sector. On the other hand, adding indigenous hardware sales and other (imported) traded hardware gives hardware a 55 percent share of the total IT market.

Table 11.2 Revenues of 200 largest IT firms by type of activity, 1994–1996

Type of activity	1996		1995		1994		Annual growth rate (%)
	PLN m	USD million	PLN m	USD million	PLN m	USD million	
Distributors	2,129.83	788.78	1,306.55	574.57	710.80	313.13	58.7
Dealers	1,149.21	427.22	705.98	311.00	496.90	218.90	39.7
Integrators	906.44	336.97	588.62	259.30	237.00	104.41	79.6
Hardware producers	739.99	275.09	399.79	176.12	279.80	123.26	49.4
Software producers	240.00	89.22	182.26	80.29	129.30	56.96	25.2
Training	50.12	18.63	37.66	16.59	22.00	9.69	38.7
Total	5,215.59	1,935.91	3,220.86	1,417.87	1,875.80	826.35	53.18

Sources: Computerworld (1996, p. 14; 1997); and author's own calculations.

Table 11.3 shows data on the performance of the 25 largest computer equipment manufacturers in 1996 based on the Computerworld survey. Their revenues from strictly defined computer equipment manufacturing are separated and presented in terms of value and percentage share of total revenue from all types of business. This may give a measure of production concentration as far as manufacturing is concerned. It is remarkable that in 1996 the top ten companies accounted for almost 80 percent of sales, and only three ten – Optimus, JTT and Posnet – for 57 percent in terms of sales of the industry strictly defined. The two leaders in PC assembling (Optimus and JTT), however, employed barely 17 percent. The figures are still more striking for Optimus, which contributed almost 40 percent of sales with only 13 percent of the sector's workforce. Thus the concentration ratio in computer equipment manufacturing is relatively high, but also biassed, in that we observe high concentration of sales and profits in the private part of this sector which must have been counterbalanced by an equal concentration of employment and losses in the state-owned companies. The explosive growth, then, can be attributed exclusively to a few private companies which, faced with increasing demand, found a way to tap financial markets – in spite of the financial crisis – and to raise private finance for expansion. This was clearly one of the main factors in the consolidation of the sector and a relatively high concentration ratio in spite of the presence of a large number of small assemblers.

Table 11.3 Main computer equipment manufacturers, 1995–1996

Company	Revenue from PC equipment 1996		Revenue from PC equipment 1995		Growth rate (%)	Employment	
	PLN m	percent	PLN m	percent		1996	1995
Total of 82/70 firms*	740.0	37	399.8	36	85.1	4,694	2,888
1 Optimus S.A.	280.9	48	160.6	47	74.9	612	475
2 Posnet	80.5	90	9.8	85	721.4	55	28
3 JTT Computer	58.9	21	42.2	24	39.6	179	152
4 Elzab Zabrze	43.7	89	–	–	–	339	–
5 NTT System	36.7	70	15.0	37	78.0	54	–
6 Baza	23.5	40	22.3	40	5.4	101	95
7 Inwar S.A.	21.6	40	12.9	40	67.4	201	155
8 Format	16.4	50	8.7	50	88.5	30	20
9 Gulipin	15.3	80	9.3	85	63.4	21	18
10 BPS	14.9	35	19.0	60	–21.5	127	116
11 Komax PW	13.4	50	–	–	–	47	–
12 Mikrotech	12.3	46	1.7	12	623.5	136	97
13 Hector	11.7	27	13.5	35	–13.3	39	–
14 Escom Poland	8.9	15	–	–	–	85	–
15 Fideltronik	7.1	80	3.4	100	100.9	154	83
16 Arma Rzeszow	4.1	40	2.6	40	57.7	19	15
17 Selcom	3.9	90	2.6	70	50.0	15	14
18 Medcom	3.4	47	–	–	–	35	–
19 HSK Data	3.3	40	3.7	50	–10.8	77	74
20 Technokabel	3.2	20	–	–	–	160	–
21 COMtech-RDE	3.2	48	2.1	26	52.4	9	11
22 MEFA Blonie	3.2	95	2.7	89	18.5	23	22
23 Infotex	3.1	60	2.8	55	10.7	15	16
24 Digilab	3.1	43	2.8	65	10.7	28	26
25 Gamatronic	2.9	40	–	–	–	26	–

Note: *82 firms reported in 1996, while only 70 reported in 1995.

Sources: Computerworld (1996, p. 9; 1997, p. 8); and author's calculations.

The other characteristic feature of the Polish PC market is a persistent dominance of domestic assemblers, a local share – over 70 percent of all PCs sold – which is not this large anywhere else in computer Europe. Only the American market shows a similar local share (but a great deal of American firms' production is outsourced from the Far East), and Western Europe's local companies show the highest share in Germany (Vobis, Escom), Holland and Italy (Olivetti), but nowhere does it exceed 30 percent. Furthermore, according to the Computerworld report data (Table 11.4), about 50 percent of PCs are being sold solely by two the largest Polish PC companies – Optimus and JTT – which have succeeded in developing their Polish brand names and have retained their market share despite a growing number of small competitive (tax and duty saving) assemblers and foreign competition.

Table 11.4 Personal computers sold in 1000 units, 1994–1996

Producer	1996		1995		1994		Change	Change
	units	share* in %	units	share* in %	units	share* in %	96/95 in %	95/94 in %
Total	390.9	100.0	336	100.0	287.6	100.0	16	17
1 Optimus	143.0	36.6	130.0	38.7	112.0	38.9	10	16
2 JTT	37.0	9.5	30.0	8.9	44.5	15.5	23	–33
3 IBM PL	23.0	5.9	17.0	5.1	6.5	2.3	35	162
4 Compaq	22.3	5.7	16.0	4.8	27.0	9.4	39	–41
5 NTT	19.8	5.1	13.3	4.0	1.2	0.4	49	1008
6 Vobis	17.3	4.4	15.0	4.5	8.1	2.8	15	85
7 DTK	15.2	3.9	12.0	3.6	9.8	3.4	27	22
8 Baza	13.7	3.5	10.5	3.1	7.3	2.5	30	44
9 Inwar	12.0	3.1	11.2	3.3	10.2	3.6	7	10
10 HP	11.9	3.0	8.0	2.4	5.2	1.8	49	54
11 Escom Pl	9.2	2.4	11.0	3.3	9.6	3.3	–16	15
12 Digital Pl	8.2	2.1	5.0	1.5	4.3	1.5	64	16
13 Dell Pl	8.0	2.0	10.0	3.0	3.5	1.2	–20	186
14 Gulipin	6.6	1.7	3.5	1.0	–	–	89	–
15 Format	5.0	1.3	–	–	–	–	–	–
16 Acer	4.5	1.2	3.5	1.0	2.9	1.0	29	21
17 Apple	4.2	1.1	–	–	–	–	–	–
18 Hector	4.1	1.0	5.0	1.5	4.6	1.6	–18	9
19 Mikrotech	3.5	0.9	–	–	–	–	–	–
20 Tulip	2.6	0.7	–	–	–	–	–	–
Others	19.8	5.1	35.0	10.4	30.9	10.7	–43	13

Note: * Totals rounded to 100.

Sources: Computerworld (1997, p. 66); and author's own calculations.

Computerworld data is based on reporting from the 50 largest companies, which are thought to supply about 70 percent of the home market; the rest is provided by small companies, so the number of PCs sold in 1996 may be estimated at more than 500,000. The amount of imported brand PCs sold on the Polish market does not significantly exceed 20 percent, and seems to be relatively stable over the three years reported. However, the data recently published for 1997 indicate that the market share of leading local manufacturers tends to decline: of 550,000 PCs sold in 1997, Optimus sold only 94,000 (17 percent), JTT – 33,000 (6 percent), and NTT – 30,000 (5.5 percent). Thus the share of the three domestic leaders shrank from 50 percent in 1996 to 25 percent. This is a significant change in the past trend, accompanied by an increasing share of total imports with declining shares of individual brands imported.

It seems that the PC demand is currently undergoing important structural shifts between different market segments: public administration and big business, SOHO (Small Office Home Office), and individual customers. The demand from the first segment is clearly declining; big institutions and big business have already been more or less computerized, and are cutting their IT budgets. SMEs also tend to rationalize their expenditure on computers, especially on expensive machines which cannot be fully utilized within their business activities. What is booming is the demand for home computers by individuals who increasingly look for more sophisticated, customized PCs (meeting Internet requirements). This is forcing the suppliers to further diversify their offers and to increase imports, which are also more diversified.

4.2 Software Industry

In 1994, the Polish parliament created a new copyright protection law, which also covered original software products, but sounded the death-knell for the software already in use. The new law resulted in an explosion in the turnover of official software market, which grew by more than four times from 1994 to 1995 (Table 11.5). Part of this was certainly due to increased sales of system and general-purpose software. However, it must be noted that system software was never the best candidate for illegal copying, given faultlessly operating hardware. On the other hand, the absence of protection favored rapid penetration by foreign suppliers of general-purpose software which, because of this 'forced dumping' easily dominated the market. Legal protection is most required for the development of application software, and particularly for customized application software, with the exception of highly customized software that cannot be used in any second application. Thus, the new law created incentives and a level playing field in these two niches both for imports and for their own product development, which remained undersupplied in the first period.

The rapid growth of the market in recent years covers software services, including software production and integration, as well as the bulk of distribution and dealing activities. However, one must be aware that trading of home-grown products was limited mainly to the niche of application software, such as in banking and enterprise management, provided by the strongest domestic competitors. Numerous weaker software houses used to combine their own products with foreign subcontracting, or trading imported (system or application) software with integration services (a rapidly growing market segment).

Table 11.5 Software services – industry data, 1991–1995

	1991	1992	1993	1994	1995
Number of companies (units)	373	530	604	623	640
Number employed	3,906	5,147	6,041	7,135	8,182
Total sales (PNL m)	114,758	281,489	402,696	667,153	2,966,935
Exports as % of sales	4.9	7.6	5.3	4.4	1.2
Equity capital (PNL m)	15,369	24,998	36,455	72,012	307,866
Foreign share as % of equity	16.8	28.3	29.8	14.1	10.2
Total assets (PNL m)	49,738	95,503	151,911	293,478	900,599
Intangibles as % of fixed assets	5.2	17.1	13.0	7.0	17.5
Pretax profits (PNL m)	7,317	21,199	36,584	43,638	173,366
Net profits (PNL m)	3,362	12,713	26,813	25,720	100,453
Productivity (sales/employee) (PNL m)	0.029	0.055	0.067	0.093	0.363
Profitability (net profit/sales) (%)	2.93	4.52	6.66	3.86	3.39

Source: Central Statistical Office. Author's calculations from balance sheet data.

As we can see from Table 11.5, the software sector clearly shows sound and rapid growth, in terms of employment, sales and profits. In 1995, an exceptionally strong market explosion (in terms of sales, equity capital and asset increase) could be observed, which was probably due not only to the stimulus coming from the new copyright protection law but also to the accelerated development of application software and integration services related to the modernization of the banking sector. Software services is certainly one of the few industries that did not report net losses over the whole transition period. Most of its capacities were not built up from scratch, but rather spun off from privatized state-owned data-processing centers. The sector exhibits relatively small foreign involvement in terms of equity, but at the same time it shows a substantial share of intangibles in fixed assets, which may be an indicator of significant dependence on arm's-length imports of foreign know-how, and a rapid assimilation of foreign technology transferred from abroad. This was only possible because of the existing absorption capacities in the form of human capital, accumulated in the sector over the previous period.

The size of the market for imported software is estimated at about USD 350 million, which is traded mainly by distributors, and this is generally standard software, because home-grown software is usually provided directly by original domestic producers. The latter is basically limited to the specific market niches of customized application software such as banking and enterprise management supporting systems. The home-grown software market is, then, much smaller in terms of turnover (amounting to around USD 100 million annually) than the home-grown hardware market. If, however, we include integration services (a market of USD 300 to 400 million), it becomes quite important and exceeds even home-grown hardware sales.

We can see from Table 11.6 that the 25 largest software producers account for about 70 percent of the domestic production, and ten of them cover as much as 50 percent, while the three leaders capture exactly 30 percent. Thus, the concentration ratio in that market segment is not as high as in the PC manufacturing sector, but seems to be substantial, and has been further increased by a wave of recent mergers. The most spectacular was that of Prokom, which formed the largest Polish group on the software market, employing more than 700 people. As might be noted, the consolidation tendency intensifies with the growth of market size and increasing foreign competition. Domestic software producers and system integrators have to be large in order to bid for large tenders, on a level footing with their foreign rivals.

Table 11.6 Main software producers, 1995–1996

Company	Revenue from own software 1996		Revenue from own software 1995		Growth rate in %	Employ- ment 1996	Employ- ment 1995
	PLN m	%	PLN m	%			
Total of 117/107 firms*	240.0	21	182.3	22	31.6	7,371	5,881
1 Prokom	36.4	18	35.9	100	1.4	750	550
2 Softbank	23.9	26	15.5	48	54.2	180	136
3 CSBI	13.2	38	9.3	35	41.9	329	289
4 Cross-Comm.	9.3	74	7.9	85	27.4	63	53
5 Macrosoft	6.9	100	2.9	50	137.9	85	44
6 Elba	6.4	100	2.3	88	178.2	87	72
7 Young Digital	6.1	100	2.4	100	154.2	33	15
8 Soft-Lab	6.0	80	1.3	40	361.5	75	58
9 IFC Poland	5.4	65	1.4	30	285.7	60	42
10 Coig	5.1	13	5.2	13	–1.9	703	888
11 CDN	4.9	84	3.1	83	58.1	49	37
12 Altkom	4.9	90	–	–	–	48	–
13 IGE	4.8	80	2.1	66	128.6	120	82
14 CIE	4.7	35	4.1	31	14.6	188	216
15 Unisoft	3.9	59	3.0	52	30	100	70
16 Yuma	3.8	78	–	–	–	95	–
17 Kamsoft	3.8	30	–	–	–	30	–
18 Comp	3.4	28	–	–	–	49	–
19 Simple	3.2	47	3.2	69	0	71	56
20 Teta	3.2	55	1.3	41	146.1	105	62
21 Kom-Pakt	3.1	60	2.8	60	10.7	48	39
22 Vulcan	2.7	92	1.9	95	42.1	41	36
23 Logotec	2.4	37	2.9	55	–17.2	36	51
24 RoboBat	2.4	96	–	–	–	42	–
25 Junisoftex	2.4	70	1.8	60	33.3	58	62

Note: *117 firms reported in 1996, while only 107 reported in 1995.

Sources: Computerworld (1996, p. 38; 1997, p. 25); and author's calculations.

It should not be surprising that none of the major domestic software firms can be identified as an original system or general-purpose software producer. However, the field in which Polish software firms are well ahead of foreign competition is in company management and financial accounting software. The reason is that they are more familiar with the conditions, quickly-changing regulations and structures of Polish enterprises. The emergence of new banks in Poland in 1991–93 spurred on the development of Polish software for banks.[214]

In the market segment of enterprise management software (MRP II), all the major world producers are present on the Polish market – SAP, Hogart, IFS, Scala, JBA, QUMAK, Ster Projekt, ISA and IBS – to name the most important players. The indisputable leader is SAP, a German software producer, specializing in application software for the largest companies. Generally, the clients of Western software suppliers are affiliates of big multinationals or the largest Polish enterprises and institutions. The major domestic competitor in that market segment is Prokom, which specializes mainly in integrated management systems for large enterprises. Quite recently it succeeded in outperforming its major Western rival, SAP, in the number of licenses sold and license revenues earned. In the segment of software for SMEs, the dominance of many Polish suppliers is still more pronounced.

In the segment of banking software, the early invasion of Western systems was soon halted due to a series of unsuccessful application solutions, as only two applications of the package IBS-90 based on Digital platform appeared to be successful. In that context, the implementation of the banking software system 'Zorba', by the Polish software house Softbank, can be regarded as the turning point for the Polish producers. As the system gained widespread popularity among the banking fraternity, Softbank became the largest supplier of the banking application software on the Polish market since 1996, even dominating Western competitors. Two other domestic software houses – CSBI and Elba – also joined this market segment successfully, and after a merger with Computerland, reached a consolidated position in bidding for major contracts. Thus the competitiveness of Polish producers of banking software seems to be particularly strong in relation to foreign suppliers.

Following the disappearance of the mainframe business, a new and important market niche, on the border between pure software services and hardware implementation, emerged for domestic computer companies – integration. To some extent, system integration is a substitute for the mainframe business where networks based on workstations perform similar functions. The most spectacular failure by Bull to complete the contracted installation for the Polish tax administration system (POLTAX), which was a result of their lack of experience as a system integrator in Poland, reinforced

---

[214] Estimates by the Polish Software Association show that the share of Polish software houses in the market is in excess of 50 percent. The leaders include Prokom (partner to Informix), CSBI (British–Polish joint venture, part of the CSB Group, developing products based on Progress software tools), Softbank (where ICL primarily held a majority stake), Decsoft (an important partner of Oracle and Digital), and Macrosoft (developing original software solutions that meet the requirements of industrial enterprises).

the bad reputation of Western companies in this area.

Table 11.7 Main integrators, 1995–1996

Company	Revenue from integration 1996		Revenue from integration 1995		Growth rate (%)	Employ- ment 1996	Employ- ment 1995
	PLN m	%	PLN m	%			
Total of 131/152 firms*	906.4	78	588.6	33	54.0	9,156	7,328
1 Prokom	155.6	77	48.1	67	223.5	750	550
2 Computerland	125.3	72	73.5	72	70.5	238	160
3 Apexim	47.8	91	41.4	90	15.5	153	180
4 Digital Polska	35.1	59	25.9	90	35.5	100	–
5 Optimus	35.1	7	20.5	6	71.2	612	475
6 COIG	34.3	87	10.1	25	239.6	703	888
7 IBM Polska	31.0	50	10.7	50	189.7	184	–
8 ATM	27.7	69	21.5	65	28.8	106	105
9 CCS	22.8	100	9.4	65	142.5	107	–
10 Lumena	22.4	80	20.1	80	11.4	46	43
11 Sprint	21.2	93	–	–	–	211	–
12 Solidex Ltd	20.6	90	–	–	–	50	–
13 Consortia	17.7	85	14.3	78	23.8	67	65
14 Telefon 2000	16.5	42	12.3	42	34.2	204	195
15 Ster-Projekt	15.1	30	3.5	15	331.4	96	58
16 Qumak Intern.	14.8	98	12.2	100	21.3	67	76
17 Samba	14.7	70	8.5	65	72.9	84	80
18 Koma	14.6	32	–	–	–	170	–
19 Sekom	12.7	62	6.7	68	89.6	23	–
20 CSBI	12.6	35	4.0	15	215.0	329	289
21 Koncept	12.1	65	10.1	64	19.8	205	199
22 Inwar	10.9	20	8.1	25	34.6	201	155
23 Decsoft	10.9	60	7.2	65	51.4	58	48
24 Apple Poland	9.6	25	7.3	25	31.5	54	48
25 Emax	9.1	35	7.2	30	26.4	112	–

Note: *131 firms reported in 1996, while only 152 reported in 1995.

Sources: Computerworld (1996, p. 10; 1997, p. 14); and author's calculations.

A number of similar examples confirmed this opinion. Without sufficient local knowledge, Western integrators would take advantage of their position in supplying expensive original hardware with packages of disintegrated software pieces (in the context of environment requirements), which resulted in never-ending projects. This opened a market niche in which one of the largest Polish system integrators, Computerland, was established in 1990. Apart from Computerland, there soon emerged many other system, network and application integrators (Table 11.7).

The integration business expanded more rapidly than other IT markets (at a compound rate of 80 percent in 1994 to 1996), giving rise to many new establishments, as well as to the entrance of other companies, well established in software production, telecommunications, or even PC manufacturing. This may be the reason for the lower concentration ratio here than in other IT activities, although the three leaders again account for more than one-third (36 percent), while the ten largest companies account for 60 percent, and the ratio tends to increase further. It is obvious that with the growth of the market, projects become bigger and more expensive, which requires more funding on the part of the bidder. On the other hand, there are still a number of smaller projects to be undertaken which are the domain of smaller, vertically specialized integrators. The market tends, then, to be shared – as in Western countries – by large players such as Prokom and Computerland, and niche integrators such as Softbank. However, foreign integrators are almost absent from the top of the ranking list, and it should be noted that of the ten largest IT projects implemented so far in Poland, seven were assigned to Polish integrators, and only three to foreign companies.

5. SOURCES OF GROWTH AND INNOVATION: EVIDENCE FROM CASE STUDIES

5.1 A Crucial Role for Technology Transfer

To analyze the determinants of the emergence and rapid growth of Polish computer and software companies, we turn to case studies of the domestic market leaders in the two industries: Optimus and JTT Computer for computers and Prokom, Computerland and Softbank for software. It is significant that in all of these cases, foreign direct investment was either totally absent or played a secondary role, not to mention the fact that the government's S&T policy was simply non-existent. Although the average FDI ratio for the computer sector is not low, and is even increasing, foreign investment penetration was focussed mainly on distribution and sales-supporting networks, which were oriented towards market niches of professional specialized equipment (mainframe and workstations). In the software sector the FDI ratio initially grew rapidly over the first three years and then declined equally rapidly. This means that foreign capital was used only temporarily and to a degree which allowed domestic software firms to preserve their independence. The large technological gap must have been bridged by other channels of technology transfer, in particular through *non-equity strategic cooperative agreements* with leading Western IT companies. Also, the principal sources of growth in terms of market and funding remained domestic rather than foreign as both indigenous hardware and software were almost all sold locally, and the expansion of relevant production capacities was financed either internally or domestically.

Actually, know-how transfer through non-equity cooperative agreements requires a high level of learning capacities on the part of recipients, but the industry-specific asset was there and could be redeployed easily. Under conditions of liberalized foreign trade, the newly established companies usually started by trading imported computer equipment, components and software products. Although their main business line used to be distribution, they accumulated vast professional expertise in computer technology, which was then capitalized while assembling own brand PCs or developing own software. Trading complex products requires complex knowledge, and similar to learning by doing or learning by using, can become an important source of learning: *learning by trading*.

5.2 The Development of Computer Companies

Learning by trading was exactly the case with Optimus, established in Nowy Sacz in 1988 as a family company, operating in a private home and producing software systems supporting company management (Optimus 1995, 1996). Complementary to the produced and sold software, the company started to import and resell PC hardware from Germany which led finally to assembling PCs from components imported first from Germany and then from the Far East. Following a price war against its main rivals on the domestic market (in 1992) and having adopted a quality improvement strategy, the company succeeded in capturing PC market share of more than 40 percent in 1994, which also helped to transform it from a reseller of imported commodities to an assembler and seller of OPTIMUS brand PCs. In 1993, the company extended its production facility to a capacity of 200 thousand computers per year, and its distribution to five local branches, 26 subsidiaries, and about 1,200 dealers. After six years, it was listed on the Warsaw Stock Exchange, and had direct access to both domestic and international capital markets. Over a period of eight years, Optimus grew from a family firm to a relatively large holding company, employing about 500 people in its main PC manufacturing plant (capacity of 300 thousand PCs per year), and offering high-quality PCs at competitive prices. In 1995, the company captured 35 percent of the Polish market or about 5 percent of the Central and East European PC market (ahead of IBM, HP, Compaq, and other world leaders in the computer industry).

A similar success story can be found in JTT Computer, established in Wroclaw in 1990 as a private partnership company for importing and trading computers and computer-related equipment (JTT Computer 1995, 1996). It was founded by students who imported and traded Commodore computers from a German-based Commodore branch and became an official Commodore dealer for Poland in 1991. The company focussed primarily on distribution of hardware, but in 1993 it started assembling its own brand ADAX, which captured at its peak a share of 16 percent of the home market. Despite the success in launching its own PC model, the distribution of computer equipment remained the main line of business and still accounts for up to 75 percent of sales, while ADAX sales account for only 25 percent. The company's competitive edge rests with its sales network on a holding structure consisting of 15 affiliates around Poland and two subsidiaries abroad. The company management focussed primarily on financial engineering and sales logistics. As a result, JTT has become the unquestioned leader among computer-equipment distributors in Poland and – according to its management – the largest independent (from foreign control) computer distributor in Central and Eastern Europe.[215]

The key to the success of both Optimus and JTT surely rests within their networks of cooperative agreements with world leaders in computer technology. Optimus deliberately rejected any dependence on foreign financing, and being listed on the Warsaw Stock Exchange, it was capable of raising capital from domestic sources, to continue its expansion strategy.[216] Optimus gained access to world technology by extending cooperation with leading world computer companies such as Seagate, Maxtor, Seikosha, NEC, Intel, Microsoft, Goldstar, Samsung, Hewlett Packard, Western Digital,

---

[215] The distribution of imported computer peripherals and components covers products of various foreign manufactures, for example, Daewoo (monitors), Citizen (printers), Seikosha, Panasonic, Xerox, Epson, Oki, IBM, Hewlett Packard, Intel, Fujitsu, Seagate, Merlin Gerin, Mitsumi, QuickShot, Aztech, Genius, Sony (monitors), Conner, Creative Labs, Logitech, ViewSonic, Qume, Number Nine, DPT, AMD, APC, AOC, Boca, BTC, and Acer (PC components).

[216] It must be noted that after some rounds of external financing, the initial owners still hold a stake of 60 percent, with 80 percent of the voice. The Optimus strategy was to look for technological rather than market or financial foreign partners. OEM was preferred to distribution, trade credit to joint ventures or FDI. The focus was rather on technology absorption than on financing.

Adaptec, Aztech, Lexmark (IBM spin-off) and Philips.[217] Similarly in JTT, international cooperation is carried out entirely on a non-equity basis. Prevailing legal forms are distribution and OEM agreements, although the latter are generally regarded as more beneficial for Western partners than for Polish distributors, because many customers are still not willing to pay higher prices for foreign brand names of equal quality. However, the knowledge spillover effect for the company remains important.[218]

As the evidence of two major domestic PC producers suggests, the most important technology transfer channel and sources of innovation were *learning by trading* and *cooperative agreements* with leading world computer companies. Science and technology policy by the government played no role in the development of the industry simply because it was non-existent. In-house R&D systems were of negligible size, since in both companies only a small staff was assigned to such tasks as technological scanning (observing world trends in computer technology), testing samples of new components to be imported, setting standards for quality control and quality assurance, and developing new customized hardware configurations to be assembled. The reason is that PC manufacturers mainly assimilated innovations embodied in imported inputs (components), supplied in a standardized form (perfectly codified knowledge) on world markets. The indigenous innovations introduced were generally minor incremental improvements; they were non-patented, and usually built upon the once-and-for-all technology and know-how transfer from the partner company.

The characteristic dominance of local PC producers (distinguishing the Polish market from other Eastern European markets) arose primarily from low-cost comparative advantage of local assemblers (*vis-à-vis* foreign competitors) on a domestic market of relatively large effective size as compared to other East European countries. The PC market is by its nature rather homogeneous and may easily be exploited even by small assemblers

---

[217] The cooperation with Microsoft (OEM since 1991) provided for a transfer of the complete generic code of DOS, which enabled free modification and customizing of the operating system. A strategic cooperation agreement with Intel was concerned with the supplies of assembled parts and components and enabled an early introduction of Pentium-based computers onto the Polish market. In 1995, Optimus became an authorized value-added reseller of AT&T structured cabling Systimax. In 1997, the cooperation with Microsoft was extended to a joint production of the Optimus Microsoft Business PC, a fixed configuration designed to serve small business enterprises. Finally, a joint venture with Lockheed Martin (USA) on coproduction of network software systems and a hardware package for air force command and flight controlling was set up.

[218] It has concluded cooperative agreements with: Microsoft (OEM-1995), Micrographics (OEM), Intel (OEM–1995), Hewlett Packard, Seagate (OEM), Daewoo, Citizen, Digital, Fujitsu, Merlin Gerin, OKI, Panasonic, Creative Labs, Aztech, Logitech, Acer, ViewSonic, Qume, Number Nine, DPT, and IBM (strategic partner in manufacturing fiscal cash registers).

provided they get access to a good distribution network and appropriate know-how. The latter was assured through acquiring codified knowledge in imported inputs combined with learning by trading and cooperative agreements. Financial constraints in terms of capital requirements initially played a minor role, as PC assembling is not a highly capital-intensive activity. This explains why the largest Polish PC manufacturers emerged as purely greenfield creations which were able to survive and grow independently without significant external funding.

5.3 The Emergence of Software Companies

In the software business the situation was somewhat different. Producing software is a labor- or human-capital-intensive business rather than physical-capital intensive. But because of the specific cost structure, developing software (also integration services) involves large amounts of financial capital to make the business work, and this with a high volatility of financial expenditure. Apart from technology transfer through cooperative alliances (as in the computer industry), Polish software companies also needed fresh capital inflow, which made them more dependent on external funding sources (sometimes from a foreign partner). But their competitive advantage consisted in the high degree of product differentiation, rather than a homogeneous market, which required more knowledge of time and place for creating original customized applications. These companies did not attempt to compete on the system software market, but deliberately sought to exploit opportunities in application software, where launching a differentiated product to fit customers' needs would give a better chance of survival. The basic input for emerging software enterprises – namely, human capital – came from former state-owned data-processing centers (ZETOs).

Prokom Software, established in 1987 with the aim of designing complex information systems for industrial and institutional applications, is a good example of that strategy. The company used sophisticated financial engineering to raise expansion capital from passive foreign investors and to preserve its independence, before finally being listed on the Warsaw and London stock exchanges in 1997. A series of mergers and acquisitions transformed the company into a holding of software houses which provide complex information systems based on its own software (18 percent of turnover) and integration services (77 percent) for big companies, banks and governmental institutions. Prokom is now an unquestioned leader in producing original, domestically developed software, in particular, systems designed for financial institutions and large corporations.[219]

Since the very beginning, Prokom has actively sought international cooperation agreements with foreign software and hardware producers. A crucial decision for the firm's future was made when the operating system Unix and relational database management system Informix (4G) were chosen as the basic tool for development and designing of applications. As a consequence, Informix (second leading world producer of tools for relational databases) became its strategic partner and Prokom happened to be the first Polish distributor of Informix softwàre (in 1992 developing the Polish version).[220]

A similar strategy of combining financial engineering with cooperative alliances can be found in Computerland, established in 1990 as 'Scandia Computer' by a Swedish investment company (specialized in information technology) and the founders of Prokom. Oriented primarily towards trading in well-known brand-name computers, providing software and installation for institutional customers, the company was renamed ComputerLand Poland under the franchise contract signed a year later with ComputerLand Europe Operations S.A., a subsidiary of Vanstar Corporation (USA). With support from other financial investors (the Polish American Enterprise Fund and the Polish Private Equity Fund), the company attained the capital structure of a venture capital enterprise with majority-holding passive investors and active minority-holding managers. In 1995, it became the first Polish IT company listed on the Warsaw Stock Exchange, and two years later acquired a few smaller IT firms while exchanging the franchise contract for equity in the merged company.

Over a period of six years, Computerland grew from a small company with a book value of USD 100 thousand to a holding valued at USD 100 million on the stock exchange, with a turnover of about USD 50 million in 1995. Apart from dealing in various configurations of hardware it mainly provided system integration services (LAN, WAN). The core of the business is adding

---

[219] Its own package of integrated module systems supporting enterprise management (FK'X, GM'X, KP'X, TPP) of MRP (manufacturing resource planning) type, developed since 1989, has already been implemented in 100 institutions; it has earned more revenue in license payments in 1996 than the company's most aggressive foreign rival SAP Polska (subsidiary of the German-based world leader in business software) was able to cash in for the comparable system R/3.

[220] The usage of a relational database management system enabled the development of integrated management systems for financial institutions since the hierarchical and network databases proved inefficient and insecure. As both software producer and integrator, the company also found other partners in related businesses: Westmount, Uniplex, Computer Associates, SCO, Century Software, AT&T, Alcatel, Madge, Cisco, LANnet, Mod-Tap, Motorola, CrossComm, Printronix, Computone, 3COM, Wyse, Legrand and Rittal, Hewlett Packard, IBM, DEC, ICL and Compaq.

value to the supplied hardware of leading world producers, based on detailed knowledge about the specific needs and demands of clients, as well as the ability to develop solutions based on multivendors' offers. Thus the upstream cooperation with hardware suppliers was crucial for the development of the company, which as early as 1991 concluded cooperative agreements with IBM, Compaq, Hewlett Packard and AT&T, and later in 1996 also with two software partners – Microsoft and Novell.

In contrast to Prokom and Computerland, Softbank appears to be focussed on software production rather than integration services, and is highly specialized in banking software. The company's strategy also differs in that it combines foreign equity involvement with cooperative alliance. Although it was established in 1989 by a group of banking professionals and initially financed exclusively from domestic capital, its expansion was heavily dependent on a foreign partner, the British IT concern ICL. In 1993, a joint venture with ICL formalized the cooperation between the two companies, and built up foundations for continued transfer of state-of-the-art solutions in banking information technology (by then ICL already had more than 300 installations in Polish banks). A year later, ICL took over a 51 percent stake in Softbank, which got immediate access to the second-largest IT group in the world – Fujitsu, of which ICL had already been a member for some time. Additionally, Softbank was made an exclusive supplier of ICL equipment to the Polish banking sector. However, in 1996, facing growing competition and mergers in the software industry, Softbank decided to raise capital through the IPO, thereby reducing the stake of ICL below 50 percent, giving the Polish party more control over the enterprise. This is a unique case where the involvement of a foreign investor has been reduced during the expansion of a local software company as necessary finance became available from the domestic capital market.

The equity relationship with ICL did not inhibit extending cooperative agreements with other foreign partners. The partnership of Informix provided the company with the fourth-generation relational database management system (RDBMS) which became a basic tool for Softbank's most successful applications of Zorba INX (retail transactions automation), offered for the first time in 1996. A cooperation agreement with an American company – IFS (Integrated Financial Systems) opened further access to a worldwide standard information system for on-line bank machines and electronic points of sale (certified by VISA, Europay, MasterCard, American Express and many others), and led to the proprietary development of the SOFTKART system for management of bank machines and electronic cards. The company also concluded other strategic cooperation agreements with the well-known international enterprises (Oracle, Cray Communications, Shared Financial

Systems, Stratus Computers Inc., Micro Focus, and Hewlett Packard).

6. CONCLUSIONS AND IMPLICATION FOR S&T POLICY

It follows from the analysis above that the role of S&T policy in the development of the computer industry changed fundamentally after 1989. While the local mainframe sector collapsed altogether and this demand segment was being completely covered by imports, any governmental interference to revive disappearing production directly was unproductive and doomed to failure in the face of foreign competition. The marketplace became the main driving force for industrial restructuring in the computer and software sectors. Liberalized foreign trade increased the competitive threat from abroad but also opened windows of opportunity for intensified technology and know-how imports by newly established enterprises. Learning by trading and international cooperative agreements became the main channels for inward technology transfer. Furthermore, radical changes and global fragmentation of the production cycle in computer technology created market opportunities, in particular in PC assembling, customized applied software and integration where emerging local firms were able to exploit their low-cost comparative advantages and existing industry-specific input (human capital). While PC-assembling companies managed to attain sustained growth from accumulated current earnings, software firms were forced to implement more sophisticated financial engineering and to seek foreign investors for funding. This is the whole story and the key to successful restructuring of the Polish IT industry within a relatively short period.

6.1 Computers

To encourage further growth and to maintain local technological competencies in that sector, it seems necessary to create favorable conditions for direct international cooperation of domestic enterprises with leading world computer manufacturers. The best solution would be to attract one of the major component producers to locate a production facility in Poland, which might also improve the comparative advantage of local PC assemblers. The accession of Poland to the EU will create sound opportunities for such a location in the longer perspective. An attempt to negotiate with Intel on such a venture has already been undertaken without success, but another project to locate Motorola's integrated circuits facility in Poland is being considered.

So long as real production activities in the supercomputer business cannot be reestablished immediately due the large technological gap, any form of participation of local agents in international R&D programs designed for information technology (including supercomputers) should be regarded as a rare opportunity for maintaining or building up local technological competencies in this domain. The government should sponsor and facilitate any cooperation of R&D institutions or enterprises with foreign partners, in particular within such EU programs as ESPRIT or Framework, which can now be accessed by domestic entities.

As far as the PC assembling industry is concerned, where unhampered access to world component suppliers and technical cooperation with world technology leaders in the industry is of utmost importance, the government's policy can play only an indirect role in facilitating trade and cooperation. The point is to create a level playing field for domestic producers to support their price and quality competitiveness against foreign rivals. Tax and tariff policy has a crucial impact on the competitiveness of the computer-assembling business where relatively small profit margins prevail. While ready-made PCs are imported mainly from the EU, and Poland is obliged to reduce customs duties due to the European Agreement, most components come from outside the European market and are subject to high import tariff rates. The solution adopted so far has been to introduce duty-free quotas in 1993 to ensure low-cost imports of components for local PC manufacturers. This still applies, but the regulation is temporary and should be reconsidered in the course of accession negotiations. With the absence of local component manufacturing, there is no reason to maintain tariff protection which favors EU competitors. However, making component imports duty free would be in conflict with the EU tariff policy. Thus to guarantee a level playing field for Polish PC makers will not be easy without any domestic component manufacturers, and the industry might become another sensitive sector as far as common tariff policy is concerned.

The other indirect measure for governmental science and technology policy supporting the development of the domestic computer industry is the state procurement policy. It is an instrument which can be used to selectively promote those producers who comply with high-quality state-of-the-art technology, that is, by applying ISO 9000 standards. This may stimulate the competition along quality axes, which encourages the local producers to keep up with world quality standards. Generally, state institutions purchase computer equipment in large quantities. Thus, concluding a so-called *general supplier agreement* with a chosen manufacturer enables him or her to enjoy scale effects in production, which is of great importance in a relatively small domestic demand compared to Western computer markets.

Supply of an educated workforce is also one universal policy instrument for supporting domestic computer and software manufacturing, which is a long-term precondition for the development of any high-tech industry. This can be achieved by giving legal and financial support to education institutions, both public and private, which provide education in computer and information technology. Here, the spillover effect may be the most assured, and incurred expenditures will not be lost. On the other hand, the private investment in this domain may be insufficient for rapid technology assimilation, as well as for attracting the required FDI into the sector. An educated workforce is the most crucial constant factor which makes the country attractive to foreign investors, particularly in high-tech industries.

6.2 Software

Direct involvement in the development of the software industry by the government has been limited over the last few years. However, an 'indirect' science and technology policy for the software sector would be advisable. First, the crucial importance of international cooperation easing technology transfer should not be underestimated. This could be supported by the legal regulations regarding the protection of intellectual property rights, in particular copyrights for software products. As we have seen, the turnover of the industry increased dramatically following the introduction of a copyright protection law in 1994. It may be expected that the transfer of *generic* technologies will also be enhanced by more rigorous execution of copyrights. The same must be true regarding the execution of civil and contract commercial law in relation to non-equity agreements, which constitute the major basis for know-how transfer in the software industry. The state thus has an important role to play in providing adequate legal regulations in this specific area, not only universal solutions for the whole economy.

Second, the financial requirements for software development should not be neglected. High and volatile financial expenditures are hardly suitable for bank financing because they lack adequate collateral. A sophisticated and very advanced capital market would be necessary to provide flexible funding. But in its absence, the government might support or even set up venture capital firms oriented towards project financing of domestic software companies. The other possibility is an appropriate state procurement policy easing access to governmental contracts for consortia of small and medium-sized software companies which, acting alone, could not sustain the burden of project financing.

In conclusion, there is not much scope for *direct* science and technology policy involvement, given the current state and main development factors of the IT industry in Poland. However, this is not to say that there is no place for the government to influence the competitive position of this highly dynamic sector of the economy indirectly. Instead of direct allocational policies, an indirect policy oriented towards creating the *functional infrastructure for the scientific and technological development* of the industry should be recommended. This would involve supporting FDI and participation in international IT programs, where – as in mainframes – domestic capabilities lag far behind the world technological frontier. Appropriate trade policy may create a competitive, level playing field for the upstream cooperation of PC manufacturers with embodied technology suppliers from abroad. State procurement policy should serve as an instrument of competition policy enforcing high-quality standards among domestic PC manufacturers as well as software suppliers. The general supply of an educated workforce would prevent future shortages of this crucial input. It may be expected that such a functional S&T policy would be free from the possible allocational distortions and protective barriers that would only cut off local producers from world technology sources. At the same time, functional infrastructure would prove conducive to the emergence of a national innovation system in the domestic IT industry.

BIBLIOGRAPHY

Computerworld (1994), *Raport Specjalny* (13), IDG Poland S.A.

Computerworld (1996), *Raport Specjalny* (24), IDG Poland S.A.

Computerworld (1997), *Raport Specjalny* (32), IDG Poland S.A.

Bitzer, J. (1997), 'The Computer Software Industry in East and West', DIW Discussion Papers (149), Berlin.

Dyker, D. and J. Perrin (1997), 'Technology Policy and Industrial Objectives in the Context of Economic Transition', in David A. Dyker (ed.), *The Technology of Transition*, Budapest: Central European University Press, pp. 3–19.

JTT Computer S.A. (1995), *Raport Roczny 1995*, Wroclaw: JTT Computer.

JTT Computer S.A. (1996), *Raport Roczny 1996*, Wroclaw: JTT Computer.

Kolczynski, M. (1994), 'Komputery w Polsce i na swiecie w polowie lat 90', mimeo, Uniwersytet Warszawski, WNE, Warszawa.

Optimus S.A. (1995), *Raport Roczny 1995*, Nowy Sacz: Optimus S.A.

Optimus S.A. (1996), *Raport Roczny 1995*, Nowy Sacz: Optimus S.A.

Targowski, A. (1980), *Informatyka. Modele sytemow i rozwoju*, Warszawa: PWE.

Teleinfo (1996), *Raport 1996*, Warszawa: Laborpress.

Teleinfo (1997), *Raport 1997*, Warszawa: Laborpress.

Part III

Summary and Outlook

12 Main Findings and Perspectives for Innovation Policies in Eastern Europe and the West

Christian von Hirschhausen

1. INTRODUCTION

Each of the preceding chapters has highlighted specific aspects of the integration of Eastern European production structures into international production and innovation networks. When socialism started to crumble in Eastern Europe in the late 1980s, few individuals, enterprises or governments would have anticipated that only ten years later, economic life would be turned upside down, the socialist production structures destroyed, and the newly emerging industry structures absorbed by international patterns of specialization and division of labor. Today, it is normal to see Eastern European patents and products on international markets under conditions of direct competition rather than state planning, and Western technology and products offered in Eastern Europe as well. Competition between Eastern and Western innovations and products has intensified, but so, too, have the network structures into which Eastern European firms were absorbed or which they developed from scratch. Along with the internationalization of innovation, production, and trade comes the subjective feeling of 'normality' currently developing in the region. Has it not become commonplace, for example, to move freely between capitals such as Prague, Bucharest and Moscow, which ten years ago were still inaccessible on the other side of the Iron Curtain? This normalization may even lead some observers to underestimate the findings presented in this book, in particular the *revolutionary* nature of the globalization underway in Eastern Europe.

Parts I and II of this book have analyzed the observed phenomena through the lens of changing patterns of innovation during the systemic change from socialism to some form of a capitalist market economy. The breadth of the analytical sector studies, linked to the conceptual framework, leads to one main conclusion: *during the last decade, national science and technology systems did not play an important role in the restructuring of industrial sectors or of enterprises in Eastern Europe.* The internationalization of industry and innovation in Eastern Europe has progressed largely outside the science and technology fragments inherited from socialism. The sectoral studies have highlighted specific aspects of the international integration of post-socialist production. Not all case studies come to the same conclusion, but a certain convergence exists: integration has taken different forms and speeds, but it is a common feature throughout the region. Indeed, whereas the empirical evidence presented here may not be fully representative, it is confirmed by studies of a similar scope arriving at similar results (Zloch-Christy; 1998, for a different interpretation, see Martin 1998).

In this final chapter, the main results of the book are summarized and some general conclusions derived, both in terms of economic research and policy recommendations. At a conceptual level, it is argued that the hopes invested in the science and technology 'potential' of Eastern European countries were ill-founded. Indeed the very notion of national 'science and technology policy systems' is inadequate in the post-socialist context, as it obscures the fact that the new networks in Eastern Europe emerged to a large extent through the *internationalization* of the sources of innovation at an *enterprise* level (Section 2). Section 3 stylizes the main features of the systemic change from post-socialist science and technology systems to globalized innovation networks: here six theses are formulated that characterize the new nature of innovation. An interpretation of the empirical sector and case studies of Part II is provided in Section 4. Section 5 derives a set of policy implications for innovation and industrial policies in and towards Eastern Europe. Finally, Section 6 identifies what implications the Eastern European developments might have for innovation policies in Western countries.

2. FROM A SOCIALIST S&T PERSPECTIVE TOWARDS A COMPETITION-ORIENTED INNOVATION PERSPECTIVE AT THE ENTERPRISE LEVEL

The key reason why the S&T 'potential' of Eastern European countries was misjudged is that the very concept of 'science and technology' is not an economic one. It originates from a *materialistic, non-monetary* vision of how the world is supposed to function: it assumes that a certain volume of raw materials, including human knowledge, is transformed into consumer products through certain transformation processes. The process of transformation largely remains a black box, to which the label 'science and technology system' is assigned. This materialistic, quantitative approach is applied under *all* circumstances, regardless of the specific economic system or historical period in which a certain country may find itself. In fact, as Chapter 2 has shown, the 1969 UNESCO definition of science and technology was an attempt to *unify* socialist and market-economic approaches in the fields of knowledge and innovation. Thus, 'S&T-ology', as we may call this discipline, sees socialist production processes in the very same light as capitalist production. The same set of indicators is applied to both highly developed countries and developing economies. S&T-ology is input oriented: it counts the physical quantity that enters the black box, while it usually ignores economic notions which can be expressed in monetary terms, such as 'efficiency' or 'profit'.

However, the defining characteristic of transformation in Eastern Europe has been precisely the radical *systemic change* from the socialist to the capitalist logic of production and innovation. Post-socialist restructuring is thus characterized by a radical change of links between the non-monetary *socialist* mode of production and distribution and the monetized, profit-oriented *capitalist* production logic (Hirschhausen 1996). S&T-ology is not a useful tool to interpret this dynamic process: by its very nature it ignores the monetary aspects of post-socialist systemic change and thus also ignores the very core driving force of industrial restructuring.

In the new context of capitalist market economies in Eastern Europe, albeit emerging ones, it seems more appropriate to consider S&T resources as one element among others that determine the *innovative* capacities of enterprises. Innovation is not an objective or a value by itself, but rather is one parameter of enterprise strategies, or as it was called in Chapter 3, one axis of competition. Industrial enterprises may use innovation as a means to establish temporary monopolies in certain market segments. However, they have many other competition axes at their disposal, both downstream (for example, price, trade mark, timing) and upstream (for example, access to financial, natural and human resources, equipment and codified knowledge).

This change of perspective has two important consequences for the analysis:

1. The setting-up or maintaining of S&T capacity to enhance innovation cannot by itself be a policy objective. Instead, it has to 'compete' with other policy measures that are likely to enhance the competitiveness of enterprises in a more efficient manner, such as competition policy, trade liberalization, or regional policy.

2. Any innovation policy must ultimately be judged by the degree to which it provides goods (material or immaterial) for which industrial enterprises express a *demand*, that is, a willingness to pay. In other words, the usefulness of most elements of the industry-oriented S&T system can be evaluated by the degree to which they are being paid for by enterprises. In contrast, *external* and *spillover* effects, that is, the creation of additional value without additional expenses, can be no guideline for innovation policies. These spillover effects are difficult to quantify and impossible to target in the first place. Thus, they are subject to misinterpretation and the worst kinds of political manipulation. No innovation or S&T policies should be based on vague hopes of creating 'spillovers'.

It can be concluded that traditional, quantitavist S&T-ology is not appropriate to analyze the changing nature of innovation in post-socialist Eastern Europe. The emerging competition between industrial enterprises, in which innovation is but one strategic parameter, cannot be understood with traditional S&T indicators. In fact, a purely quantitative approach to S&T analysis reveals nothing on the specifics of the post-socialist restructuring of innovation activities. It is therefore proposed that the use of the S&T terminology and approach be abandoned. It is replaced here by a vision of *innovation* and innovation policies as a determinant of competition and enterprise strategies. The concept of a *demand-derived innovation policy* (developed in Chapter 2) probably best describes the new perspective. Demand orientation means that *monetary demand* should be the ultimate criteria of the success of innovation activities. An enterprise perspective is most conducive to providing the information necessary to evaluate the efficiency of an innovation policy measure.

3. MAIN RESULTS IN STYLIZED FORM

Within the complexity of ten years of industrial restructuring and innovation in Eastern Europe, some regularities seem to exist, which can also be identified in the empirical studies presented in Part II. These are presented in the following six 'stylized results'.

- **The collapse of the socialist production system led to a radical restructuring at the enterprise level; as a result, the input-oriented, socialist S&T system, too, was not only restructured, but literally disappeared**

Earlier empirical work has shown that there can be no 'gradual' restructuring in the post-socialist context (Bomsel 1995; Hirschhausen 1996). The socialist mode of non-monetary production imploded after socialism had been abandoned and capitalist constraints had been introduced. This also applies to each production unit and thus to the entire institutional structure: former socialist factories and combines fell apart, new capitalist enterprises were created. The key to understanding post-socialist reform is in studying the process of enterprization and the integration of these enterprises into national and international networks.

With the collapse of socialism, the socialist S&T system disintegrated as well. The introduction of monetary constraints on a dominant part of former S&T activities destroyed the coherence that such a system might have had during the socialist period. Given the political decisions leading to the collapse of the socialist system, there was no way that the destruction of socialist S&T systems could have been avoided. Finding such disappearing S&T systems in Eastern Europe is not just a metaphor: anyone associated with these S&T institutions during the last decade has witnessed the implosion of the system; he or she has also personally followed the harsh reorientation and search for survival of institutes and even the individual researchers. Indeed it is difficult to identify S&T institutions or individuals who have not experienced a break in activity between their socialist and post-socialist existence.

With the abolition of the strict socialist separation between the conception of innovation and the production process, many elements of the socialist S&T system (that is, the research institutes and science academies) have striven to transform themselves into commercial enterprises. The changes of the socialist S&T system can be categorized by the *degree* to which the individual elements have been transformed, that is, either to become part of a new, demand-oriented innovation system, or to remain on the supply-oriented trajectory, largely outside monetary constraints. In practice, fragments of a 'mixed' system emerged from the integrated socialist S&T system. Generally speaking, these fragments can be categorized into (i) *'enterprized' innovation firms* and (ii) *research dinosaurs*. The latter have proved to be resistant to change, and in some countries have developed an astonishing survival reflex; however, their contribution to economic transformation and innovation is low. For the newly emerging innovation enterprises, be they independent or part of a larger conglomerate, *financing* is the major driving force for restructuring. In general terms, the restructuring of socialist S&T systems can be characterized as a radical case of 'creative destruction'.

- **Post-socialism led to a devaluation of the socialist innovation potential, a part of which could be redeployed to other areas**

As a result of the creative destruction at industry and enterprise levels, the innovation 'potential' inherited from socialism is of limited value in the new context of market economies. As of the end of the 1990s, socialist industrial capacities have almost all disappeared, and have partly been enterprized to become new, capitalist capacities. Physical capital was almost entirely devalued. However, certain non-specific parts of the former system can still be used, although they have to be redeployed to other areas. In cases where few complementary assets are required, the redeployment of human capital is relatively straightforward. This is the case, for example, in the software sector. Where more complicated network structures prevail, the redeployment may be more difficult or even impossible, as with telecommunications equipment. It is worth noting that some elements of the former S&T system may also be useful in cases of creating new activities from scratch; this is mainly the case with non-specific, entrepreneurial human capital.

- **The end of transformation: distinct patterns of enterprise restructuring and systemic reform in CEE countries and post-Soviet CIS countries**

Ten years after the beginnings of systemic transformation in Eastern Europe, one can observe an increasing division between different national trajectories of structural reform: the advanced reforming countries of Central and Eastern Europe, the so-called accession countries about to enter the EU, have achieved a profound reorganization of industrial structures and enterprises. In contrast, most of the CIS countries have not. Very different patterns of transformation, or 'transition' as it is called by the mainstream, have emerged in these two regions: in the advanced CEE countries, enterprization is complete and new industrial structures are now firmly established, including links with enterprises worldwide. The results have quickly become apparent: growth rates of industrial production have stabilized and the integration of CEE enterprises in European markets is accelerating (see Chapter 3). Today, the main policy question is one of refining regulations, to 'grease' the economic system in order to make it function more smoothly.

In contrast, enterprization and restructuring in the CIS countries – in particular the European ones (Russia, Ukraine, Belarus) – has *not* proceeded sufficiently to reveal new, stable network relations. Institutional conditions such as inter-enterprise debt, absence of laws or their application, macroeconomic instability and inconsistent industrial policies are insufficient to provide a stable framework. In 1999, the decline in output has hardly been halted. The state remains a major industrial player, be it through direct ownership or indirectly through sectoral regulation and tariffs. In more general terms, it is unlikely that the CIS countries will adopt the institutions of a capitalist market economy. Instead, they seem to be headed towards a kind of *post-Soviet* mixed economy, without any clear distinction between state action and the economy. The time when 'Eastern Europe' could be used as a synonym for the entire region is clearly over. Today, a different set of hypotheses has to be used for reforming CEE and for CIS countries.[221] This is what we have called the *end of transformation* (Hirschhausen and Waelde 1999). Although somewhat controversial when first formulated a couple of years ago, the hypothesis of the 'end of transformation' is now generally accepted even by the mainstream research and political thinking on Eastern Europe.[222] It also implies that different approaches to innovation policies are required in the two regions.

- **Innovation and catching-up of Eastern European enterprises is facilitated by international integration**

In the Eastern European, post-socialist context, national innovation or S&T systems did not have a strong impact for enterprise restructuring. Independent (for example, national or regional) problem-solving strategies have been largely unsuccessful. Successful restructuring in post-socialist Eastern Europe depends mainly on the access to markets, knowledge and technology. In other words, it depends on the integration in *international* innovation, production and sales networks. This network integration can have different focusses at the outset: one can distinguish *market* integration, which is only downstream oriented, *production* integration, which is the internationalization of production processes as in the case of shipbuilding, and *innovation*

---

[221] This clear distinction does not hold for the second-tier CEE countries, where some transformation may still be taking place, for example, Bulgaria or Romania.

[222] The reorientation of two of the most respected journals of transition research is representative for this development. The journal *Economics of Transition*, in an attempt to provide a new focus to the journal, stated that 'in some important respects these [Central European countries undergoing transition towards a market economy, especially those on track for early accession to the EU] countries can be studied in the same terms as one would study the relatively developed countries of Western Europe. . . . Other countries, especially in the CIS, are much further behind in their reforms.' (*Economics of Transition*, 7 (1), p. i). The journal *Communist Economies and Economic Transformation* has even dropped the 'transformation' aspect from its title, to become simply *Post-Communist Economies*, 'because of a growing feeling that the major processes into which transformation has generally been divided – stabilization, liberalization and privatization – have in substantial measure been completed' (journal announcement, early 1999).

integration, which is covering the upstream innovation process as well, as in the case of the car industry.

It cannot be concluded, however, that market integration is less valuable than innovation integration, as some of the literature on Eastern Europe as a cheap production location asserts. Market integration – often taking the form of outsourcing towards Eastern Europe – may be the first step in a deeper integration process which is yet to come, as is the case with computer development. Therefore, innovation policies should not favor activities for which a deeper integration process may eventually be expected.

- **Successful enterprization and innovation was a collective process that cannot be reduced to a single critical factor**

There is no such thing as a single successful innovation policy to optimize the process of enterprization and internationalization. Rapid ownership change towards efficient structures of corporate governance is certainly conducive to market-oriented restructuring, as is a regional approach to overcoming socio-economic obstacles at the local level. It goes without saying that a stable institutional and macroeconomic environment also helps restructuring. But none of these necessary factors is *sufficient* for success. The same is true for the internationalization of innovation networks; while this has been a decisive factor in most cases of rapid restructuring, it does not guarantee *per se* the emergence of new, efficient network structures.

- **For the development of new innovation activities, it generally does not matter whether the network organizer is domestic or foreign**

It is sometimes argued that the depth of emerging networks depends on the nature of the network organizer (Radosevic 1997): *foreign-led* restructuring is supposed to lead to rapid, international networking but also to *shallower* network structures; in contrast, *domestic-led* restructuring may take longer but also leads to more *stable* network relations. This implies that by providing domestic enterprises with more time to develop 'organically', economic policies such as temporary trade protection can favor the long-term development of *nationally*-based networks.

Empirical evidence does not confirm this hypothesis. First of all, in the phase of post-socialist creative destruction, it is impossible to make a clear distinction between shallow and stable network relations and little can be said about their dynamics. In most cases it is also unclear *who* is the real network organizer. Before policy-makers have identified network structures, these may have already changed in reality ('shooting at moving targets'). But, most importantly, as *all* networks develop from scratch, the distinction between foreign and domestic network organizers loses its significance: all new network organizers can be considered to be foreign in the sense that they are external, that is, coming from outside the former networks and developing qualitatively new relations. If this is the case, it is hard to justify policy measures that restrict the international access of national enterprises in order to enhance the domestic innovation capacities.

4. EVIDENCE OF THE GLOBALIZATION OF INDUSTRY AND INNOVATION IN KEY SECTORS IN EASTERN EUROPE

The results stylized above have been derived in part from the empirical studies presented in Part II. The interpretation of the 'hard facts' of sectoral restructuring was, in turn, influenced by the general hypotheses emerging in the course of the project. This virtual circle generated the central focus of the book on the *globalization of industry and innovation taking place in Eastern Europe*. In the following survey of industrial restructuring in Eastern Europe, the extent to which this globalization process is present in some of the key sectors is examined. The results of the sector studies are also checked against the main results laid out above (see also Table 12.1 for a summary).

4.1 The Car Industry: Phoenix out of the Ashes

The car industry in Eastern Europe is a case of both radical restructuring in the post-socialist context and a very quick integration into *international* multi-layer R&D, production and sales networks. It is taking place simultaneously with the restructuring and expansion of the car industry in the main producing regions (USA, Western Europe, Japan) into the global economy through direct investment, strategic alliances and mergers. A review of the three most advanced post-socialist countries (Poland, Hungary and the Czech Republic) shows that none of the socialist capacities or networks are in place any longer. The country that did not even have a car industry – Hungary – is about to become a highly productive car-assembling country. Labor cost advantages more than offset the lower efficiency and quality – which are rapidly improving in any case – to attain international standards: Skoda (Czech Republic), FSM-Fiat (Poland) and Magyar Suzuki (Hungary) all sell their cars on Western European markets. Whereas the adaptation of car industries in Eastern Europe has largely been achieved, the post-Soviet countries have so far been largely excluded from the integration process.

Enterprization has made hardly any progress in Russia, Ukraine, Belarus or Uzbekistan. The markets have remained protected, even if there is a growing demand for high-quality cars. Laws on privatization and sales of assets to foreigners have not helped the investment of foreign capital in these countries.

Modernizing Eastern European enterprises, or creating them from scratch, relied on a set of complex factors: not only the restructuring of existing firms, the liquidation of obsolete assets and the development of new functions, but also the development of a strong network of subcontracting companies and the reliance on skilled labor, new services and financing. The leading actors in this process of transformation were clearly the dominant *international* car groups, who were investing, buying or selling in Eastern Europe. Enterprises owned by foreign investors were able to restructure more quickly, create new markets and link the local business to global strategies. In contrast, the car industry in those countries that followed a domestic-led restructuring have fallen behind their international competitors.

The above analysis leads to the following policy implications: the automotive industry in Eastern Europe does not need to rely on high technology to remain competitive in its dominant segments. International car manufacturers established in Poland and the Czech Republic, for example, will not delocalize their R&D activities towards these countries, but will keep them at their headquarters, with a possible exception in the case of Hungary. This trend is consistent with the international development towards concentrating rather than fragmenting R&D. The FDI-based development of the Eastern European car industry does not imply the absence of links to the newly emerging domestic innovation system. Technology transfer is certainly eased by the skilled workforce and engineering capabilities. Domestic supplier networks become more important over time. The situation in Eastern Europe may be compared to the UK, a country which no longer has any domestic car producers and where the appropriation of know-how has generally been facilitated not by setting up specific S&T institutions but by the accumulation of experience gained through the cooperation with foreign car manufacturers. Potential remaining tasks for a technology policy are of a general scope: one example would be helping firms, especially SMEs, to have access to information about processes, innovations and markets, in order to reduce the asymmetry between big enterprises and subcontractors, and thus to lower the barriers to entry. Also, the curricula of technical education might be looked at and updated to supply a more qualified workforce.

4.2 The Shipbuilding Industry between World Markets and Post-Soviet Stagnation

The case of the shipbuilding industries shows how the restructuring of a supposedly heavy industry in Eastern Europe depended on the integration of shipyards into international networks characterized by high-tech, information-dominated, logistically intensive processes. In this industry, supplier networks are playing an increasingly crucial role in the development and the production of ships, covering as much as 70 percent of the added value. With the collapse of socialism, the socialist mode of ship production as a prime strategic military activity collapsed as well. Production had to be reoriented towards international markets where Eastern European yards now compete with Western capitalist yards worldwide. Therefore, the restructuring from highly integrated shipyards towards non-integrated production structures with an efficient supplier network was the basic condition for successful restructuring. These non-integrated production structures further enable the Eastern European shipyards to compensate for their disadvantages in equipment through the purchase of required parts from Western producers. The technological gap turned out not to be a problematic factor for restructuring. In the segment low- and medium-complexity ships, price is the main competition axis; thus, more-complex equipment has to be imported by almost all shipyards around the world. Innovation as a collective process is characterized in this sector by a mixture of internal sources such as design bureaus and R&D departments, as well as external sources such as suppliers and research institutes.

A net difference can be observed between the modes of restructuring in an advanced reforming country, for example, Poland, and post-Soviet countries such as Russia and Ukraine. For example, the two most advanced Polish shipyards have integrated international supplier and downstream networks, such as shipping companies and finance, and are competing successfully on international markets. A specific innovation policy is not needed as there is no evidence for upcoming constraints through proprietary technology, and financial restructuring is well under way. Ultimately, a diversification from low- to medium-complexity ships seems likely. In contrast, Russian and Ukrainian yards are blocked in their enterprization by the institutional framework – for example, their non-monetized economies, rigidities in local labor markets and unstable legal conditions. This leads to high costs and low international competitiveness; restructuring remains a local process. The Russian and Ukrainian governments might consider abandoning their insufficiently targeted S&T policies. Import tariffs for equipment and local-content obligations might be softened as they reduce rather than support the competitiveness of domestic shipyards. An acceleration of the enterprization process is needed if shipbuilding is to have a future. Innovation policies should be aimed at creating conditions conducive to local restructuring at enterprise level.

In general, there is little evidence of market failures which would warrant state support for national shipbuilding; nor can the lack of absorptive capacity justify direct support to local or national production networks. The prospects for shipbuilding in Eastern Europe and the CIS are good, though this does not apply to all shipyards equally. The example of Poland, which emerged as the fifth-largest shipbuilding country worldwide, shows that the potential can be put to work once the external conditions favor restructuring. Other shipbuilding countries such as Croatia or Romania may eventually follow this example.

4.3 Food Processing in Eastern Europe between Family Production and Multinational Groups

Like many other activities, food processing did not exist as an independent economic sector during socialism. Instead, food-processing activities were usually integrated into the agricultural sector, where they were treated as an internal service. The primary task of agriculture was the provision of the population with sufficient *quantities* of food, which particularly in the Soviet Union was still not always achieved. Hence, food processing was treated only as a low priority. Correspondingly, the investments were low and the few combines were badly equipped. The S&T base was small, not only in food processing itself but also in the supplying industries such as machinery and chemicals which produced products far below international standards. There was a high level of integration of the different stages of the food chain in the former system. Thus, post-socialism can be seen as a way of creating a new independent, non-integrated food-processing industry. During the enterprise development process, the different units of the former combines and the agricultural and the processing activities have indeed been separated.

The speed of transformation of CEE and CIS countries is different. Most of the CIS countries still have problems guaranteeing their population a supply of the most basic food; thus food processing is still of low importance. In contrast, in the reforming CEE countries, food processing has become a real competition factor between enterprises: a rising demand for broader product ranges can be observed. These growing markets for food-processing enterprises are also the reason for the significant amount of FDI that the CEE countries have attracted in recent years, as is the case with Hungary, the only country to have had a relatively highly-developed processing activity in the

1980s. The main sources of innovation are Western enterprises, which appear in the form of suppliers of equipment, foreign investors or subsidiary enterprises.

The scope for an explicit innovation policy in favor of this newly emerging sector is quite limited, due to the food-processing industry's high dependency on demand. The development of the industry and its process of catching up technologically are based mainly on *technology transfer* from Western countries, which are becoming a basis for the development of domestic capacities. Thus, it is necessary for policy to allow free access to markets. In the CIS countries, the satisfaction of the population's basic need for food is the condition for a developing food-processing industry; otherwise markets remain locally segmented and no general, nationwide development is imaginable.

4.4 Telecommunications: A Difficult Catching-up Process

Telecommunications, too, had to be created from scratch in post-socialist countries. Under socialism, private applications and services hardly existed, and the underlying equipment sector was poorly developed. By contrast, in capitalist market economies, telecommunication services and equipment have developed particularly rapidly in the 1980s and 1990s, mainly due to the broadening of flexible multimedia networks and the far-reaching liberalization of the sector. By deciding to adopt international service standards, Eastern European countries decided to abandon socialist networks. The creation of equipment enterprises and the transformation of former monopolist service providers has so far been dominated by foreign investment, introducing most of the technical and regulatory know-how. Given the greater importance of telephone users, the forces protecting equipment manufacturers and their technology links were quickly pushed aside, and a rapid *technology transfer* took place in the import of equipment from abroad. The adjustment was to some extent hampered by initial domestic procurement rules and the requirements for joint ventures. The level of domestic equipment production is more closely linked to local production costs; their connection to the international manufacturing process is linked, then, to domestic demand.

If one approaches the market from the perspective of *demand-led growth*, then it becomes clear that the overall macroeconomic framework on the one hand, and sector-specific conditions such as the regulatory framework and treatment of foreign direct investment on the other, have tremendous consequences for the development of the basic access networks and related services. The Eastern European countries show different approaches to this sector, ranging from opening the market to dominant foreign investors (for example, Latvia and Hungary) to a much more state-controlled approach (for example, Russia). In CEE countries, skewed demand for modern telecommunication services was oriented mostly towards imported technology from the West, leading to a rapid pace of modernization. For Russia, on the other hand, the lack of a clear macroeconomic and regulatory strategy and the subsequent lack of foreign direct investment led to a much smaller demand for equipment, including imported equipment, and for the associated S&T links. Therefore a slower adaptation process on the network and on the equipment side resulted.

One generally applicable innovation policy is the streamlining of the regulatory framework and the facilitation of direct foreign investment. Both could have consequences for the development of the basic access networks and related services; hence, they also have a direct impact on the equipment market. Strategic investors have played a key role as network organizers in CEE countries, with regard to both local networking and the internationalization of equipment supply. The cases in which domestic equipment producers were protected (for example, by local-content obligations) do not seem to have had beneficial results (for example, Poland). This might be different in Russia, where the investment necessary to upgrade the bulk of the domestic networks is of a much higher complexity, and will not be financed from abroad.

4.5 Software, a New Industry and New Enterprises

Computer software is another case of profound reorganization of industry and innovation structures. Under socialism, 'software' did not exist as a product, only as a fully-integrated service. With the end of socialism, a lack of competitiveness in relation to the newly emerging imported products resulted in the collapse of the national production structures and the necessity for international networking. The rapid introduction and absorption of new international hardware technologies after the collapse of socialism required a completely different kind of software, not only in terms of the software technology used, but also in terms of the areas of application. The human capital of the Eastern European countries in software technology was devalued to a certain extent by this development. Former employees of the specialized software departments left their positions or lost their jobs through the closure of the departments or host institutions, and moved to the emerging software sector.

About three to four years after the collapse of the old system the degree of integration began to increase more quickly, from pure market integration to product and even innovation integration. With the development of the computer market, the demand for more complex software solutions increased and led to more sophisticated activities on the part of Eastern European software enterprises. Domestic enterprises started to develop software with low standardization and custom software locally, and to offer services such as implementation, installation, adaptation and training. The further development of Eastern European software enterprises into these more sophisticated activities was based on *technology transfers* by their agreement or cooperation partners. The new Eastern European software enterprises, the overwhelming majority of which are greenfield creations, now dominate the market segments for software with low standardization, adapted software and small-scale custom software projects. Furthermore, the segment for computer-connected services such as installation, implementation and training is also dominated by domestic enterprises. In these segments, the competition advantages of domestic enterprises – for example, the knowledge of language and culture and personal contacts – come into play. The remaining segments are dominated by the well-known international software companies.

The software sector was not a specific target of any of the Eastern European governments' innovation policies, and indeed, there seems to be no need for this. Among the political measures were the introduction of patent-protection laws which, however, lack rigorous enforcement. Possible starting points for a public policy could be the provision of specific parts of the infrastructure, for example, the introduction of standardization procedures and quality standards, or the improvement and enforcement of the telecommunication and patent protection laws. Another important element of public policy is the modernization of education by importing knowledge of modern computer technology. An indirect source of support may come from higher institutional stability, which would provide longer planning horizons to software users.

4.6 Personal Computers: Emergence of National Champions

The restructuring of the Eastern European computer industry is to a certain extent a success story: domestic enterprises developed international supply networks from scratch and applied their own ingenuity to emerge among the domestic market leaders. Under socialism, the production of computers and required components was strictly state controlled due to its importance for the military-industrial complex and state institutions. This system collapsed with monetization and the introduction of international competition. The former socialist computer producers either closed down entirely or switched to other activities. This process released personnel into the newly emerging private computer industry dominated by greenfield creations. Initially, the new enterprises started to trade in Western computers, computer components and suitable software. After having gained some experience in this business, they started to assemble PCs themselves. The required components were imported from the Far East or the USA. The trade activity continues to remain an important part of the domestic business, but with the development of the computer markets, services gained in importance.

The immediate availability of technology allowed the new enterprises to catch up with technology through the S&T systems of their foreign suppliers. This gave both computer enterprises and their customers the opportunity to use state-of-the-art computer technology immediately. The fact that only PC assembling is carried out in Eastern European countries should not be seen as a negative development, because it is in line with global PC production structures. In the market segments for higher-class computers, the existing production and R&D structures were not competitive and therefore collapsed. The present innovation networks of Eastern European computer enterprises are international, and domestic sources have little importance. International developments show no sign that this will change in the near future.

Given the low barriers to entry and the smoothness of the restructuring process thus far, there seems to be little opportunity for a public policy to support the development and improve the competitiveness of the domestic computer industry. The 'new' computer industry is active exclusively in the assembly of PCs, for which R&D capacities are not required. Thus Eastern Europe emulates most Western countries, where R&D capacities for PC technology are also small, and still decreasing. The role of the state is limited to being that of a customer, for example, for the automation of administration, introduction of IT in schools and universities, and as a provider of education opportunities. There are no signs that an industry for sophisticated computer components such as graphic devices and hard disks is about to emerge. The internationalization of Eastern European computer production and innovation networks has largely been achieved.

Table 12.1 Survey of main results and application to sector studies

Stylized results/ sector studies	1) Collapse of socialist science and technology systems	2) Devaluation of socialist innovation potential	3) Distinct patterns of restructuring between CEE and CIS countries
I) Car industry	yes (no continuity possible between S&T for 'Trabant' and 'Cinquecento')	largely (some conversion to new capacities possible)	yes (due to globalization in CEE, domestic orientation in CIS)
II) Shipbuilding	yes (due to abandoning of the socialist, military-oriented S&T system)	largely (conversion from military to civil and market-oriented products difficult)	yes (due to institutional normalization in CEE and heavy Soviet legacy in CIS)
III) Food processing	yes (new economic activity requires new assets)	– (food processing non-existent in the socialist period)	yes (CEE: approaching international standards; CIS: hampered by incomplete food chain)

Stylized results/ sector studies	4) Necessity for international integration	5) Innovation as a collective process	6) Irrelevance of the origin of the network organizer
I) Car industry	yes (need for internationally established network organizer)	yes (required by highly complex network structures)	no (foreign led more likely to succeed)
II) Shipbuilding	yes (international technology a necessary condition for market access)	yes (absorptive capacities strong in Eastern Europe)	yes (what counts is market orientation)
III) Food processing	largely (catching-up facilitated by technology transfer)	yes (upstream and downstream linkages crucial)	yes (final demand as key determinant)

Stylized results/ sector studies	1) Collapse of socialist science and technology systems	2) Devaluation of socialist innovation potential	3) Distinct patterns of restructuring between CEE and CIS countries
IV) Telecommunication (services and equipment)	yes (quantum leap makes socialist S&T obsolete)	– (equipment: yes; services: some transfers possible)	yes (CEE: foreign-led modernization; CIS: domestic-led muddling-through)
V) Software	– (no 'software' industry in socialism)	no (existing skills were the basis for new software industry)	no (gradual differences only)
VI) Computers	yes (from socialist computer systems to pure PC assembling)	yes (innovation takes place in components, not in assembling)	no (gradual difference only: market penetration of PCs much stronger in CEE than in CIS)

Stylized results/ sector studies	4) Necessity for international integration	5) Innovation as a collective process	6) Irrelevance of the origin of the network organizer
IV) Telecommunication (services and equipment	yes (due to new technological and regulatory requirements)	yes (absorptive capacities crucial)	no (foreign leadership required for catching-up)
V) Software	yes (no domestic-based catching-up possible due to technology requirements)	yes (key factor: adaptation of international technology to the domestic situation)	yes (hardly recognizable borders between 'foreign' and 'domestic' software enterprises
VI) Computers	yes (no domestic development possible without access to components and design)	no (PC assembling is low-tech, other computers no longer produced)	yes (domestic- or foreign-led networks compete with each other on an equal basis)

5. POLICY IMPLICATIONS FOR EASTERN EUROPE

Are the sectoral analyses and case studies presented in Part II representative? Some sectors generally considered essential for the industrial restructuring of Eastern Europe are not covered, such as research-intensive sectors (for example, pharmaceuticals) and also traditional heavy industries where these countries might have a competitive advantage (for example, steel, metallurgy, mining and petrochemicals). Also, not all former socialist economies have received the same coverage as the advanced reforming countries of Eastern

Europe and the large CIS countries upon which this book is focussed. It is assumed that not much additional insight is gained from analyzing countries in-between, for example, Romania or the Slovak Republic. However, notwithstanding the lack of full coverage (upon which no research can ever be based), we contend that a set of generally valid *policy implications* can be derived for Eastern European countries. They also concern Western policies towards the region:

- Given the collapse of domestic S&T systems in post-socialist countries, the internationalization of innovation, production and sales networks in Eastern Europe was and remains a condition for the reemergence and development of efficient enterprise and innovation structures within each country. This globalization process should be supported by economic policy if possible, rather than be hampered by domestically-oriented policies.
- The scope of national S&T analysis and policies in post-socialist Eastern Europe is sharply reduced. The breakdown of the socialist S&T systems and the emergence of international production and innovation networks make nationally targetted policies largely superfluous. Should innovation policies be continued, they are best carried out at a supra-national level, the extension of which depends upon the nature of the innovation network.
- Industry-specific innovation policies are unlikely to succeed. The post-socialist process of creative destruction leads to a redefinition of the borders between enterprises and sectors. 'Shooting at moving (industry) targets' is already difficult in economies with stable sectoral structures; under Eastern European conditions, it was and remains impossible.
- Innovation policies for the East have to take into account the fundamental institutional differences between established Central and Eastern European market economies and post-Soviet mixed economies. In the former, the internationalization of innovation networks is almost complete, and only marginal policy measures may be required; in the latter, the most efficient innovation policy would be to facilitate the process of enterprization at the local level.
- In no post-socialist country should innovation policies be based on the notion of a presumably high 'technological potential', but instead on the real existing competitiveness of newly emerging enterprises and networks. It is market demand that determines the value of technological capabilities. And it is not in Eastern Europe that 'high-tech' activity is likely to produce the highest profits. Stated differently: there is neither a need nor a perspective for a Silicon Valley either in Croatia or anywhere else in Eastern Europe. The use of the socialist, that is, non-monetary, concept of

'potential' might be abandoned and replaced by a sound competition analysis in the framework of a capitalist market economy.

- There is not one best trajectory for technological restructuring and catching-up. In particular, the use of so-called 'high-technology' is neither a prerequisite for modernization nor a guarantee for its success. By contrast, technological catching-up may start by simply providing low-priced capacities for outsourcing, for example, in the textile business. The bad image that 'low-tech' activities have in Eastern European governments and public opinion should not lead to mistreatment of these sectors. A job created in the clothing industry can be just as valuable as one in the pharmaceutical industry, and the former might even be more promising for modernization and international competitiveness. In any event, state policies have only a marginal impact on emerging patterns of restructuring: therefore they should not put all their eggs in one 'high-tech development' basket.
- There is no such thing as a single best innovation policy. Specific policy measures can be defined only for concrete cases, that is, specific countries, enterprises, and so on at a certain point in time. Common policy conclusions, such as to 'provide support for small and medium enterprises', are difficult to apply.
- Technology is not the main obstacle to successful enterprise reform. Instead, the success of enterprization depends on a wide range of factors, for example, financing, organizational change, market development and so on. In most relevant cases in Eastern Europe, technology can be considered to be a generic, tradable good which is available on world markets. The adaptation of this technology then depends only on absorptive capacities, which are generally abundant in Eastern Europe.
- Technical education, too, is subject to radical change and should therefore be adapted to the prevailing situation. An overhaul of curricula is necessary to keep up with international technical standards.
- Last but not least, this book has produced a conceptual result: the concept of 'science and technology' is not appropriate to reflect the systemic change under way in Eastern Europe. It implies a positive connotation of S&T as having a value *per se*. While this was true under socialism, the ultimate rationale in a capitalist market economy is the creation of monetary value. This implies that the value of the S&T system, too, is judged ultimately by monetary criteria. Thus, there is no possible continuity between the socialist and the capitalist notion of S&T. With the end of socialist S&T systems, new, money-driven systems of innovation emerge. However, innovation is but one of an enterprise's competition axes. The traditional, quantitatively-oriented research on science and

technology issues, which we have called 'S&T-ology', largely ignores the monetary aspects of post-socialist systemic change; thus, it misses the central driving force of industrial restructuring.

6. OUTLOOK: NEW PERSPECTIVES FOR INNOVATION POLICIES IN THE WEST

The analysis of Eastern European industry restructuring opens up new perspectives for innovation policies in the Western world as well. By way of their flexibility in the recombining of assets in new enterprises and industries, the developments in Eastern Europe may prefigure some of the trends emerging more slowly in other regions of the world, for example, Western Europe and North America. Indeed, Eastern Europe has become a 'laboratory' for new patterns of industrial restructuring. This had significant results in the case of shipbuilding, for example, where several Polish shipyards gave an impressive lesson on modernization to the ailing Western shipbuilding industry. Likewise, the emerging duality of Eastern European software markets foreshadows a similar development in other regions of the world, with few tailor-made individual products by domestic producers, and a dominance of truly global software for standard applications. Other examples are presented in Part II of this book.

Thus, the lessons from Eastern Europe may sound an alarm for innovation policy-makers elsewhere. The need for a drastic change in innovation policies from a supply to a demand orientation was easily detectable in the Eastern European context, with the immediate disappearance of socialist networks. However, is not the situation in most Western countries similar – though more gradual – with decreasing state budgets and growing internationalization of R&D and production networks? And, if we have shown that nationally-oriented innovation policies have only a limited impact upon the restructuring of industry in Eastern Europe, could not the same be true for the West?

The lesson from Eastern Europe for the West may therefore be to replace the supply-oriented approach to innovation policy with a *demand-oriented* approach. In the absence of an established link between fragile and highly-aggregated S&T statistics and other economic indicators, a purely supply-oriented approach is hard to justify. Instead of simply proposing Western approaches to the East, the West may learn from the Eastern experience: innovation policies should be critically reassessed using a demand-oriented approach. The globalization of industry and innovation observed in Eastern Europe may thus become a determinant for innovation policies in the West as well.

REFERENCES

Bomsel, Olivier (1995), 'Enjeux industriels du post-socialisme', *Revue d'Economie Industrielle* (72).

Hirschhausen, Christian von (1996), 'Lessons from Five Years of Industrial Reform in Post-socialist Central and Eastern Europe', *DIW Quarterly Journal of Economic Research*, **65** (1), pp. 45–56.

Hirschhausen, Christian von and Thomas Waelde (1998), '*The End of Transformation*', Paper presented at the Annual Conference of the Verein für Socialpolitik, Rostock, September.

Martin, Roderick (1998), 'Central and Eastern Europe and the International Economy: The Limits to Globalisation', *Europe-Asia Studies*, **50** (1), pp. 7–26.

Radosevic, Slavo (1997), *Foreign and Domestic-led Modernization in Industrial Sectors in Russia, Ukraine, Poland and Hungary: Dynamics, Strategies and Lessons*, Brighton: Proposal for Inco-Copernicus Program.

Zloch-Christy, Iliana (ed.) (1998), *Eastern Europe and the World Economy*, Cheltenham, UK and Northampton, MA, USA: Edward Elgar.

Subject Index

Automotive industry 60f., 64f.,
68, 71f., 87, 89, 95, 104ff.,
115ff., 123ff., 324

Bankrupt, -cy 5, 288
Belarus 26, 43, 47, 54, 89, 274,
320, 324
Bulgaria 47, 52, 66, 70f., 81,
134, 141f., 163, 196ff., 202f.,
221, 321

Capitalism 14f., 24, 28, 147
Combines 2, 6, 43f., 148, 252,
278, 308, 319, 326
Commonwealth of Independent
States (CIS) 5, 28, 43, 45ff.,
55, 67, 75f., 79, 111, 117, 125,
146, 157, 165, 175, 183,
201ff., 211, 213, 217, 221f.,
236, 240, 242, 265f., 271, 320,
321, 326f., 331ff.
Competition axes 25, 40, 42, 62,
72, 76, 111f., 130, 132, 232ff.,
239, 259, 261, 263, 267, 276,
317, 325
Computer
enterprise 258, 265, 270, 274ff.,
330
industry 189, 195, 237, 257f.,
264f., 269f., 274ff., 278,
283f., 286ff., 302, 304, 306,
309f., 329f.
Coordinating Committee for
Multinational Export Controls
(COCOM) 17, 198f., 201,
208, 222, 237, 287
Corporate governance 74, 78f.,
157, 290, 322

Council for Mutual Economic
Assistance (CMEA/
COMECON) 1, 26, 66, 95,
97ff., 117, 124, 143, 174,
196ff., 197ff., 205, 207, 210,
217, 219, 221f., 264, 269, 270,
274, 286ff.
Croatia 66, 134, 141f., 146, 163,
218, 326
Czech Republic 29f., 43, 48, 52,
60, 65, 67, 69ff., 74, 81, 89,
90, 92f., 116, 177, 195, 201,
217, 228, 240f., 244, 249ff.,
258, 268ff., 273, 323f.

Education 1, 14, 16, 24, 29, 68,
73, 79f., 123, 125, 140, 244,
249, 252, 254, 279, 311, 324,
329f., 334
Electronics 40, 59, 105, 117,
130, 143, 155, 168, 194, 214,
219, 274, 288
Enterprization 43ff., 48, 143,
146, 148f., 154f., 157, 179,
289f., 319ff., 322, 325, 333f.
Estonia 2, 26, 33, 38, 48, 52,
144, 174, 176f., 180, 196, 203,
205, 210f., 228, 244, 246,
255f., 274, 277, 279f.
European Bank for Recon-
struction and Development
(EBRD) 47, 50, 55, 67, 77, 81,
267
European Union (EU) 1f., 7, 47,
50, 71, 101, 105, 118, 123,
137, 139, 143, 164f., 175, 178,
183, 194, 215f., 228, 231,
236f., 240f., 260f., 263, 267,

271, 309f., 320f.

Food processing 6f., 38, 162,
164f., 167f., 174, 181f., 326,
331
Foreign direct investment (FDI)
69, 71, 78, 80, 176ff., 182,
202, 204ff., 208, 211f., 215,
217, 219, 222f., 291f., 302,
304, 311f., 324, 326

Growth 1ff., 6, 21, 37f., 42, 45ff.,
52ff., 59, 61, 64, 70ff., 79f.,
96, 106, 116f., 119, 133, 161,
180, 186, 190, 204, 221, 223,
235ff., 252, 257, 260, 263,
272, 275, 279, 285, 288, 292f.,
297f., 302, 309, 320, 327

Hungary 2, 7, 30, 38, 50, 52, 66f.,
69f., 82, 89f., 95ff., 99, 100f.,
107, 111ff., 118f., 121ff.,
124ff., 163, 176ff., 181, 183,
187, 195, 197f., 201ff., 210,
212, 215, 217ff., 240f., 244,
254, 258, 267, 268, 323f., 326,
328, 336

Industrial
  economics 6, 37
  policy 49, 69, 97, 139, 151
Inflation 43, 75, 209
Infrastructure 22f., 31, 76, 121,
123, 125, 186, 195f., 201f.,
204f., 207, 210, 214f., 221f.,
243, 254, 287, 312, 329
Innovation networks 6f., 253,
265, 278, 315f., 322, 330, 333
Innovation system 2, 4, 6, 13ff.,
19ff., 25f., 28f., 31f., 67, 130,
137f., 228, 252f., 258, 262,

264, 266, 270, 278, 312, 319,
324
Institutions 3, 5, 15ff., 19, 22ff.,
31f., 47, 61, 68, 70, 129, 137f.,
154, 180, 186f., 193, 195, 198,
208, 210, 214, 221, 237f.,
244f., 248ff., 252, 264, 269,
275f., 288, 296, 300, 306f.,
310f., 319, 321, 324, 328f.
Investment 7, 31, 42f., 62, 64,
68f., 71f., 77f., 80, 99, 101f.,
113, 119, 121ff., 139, 145,
148f., 157, 186, 189f., 195f.,
198, 200, 202ff., 215f., 219,
221f., 254, 276f., 287, 302,
307, 311, 323, 327f.

Knowledge base 13f., 18f., 27,
32, 211, 258

Latvia 26, 33, 53, 163, 187, 196,
201, 203, 210ff., 221ff., 225,
228, 244ff., 248f., 255f.,
274ff., 276, 279f, 328
Liberal, -ism 69, 80, 99, 106,
186, 195, 221
Liquidation 213, 324
Lithuania 26, 33, 48, 53, 144,
203, 210f., 213, 228, 244,
246ff., 255f., 274ff., 279ff.

Market
  failure 157, 326
  segment 39f., 72, 76, 110f., 132,
  135, 142, 228, 231ff., 237,
  240, 242f., 249, 253, 259ff.,
  265, 267, 271f., 275, 279,
  285, 290, 292, 296ff., 300,
  317, 329f.
  structure 25, 40f., 71, 177, 189,
  192, 261, 271, 289

Market economy 4, 28, 39, 44f.,
73, 95, 115, 211, 239, 245,
283, 290, 316, 321, 334
Modes of growth 37f., 42, 45f.,
96, 116

Organization for Economic Cooperation and Development
(OECD) 9, 19f., 28, 30, 34, 62,
68, 78, 82, 127, 139f., 143f.,
148, 159, 164, 176, 183, 195f.,
231, 256, 280

Poland 2, 8, 28, 30, 38, 43, 51,
53, 65ff., 70f., 73, 80, 82,
89ff., 100, 116, 118, 130,
133ff., 141f., 144, 146, 148,
150, 154, 157, 163, 176f.,
195ff., 199, 202f., 205, 210,
213, 218, 221, 238, 240f., 244,
255f., 258, 264, 267f., 272,
275, 280, 283ff., 290, 294,
299ff., 307, 309ff., 323ff., 336
Production networks 7ff., 23, 63,
70f., 96, 150, 157, 252, 274,
326, 335

Research and development
(R&D)
personnel 270
expenditures 3, 30, 123
Romania 43, 47, 53, 66, 70f., 81,
89, 98, 134, 141f., 144, 146,
163, 197, 202f., 321, 326, 333
Russia (Russian Federation) 7, 29,
43, 47, 60, 65ff., 69ff., 75f.,
78ff., 82, 89, 94, 116, 130,
134, 140ff., 144, 146, 152f.,
156, 159, 163, 187, 195ff.,
196f., 200ff., 209, 211ff., 216,
221f., 240f., 255, 258, 267f.,

275, 320, 324f., 328, 336

Science and technology (S&T)
concept 6, 14f., 40, 43, 50, 61,
64, 110, 115, 137, 189, 217,
228, 231, 235, 316, 318, 334
demand for 14, 22, 27, 213, 214
evaluation 15
indicators 28f., 318
policy 21, 23, 30f., 33, 74, 77,
80, 123, 148, 151ff., 256,
285f., 302, 309, 312
supply of 20f.
system 1, 23, 41, 79, 80, 157,
178ff., 318ff., 330f., 333f.
Shipbuilding 6f., 27, 65, 129ff.,
133ff., 146, 148ff., 321, 325f.,
335
Slovak Republic 66f., 70, 89f.,
116, 197, 203
Slovenia 2, 54, 66, 70, 71, 81,
89f., 116, 163, 199
Socialism 1ff., 6, 13, 15, 19, 23f.,
26ff., 32, 37, 43f., 48, 50, 65,
140f., 147, 156, 167, 174, 228,
238, 240, 242, 245, 250, 252f.,
258, 264ff., 270, 274f., 278,
315f., 319f., 325ff., 330, 332,
334
Software
enterprises 230, 233, 235,
239ff., 245ff., 250f., 253,
306, 329, 332
industry 8, 227, 238, 254, 258,
284, 288f., 308, 311, 332
sector 209, 227f., 230, 236ff.,
243ff., 245ff., 249f., 252f.,
292, 297, 303, 309, 311, 320,
328f.
Soviet Union (USSR) 4, 26, 50,
66, 146, 148, 152, 156, 196f.,

199ff., 211f., 214, 224, 254,
264, 274, 286, 326
Stock market 206

Technological
  paradigms 13f., 18f., 22, 27, 32,
    166, 278
  trajectory 14, 18, 27, 32, 265,
    278, 283
Technology transfer 27, 32, 66,
  73, 143, 154, 186f., 195f., 199,
  202, 205, 218f., 221ff., 239,
  242, 253, 298, 303, 305f., 309,
  311, 327, 329, 331
Telecommunications 7, 185,
  187ff., 194f., 201, 209ff., 216,
  220f., 254, 327ff.
Trade 8, 19, 37, 45, 47, 75, 77,
  104, 116, 121, 125, 133, 153,
  177, 185, 197, 201f., 204,
  210f., 214, 218, 222, 238f.,
  246f., 250, 252f., 265, 274f.,
  288, 303f., 309f., 312, 315,

317, 322, 330
Transformation 1f., 4ff., 14, 24,
  29, 32, 38, 41, 43f., 46ff., 73,
  78, 147, 186f., 195, 202,
  210ff., 215, 222, 228, 257,
  283, 285, 292, 317, 319ff.,
  324, 326, 327
Transition 65, 71, 78f., 83, 95f.,
  116ff., 124, 168, 174f., 180f.,
  215, 283f., 298, 320f.
Transport 104, 122, 133, 147,
  152, 277

Ukraine 7, 43, 45, 47, 50, 54, 71,
  89, 125, 134, 140ff., 144, 146,
  153, 159, 203, 320, 324f., 336
United Nations Educational,
  Scientific and Cultural
  Organization (UNESCO) 14f.,
  33, 35, 317

World Bank 51, 127, 162, 163,
  184, 203, 224, 267, 277, 281

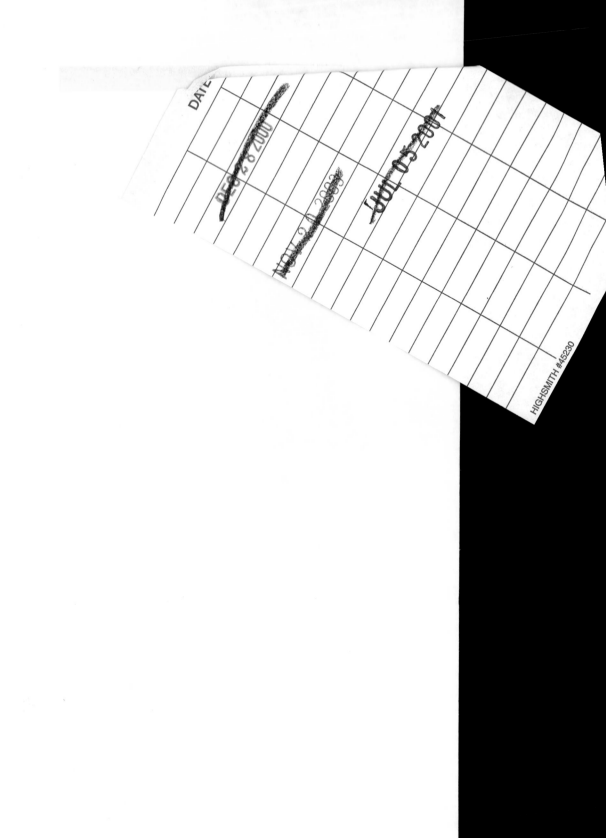